THE PROGRESSIVE WORLDVIEW

VOLUME I

THE HISTORY OF PROGRESS

FROM THE SCIENTIFIC REVOLUTION TO THE TWENTIETH CENTURY

ANDREW CARLSON, PHD

Copyright © 2023 Andrew Carlson, PhD

ISBN: 979-8-9893727-1-3

All rights reserved. No part of this publication may be reproduced, distributed, or transmitted in any form or by any means, including photocopying, recording, or other electronic or mechanical methods, without the prior written permission of the publisher, except as permitted by U.S. copyright law.

andy@theprogressiveworldview.com

For privacy reasons, some names, locations, and dates may have been changed.

Book cover and interior design by Mirko Pohle

First Edition 2023 in the United States

PWV Publishing

CONTENTS

———

INTRODUCTION

———

I am a progressive. This means, of course, that I take a progressive stance on a whole range of social, political, economic, and moral issues. I am for building bridges between diverse groups and welcoming in the stranger, not building walls to keep others out. I favor raising both the minimum wage and the corporate tax rate to bring about greater equality. My view of human life makes me pro-choice, pro-gun control, and anti-death penalty. And I believe climate change is real, largely human-caused, and a grave threat to our children and their descendants. Still, the fact that I can check all these boxes on the progressive scorecard is not what I mean, first and foremost, when I say that I am a progressive. Or more precisely, I do not believe that taking these political positions is what *makes* me a progressive. These stances, rather, are the *effect* of a deeper set of convictions I hold about our world: where it came from, where it is headed, how it operates, and the place human beings occupy within it.

For at the end of the day, I believe in progress. I believe in the *reality* of progress. I believe progress is the way of the world—the general trend, not just of human history, but of cosmic history. And I believe in the *possibility* of progress. I believe we have not just the opportunity, but the moral obligation to participate in our world's progress. At whatever stage of local or global progress we happen to find ourselves, we are responsible for helping our world take its next steps forward.

This is not a light responsibility to assume, for experience has shown that progress is hard. Progress is slow, often interminably slow. Progress is messy and wasteful, typically involving more false starts and blind alleys than actual steps forward. And not infrequently, progress is painful, even tragic. Nevertheless, I believe our universe has a bias in favor of progress. I believe that, if we take a long enough view, the universe is constantly striving to move *forward* and *upward*. Progress is, therefore, the lens through which I view the world; it is my worldview. Even when things are difficult—when my own life does not seem to be going anywhere, or when the world around me appears to be standing still, if not moving backward—it is a faith in progress that keeps me going.

Which prompts the question: What is progress?

The Progressive Worldview is my attempt to answer this question. It is a big question, so *The Progressive Worldview* will span three volumes, with the current volume, *The History of Progress*, being the first. As its title suggests, this initial volume traces the history of the progressive worldview, from its first appearance early in the seventeenth century through the end of the twentieth century. The second and third volumes of *The Progressive Worldview* will be my attempt to articulate an updated version of the progressive worldview that continues to be relevant and compelling here in the opening decades of the twenty-first century, even amid a young century that seems to be intent on proving just how hard progress can be.

Three major theses will guide and structure the current volume's exploration of the history of the progressive worldview. The first thesis is that, as the progressive worldview has emerged and evolved over the past four centuries, the single most significant factor driving and shaping its development has been a series of concurrent advances of the modern natural sciences. In fact, the whole notion that the world can be regarded as moving forward and upward—as opposed to going round and round in circles or sinking ever further into decline—first arose in the wake of the Scientific Revolution of the seventeenth century. For over fifteen hundred years, Western society had labored under the weight of a declinist spiritual narrative that portrays the present order as hopelessly corrupt and just heading further downhill. With no one having much reason to hope tomorrow will be better than today, at least as long as we remain in this life, learning stagnated across the medieval period. The study of the natural world, in particular—the bodily realm of sin and corruption, soon to be destroyed—was badly neglected when not actively suppressed.

But then, early in the seventeenth century, a scattered group of bold and curious thinkers set aside their Bibles, their Aristotle, and their general reliance on established authority, and instead began to apply their own powers of reasoning to the study of the world around them. Within decades, they were achieving impressive results, and by century's end, these "scientists"—as this new variety of scholar came to be known—had learned more about the natural order in one hundred years than all the philosophers and theologians of the previous two thousand years. Suddenly, progress in the study of nature was not merely possible; it was happening every day, with further progress appearing to be assured by a modern scientific method that had a perpetual grasping for ever more knowledge built right into it.

Over the seventeenth century, this new form of intellectual progress was of interest mostly to Europe's relatively small intellectual class. By the eighteenth century, however, a growing number of inventors, engineers, and industrialists had begun to demonstrate that, once you have properly discerned the laws of nature, you can use this knowledge to start reshaping nature to better align with our human ends, specifically by inventing, refining, and commercializing new technologies that more efficiently meet our natural wants and needs. As this began to happen, average living standards in Europe and North America began to rise—at first very slowly, and initially among those classes not stuck at the bottom of the socio-economic ladder—but eventually more quickly and broadly. And thus, for the first time in human history, a sizable portion of the population began to live above a bare subsistence level. Increasingly, moreover, people could use their rising incomes to purchase a variety of novel goods that had never been available, even to royalty. All of this means that tangible, measurable progress was starting to come into view, not just for society's elites, but for many average people.

If the origins of the progressive worldview can therefore be traced back to the birth of modern science and the intertwining technological and commercial revolutions the Scientific Revolution made possible, it did not take long for the savants and statesmen of the Enlightenment to start applying the concepts and methods of the modern physical sciences to such humanistic disciplines as political science, economics, psychology, and moral philosophy. Most significant among these concepts was that of universalism. Indeed, the second major thesis guiding this book is that universalism is the concept that most deeply underlies the progressive worldview in both its scientific and moral aspects, thereby linking these two sides of the progressive coin.

To briefly anticipate this argument, following Aristotle, the scholastic philosophers of the Middle Ages had long maintained that every substance in the world—every discrete thing; every rock, tree, and animal—has its own individual nature, distinct from that of other substances. Beyond guiding the scholastic investigation of nature, such as it was, this Aristotelian metaphysics provided a convenient means of explaining and justifying the existing feudal system: kings are born with a regal nature, whereas peasants inherit the servile nature of their parents, so all is right with the world, or as nature intended, when kings are ruling and peasants are serving.

Against this medieval backdrop, it represented a major conceptual shift when Galileo proposed his law of falling bodies. No longer focusing on the individual natures of particular falling bodies, Galileo was positing a single, universal law of nature that determines how every heavy body falls, everywhere and at all times. Following Galileo's lead, such modern political and moral philosophers as Thomas Hobbes, John Locke, and Immanuel Kant began developing a doctrine of moral universalism asserting that all people are bound by the same universal moral principles. Crucially, this equality before the moral law also implies that all people ought to be *treated* as equals—as possessing the same degree of moral worth and dignity. Thomas Jefferson may have captured this conviction most eloquently when he wrote in the Declaration of Independence, "We hold these truths to be self-evident, that all men are created equal, that they are endowed by their Creator with certain inalienable Rights, that among these are Life, Liberty, and the pursuit of Happiness."

The third thesis guiding *The History of Progress* is that the four-hundred-year history of the progressive worldview can be divided into two major periods, corresponding to what I will call the first two iterations of this worldview. We have already touched on the first period, covering the seventeenth and eighteenth centuries, and thus spanning the Scientific Revolution, the Enlightenment, and the first concrete attempts by American and French revolutionaries to remake society in accord with the principles of universalism. In its scientific aspect, the worldview that arose out of this period came to be defined by the model of the universe Isaac Newton presented in his *Principia Mathematica*: a rational, interconnected system of universal laws. These laws allow for various forms of local motion within nature, but as Newton saw it, nature itself remains augustly unchanging in its most fundamental structures.

As the thinkers of the Enlightenment then applied Newton's insights across the whole intellectual landscape, they came to regard the various forms of progress European society was suddenly making—scientific, technological, commercial, political, moral—as forms of local motion that Newtonian physics allows, all driven by the faculty of human reason. According to the worldview that arose out of this period, therefore—the first iteration of the progressive worldview—human reason is the primary driver of the world's progress, while the Newtonian universe provides the stable, rational arena within which reason can make its progress.

Over the nineteenth and twentieth centuries, the progressive worldview underwent a major transformation as scientists in a number of disciplines began to discern that the universe is not, in fact, as stable and unchanging as Newton had believed. On the contrary, our world has been undergoing a series of profound changes for a very long time, as emerging knowledge in such fields as geology, biology, thermodynamics, and cosmology was making increasingly clear. And many of these changes point unmistakably in the direction of progress. This includes, over the past 6 million years, the evolution of a very smart ape that would eventually come to dominate the planet, logging such achievements as authoring *On the Origin of Species*, the Emancipation Proclamation, the theory of general relativity, and the "I Have a Dream" speech. Accordingly, as a second iteration of the progressive worldview took shape over the nineteenth and twentieth centuries, this worldview came to regard human reason not so much as the primary driver of the world's progress as one of its most distinguished products, with human beings now merely doing their part to carry forward a universal story of progress that has been playing out for close to 14 billion years.

In its political and moral aspects, the second, more dynamic iteration of the progressive worldview came to be shaped by a growing recognition on the part of progressively minded thinkers, leaders, and activists that, even with a democratic system of governance in place, the existing social order would still need to be changed in profound ways if the progressive ideal of moral universalism was to be fully realized. Limiting our discussion to the case of the United States, the situation progressives inherited at the beginning of the nineteenth century was roughly thus. The philosophers of the Enlightenment had done a brilliant job of abstractly defining the ideal of moral universalism. The American founders, meanwhile, had done an impressive job designing a democratic system of government that was not only stable but that also began to lend the ideal of moral universalism concrete reality—within, that is, the demographic subgroup that had always dominated European society: straight, White, able-bodied Christian males. What these Enlightenment-era progressives almost uniformly failed to grasp is how far short they fell from completing their own self-appointed task of instituting a truly universalistic social order.

Over the course of the nineteenth and twentieth centuries, progressives from a wide array of demographic backgrounds increasingly came to realize that the greatest practical impediment to realizing the progressive ideal of universalism is the age-old propensity of human beings to divide themselves into subgroups based on any number of economic or demographic factors, with the more powerful groups then subjugating everyone else, claiming a wide range of exclusive privileges for themselves at the direct expense of those beneath them in the resulting social hierarchy. As this social reality set in, the progressive moral project—as conceived under the second iteration of the progressive worldview—came to involve drawing one traditionally marginalized group after another into the social mainstream, according its members the full slate of rights, opportunities, and moral dignity originally promised to them by such documents as the Declaration of Independence, though never delivered, with the ultimate goal of one day realizing the universalistic dream Martin Luther King described on the steps of the Lincoln Memorial in 1963.

As should be clear by now, the sort of progressivism *The Progressive Worldview* takes for its topic is not the narrow form that has come to distinguish the progressive wing of the contemporary Democratic Party of the United States from its moderate wing. In the very broad sense of progressivism I will here be discussing, Hillary Clinton and Joe Biden are progressives just as much as Bernie Sanders or Elizabeth Warren. But so, too, are many American conservatives of a more traditional bent, whose small government, pro–free market vision animated the Republican Party over the second half of the twentieth century—think here of William F. Buckley, Jr., Milton Friedman, or Ronald Reagan. The political views of these Republican figures may have fallen to the far Right end of the spectrum of possible progressive views, but all three were committed to the Enlightenment institutions of liberal democracy and the market economy, while at least paying lip service to the principle that all people are created equal.

Emphatically, the same *cannot* be said about the Republican Party of the early twenty-first century, particularly since the rise of the Tea Party and the ascendancy of Donald Trump. And at various points in the second and third volumes of *The*

Progressive Worldview, I will consider the populist turn the American Right has recently taken, along with the implications this development has had for the social and political landscapes American progressives must now navigate—a situation echoed in many other countries around the world today, including both those with democratic regimes and those under authoritarian rule. Indeed, the fact that large segments of the global population appear to be falling back into the sort of tribalistic, hierarchical thinking that was more characteristic of the premodern political order has lent a particular urgency to my task of detailing the history of the progressive philosophy that first led the world to see a way past such thinking. It has also convinced me that the progressive worldview is now due for a third iteration, one that is adequate to the technological, political, economic, and social conditions of the twenty-first century.

Attempting to articulate such an updated conception of the progressive worldview—once again by drawing heavily on the insights of the cutting-edge sciences of the day—will be the task of the two final volumes of *The Progressive Worldview.* Here in *The History of Progress,* I will resist the urge to dive into the minutia of contemporary politics and keep my focus on the very big picture: that of a universe that has been making progress of one sort or another for nearly 14 billion years, leading up to our own contemporary attempts to help the universe take its next step or two forward.

CHAPTER 1

TELLING STORIES ABOUT OUR WORLD: CYCLICAL, LINEAR, AND DECLINIST WORLDVIEWS

As noted in the Introduction, holding a progressive worldview means viewing the world, in its fundamental trajectory, as moving *forward* and *upward*—as gradually getting *better* over time, notwithstanding what may be frequent setbacks. Yet, this is by no means the only way the world can be viewed. In fact, as far as worldviews go, the progressive worldview is a relative latecomer. Briefly considering a few of its most significant precursors will help us to appreciate just how novel the progressive worldview was when it started coming together in the seventeenth century.

Cyclical Worldviews

As best we know, virtually all the world's oldest cultures viewed the world as cyclical in nature, for obvious reasons.

Living much closer to nature than we do today, prehistoric peoples saw the sun disappear every evening, but then rise again in the morning, just as they watched the world grow cold and die every winter, to be followed by warmth and new life every spring. The animals around them navigated a similar traverse, moving from birth, growth, and maturity to decline and death, with the cycle repeating itself for the new generation spawned during the period of maturity. Of course, human beings were tied to this same life cycle, underscoring the fact that they were part and parcel of nature, and that the fundamental tendency of nature is to travel in circles—rising and falling, living and dying, ebbing and flowing, waxing and waning—always cycling back to the same state. Indeed, when night fell and early peoples were presented with the spectacle of the heavens, they were showered with images of cyclical constancy: the moon appearing and disappearing every twenty-eight days, the stars completing a grand circuit across the sky every year, and even the planets traveling in paths that were more complicated, but regular enough for ancient cultures to discern their patterns and predict their movements.

Given our ancestors' proximity to nature, when they began telling stories about their world—constructing mythologies, we would now say—it is not surprising that many of the spirits, forces, and deities who populated these stories were personifications of natural processes. Gods of the sun and goddesses of the moon made their regular rounds. Rain gods and fertility goddesses bestowed life when they were well pleased—although they could also choose to with-hold their gifts when vexed. And whole pantheons came to represent such natural phenomena as rivers, mountains, seas, animals, the seasons, and even death. Because people had little control over their environments in this pre-technological era, they made sacrifices to these deities, hoping to mollify them into performing their customary tasks: yielding meat on the hunt or bringing rain to the fields, blessing young women with children or young men with strength, restoring health to those struck down by sickness. These deities were often terrifying, being as capricious on a day-to-day basis as nature, herself—which explains why many primitive cultures were willing to go to such horrifying lengths as human sacrifice to appease them. Yet, fickle personalities notwithstanding, the gods also had a long-term constancy that doubtless provided our ancestors with a sense of metaphysical comfort. Day to day, life was a confusing, unpredictable, frightening struggle. Eventually, however, the rains *do* return, women *do* bear the next generation, and plagues *do* run their course, thus suggesting that the ups and downs of daily life are little more than a passing dream, whereas the world's true reality lies in its deeper, unchanging core. Again, this constancy is modeled by the heavens above, which naturally came to be seen as the dwelling place for many of the gods whom early peoples worshipped.

In the second millennium BCE, strongly cyclical local religions on the Indian subcontinent began coalescing into the Vedic religion, later spawning Hinduism, and then—over the course of the first millennium BCE—such major offshoots as Buddhism, Jainism, and Sikhism. While these religions differed in their theological details, they were united by a belief in *samsara*. *Samsara* can be translated variously, most often as "wandering" or "world," but it denotes an unending circuitous movement. *Samsara* is visually represented by the Wheel of Life, which carries the world up, but then draws it back down, crushing any individuals who would try to fight against it. With *samsara* thus being the way of the world for Hinduism and its progeny, it also came to be seen as the primary shaper of human life. Specifically, because death is always seen to be followed by new life in nature, the belief arose that human death is also not final, but rather we are reincarnated, often as human infants, but sometimes as newborn animals of other species. While most of us cannot remember our previous lives, we carry our *karma*, or moral character, with us. Our *karma* is shaped by how we conduct ourselves, and it then affects our rebirth: those who live exemplary lives are reborn into more desirable circumstances, such as a higher social caste, whereas those who live meanly are born into worse circumstances, such as the thief who might be reincarnated as a rat.

While the Vedic belief system therefore teaches that individuals can make slow progress towards bettering their condition over a series of lives, this improvement is still only relative. The first of the Four Noble Truths of *samsara* is that all of life—the entire cycle—is characterized by suffering. The Wheel of Life, in other words, may carry us up and down, but not only the down times are difficult. Rather, the whole turbulent journey is one of suffering. As long as we ride the Wheel of Life, therefore, we will never know true peace, since even the upturns will be fleeting and uncertain, while the downturns will be inevitable and devastating. It is thus not surprising that Hinduism and its offshoots developed a notion of *moksha* or *nirvana*, which implies a liberation from the ups and downs of *samsara* through a return to *brahman*, the unchanging, immobile, ultimate ground of all reality. Different Vedic traditions laid out different paths to *moksha*, with some stressing moral practice and others counseling meditation or other spiritual disciplines. All agreed, however, numerous lives of dedicated effort must be spent before a soul can free itself from the cycle of life and death. Only then will the soul achieve a peaceful stability approximating that of the night sky above.

If it is not hard to see how the regular patterns of nature would produce a worldview that was generally cyclical, how did this translate into such a fatalistic outlook for the practitioners of the Vedic religions, believing that individuals have virtually no control over their own fates—at least in the context of the current lifetime—and that the entire cycle of the Wheel of Time is characterized by suffering? The answer is that, not just for people in India, but for virtually everyone across the ancient world, life was simply this way. Gradual improvements in agriculture notwithstanding, everyday life continued to be extremely challenging and stressful for most people, not least because they remained highly dependent on nature for their existence yet possessed no control over nature's forces. If the rains came, crops grew and everyone ate; if there was an extended drought, people starved. Sickness came out of nowhere, and it was just as likely to kill you as run its course and fade away, no matter what sacrifices you might offer to the gods. And of course, not even the healthiest people could avoid eventually growing old and dying.

None of this, moreover, ever changed. As much as everyday life may have been a frenetic scramble for subsistence, the larger world remained essentially static. Not only did the same cycles of nature ever repeat, but modes of human social organization and governance were so deeply ingrained in the collective consciousness that no one, not even a king or a prophet, could imagine altering them significantly. To be sure, when we look back on this era, calling upon the sweeping view of history we have acquired in modern times, we can see that something like the rise of the Vedic religions produced meaningful changes for the cultures affected by it. Yet, such cultural transformations took hundreds, if not thousands, of years to occur. And ancient peoples had no history books to tell them what had happened more than a few generations prior; by our standards, at least, they lacked historical consciousness. From the perspective *within* such a culture, the world simply did not change enough over the course of a single lifetime for anyone to register the change— beyond the regular ebb and flow of nature, harrowing enough in itself. Thus, to the extent that people longed for an escape from the rise and fall of the Wheel of Time, they would natu- rally not expect this change to arise within the present order. They could only dream of a peace that would one day come through a transcendence of that order—through a radical transformation of their way of being into something that better resembled the calm stability of the stars.

Whether Greek mythology borrowed directly from Vedic sources, or these two traditions developed their respective mythologies out of a similar life experience, it is not difficult to find echoes of the cyclical Vedic worldview in Greek writ- ings. Hesiod, for instance, an epic poet of the eighth century

BCE and a contemporary of Homer, describes a series of ages through which the world cycles. These start with the Golden Age, during which people live in peace, stability, and abundance, then progress through the increasingly coarsening Silver, Bronze, Heroic, and Iron Ages. The last of these ages is characterized by warfare, brutality, and scarcity; it is the age we currently occupy. A few centuries after Hesiod, Plato was one of the first great representatives of a new type of Greek thinker—philosophers, who began trying to move beyond the mythical mode of storytelling to establish a more rational means of describing our world. Plato nonetheless referred back to the Hesiodic cycle. It is sometimes difficult to know exactly what Plato believed, since he wrote in dialogue form and his characters express a variety of views that he may or may not have shared. Nevertheless, his works invoke images of cyclical motion frequently enough that it seems likely he believed the world perpetually moves through a series of ages, perhaps as influenced by the movements of heavenly bodies. Notably, Plato introduced the notion of the "Great Year," the time required for the sun and planets to complete enough circuits across the sky that all return to their original configuration; the Platonically inspired poet W. B. Yeats later calculated this period to be around 26,000 years. Presumably, the completion of a Great Year would be a time of renewal for humankind, when a new Golden Age could begin.

On a similar cyclical note, Plato's favorite protagonist—his real-life teacher, Socrates—frequently observes that the human soul is not just immortal, but is reborn through a series of reincarnations. What Plato is best known for, however, is his Theory of Forms. While not exactly a cyclical doctrine, the theory draws upon the same intuition that cyclical myths sought to express: even as life is beset by perpetual change, often confusing and not infrequently threatening, all of this flux is underlain by a deeper, more orderly, unchanging reality. In Plato's case, he arrived at this conviction through reasoning. Consider, for instance, the trees around us. We see that an individual tree may grow to a great height, yet one day decays or is chopped into firewood. But what it means to be a tree—the form of the tree—does not change, even as individual trees come and go. Individual trees must therefore be mere shadowy reflections of a deeper reality, which Plato located in an unchanging realm of Forms. He was never able to fully explain what exactly the Form of the Tree is or where it resides. Over the course of the Platonic dialogues, Socrates tries a number of different accounts of the Forms, none achieving perfect clarity. Nor, Socrates points out, should this surprise us. Because we spend so much of our lives immersed in the fleeting, delusive world of appearances, all we can do is catch brief glimpses of the Forms here and there, and only after tremendous intellectual effort. Imperfect as our experience of the Forms may therefore be, Plato also clearly regarded such contemplation of the Forms as the highest possible human endeavor. This was his *moksha*, his escape from the turmoil of everyday life, although—reflecting the rising spirit of Greek rationalism—this transport to a realm of transcendent peace and stability was to be achieved, not through religious devotion or spiritual practice, but through the disciplined exercise of our powers of reasoning.

Plato's most illustrious pupil, Aristotle, was far more

practical and more focused on this world than his teacher. Thus, if Plato thought philosophers were at their best when engaging in flights of pure reason, Aristotle could be considered the first empirical scientist in the Western tradition, focusing his attention on such ordinary objects as rocks, trees, and animals. Accordingly, Aristotle does not provide us with the same sweeping images of the cosmos as we find in Plato's dialogues. Nevertheless, Aristotle's philosophy has a quiet, cyclical character all its own, even if we must work harder to tease this out. In any case, we need to at least mention Aristotle here, given the prominent role his metaphysics would ultimately play in medieval philosophy, such that its *rejection* by early modern thinkers would be one of the crucial spurs to the Scientific Revolution and the progressive worldview it inspired.

In his defining metaphysical move, Aristotle accepted Plato's argument that "what it means to be a tree" is what remains constant, yet he rejected his teacher's claim that Forms must therefore reside in some ethereal realm transcendent to nature. Rather, Aristotle argued, everyday objects such as rocks, trees, and animals contain their forms or natures within them. Obviously, Aristotle had no conception of DNA, yet he seems to regard an object's form as a sort of immaterial DNA, containing all the properties that define the object as that type of object, and a plan for its development. Hence, the acorn grows into an oak tree, with its broad leaf canopy and other characteristic features, because the acorn already contains the oaken form within it, even before it has begun to sprout.

This account of inner forms or natures gives Aristotle's

metaphysics its strongly teleological character. In Aristotle's account of the world, the movements we observe are not generally blind groping or the random collision of atoms in the void. Rather, actions are generally directed towards determinate ends, specifically, the ends that particular objects contain within them, in virtue of their forms. This teleological movement, in turn, makes room for a certain notion of progress in Aristotle's philosophy: an object is making progress when it is moving toward fulfilling its inner nature. A young lion, for instance, makes progress when a series of successful hunts provides it with the nutrition required to grow into a more mature lion. That said, this type of progress does not bring the lion to an actual end state, where it could stop striving and rest on its laurels. On the contrary, the mature lion must keep hunting and killing prey, not just because it always needs more calories, but because *this is what lions do*; hunting and killing prey *is what it means to be a lion*. And yet, even successfully fulfilling one's inner nature in this fashion is only a transitory achievement, since maturity is inevitably followed by decline and death. And thus, while the teleological nature of Aristotle's philosophy does lend a real directedness to the world he describes, it does not suggest a one-time, linear movement from point A to point B. Rather, striving to fulfill one's inner form or nature represents the upward arc of a turning wheel, sure to be followed by a downward turn.

If Aristotle focuses most of his attention on the here and now, his philosophy ends up describing a similarly cyclical world when he ventures into more metaphysical territory. Noting that an obvious reason why an object moves the way it does every day is because something has pushed it from behind, with this pusher having presumably been pushed by something behind it, Aristotle argues that this regress cannot continue forever, or else nothing could have initiated this chain of movements in the first place. In the closest Aristotle ever comes to practicing theology, therefore, he suggests the universe must be anchored by some sort of "unmoved mover." This quasi-deity does not set the universe into motion by giving it a push from behind. Rather, it exerts more of a force of attraction, pulling things towards it, in the sense of being the ultimate end towards which things strive. Once again, however, this "end" is not an *end state*, which the universe could reach and then stop striving. Aristotle thought it was logically possible for the universe to have either a beginning or an end. If, after all, the universe began at some time, then what was occurring before its birth? Likewise, if the universe were to end, what would happen after that? Hence, the world must be eternal, with the unmoved mover exerting a constant attractive force that keeps everything moving forever, rather than allowing the universe to grind to a halt.

This perpetual motion is observed most clearly, of course, in the heavens. And this points to another distinctive feature of Aristotle's philosophy: his claim that the celestial and mundane orders are governed by completely different principles. The most notable difference is that bodies here on earth, when left to their own devices, will tend to move in straight lines. The motion that comes naturally to celestial bodies, conversely, is circular, as evidenced by the circular orbits around the earth of the sun, moon, stars. (The Egyptian astronomer Ptolemy would later augment Aristotle's model of the universe to show that even the planets could be seen to move in a circular fashion, with their stuttering movement across the sky being explained by a series of epicycles embedded in the larger cyclical paths they follow.) In any case—borrowing an argument from Plato—Aristotle notes that the motions of mundane and celestial bodies are not just *different* from one another. Rather, circular motion is *better* than linear motion, because it is more perfect: A circle loops back and completes itself, whereas the movement tracing out a straight line is never finished. Presumably, therefore, the unmoved mover's first job is to keep the celestial realm moving in its perfect circles, while we do our best to approximate this circular movement by living in accord with a variety of natural cycles here below. Unlike Plato or the Vedic mystics, the ever-worldly Aristotle never suggests any paths by which we might simply leave our mundane condition behind and take up residence in the world's higher, calmer, more perfect region. Nevertheless, since all the world comprises substances and their forms, we can at least achieve some degree of harmony with the larger universe by doing our best to fulfill our own personal forms or natures, whatever these might be.

The Linear Worldview of the Ancient Hebrews

If most of the ancient world remained firmly rooted in a cyclical worldview, a small group of Semitic tribes in the Middle East was feeling its way towards a very different way of conceiving the world and the flow of time. This shift was by no means a clean break with the past, nor was it accomplished overnight. Nevertheless, the foundational narrative the Hebrew people began to tell—recounting where they came from as a people, where they were headed, how the world works, and what place human beings occupy in the world—started taking on a decidedly more linear character. This narrative was cobbled together over a span of nearly a thousand years, starting sometime before the tenth century BCE, with the earliest stories handed down orally for hundreds of years before being written down. Sometime between 600 and 400 BCE, the various books composing the story were collected into the Tanakh, or Hebrew Bible, with new material still being added until as late as 200 BCE. A few centuries after that, the Tanakh became the source material for the Christian Old Testament.

What made this Hebrew narrative more linear than cyclical? The hallmark of the linear conception of time is non-reversibility. In a cyclical world, things may change, but if you wait long enough, they will return to their original state. Hence, nothing is permanent in a cyclical world; nothing is done that cannot be undone, and probably will be at some point. The sun god may perish at the end of the day, but he is sure to rise again the next; the current generation may head towards old age and death, but the next generation will relive the joys of youth. In the story the Hebrews began to tell about their world, conversely, certain events take place that change things forever, with no going back to the previous state, and unmistakable differences between the time before and the time after. This happens most emphatically with the narrative's opening words: "In the beginning, God created the heavens and the earth." Whereas most ancient cultures assumed the world had always been around, forever tracing out the same circles, Genesis tells of a dramatic starting event. First there was nothing, then there was a world. Needless to say, things have never been the same since.

As the Hebrew narrative continues, it is frequently punctuated by similar non-reversible events. Adam and Eve disobey God and are kicked out of paradise, never to be allowed back in. Posted before Eden's gate, an angel with a flaming sword drives the point home: There is no going back to the ways things were before. When God, a few chapters later, nearly destroys the whole world in a flood, he promises Noah he will never do this again. Thenceforth, God places certain limits on his own actions, thus adopting a different relationship with his creation. Some generations hence, God tests Abraham's loyalty by commanding him to sacrifice his son, Isaac, granting a reprieve only when it has become clear Abraham is quite prepared to obey. God then makes another covenant, this time telling Abraham his descendants will be as numerous as the stars. From this time on, the Abrahamic line occupies a unique status as God's chosen people. And when God hands Moses the Ten Commandments, the people of Israel thenceforth have a law to live under. They may violate that law—and they often do—but there are now consequences for this, so people's lives are measurably different before and after the giving of the law.

As Thomas Cahill points out in *The Gifts of the Jews*—a book devoted to this shift in Jewish thinking from cyclical to linear time—the linear nature of the Hebrew narrative is heightened by that fact that its protagonists are not just personifications of natural phenomena, but individuals with personalities, histories, and emotions. When the sun god brings light and warmth in the morning, he is just doing what he has always done: this god's whole being involves nothing but bringing light and warmth. When God commands Abraham to kill Isaac, however, this comes only after Abraham and his wife, Sarah, have both lived to nearly a hundred years old without being able to conceive a child; suddenly, they are surprised to learn that Sarah is pregnant. Abraham must therefore have loved Isaac even more than most men love their sons, which makes God's command to kill Isaac all the more monstrous. The fact that Abraham was nonetheless prepared to obey God demonstrates the incredible, even irrational, faith he places in God. Taking all of this together, the Abrahamic drama has so many unique circumstances, characters, and dynamics that it could not possibly repeat itself, much less on a periodic basis. This was rather a one-time event, with a distinct before and after, and with effects felt to the present day, given that not just one major world religion, but three, trace their founding back to Abraham's seminal display of faith.

If the linear character of the Hebrew narrative thus clearly implies that time is moving *forward*, with there being no chance of going *back*, much less round and round in circles, this movement still does not have a clear *upward* or *downward* trajectory. This story contains no overriding sense that things are consistently improving or worsening over time, whether for the world as a whole or for the Jewish people in particular. There was the initial act of creation, of course, which God proclaims to be good. But this was followed almost immediately by Adam and Eve's eviction from Eden, which can hardly be viewed as a positive development. When God later covenants with Noah never again to destroy the world, this is perhaps a sign of progress, suggesting God has undergone some sort of moral growth. Yet, the telling words here are "never again." They underscore the fact that God has just nearly wiped out all of humanity—nor is this the last act of genocide God commits in the Hebrew Bible, even if future massacres are typically limited to a few thousand people. And while the story of the Exodus is an uplifting saga of freedom wrested from oppression that has inspired many liberation movements ever since, within a few hundred years of the escape from Egypt, the people of Israel were back in captivity in Babylon, just as they would later come under the yoke of Roman rule.

If the events of the Hebrew narrative therefore lack a clear upward or downward trajectory, the shift to a linear view of time did, however, allow its authors to introduce one key element into the Jewish worldview that was a rare commodity in the ancient world: hope. With a cyclical worldview, you may hope to catch an upturn of the Wheel of Life, but this is a tainted hope, since you know that eventually the wheel will drag you back down. That is why it is best, in this worldview, simply to concede that all life is suffering and to seek some sort of escape from the whole cycle of ups and downs. Nor, as mentioned before, was this an irrational or inappropriate response to the everyday reality most people faced in the ancient world. As a rule, there was very little chance that things were going to change significantly over the course of anyone's lifetime, whether with respect to technological know-how, material well-being, or social organization. So why not just hunker down and try to get through life without fighting against the tide? Such a resigned attitude can also help reinforce this very stasis, preventing people from recognizing and grabbing those opportunities for change that do occasionally present themselves, even in the most rigid societies.

In the Hebrew narrative, events are by no means always positive. Many terrible things happen, as often as not with God as their author. And yet the narrative also gives numerous examples of improvement over time—lasting material betterment. Sometimes it takes most of a person's lifetime for noticeable change to occur, as with Abraham and Sarah having to wait for their exceptional child, or Moses leading his people through the desert for forty years, to within sight of the promised land. Nevertheless, having a vision of hope—believing that positive change is possible, no matter how long it may take or how difficult it may be—can dramatically alter a culture's outlook. It can, when circumstances allow, become its own self-fulfilling prophecy, giving people the courage and fortitude they need to make it through the desert, sustained by a faith that one day they will arrive in the land of milk and honey, if only they can stay the course.

This sense of hope is particularly pervasive in some of the later books of the Tanakh—namely the prophetic works. These books contain no shortage of gloom and doom regarding the current state of the Hebrew people, as they faced both external threats and internal corruption. Yet, these books also look to a brighter future, to be realized through the imminent coming of a messiah, or savior. Many of these books were written during the period of Babylonian captivity, when the people of Israel really needed a savior. Notable, however, is that although the Hebrew prophets clearly believed the messiah would come from God, the salvation they sought was not some sort of *samsara*—not an escape from the present metaphysical order. Rather, they foresaw that the messiah would transform the present order, freeing the Jews from captivity, rebuilding the temple in Jerusalem, and putting Israel back into control of its own fate as a proud and prosperous nation. This belief—the conviction that lasting, significant change can be made within the present order—is a product of the linear view of time. And this way of viewing time, with its hopeful vision of a better future, forms the ultimate "gift of the Jews" that Cahill references in his title, a gift the ancient Hebrews bequeathed to the rest of the world.

The Declinist Worldview of Traditional Christianity

The belief that meaningful change can be brought about within the present order appears to have been shared by a certain carpenter from Nazareth whom a small band of Jews came to regard as the long-awaited messiah. As Jesus traveled around Israel, he performed numerous wonders, thereby strongly suggesting that he was no ordinary human being, but rather someone close to God. The heart of his message, however, lay in this world, in challenging the structures of oppression and bigotry built into both social convention and Jewish law. Taking the side of the weak, the poor, and the ostracized, Jesus railed against the rich and the powerful, arguing that while their fine robes and domineering behavior might win them approbation in society's eyes, they were hypocrites and vipers in God's eyes. Just as Jesus overturned the tables of the money changers in the temple, he sought to overturn the established social order—or at least sidestep it—by establishing an alternate kingdom in which lepers, prostitutes, and tax collectors were accorded just as much respect as kings and priests. This message was, of course, deeply threatening to both the Jewish hierarchy and the occupying Roman administration, which is why these two authorities conspired to execute Jesus.

To be sure, Jesus did not just speak about reforming the current social order or about realizing the Kingdom of God on earth. He also sometimes referred, albeit rather cryptically, to a life after death that was specifically *not* reincarnation into the present order, but rather—in the spirit of linearity—a permanent transport from the imperfect world here below to an unchanging heaven above. Jesus also spoke, even more cryptically, of a time not too far hence when the entire present order would be destroyed, with those who hearkened to his message being transported upwards to dwell with God forever, while those who opposed him would be condemned to eternal hell. For the small "Jesus movement" that persisted after Jesus's execution, in the face of sometimes brutal persecution, the notion of reforming the present order must have appeared, not just daunting, but downright impossible. The dream of metaphysically escaping the present order, conversely, would have provided immense relief—to say nothing of the thrill of imagining one's persecutors getting their just desserts. It is not surprising, therefore, that over the early centuries of the Common Era, many in the Jesus movement came to focus on the otherworldly aspects of Jesus's teachings. The die was therefore cast, such that even when Christianity began to coalesce into an actual religion, rising first to a position of respectability, then of power with the conversion of the Roman emperor Constantine in the fourth century CE, many Christians had come to regard the core promise of Jesus's teachings as being salvation, not *within* this world, but *from* this world. This understanding became orthodoxy by the early fifth century with the writings of the towering figure of early Christian theology, Augustine, Bishop of Hippo.

Augustine is crucial to our discussion of the differing trajectories worldviews can have, as his doctrines of original sin and substitutionary atonement gave the Christian narrative its distinctively downward vector. Much of this story is familiar to us from the Tanakh. In the beginning, God created the world, and it was good. God then created Adam and Eve in the Garden of Eden, which was paradise. But the first couple sinned by violating God's direct commandment, and thenceforth were banished from the Garden, condemned instead to a life of struggle and suffering. It was here that Augustine offered a novel interpretation of this Hebrew story, arguing that all of Adam's descendants inherited this same sin. This means we are all sinners, rightfully condemned for the original sin of Adam, which we still bear within us. Yet, even more significant is the effect this original sin has on our current actions: it corrupts us into committing further sins of our own. Thus, we are like alcoholics whose addiction leaves us unable to resist another drink, sinners whose sinful condition renders us incapable of resisting an ever deeper slide into sin. With all of us, therefore, actively hastening our own descents into the mire, the larger world is locked in a downward spiral from which it cannot right itself. The good news, however, is that while we have not done anything to merit any grace, God in his mercy sent his son Jesus into the world to take our sins upon himself and submit to death on a cross in our stead—substitutionary atonement—thereby making it morally justifiable for God to forgive our sins, provided only that we repent and request this forgiveness. The need for universal condemnation having thus been transcended, when Jesus rose from the dead and ascended into heaven, he could bring with him those choosing to follow. To bring finality to this cosmic drama, Jesus would return at the close of the age—presumably not far off—to complete what had been the self-destruction of the present order, performing a final separation of the wheat from the chaff and building a New Jerusalem in which the faithful could dwell blissfully for all eternity, while casting those who still refused to repent into an unquenchable lake of fire.

Note that this narrative does contain certain elements of the old cyclical stories. Both the resurrection of Jesus and the creation of a New Jerusalem (essentially a new Eden) harken back to countless older stories of death and rebirth. Nevertheless, the Christian foundational narrative—like the Hebrew narrative from which it arose—does not repeat itself periodically. It is instead a one-time, non-reversible series of events with a distinct beginning, middle, and end. In fact, the Christian story takes the open-ended Hebrew narrative and gives it a more distinct endpoint, even if the precise date of this endpoint appears to have slipped past original expectations. Bolstering the linear character of the story is a central protagonist who may share in the divinity of the transcendent God yet who is also exceedingly human, having a life story filled with the sorts of personal details that do not readily admit to repetition—being born in a stable to a specific mother and father, for instance, during the time of the rule of Herod the Great. Unlike the Hebrew story, however, which is marked by constant ups and downs, the Christian story—particularly as interpreted by Augustine—portrays a world that has been sliding ineluctably downward ever since its first moments. And with the doctrine of original sin rendering it metaphysically impossible for the world to pull itself out of this decline, little hope is left that anything can meaningfully improve within the current order. Accordingly, the hope Jesus does provide is that we can be transported to a completely different order, one where, "God will wipe every tear from their eyes, and there will be no more death or sorrow or crying or pain"—a transformation so radical it can only be accomplished *through* our deaths, whether individually or through the complete destruction of our familiar world.

As the Church grew in power and began to dominate European social, political, and intellectual life, its declinist worldview came to shape Western thinking for well over a millennium and a half, with profound implications for all of European society. One of the most immediate effects of this declinist worldview was the loss of learning that characterized the early medieval period. The Dark Ages may not have been quite as dark as once thought, with the isolated scholar here or there—usually tucked behind the walls of some secluded monastery—continuing to do little bits of intellectual work. Nevertheless, untold numbers of Greek and Roman texts were simply lost to the European world, and the scholarship that did take place focused almost exclusively on theology, and specifically on questions of the nature of God and our immortal souls. The study of the physical world, in particular, came to a standstill. If, after all, the world around us is hopelessly corrupt and soon to be destroyed, what good can possibly come of studying it? Indeed, what good can come from exercising our human powers of reasoning, at all, since any knowledge not given to us directly by God is just guaranteed to lead us deeper into sin?

With intellectual effort therefore slowing to a crawl, innovations in the social, political, or economic orders were simply not contemplated, much less implemented. Instead, Europe settled into a rigid feudal order where kings and lords ruled over their peasants with virtual impunity, yet everyone was locked into their particular place in the social hierarchy by the accident of birth. The vast majority of the population pursued a subsistence living through farming, but since peasants owed a significant portion of their meager harvest to the local lord in feudal dues, even subsistence could be threatened by a single bad stretch of weather or a crop infestation. Warfare was common, and while a lord theoretically had the feudal obligation to provide his peasants with military protection, he also had the power to conscript them into military service, thereby pouring their lives into his petty squabbles with the neighboring lord. With everyday life being so bleak, when lords and peasants engaged in the one experience they shared—going to the local cathedral to hear mass—it is unlikely anyone thought to dispute the priest's message that the world around us was on its way to hell, with the only hope for an improved condition coming after our deaths.

By around the twelfth century, the European mind did begin to stir itself. Notably, a large number of Greek philosophical texts—long lost to the West, but preserved in Islamic libraries to the east—began trickling back into Europe, thereby helping re-ignite an interest in learning. Thomas Aquinas took the lead in synthesizing Christian theology with the newly rediscovered physics and metaphysics of Aristotle, at the same time providing scholars with theological cover for the renewed study of nature: Aquinas argued that because God had created the world and proclaimed it good, reading the "Book of Nature" gives us one more path to knowing the mind of God, even if this path would always be subordinate to studying the revealed Word of God. Over subsequent centuries, the modern university system came into being through the founding of such Church-sponsored institutions as the Universities of Paris, Bologna, Oxford, and Cambridge. Theology remained the king of disciplines, but physics ultimately found a place in the standard university curriculum. For reasons we will consider in the next chapter, the approach taken to the study of nature within "the schools" was not terribly productive; hence, the loss of natural knowledge that characterized the Dark Ages was replaced more by stasis than actual progress. Nevertheless, the study of the natural world was at least back on the table.

The Italian Renaissance of the fourteenth through seventeenth centuries added more life to Europe's reawakening cultural and intellectual scene, particularly through a dramatic flourishing of the arts and other "humanistic" disciplines. While invigorating in many ways, this movement did little to challenge the downward trajectory of the worldview handed down from the Middle Ages. For one thing, the Church continued to dominate cultural life, particularly near its seat in Rome, and thus the story of the paradise lost was never far in the background. Moreover, both the arts and the scholarly disciplines of the Renaissance were dominated by classicism, the driving goal of which was to rediscover and recreate the accomplishments of ancient Greece and Rome. This obsession with all things classical essentially gave rise to a second declinist narrative, complete with its own Golden Age and fall: the heights of creative and intellectual achievement were reached by the ancients, with the abandonment of classical culture plunging Europe into the darkness of the early medieval period. Indeed, the term "dark ages" was coined, and given its pejorative connotations, by Renaissance scholars who hoped to regain paradise by resuscitating the cultural glories of the past.

In northern Europe, meanwhile, Martin Luther shook up religious life in 1517 by nailing a series of ninety-five theses critical of the Roman Church to the door of Wittenberg Cathedral, thereby sparking the Protestant Reformation. Luther's most immediate objection was to such contemporary Church practices as the sale of "indulgences"—essentially promises of future salvation in exchange for donations to Rome today, needed to fund the building of Saint Peter's Basilica. More broadly, Luther argued that parishioners should not have to go through the hierarchy of the Church to reach God, but rather every individual was capable of foster-ing a direct relationship with their creator. This re-thinking of the relationship of God and humans created a space for individual thought and conscience that would eventually help shape much of modern thinking. In the short term, however, Luther and such fellow reformers as John Calvin wholeheart-edly embraced Augustine's doctrine of original sin and the resulting declinist narrative, insisting that salvation can be won only in the next life, and only through a belief in the grace of Jesus Christ, not through any sort of works we might perform of our own agency, whether in the intellectual, polit-ical, or moral spheres.

As it happens, the individual's inability to bring about meaningful change in their lives corresponded to the every-day reality faced by the majority of people living across Europe, where life remained essentially grim. All but a small elite lived under conditions that we would now consider extreme poverty. Nutrition was poor, sanitation unheard of, and very few people could afford what medical care was available—which probably made them the lucky ones, given the success rate most physicians could boast. Disease was common, and catastrophic plagues periodically killed large numbers of people, with the Black Death of the fourteenth century reducing the European population by an astound-ing 30 percent to 60 percent. Social mobility was essentially non-existent, as the feudal system provided no realistic path by which a person born a peasant could ascend to the nobil-ity. Wars were common, and the Reformation increased their frequency and destructiveness by pitting Catholic and Prot-estant princes against one another in a series of devastating, continent-wide wars that had as much to do with theology as territory. These religious wars, in turn, helped prod the loose-knit feudal kingdoms of the Middle Ages to consolidate into more centralized nation-states, thus giving monarchs a power that was even more absolute than before. For most Europeans, therefore, everyday life was a struggle, with little realistic hope of improvement within a person's lifetime. It is little wonder, therefore, that the declinist worldview preached in both Catholic and Protestant churches continued to ring true for the mass of Europeans, who continued to place their hope, such as it was, in an afterlife that promised a radical departure from the present order.

It should be noted that this widespread fatalism was not unwelcome to the lucky few who happened to occupy the upper ranks of European society, whether in the political or ecclesiastical hierarchies. Any declinist ideology, after all, will naturally be conservative in character: setting out from the belief that things are getting worse over time, the declinist view implies we should do everything in our power to arrest the slide, including freezing social conditions as they are. In a European political order where a small number of kings, popes, lords, and priests wielded a tremendous amount of power and privilege over everyone else, this meant preserving, if not sharpening, these inequalities. Thus, to the extent that the average subject did not believe the current social order could possibly be changed, this helped preserve and strengthen the power of the ruling classes. Yet, this convergence between the prevailing declinist worldview and the interests of the ruling classes was not merely a lucky coincidence. On the contrary, the priests—under the watchful eye of the king and his nobles—provided the uneducated masses with their only vision of a world larger than the fields they plowed. The priests, more specifically, were charged with providing everyone with a narrative detailing where the world comes from, where it is headed, how it operates, and what place human beings occupy within it. It was quite natural, therefore, that over time they would slant the stories they told in favor of maintaining the status quo, slanting them to preserve or augment the power and privilege that both the political and the ecclesiastical hierarchies enjoyed.

To be clear, neither medieval European priests nor even the kings they served had an absolute free hand in the sorts of stories told about the world. Throughout medieval Europe, the traditional Christian narrative was the only foundational story most Europeans had ever heard, while being thoroughly interwoven into all of Europe's social traditions and governing institutions. Beyond this, however, it provided large numbers of people with metaphysical solace amid a very difficult life. Outside of a few small Jewish communities, therefore, no one in medieval Europe had much reason to question the received Christian narrative, or *wanted* to question it. Finally, as a story that had been written down for over a millennium, it was not able to be changed ad hoc. All of that said, the biblical stories still left plenty of room for creative license in exactly *how* they were retold and interpreted. It is unsurprising, therefore, that most priests would tend to favor the interpretation that best promoted their own interests, and those of their political patrons, which meant maintaining Europe's highly stratified socio-political system, while discouraging any thoughts of significant social change.

And given the Christian narrative they were handed, the best way the priests could do this was to downplay the scriptural passages in which Jesus called the rich and powerful to account, instead hammering home the Augustinian message that the current order is so hopelessly corrupt as to be not worth fixing, with our best course therefore being to keep our heads down, do whatever is commanded by our lord in heaven and the lord in the manor down the road, all while placing our hopes for reward in the next life.

As self-reinforcing as medieval Europe's declinist worldview therefore was, by the middle centuries of the millennium, a few cracks had begun to appear in both this worldview and the ossified social order built around it. An emerging merchant class—with members neither peasants nor lords—began opening a space for the acquisition of wealth and power outside the feudal system. These same merchants traveled extensively, bringing exotic goods and stories back with them from abroad. Indeed, kings' and merchants' lust for acquisition fueled an era of exploration and discovery that multiplied the size of the known world several times over. In addition to gold and silver, explorers returned home with biological and mineral specimens never previously seen or documented in Europe, thus suggesting that the knowledge of the ancients had not been as complete or perfect as Renaissance scholars thought. And in the sixteenth century, the Polish astronomer Nicolaus Copernicus advanced the surprising claim that the Earth does not remain stationary beneath our feet, with the celestial bodies revolving around it, but rather the sun remains motionless at the center of the universe, while the Earth, planets, and stars all travel in circular orbits around it.

When Copernicus first published his theory in 1543, the final year of his life, it did not actually create much of a stir at the time; his writings were not placed on the Inquisition's Index of banned books until some fifty years later. Only when the heliocentric model of the solar system started gaining some influential followers did its full implications began to sink in for Europe's ruling powers. For one thing, the Copernican theory directly contradicts the geocentric model of the universe Ptolemy had adapted from Aristotle's writings in the second century CE, which meant Copernicus was claiming to know more than two revered ancient authorities. More significantly, the heliocentric model challenges the Genesis account of creation by suggesting that human beings do not stand at the center of the created universe, whether literally or figuratively: Can we really be God's chosen creatures if we spend our time flying around space on the third planet from the sun? Most significantly of all, however—though no one could have recognized it at the time—Copernicus's new theory presaged a new approach to the study of nature that would coalesce over the seventeenth century and beyond. Leaving behind the barren disputations of scholastic philosophers, the modern scientific method would become an engine for the acquisition of new knowledge, thus giving rise, first, to a notion of sustained intellectual advance, then to an entire worldview shaped by a dynamic, not of cyclicality or decline, but of continuous ascent or progress.

CHAPTER 2

THE SCIENTIFIC REVOLUTION: THE BIRTH OF PROGRESS

This chapter examines how modern science changed the study of nature, and how this inspired a new way of looking at the world, built around the notion of progress. To understand why the Scientific Revolution was so revolutionary in the seventeenth century, however, we first need to consider what it was a revolt *against*. First and foremost, it was against the philosophy of Aristotle, as appropriated by Christian theologians of the late medieval period. We will therefore briefly return to Aristotle and his medieval interpreters, focusing on their approach to the study of nature, before considering how the modern scientific method that arose over the seventeenth century would eventually lead, not just to the progressive worldview, but to the modern world.

The Scholastic-Aristotelian Approach to the Study of Nature

As the previous chapter noted, the rediscovery of Aristotle's physics and metaphysics in the twelfth century spurred a revival of the study of nature in Europe, and for the next five hundred years, virtually all "natural philosophy" was conducted within an Aristotelian framework. Because most of this work was done within church-sponsored universities, or "the Schools," it came to be known as the scholastic, or scholastic-Aristotelian, approach to nature. As similarly noted in the last chapter, this way of doing science was markedly unproductive. That is not to say absolutely nothing new was learned about nature over the medieval period. Still, the pace of learning was extraordinarily slow, and its reliability was virtually nonexistent, with numerous false claims being accepted alongside truthful claims for centuries, and no one being able to tell the difference. To see why the scholastic-Aristotelian approach was so unproductive, let us first consider Aristotle's metaphysics in more detail.

For Aristotle, as previously noted, the world was composed of substances. By "substance," Aristotle did not mean anything fancy. He just meant things. This table, that rock, this oak tree, that human being are all substances. And as we saw, whereas Plato had argued that things are what they are because they somehow participate in an archetypal, otherworldly Form, Aristotle believed that things contain their forms within them: An oak tree is an oak because it has the form of an oak. This form or nature is not a physical component of the object. Rather, it is the principle that gives the object (1) its essential unity—it is *one* oak tree, a discrete, self-contained object distinct from the tree next to it; (2) its identity—it is an *oak tree*, not an elm tree, a rock, or a human being; and (3) a dynamic plan for its development—the acorn is already striving to be a mature oak, as guided by its inner form. A substance gains the second of these components, its identity, from the properties that define its essence. Aristotle defined human beings, for instance, as "rational animals," with animality implying a list of properties we share with other sentient beings, whereas rationality is the property that sets us apart from other animals. All these properties help compose our essence, although rationality most truly defines the human essence. Individual people may well have other properties that apply to them, such as "dark-haired" or "tall." Such properties do not affect our basic humanness, however, so they are classified as accidental, rather than essential, properties. It goes without saying that accidents do not merit careful study, since they can come and go without changing the essential nature of a particular substance.

Given that the world comprises substances with properties, it follows that the study of nature should consist, first and foremost, of examining physical objects one by one, cataloguing them, and making lists of their essential properties. And this, in fact, is what Aristotle did, making some of the world's first empirical studies of various types of natural objects. He even charged his former pupil, Alexander the Great, with sending back interesting specimens from his far-ranging conquests. This was certainly a reasonable first step toward gaining a rational understanding of nature. The downside of this approach, however, is that it is very slow and incremental. Simply put, a huge number of different types of object exist out there, so if you study each one by one, in isolation from all the others, it is going to take a very long time to amass a significant body of knowledge. No matter how much detail you may gather about one type of object, this still only tells you about that type of object, with there still being countless other objects out there, about which you have learned nothing.

Significantly, what is *not* studied on the Aristotelian approach to nature are the relations between things. Because individual substances each have their own essential unity, they are fully discrete from one another: This chair is this chair, and that table is that table, and never the twain shall meet, since each carries its own form within it. Granted, at any given time, it may be true that, "This chair is sitting in front of that table." Still, "sitting in front of a particular table" can only be an accidental property of a chair; it is not an essential property since the chair would still be a chair if it were moved away from the table. Relations thus having nothing to do with things as they are in themselves, they are deemed unworthy of careful study. The result, again, is that you can study chairs for as long as you like, but this will tell you nothing useful about tables—nor about oak trees, rocks, or people. Nor will your study of chairs tell you anything about the ways chairs and tables typically interact; for instance, people often sit in chairs placed before a table. All in all, therefore, the acquisition of knowledge remains a slow, incremental process on the Aristotelian model, and one that still does not tell us everything we might like to know about our subject matter.

To be fair, there is one way in which Aristotle did consider the specimens he studied in relation to one another. When cataloguing natural objects, Aristotle did not simply jot their names in a book. Rather, he organized them into systems of genera and species based on their similarities and differences.

Thus, because human beings are sentient creatures that can move about under our own power—a property we share with other animals—we belong to the overarching genus of animal. We further share such specific traits as warm-bloodedness, live birth, and lactation with other mammals, so we belong to the sub-genus of mammal, as distinguished from other sub-genera such as amphibians, insects, or birds. Our rationality, meanwhile, sets us apart from other mammals, and indeed from all other animals, so this is what defines us as a distinct species. For Aristotle, this tree-like division of things into genera and species was not merely a convenient system of classification that we, as observers, subjectively apply to the objects around us. Rather, this classificatory system has an objective existence of its own, reflecting the logical structure of reality. To better navigate the world's logical underpinnings, therefore, Aristotle further studied deductive logic, a discipline that allows us to draw conclusions about the properties of individuals based on their membership in larger genera or species.

The basic form of deductive argument is the syllogism; Aristotle gave us its classic example. "Socrates is a man. All men are mortal. Therefore Socrates is mortal." The advantage of this form of argument is its absolute certainty. If the argument's two premises are true, then it is absolutely, positively certain that the conclusion will also be true, solely in virtue of the argument's form. The problem with deductive logic is that it cannot really teach us anything we do not already know about the world. For instance, if we know Socrates is a man—as required to assert the initial premise in the syllogism above—then we must have known, at least implicitly, that he is mortal. Were Socrates still alive today, some 2,600 years after his birth, we might consider him a god or a demon, but we never would have classified him as a man. Hence, while the conclusion, "Socrates is mortal," may well be true, it is not novel; it has not advanced our knowledge of the world.

To be sure, if you tell me a wombat is a mammal, and I know that all mammals bear their young live, then even if I have never witnessed a wombat birth—even if I have never heard of this animal—I can nonetheless conclude that wombats bear their young live. Accordingly, my *personal* knowledge has been extended through this act of deductive reasoning. Nevertheless, *someone* must have watched wombats bearing their young live, or this animal never would have been classified as a mammal in the first place. The syllogism in question has therefore done nothing to extend our *collective* knowledge. (Nor have we touched on the problems presented by the platypus, an egg-laying mammal.) In any case, as useful as deductive logic may be in helping us organize our knowledge and maintain its coherence, it does not, in itself, add anything to this knowledge. Thus, deduction is unlikely to enrich or invigorate the slow, incremental study of nature that Aristotle's doctrine of substance implies.

To his credit, Aristotle did at least find time in his busy schedule to go out and study a wide variety of natural specimens, noting and recording their properties. But when his scholastic successors later revived his substance-based approach to nature, they generally omitted this key step of empirical observation. The primary mode of instruction used within scholastic institutions was "disputation," whereby two professors would be assigned to debate a proposition before the class, one given the affirmative stance, the other the negative. Various forms of argument were recognized as valid means of scoring points within the debate. One was deductive logic, limited in ways we have already seen. Another was the appeal to authority. Of course, scripture was always the safest authority to cite, but when the proposition being debated concerned the natural world, Aristotle—usually referred to in debate transcripts simply as "The Philosopher"—was the go-to authority. The problem, of course, is that Aristotle was just one man, and he had made his observations some two thousand years prior, so he had not really managed to amass many empirical facts. Some of the facts he did record, moreover, or else the conclusions he drew from these facts, were wrong. Medieval scholars, meanwhile, almost never went outside to examine the rocks or flowers or celestial bodies they were debating. This left them with no objective means of determining whether the assertions they debated were true or false. Disputations thus devolved into little more than rhetorical contests, with the prize generally being given to the most verbally gifted professor, notwithstanding the fact that no one's knowledge of the natural world had been advanced in the slightest.

All of these deficiencies notwithstanding, the scholastic-Aristotelian approach to the study of nature remained dominant within the Schools throughout the late medieval period. Until well into the seventeenth century, therefore, if you wanted to receive any sort of formal training in natural philosophy, you would be taught scholastic-Aristotelianism. By the beginning of the seventeenth century, however, a handful of thinkers, mostly working outside the Schools, had begun to see the many weaknesses of the scholastic approach while groping their way toward a new, more productive means of studying nature.

The Search for a New Method

To the natural philosophers of the early seventeenth century who were frustrated with Aristotle and his medieval successors, it seemed clear that the key to unlocking the secrets of nature was to find the proper method, then rigorously follow it. They disagreed only about what the proper scientific method was. At risk of over-generalizing, we can say these forerunners of the Scientific Revolution split themselves into two camps, largely along geographic lines, with those in the British Isles favoring an empirically-based approach to nature, and those on the European continent inclining more toward rationalism. Both sides had their great champions; we will here mention only the most prominent representative of each camp.

Francis Bacon, onetime Lord Chancellor of England, was more of a statesman, orator, and writer than a practicing scientist, but in works such as the *Novum Organum* and the *New Atlantis,* he began laying out a program for scientific research that harkened back to Aristotle in many ways—though contrasting sharply with the watered-down Aristotelianism of the scholastics. Most notably, Bacon stressed the importance of empirical observation. He rejected any approach to nature that begins with a metaphysical doctrine, then attempts to squeeze the phenomena we observe under it.

Rather, before we even start trying to explain nature, Bacon argued, we should make a grand survey of all known natural objects and phenomena, recording everything we can observe about them, to give scientists an objective, unbiased data base from which to begin their theorizing. The information recorded might include lists of the properties generally associated with particular types of objects, per Aristotle. Yet, it would also include such "accidental" properties as when and where a particular phenomenon tends to arise, what other phenomena usually accompany it, and what phenomena with which it is never seen. In a sense, this would be an intensified version of Aristotle's first forays into empirical research. Recognizing the great magnitude of this task, however—far beyond the capabilities of any one researcher—Bacon advocated for the creation of a scientific establishment, to be organized and funded by the state, since the state would be the ultimate beneficiary of any new learning this endeavor might produce.

As much of an accomplishment as this initial survey of known phenomena would be, Bacon saw it as only the beginning of the scientific endeavor. A massive amount of data having been collected, scientists could then start analyzing and drawing broader conclusions. This would be, Bacon suggested, mostly through inductive reasoning. Induction is essentially the converse judgment as deduction: Whereas deductive reasoning moves from the general to the particular—from "All men are mortal" to "Socrates is mortal"—inductive reasoning moves from the particular to the general. Thus, if I observe that this crow is black, and this crow is black, and that crow is black, I may venture the more general assertion that *all* crows are black. The scholastics had long turned their noses up at inductive reasoning, since it lacks the certainty of deductive judgments: For all I know, the next crow I see may be white, which would nullify my general claim about all crows being black. What Bacon recognized, however, is that scientific claims do not have to be absolutely certain to be objective and useful. Most crows really are black, and determining this through empirical observation meaningfully advances our knowledge about birds. Nor does the fact that we occasionally stumble across an albino crow invalidate our knowledge of crows; doing so enriches it. For now we know even more about crows—that they are usually black, but occasionally white—and this can drive our research forward by spurring us to investigate why crows end up the color they do. Indeed, Bacon argued, research should ultimately be directed toward learning, not just what properties things have, but the causes of these properties. If I observe, for instance, that crows with two black parents are never white, whereas crows with at least one white parent are often white, I can risk the inductive judgment that parentage—rather than, say, a bird's diet—is the cause of a crow's color.

Continuing to outline his program, Bacon advised that, after putting forth an inductive judgment, we should return to observation to see whether the general claim being proffered is borne out by experience. And if nature does not readily provide us with the observations required for this, we can devise experiments that do. To be sure, when we perform such empirical testing, there is always the chance that nature will contradict a general claim just put forward, thereby invalidating it, fully or partially. And no doubt this is frustrating. But this setback then impels us to look for ways to correct or refine our original claim, and this may well lead to knowledge that is not only more solid than what we had before but that also covers something we had not previously known: We have extended our knowledge. In sum, therefore, Bacon argued that what is required for the study of nature to be both fruitful and rigorous is not the absolute certainty of deductive logic, sterile in its clinging to what is already known. Rather, we need the brasher, more exploratory judgments of inductive logic—just reined in by the objective check that comes from continually returning to empirical observation.

Across the English Channel, the Frenchman René Descartes agreed with Bacon that deductive logic does not generally produce new knowledge. Descartes was not so quick, however, to give up on the goal of certainty in science. On the contrary, this widely-recognized father, not just of continental rationalism but of modern philosophy in general, made a career of seeking certainty. His most well-known assertion was, "I think, therefore I am"—a claim meant to be so absolutely, certainly true that it could not possibly be doubted. (If I doubt I exist, this means I am doubting, yet I must exist to be doubting, thus confirming that I exist.) In his *Meditations on First Philosophy*, Descartes uses this single, indubitable truth as a foundation upon which to build a whole raft of philosophical assertions, all of which he claimed to be equally certain.

Striving to bring this same level of certainty to the work he did within a variety of scientific disciplines, including optics, mechanics, and anatomy, Descartes argued that the way to achieve certainty in science is through a careful application of method. And indeed, two of his earliest works, *Rules for the Direction of the Mind* and *Discourse on Method*, were devoted specifically to the question of how we ought to study nature, or really anything. For the history of science, Rule Five from *Rules for the Direction of the Mind* proved to be among Descartes's most influential contributions:

> The whole method consists entirely in the ordering and arranging of the objects on which we must concentrate our mind's eye if we are to discover some truth. We shall be following this method exactly if we first reduce complicated and obscure propositions step by step to simpler ones, and then, starting with the intuition of the simplest ones of all, try to ascend through the same steps to knowledge of all the rest.

This general approach to science has come to be known as "reductionism," and its basic insight is straightforward. When we observe the natural phenomena around us, many of them are extremely complex and confusing, to the point that, if we were to set out trying to explain them in all their complex entirety, we hardly even know where to begin. The trick, therefore, is to break a complex phenomenon into simpler components and, if necessary, break these components into even simpler parts. Eventually, we will arrive at a subject matter so simple that the mind can grasp it with intuitive clarity. With a set of indubitable building blocks thus having been established and fully comprehended, we can start putting the pieces back together; we essentially reconstruct the more complex phenomenon in step-by-step fashion, until we arrive back at our original subject matter. Now, however, we are able to offer a clear and comprehensive explanation of the phenomenon, the confusion and obscurity that first cloaked its inner workings having been stripped away.

But how, more precisely, do we go about "breaking down" the natural objects we wish to study? For Descartes, the answer was not necessarily to dissect phenomena into smaller and smaller physical parts. Rather, he preferred to proceed by a method of abstraction. Having received a scholastic education, Descartes was familiar with the distinction between essential and accidental properties. When he turned to the study of physical bodies, therefore, he asked which of their properties are essential, and which are accidental. The bodies we observe all have some color to them, yet take away a body's color, and it is still a body, albeit transparent. The same goes for the smell associated with a body, or its temperature, or its taste. Even a body's hardness—the fact that it resists other bodies moving into the same space it occupies—can be abstracted out, and there will still be something there, even if just a ghostly geometric shape. Take away this shape, however, or more generally the fact that the body is extended in space, and there will be nothing left; there will be nothing within which such properties as color, temperature, or hardness could be housed. The essence of physical bodies, Descartes concluded, must lie in their extension, with their essential properties therefore being those that can be expressed in the geometric terms of size, shape, number, and motion. Other observed properties are merely accidental, so their study is secondary. In fact, if accidental properties are to be given a scientific account, they must be derived from the body's more foundational geometric properties.

Having reduced physical bodies to their geometric shape, Descartes was in a position to leave his scholastic roots behind and kick his new rationalistic approach to the study of nature into high gear. Recall, once again, that while deductive logic ensures formal certainty, it does not produce fresh knowledge because it merely draws properties out of concepts that were already there. "Mortality" was already included in the concept of "man," so we are merely drawing this fact out when we conclude that Socrates, the man, is mortal. Consider the concept of the triangle, however. It is defined by a relatively basic set of properties, such as, "closed rectilinear figure," "three sides," and "three angles." Nowhere does the concept of the triangle contain the fact that its three angles will add up to two right angles, or 180 degrees. Nevertheless, geometers since Euclid had been using simple, intuitively clear proofs to demonstrate this fact, along with many others, about triangles. Such facts are not contained within the concept of the triangle, and thus a particular fact may never have been noticed by any previous mathematicians. Nevertheless, such facts can be demonstrated with absolute, intuitive certainty. Geometry therefore retains the certainty of deductive logic while also allowing for novelty, or the discovery of new knowledge. And this means—Descartes cheerfully concluded—that if physical objects can be reduced to their geometric shapes, researchers can unlock the secrets of nature simply by sitting at their desks and doing geometry!

This, in fact, is how Descartes conceived the scientific project, and as an accomplished mathematician, another key contribution he made to the advancement of science was his invention of analytic geometry. Introducing the Cartesian coordinates that now bear his name, Descartes developed the means by which we describe lines, curves, and other geometric shapes using algebraic equations, thus promising to bring additional precision and certainty to the study of nature. And because Descartes and his fellow mathematicians were enjoying such success in discovering mathematical truths that were novel, yet objectively certain, Descartes believed the study of material nature could proceed at a similar pace, perhaps even unlocking all the major secrets of nature—and thus essentially completing the project of science—within his lifetime.

Of course, this is not how things worked out. The subject matter of science turned out to be far vaster and more complex than Descartes had ever imagined. His rationalistic approach, moreover, had key deficiencies that not only slowed his progress but rendered many of the specific accounts he developed of natural phenomena just plain wrong. It turns out, for instance, that the mechanical interaction of bodies simply cannot be explained by reducing them to empty geometric figures. Rather, the investigator must have a way to describe the forces that fill bodies and impel them through space—an extra-geometric term Descartes's geometric physics could not accommodate. More generally, while Descartes paid lip service to the importance of empirical observation and experimentation, he did little empirical work himself and did not provide much guidance for integrating empirical findings into the work of theory. Having such an empirical check would have told Descartes, for instance, that the rules he devised to describe the collisions between two elastic bodies were wildly inaccurate. Lacking such a check, Descartes failed to articulate many more enduring scientific truths than his scholastic predecessors had managed. Nevertheless, his general approach of reductionism, combined with the more specific application of mathematics to the natural world, left a huge imprint on the development of modern science.

What was needed, therefore, was some way of combining Descartes's rationalistic, mathematically-based approach to nature with Bacon's empirical, inductive approach. In fact, even as Descartes was doing his work, an Italian astronomer had started groping his way toward just such a synthesis.

The First Modern Scientist: Galileo

If Bacon and Descartes were philosophers at heart, at their best when they focused on questions of method, Galileo Galilee was the first great example of what we would now call a "working scientist," more concerned with the results he was getting than with strict fidelity to any particular method. And the results he logged were impressive, in both the empirical and theoretical realms. As an observational astronomer, Galileo built his own telescope and used it to study celestial objects with a precision previously unachieved. So doing, he discovered that Venus has phases, Jupiter has moons orbiting it, and the surface of the sun is marred by sunspots. All these observations lent credence to the Copernican model of the solar system, which Galileo openly supported early in his career. The Church having grown touchier on this issue, Galileo was ultimately placed under house arrest and forced to partially recant his heliocentric views—a concession he probably made so that he could continue his other scientific work. In any case, the high drama of his astronomical work notwithstanding, even more significant for the history of science was the study Galileo made of falling bodies.

Prior to Galileo, the conventional wisdom on falling bodies could be traced back, of course, to Aristotle. Observing that if you release a feather from one hand and a rock from another, the rock will fall faster, Aristotle had suggested that, as a rule, heavy bodies tend to fall at speeds that are, first, constant and, second, proportional to their weight. This rule follows fairly directly from Aristotle's larger account of nature. Given that Aristotelian substances carry their properties around within them, heavy bodies will fall when released because they possess a tendency to move earthward. With a body's weight therefore being nothing but a measure of how hard the body strives earthward, we may conclude that the heavier the body is (the harder it strives earthward), the faster it will travel when released. And once the body is moving, its inherent degree of striving will not change, so neither should its speed. Because these results could be deduced from the metaphysics of an authority as well-established as Aristotle, and because empirical observation played such a minor role in scholastic science, no one had thought to test Aristotle's account of falling bodies for over two thousand years. Galileo, however, had doubts.

According to popular legend, Galileo climbed to the top of the Leaning Tower of Pisa and dropped heavy objects of varying weight off it. When they all landed at approximately the same time, this demonstrated that bodies of different weights fall at the same speed, not at speeds proportional to their weight. This story is likely apocryphal: in an era prior to the invention of stopwatches, bodies in freefall travel far too quickly to be studied carefully. One of Galileo's strokes of genius was therefore not to simply go out into nature and observe what he found there, but rather to devise an experiment that forced nature to answer the specific questions he had, under strict conditions that would allow him to observe carefully and record the results. In this case, Galileo propped up one end of a long board to create an inclined plane, down which he could roll steel balls of varying weights. These balls still fell earthward, but they rolled slowly enough that Galileo could measure their rate of fall using the most reliable time-keeping instrument available to him, his pulse. Performing this experiment many times with balls of varying weight, he was able to definitively show that an object's weight has no bearing on the rate at which it falls, provided only that you abstract out such extraneous factors as friction and wind resistance.

With this result, however, Galileo was just getting started. He further discerned a regularity in the total distance a steel ball has rolled, as compared to the time it has been traveling. Significantly, however, distance traveled is not directly proportional to time traveled, as we would expect if bodies fell at a constant rate. Galileo's empirical experiments showed, rather, that total distance traveled is proportional to the *square* of the time a body has been falling: If a steel ball rolling for 1 second travels 1 foot, after 2 seconds it will have traveled 4 feet, after 3 seconds it will have traveled 9 feet, and so forth. Putting this result into algebraic form, Galileo formulated the first version of the law of falling bodies, $s = at^2$, where s is distance, a is a constant, and t is time. The implication is that, rather than bodies *falling* at a constant rate, they *accelerate* at a constant rate. And the even broader conclusion Galileo drew from this result is that when *any* force (including, but not limited to, gravity) is constantly applied to a body, this will cause that body to accelerate at a constant rate, other factors being equal.

What exactly had Galileo achieved? In many ways, the fact that he had managed to correct a two-thousand-year-old mistake regarding the rate at which bodies fall was among the least significant results of this exercise. How often do we even care how fast a particular body falls? Far more significant was the process of discovery that Galileo undertook to achieve this result. First, he began his work as Bacon counseled, not by accepting what the authorities had already decreed about some phenomenon, nor by applying deductive logic to an established metaphysical system. Rather, Galileo turned directly to empirical observations, and large numbers of them. Having studied numerous cases, Galileo then noticed a pattern or regularity among them. This led him to suggest a claim that moved more in the direction of induction than deduction: He moved from observing that *this* body falls at a certain rate, and *that* body falls at the same rate, and *that* body falls at the same rate, to conclude, "*All* bodies fall at this same rate." Note, however, that the claim he put forward was not exactly of the "All crows are black" variety, as would have been expected under Aristotle's substance-with-properties metaphysics. Instead, Galileo proposed an algebraic equation that describes a functional relationship between two factors that would have been considered accidental in the Aristotelian world, time of fall and distance traveled. To arrive at this equation, Galileo had to perform the sort of reduction that Descartes's method prescribed, abstracting out everything not strictly relevant to the problem at hand, including the type of body falling, its propensity to generate wind resistance, and even—it turns out—its weight. This left Galileo with a set of factors, including time, distance, velocity, and acceleration, all of which could be measured and thus expressed in quantified form. And this in turn allowed him to apply the tools of geometric and algebraic analysis to the empirical data collected. For Galileo to generate his famous equation, however, he still needed to make one more leap that was not, properly speaking, either deduction or induction.

Here, we need to pause and introduce a third form of judgment, one that neither Aristotle nor the scholastics had included in their accounts of logic. Indeed, this form of judgment was so underappreciated that it would not be given a proper name until two hundred years after Galileo lived. In the late nineteenth century, the American philosopher Charles Sanders Peirce coined the term "abduction" to capture this third form of judgment. Unfortunately, Peirce's attempts to explain abduction can be quite impenetrable, and he repeatedly changed his story, so I will here suggest an account of abduction that is perhaps less nuanced than Peirce's, but, I hope, more graspable.

Experience often presents us with a flood of data. This can be sensory data, linguistic data (words and sentences), strings of numbers, or any other sort of information. As curious, reasoning beings, we naturally try to make sense of this morass of data. We try to grasp certain patterns we identify so that we do not just face a disjointed array of impressions but rather can hold it all together in some sort of conceptual unity. Just think about looking up at a cloud and trying to grasp its swirling manifoldness in a single concept. "It's an elephant! No, wait, it's a horse!" In throwing out these concepts, the mind is not proceeding deductively. The cloud does have four long wisps coming down from it, and we know that all elephants have four legs. Still, these two facts are not enough to let us "deduce" the cloud is an elephant. Nor is the mind proceeding inductively; it is just viewing a single cloud, after all, not offering up a generalization after viewing many. Instead, the mind is just allowing its gaze to sweep over the data, keeping an eye out for discernible patterns. Perhaps a pattern it stumbles across triggers associations with some other object the mind has previously observed, like "elephant." Or maybe it is some wholly novel pattern. In any case, the mind just starts throwing concepts out there to see if any fit the data. If a concept does not fit—"Wait, there's no trunk; it can't be an elephant"—the concept is withdrawn and another is tried, until finally one is struck upon that does fit the data well. "OK, it's a horse." This concept is retained and used to grasp the data, at least until another concept proves to be a better fit.

It is not difficult to see why abductive judgments were not mentioned in the classical logical canon. If induction lacks the certainty of deduction, abduction seems to be little more than an outright guess, coming with no guarantee it will strike upon the right answer. In fact, for something like finding patterns in a cloud, it is not even clear there is a "right" answer out there for anyone to discover. Do abductive judgments, then, have any objectivity to them, and do they even merit being called "judgments"? In fact, they do. For one thing, abductive judgments are not completely random or capricious. Rather, they are guided, at least in their general outlines, by the data: If I see a cloud with four smaller wisps protruding down from it, this may not unambiguously tell me the cloud is a horse, but I will probably not venture that it is a battleship or an ice cream cone. And while it is true we have no guarantee that any particular concept we propose will fit the data well, once we have thrown the concept out there, we do have real data to compare it against, so we have an objective means of determining how snug the fit is and the freedom to discard any concepts that do not fit the data well. Note, however, that to decide whether a proposed concept should be retained, we do not even need to ask whether the concept is perfectly "right." We just need to ask whether it helps us make sense of our experience more efficiently. When we look up at the night sky and see an archer in the stars, for instance, this abductive judgment is, strictly speaking, "wrong," insofar as no giant people live in the sky. Nevertheless, this way of regarding the stars helps us organize our view of the night sky. And thus, because the concept of the archer fits the data fairly well, and it is helpful to us, we retain this concept, utilize it, and share it with others.

If abductive judgments are therefore a bit more free-wheeling than either deductive or inductive judgments, unabashedly coming with some risk of error, they have the advantage of allowing us to introduce true novelty into our knowledge. For a more consequential example, let us go back to Copernicus's suggestion that the Earth revolves around the sun. To strike upon this notion, induction was obviously of no help to Copernicus. He was not observing many Earths revolving around many suns and concluding from this that all Earths revolve around the sun. On the contrary, he had just one Earth to observe—and from our vantage point, informal observation suggests a stationary Earth far more than a stationary sun. As far as deduction goes, meanwhile, Copernicus did have one generally accepted initial claim: "All heavenly bodies travel in circles." This was a claim that Copernicus did not question, and it probably helped him make the leap to the notion that perhaps Earth is not stationary, but rather travels in a circle, as the moon appears to. Still, deduction alone could not get Copernicus to this conclusion— all celestial bodies travel in circles, Earth is a celestial body, therefore Earth travels in a circle—for the accepted wisdom held precisely that Earth is *not* a celestial body, but rather a mundane object, with its own distinctive, rectilinear mode of traveling through space.

What Copernicus had to work with, therefore, was a rough pattern suggested by experience. The moon appears to travel around Earth in a circular path, and the planets appear to travel around Earth in *something like* a circular path. Still, this pattern was not fitting the planets very well, due to their retrograde motions. For some time, astronomers had been following Ptolemy in abductively proposing that perhaps the cyclical orbits planets follow contain smaller epicycles within them. Improved observations were just forcing astronomers to add more epicycles within epicycles to make these models work—and they still did not provide a perfect fit to the data. Copernicus therefore began playing around with other scenarios. He doubtless quickly discarded any obvious mismatches, such as heavenly bodies traveling in triangular paths. But then he struck upon a notion that was elegant in its simplicity, while fitting the data pretty well: Earth is not stationary, but rather it travels around the sun in a circular path along with the other planets. He latched on to it and began spreading the word to others.

In fact, Copernicus had not yet arrived at the "right" answer, for later observations would show that the Copernican model of circular planetary orbits still does provide a perfect fit with the data. It was Johannes Kepler, a century later, who determined that planets, including Earth, actually travel in ellipses around the sun. Indeed, Kepler provides us with an even clearer example of abductive reasoning: His notes show he tried out some twenty different mathematical descriptions of planetary paths before striking upon the ellipse as the equation that best fits the data. In trying out all these possibilities, Kepler was clearly not "just guessing," insofar as the equations he tested were strongly informed by both the general Copernican insight of heliocentrism and the improved observational data Kepler's mentor, Tycho

Brahe, had painstakingly gathered. At the end of the day, however, these various equations *were* guesses, thrown out there and then tested against the data until one was found that fit the data nearly perfectly. This method, which we could call "informed trial and error," is certainly messier than working with never-erring syllogisms, or even with inductive generalizations. As we have just seen, however, if the human mind had no means by which to advance its thinking other than deduction and induction, we would still probably believe that Earth stands still, with the other planets traveling around it.

Galileo's key insight regarding the descent of heavy bodies was similarly a product of the abductive mode of reasoning. By the time he had repeatedly tested steel balls rolling down inclined planes, confirming that each one covered a distance proportional to the square of the time traveled, he was perhaps using induction to conclude that *all* bodies—including bodies other than steel balls—fall at this same rate. Yet, to get to the point that he was performing *these* particular experiments, measuring *these* particular variables, and testing the data against *this* particular equation required that Galileo first take a major abductive leap beyond the accepted wisdom of Aristotle. Galileo first had to posit that the movement of bodies could be translated into mathematical form, and that we could expect to find some common equation that would equally well describe their disparate falls. As he then searched for this equation, we do not know whether Galileo tried out several different possibilities, most of which he had to reject, as Kepler had done. In any case, as he pored over his observational data, he must have noticed that, early in a body's fall, the distance it travels increases slowly, but then it starts to increase faster, and then it increases very fast. This must have suggested the notion of exponential growth to Galileo, and led him to playing around with squares and cubes. And when, at some point, he tried out a proportionality between distance traveled and square of the time traveled, the equation *worked*, fitting the experimental data very closely in case after case. Galileo latched onto this equation, and he thus had a new law of nature to propose: the law of falling bodies.

And this, more than anything specific Galileo learned about how quickly bodies fall, was his real contribution to the development of modern science: He proposed a new law of nature. For prior to this time, there had not really *been* any laws of nature. This claim, however, will require explanation.

The Laws of Nature

Obviously, gravity was in full effect when Aristotle lived; he had observed its influence when making his own observations on falling bodies. Still, it never would have occurred to him to discuss "the law of gravity" or "the law of falling bodies." For one thing, under his substance-based metaphysics, Aristotle located the tendency to move earthward within individual bodies. He viewed this tendency as a property, in other words, that inheres in particular types of substances—namely those composed of earth. Bodies composed of air or fire have different tendencies, which is why they generally swirl around or move upward. With every heavy body therefore containing within it an explanation for why it falls, there can be no single, overarching principle that explains the behavior of all such bodies. Granted, because many substances have similar properties, the observer can categorize them together and inductively offer generalizations about their behavior; this is what Aristotle did when he suggested heavy bodies tend to fall at a constant speed proportional to their weight. But even if this rule was correct, it was still just a general tendency, as Aristotle formulated it, not an ironclad law. And Aristotle further notes that, for any general tendencies we might observe, exceptions seem to exist. While earthen bodies typically fall earthward, for instance, very light objects, such as dust motes or feathers, seem to fly around in all directions, and even heavy bodies can be picked up by a strong wind. In these instances, we can at least suggest some reason why the general tendency of heavy bodies to move earthward had been violated, but Aristotle adds one final proviso: Sometimes things just happen by chance. Sometimes individual objects just depart from their usual tendencies, with no explanation why.

This being said, the law of nature Galileo was proposing differed from Aristotle's generalizations in at least two key respects. First, the law of falling bodies is a *law* of nature. It is not just posited as a general rule in effect for most of the time, except when it is not. On the contrary, the law of falling bodies is formulated with mathematical precision, and it is claimed that every body will follow this law precisely, down to the last decimal point, in every instance (provided extraneous influences are factored out). Second, the law of falling bodies is a law of *nature*. This law, in other words, does not inhere in particular bodies. Rather, it applies across the entire field of observation, holding true for every particular body that happens to be located within this field—which is, presumably, all of nature. Galileo had therefore stopped looking within particular objects for their distinctive natures, and instead turned his attention to *nature*, understood as the whole field of things.

Why was this significant? Recall that, on Aristotle's substance-based account of nature, substances are discrete from one another, which means the only reliable way to gain knowledge about particular types of things is by going from one object to the next, noting and cataloging the properties of each. On this approach, if you have been studying steel balls, you may well have learned how fast such balls fall, but you will have learned nothing about other types of objects, all with their own properties. And as noted earlier, when you think about how many different types of objects are in nature, this makes for a very slow, incremental process of scientific learning. Galileo, in contrast, showed that most of a steel ball's properties, including even its weight, are irrelevant to how fast it falls. These properties can therefore be abstracted out of the account of its fall. But if you can abstract out most of the properties that make a steel ball a steel ball, you can do the same with other bodies. And then—everything else having been rendered equal—you can apply what you have learned about steel balls to other sorts of objects. By measuring the rate of fall of steel balls, in other words, Galileo had thereby determined how fast a rock would fall, or a tea kettle, or a rhinoceros, or even a unicorn. And to do this, he did not have to go out and examine any of these other types of objects. Indeed, unicorns do not even have to exist to be subject to the law of falling bodies, provided we imagine them as having material bodies. This approach to nature therefore opens the door to a far more rapid expansion of knowledge than was possible under Aristotle's metaphysics. Instead of going from one of nature's countless different objects to the next, patiently recording the properties of each, we can try to discover a few simple laws that govern all of nature, and this will allow us to explain the behavior of all different sorts of things, including even those we have never seen before—including even those *no one* has ever seen before. While this approach still has an indispensable empirical basis, it gives researchers a means of leveraging their empirical observations, applying what they learn from one object to many more types of objects than those directly observed.

Of course, the elephant in the room here, which we must never forget, is that this new approach to nature lacks the certainty of deductive logic or geometric proof. For all we know, the next observation we make could show that our supposedly "universal" law does not apply universally. Counterintuitively, this possibility for error is actually one of the greatest strengths of the modern approach to nature. We could even say that if the concept of the law of nature opened the door to a potential rapid expansion of scientific knowledge, the possibility of getting such laws wrong is the engine that actually began driving this expansion of knowledge forward. Once again, with laws such as the law of falling bodies being posited as being universal, the claim is that they are true everywhere, at every time, with all of their mathematical precision. This means that when you return to empirical observation, you have a very clear standard for determining whether these new observations confirm or contradict your proposed law. Indeed, because the proposed law is claimed to be so ironclad, if even a single instance should arise in which the law is contradicted, this indicates the proposed law is not actually a law; it was not correct to begin with. Frustrating as this may be, if you are not going to give up, you must either modify your proposed law to account for the observed exception or else scrap it entirely and devise a new law. In either case, if you are successful, the result will be a law that explains everything covered by the previous law, yet which also explains the apparent exception. And this means your sphere of explanation has expanded; your knowledge has increased.

One implication of the investigative dynamic just described is that when you propose a new law of nature, the first thing you should do is try to knock it down. You should go back to empirical observation and actively try to find a counterexample that demonstrates your proposed law to be false. Admittedly, this demand probably runs contrary to human nature: Having struck upon a new and seemingly revolutionary piece of knowledge, the typical scientist will be inclined to defend this new claim tirelessly, rather than trying to knock it down. As a scientific community began to emerge across Europe, and as various means for sharing results among its members began to develop—first primarily through the exchange of letters, then increasingly through presentations at scientific societies, and ultimately publication in academic journals—you could be sure that if you put forward a significant claim, some professional rival or ambitious young upstart would put your claim to the test, doing everything they could to disprove it. If this trial by fire fails to produce contrary evidence, your claim is strengthened all the more. But if anyone does uncover problems with your proposed law, yet they go on to revise it or replace it with another law that fits the data better, so much the better. That means your work, together with that of your critic, has added to the scope and reliability of the community's collective knowledge.

The Modern Scientific Method

As other scientists in the seventeenth century began using an approach similar to Galileo's in their particular fields of study, there was no single author who sat down and wrote out "the scientific method," as we now learn it in high school. Indeed, as late as the twentieth century, scholars such as Thomas Kuhn and Karl Popper were still debating the precise details of how the scientific method works. Nevertheless, over the course of the seventeenth century, what has since come to be known as the "hypothetico-deductive method" gradually took shape and established itself as the standard method for studying nature. We have already seen most of its key steps in action, but they can here be drawn together in summary fashion.

1. Conduct initial empirical observations. As the broad outlines of your subject matter begin to come clear, your eye may be drawn to some interesting data you want to study

further. As you look more closely, certain regularities or patterns in this data may begin to suggest themselves.

2. Try to come up with a generalized rule or theory that captures these patterns and thus accurately describes or explains the particular phenomena you have been observing. When you think you have such a theory, assert it provisionally. This is the hypothetical stage of the hypothetico-deductive method.

3. Taking this new theory as a starting point, deduce certain phenomena that should occur in nature if your theory is correct. Make detailed predictions, in other words, based on the rule you have proposed. Here, finally, was the use modern science had found for deduction. These particular deductive judgments do not tell us, with absolute certainty, what is true in the world—something beyond the power of deduction, anyway. Rather, they tell us what must be true *if a given hypothesis is correct*, thereby allowing us to test this hypothesis.

4. Put your theory to the test. Perform further empirical observations, that is, with an eye to whether your predicted results come about under the prescribed circumstances. And if nature does not readily offer you such observations, devise an experiment that does.

5. Evaluate the results of this empirical test. If all your predictions have been borne out, this lends credence to your proposed theory. It does not absolutely "prove" your theory

true, since the next observation could always contradict it. Nevertheless, the more observations that bear out a theory, the stronger it grows. So, if the first round of empirical testing has been successful, return to Step 3, the deductive stage, and use your theory to predict even more detailed empirical results before proceeding to test these predictions. If, conversely, even one of your predictions has been contradicted by the empirical data, this indicates a problem. It could mean an observational problem, such as a fly on the lens, or it could mean you made an error in deducing a specific prediction from your more general theory. But it could also mean the theory itself is fully or partially wrong. In this case, it is time to go back to the drawing board, or back to Step 2, where new hypotheses are generated. If your original theory had been performing well, but was tripped up by some minor detail, you may be able to modify the theory to account for the aberration. But if the original theory had already been foundering, you may need to scrap it and propose a new one in its place.

The dynamic generated by this approach to nature is obviously quite different from that of the scholastic-Aristotelian approach. Indeed, in retrospect, we could almost say the scholastic approach was designed for stagnation and error. Even under the best circumstances, when empirical observations are being conducted—as Aristotle did—the results promise to be slow and incremental as observers laboriously move from examining one discrete object to the next. When observation is then abandoned in favor of sole reliance on deductive logic and the appeal to authority, not only is very little new knowledge generated, but there is no mechanism for ferreting out incorrect claims.

The modern scientific method, conversely, contains an impetus toward rapidly increasing knowledge—or really several of them—combined with a feedback loop to ensure that its claims remain grounded in reality. First, by starting out with empirical observation, then moving toward more general laws through a combination of induction and abduction, the modern approach encourages the formation of theories that are guided by the data but novel in their claims. Contrary to the dreams of Descartes, this empirically based approach still requires a great deal of observational work, on the massive, collective scale Bacon envisioned. Nevertheless, by turning the focus of investigation from individual substances to the relations between them, and ultimately to the universal laws describing these relations, the modern approach essentially leverages the knowledge gained through particular observations and makes it applicable to different sorts of objects across nature. And while some of the laws proposed through this speculative endeavor may turn out to be wrong, the modern scientific method mandates going back and checking any hypothetical claims against empirical reality. This closure of the feedback loop not only roots out errors but actually helps generate a forward momentum by encouraging that any deficient theories be replaced by new, more sophisticated theories that can account for all the phenomena their predecessors had explained, plus the anomalies.

As various scientists began stumbling their way toward this new scientific method over the course of the seventeenth century, the results they achieved quickly dwarfed what had been learned about nature over the entire scholastic period. We have already mentioned the work of Kepler and Galileo in physics and astronomy. Later in the century, Christian Huygens corrected the errors in Descartes's account of collisions, thereby helping establish the increasingly influential "mechanistic philosophy," which regards all motion in nature as caused by the jostling of solid bodies. Robert Boyle was an advocate of the closely related "corpuscularian philosophy," which postulates that matter is ultimately composed of unbreakable atoms that bounce around and interact with one another mechanically. Boyle helped found the modern science of chemistry, particularly through his study of the relationship between volume and pressure in gasses. In the biological realm, Antonie van Leeuwenhoek pioneered the design and use of the microscope; he was the first to observe the presence of microorganisms in pond water, as well as studying such microscopic components of the human body as muscle fibers, capillaries, and spermatozoa. William Harvey, meanwhile, translated his extensive anatomical research into the first comprehensive theory of the circulation of the blood. The towering achievement of seventeenth-century science, however, and in many ways the culmination of the Scientific Revolution, was Isaac Newton's publication of *Principia Mathematica* in 1687.

The Newtonian Model of the Universe

In a real sense, *Principia Mathematica* achieved Descartes's goal of using mathematics to articulate a complete system of nature, at least insofar as nature is regarded as a mechanical system. To get to this point, Newton—like Descartes—first had to extend the mathematics of his day, in his case by inventing differential calculus. While Descartes's analytic geometry was good for expressing simple geometric shapes in algebraic fashion, it was unable to represent many complex curves, meaning that mathematicians wishing to study these curves had to approximate them in stair-step fashion. By treating such stair-steps as infinitesimally small, calculus can represent these curves as perfectly smooth. This also renders calculus ideally suited to describing the continuous motions of bodies through space, as Newton required for his physics. And at the same time, calculus shows how the equations expressing such motion-related variables as distance, velocity, and acceleration can be derived from one another, thereby lending systematic unity to the study of motion.

With these new mathematical tools in hand, Newton laid out his famous three laws of motion. (1) A body will travel with a constant velocity, and thus in a straight line unless acted on by another body. (2) Force equals mass times acceleration. (3) For every action, there is an equal and opposite reaction. These three laws provide the foundation for Newton's mechanical system, which has come to be known as "classical mechanics." As we will see in later chapters, mechanics turned out to be inadequate for describing all of nature's phenomena; it cannot, for instance, explain the energy released through combustion, nor does it address such phenomena as electricity and magnetism. Nevertheless, when limited to the mechanical domain, Newton's equations have not been improved upon; they were used in the twentieth century to calculate the trajectories for landing the

Apollo spacecraft on the moon. In fact, this points to what may have been Newton's greatest achievement, at least from a philosophical perspective. Although Newton could not have foreseen people would one day land on the moon, he understood that the laws governing motion here on Earth *would* be applicable on the moon or anywhere else in the universe. Thus was overturned another millennia-old belief.

Recall that, since ancient times, the heavens and the earth had been viewed as completely different realms, each operating in accord with its own principles. In Aristotelian physics, the natural tendency of mundane bodies was to travel in straight lines, whereas heavenly bodies followed a more perfect circular course. Yet even before Aristotle, the stars had always been viewed as a realm of tranquil stability, the seat of unchanging eternity, in contrast to the turbulent, messy world here below, so full of conflict, suffering, and death. Legend has it that Newton was sitting beneath an apple tree, staring up at the moon when an apple fell and hit him on the head, thus prompting his realization that the mundane and celestial realms are governed by the same laws. While this story is almost certainly apocryphal, Newton did have the striking insight that the law describing the apple's fall could be used to explain why celestial bodies travel in roughly circular orbits around one another. A body like the moon, for instance, just needs to be thought of as falling toward Earth, yet not directly on a collision course, such that, even as the force of gravity continually bends the moon's path, pulling it earthward, the moon's own momentum causes it to forever overshoot the earth. Newton had no idea what the force of gravity *was* that draws both apples and moons earthward—or more precisely, that draws all heavy bodies toward one another in proportion to their mass. Nevertheless, once he had realized that the motions of mundane and celestial bodies could be described using the same equations, he was essentially able to take Galileo's law of falling bodies and use it to derive Kepler's laws of elliptical planetary motion.

For some of Newton's contemporaries, particularly those in the religious establishment, this unification of the celestial and mundane realms was doubtless unwelcome. Not only had Newton's system confirmed the heliocentric model of the solar system beyond a reasonable doubt, but by treating celestial and mundane bodies as equals, it must have felt like Newton was sullying the heavens, dragging the stars down into the muck with us. But for those gripped with the excitement of the Scientific Revolution, the perception was just the opposite. From their perspective, Newton had shown that, here on Earth—for whatever turmoil we may experience in our daily lives—the natural world operates with the same predictable stability that had long been attributed to the stars. This stable order, moreover, is a *rational* order, and thus one we can penetrate with our powers of reasoning. So, whereas Plato had believed we can use reason to catch a brief glimpse of the world's ultimate truth, although only by transporting ourselves to an otherworldly realm of unchanging Forms modeled after the heavens, Newton showed that the everyday world around us, including both above our heads and beneath our feet, is home to the unchanging laws that govern reality. And these are laws about which we can use our powers of reasoning to achieve not just fleeting glimpses, but lasting, comprehensive knowledge.

The Birth of Progress

As noted already, most of the achievements of seventeenth-century science were theoretical in nature. Even as Newton's fame spread around Europe, modern science had not yet begun to have much of an impact on people's everyday lives. Still, for many in Europe's intellectual classes, at least, the notion of a rational, stable, lawfully-governed order of nature, together with the rapid progress suddenly being made in penetrating its universal laws, could not help but suggest that human beings would soon be in a position to finally start logging victories over the turmoil and suffering that had characterized human life for so long. Indeed, this was Descartes's dream from the beginning. While acknowledging that the search for truth is worthwhile in its own right, he explicitly stated that the ultimate purpose of science is to make us "like owners and masters of nature." Admittedly, this phrase may strike those of us in the twenty-first century as hubris, after we have already witnessed several centuries of human beings trying to master nature, often fruitlessly and sometimes with devastating environmental consequences. We must remember, however, what life was like when Descartes wrote these words. If the odd technological advance over the ancient and medieval eras had, from time to time, made life slightly more comfortable, especially for those in the privileged classes, on balance, very little control had yet been achieved over nature.

As a result, people remained at nature's mercy, and nature continued to be the same terrifying, malevolent force it had always been, wreaking havoc on peoples' individual lives through disease, injury, or infirmity, and sometimes decimating whole regions through drought, plague, or earthquake.

Under such conditions, a dream of mastering nature was not megalomaniacal. It was rather the same longing for peace, stability, and escape from suffering that had led ancient peoples to look to the skies and posit an otherworldly *samsara* or heaven. Now, however, for really the first time in human history, the realistic possibility was emerging of winning some relief from nature's torments. This was not, moreover, through transport to some otherworldly realm, nor through the agency of a divine savior. Rather, this relief was to be found right here in this world, in this lifetime, by means of our own agency, and more specifically through the use of our faculty of reasoning. If nature is a rational order governed by universal laws, and if we can use our powers of reasoning to discern these laws, we can then use laws to predict how nature will behave. And if we can predict what nature will do under particular circumstances, we can start manipulating these circumstances, such that nature finally begins to work in accord with our ends, rather than constantly frustrating them. In the most general terms, this is what technology is, and while the flood of scientific knowledge emanating from the seventeenth century had not yet been translated into many technological advances, this was the promise that lay on the horizon.

Thus, even before the eighteenth century had dawned, something had begun appearing in various quarters of

Europe which, as we saw in the last chapter, had long been a rare commodity for the human species: hope. To be sure, life remained grim for most Europeans. Poverty was still endemic, and warfare was just as common as ever. Absolute monarchy remained the norm for governance, and those born into the lower ranks of society still had little chance of improving their lots. Nevertheless, a sense of optimism began to build, at least for those who followed what was occurring in the sciences. Nor was this the optimism of the Renaissance, predicated on the return to a Golden Age, when everything had been better and people had known more. Rather, inspired by the completely novel advances that had begun to take place regularly in the modern natural sciences, this was a vision that looked more forward than back—a sense that today is better than yesterday, and that tomorrow might be even better than today. These were the first glimmerings of a progressive worldview.

CHAPTER 3

THE SOCIAL CONTRACT: POLITICAL PROGRESS

Thomas Hobbes, an Englishman, was a contemporary of Descartes, with whom he shared a brief correspondence. Early in his career, Hobbes was deeply impressed by the work of Galileo, and he developed a mechanistic doctrine holding that all physical phenomena can be understood through the motions and interactions of solid bodies. Rather than engaging in the sort of experimental work Galileo was pioneering, however, Hobbes was more of an armchair theorist, so his early writings did little to advance the history of physics. His real contribution to European thought came later in his career when he turned his attention from bodies crashing into one another to the study of human beings and their interactions—something he ended up describing in equally mechanical terms. Perhaps the best way to describe the role Hobbes played in helping shape the progressive worldview that was emerging over the seventeenth and eighteenth centuries is as follows: If a worldview is a narrative that describes where the world came from, where it is headed, how it operates, and what the place of human beings is within it, and if the physical scientists of the seventeenth century were fundamentally redescribing how the world operates, Hobbes was the first great modern thinker to unflinchingly ask what this meant for the place human beings occupy in the world.

As it turns out, almost none of Hobbes's contemporaries liked his answer. It just painted human nature in a too dismal light. Nevertheless, Hobbes's work transformed modern political theory, particularly when his general approach was adopted by later thinkers, including his most influential follower in the English tradition, John Locke. This chapter will focus on the studies Hobbes and Locke made of human psychology and social organization, and on the novel political principles to which their studies led them.

The Hobbesian Dilemma

When Hobbes turned his attention to the study of human beings, the fundamental insight from which he set out was straightforward. By this time, Galileo and his colleagues in the physical sciences were well on their way to establishing that nature and everything in it are determined by certain immutable, universal laws. It follows, Hobbes reasoned, that if human beings form part of nature, we too must be determined in all our actions by some immutable, universal law or set of laws—some human equivalent to the law of falling bodies. Already, this set off alarm bells for many of Hobbes's critics. If all our actions are mechanically determined, how can we be moral actors, responsible for the decisions we make and the way we treat one another? Granted, medieval theologians had long been forced to grapple with a similar problem. Assuming God is omnipotent and omniscient, he must know what we are going to do, even before we do it. But if all our actions are therefore divinely predetermined, how can we have the free will required to be morally responsible for our actions? Still, this was at least a benevolent God, whom everyone knew to be completely inscrutable, who was responsible for foreknowing our actions. Maybe this left some wiggle room for human free will. But if human beings have no more freedom than billiard balls careening around a table, does morality have any meaning?

Things did not improve when Hobbes proposed the law that he believed must govern all human behavior. Relying on a mix of introspection, common-sense reasoning, and informal observation of both the people and animals around him, Hobbes concluded that there was only one conceivable candidate for the law of voluntary behavior: not just human beings, but all living creatures must invariably act in their own perceived self-interest. That is not to say we have no choice in what we do; circumstances often present us with many different choices. Given the choice, however, why would anyone choose to do anything but what they perceive to be in their own best interest?

Most immediately, Hobbes argued, this means living creatures will naturally seek out pleasure while avoiding pain since pleasure is a self-evident good, whereas pain is manifestly undesirable. But even more fundamentally, since experiencing pleasure presupposes that a creature be alive, the ultimate interest of any living creature is self-preservation. As it turns out, the survival instinct and the pursuit of pleasure often coincide since living organisms seem to be constructed in such a way that—as a general rule—what gives them pleasure tends to promote their survival, whereas pain indicates a diminishment of well-being. Taking all these observations together, therefore, and applying them to the specific case of human beings, we could say the "law of human behavior" appears to be that we invariably strive to act in our own perceived best interest, with self-preservation being our ultimate interest, as complemented by a natural interest we have in maximizing the pleasure we experience while minimizing the pain.

The challenge this conclusion poses to morality is again clear, and it left Hobbes facing what I will call "the Hobbesian dilemma." On the one hand, even by the middle of the seventeenth century, it was becoming clear that the modern approach to science was far superior to its scholastic-Aristotelian predecessor. And as we saw in the previous chapter, this modern approach and the sudden progress it was making depended entirely on the revelation that everything in nature is governed by certain immutable, universal laws. Anyone who was excited by the potential of modern science, therefore, would have been loath to give up the characterization of nature as a rational order governed by universal laws. On the other hand, if this characterization of nature was to be maintained, and if human beings were to be given a place in this natural order, it seemed people themselves would have to be regarded as being fully determined by some universal law. Everyday experience would suggest, moreover, that self-interest is the only reasonable candidate for such a universal law of human nature. This is an uncomfortable conclusion, however, not just for the religiously minded but for any observer, for at least two reasons. First, even if observation suggests that humans are *generally* guided by self-interest, we also witness numerous instances of people behaving in ways that we would describe as socially responsible, or even downright moral. As investigators of nature, therefore, we want to be able to explain this apparently anomalous behavior. As human actors ourselves, moreover, we want to believe we can behave in some sort of moral fashion that would raise us above the level of beasts, not to mention billiard balls. But again, if all nature is governed by mechanistic laws and we are part of nature, how is any sort of socially responsible, moral action possible?

For many of Hobbes's contemporaries, the apparent implications of this whole line of reasoning were simply too horrifying to contemplate; they declined even to engage with Hobbes, writing him off as an atheist. Descartes took a somewhat different path, sidestepping the Hobbesian dilemma through his doctrine of mind-body dualism. Descartes agreed that bodies are governed by certain universal laws of nature—which he thought could be reduced to the laws of geometry. But Descartes argued that minds, as unextended thinking things, are a completely different variety of substance than extended bodies. This leaves the mind free from the mechanistic laws that govern the extended realm, and hence free to be a robust moral actor. Unfortunately, this dualistic metaphysics runs into all sorts of theoretical problems, not least the question of how two completely dissimilar substances can interact enough for the mind to issue commands to the body, and for the body to report sensations back to the mind, as appears to happen in daily life. Hobbes, in any case, rejected the whole notion of a disembodied mind or soul as superstitious twaddle, and thus he resolved to stay the course with his mechanistic, materialistic view of nature, meaning that he had to face the moral dilemma to which his own observations had led him.

Hobbes was not, however, quite as pessimistic as his detractors made him out to be. Specifically, he did not view the dilemma he had bumped up against as the death knell for human morality. Rather, he saw it as the starting point for our moral investigations: Granting that we human beings are self-interested in all we do, how is it that we sometimes behave in a socially responsible, moral fashion?

Hobbes on the State of Nature

The preliminary answer Hobbes could suggest is that we all live in civic society, and the various societies we inhabit place any number of restrictions on our self-interested behaviors through a wide array of laws and governing institutions. But this just prompts another question: Given our inveterate self-interestedness, how did we ever come to live in these law-governed societies?

As Hobbes made his way to political theory, the question that had long driven this field was, "Whence derives the sovereign its legitimacy?" The answer inherited from the Middle Ages was the doctrine of the divine right of kings. As articulated by its most famous exponent, Sir Robert Filmer, divine right doctrine holds that, in the first few verses of Genesis, God gave Adam sovereignty over all creatures of the earth. In the generations since, this sovereignty has been divided and passed down through certain lines of Adam's descendants. Today's sovereigns therefore inherit the right to rule over their respective realms, most immediately from their fathers, but ultimately from their Father in heaven. By the same token, the most fundamental laws by which we are to live come directly from God, who literally wrote the Law on a pair of stone tablets and handed them to Moses. Mundane kings are then charged with crafting more specific laws for their subjects, as guided by a paternal care echoing that of God.

Even as Hobbes was formulating his own political thoughts, divine right doctrine was being challenged in a very real way in England. The reigning king, Charles I, was a staunch advocate of divine right theory, and he was using this doctrine to claim more absolute powers for himself. Parliament, jealous of its own authority, began pushing back, and by the early 1640s full-scale civil war had broken out. Parliamentary forces eventually captured Charles, and when he refused to negotiate a more limited monarchy, he was beheaded. Hobbes, made nervous by his connections to the royalist camp, had fled to Paris at the beginning of the war, and it was there he wrote his monumental work of political theory, *Leviathan*. The irony is that, while Hobbes was a supporter of Charles and of the monarchy more generally, his magnum opus probably did more to undermine the institution of the monarchy than had the king's executioners, since the novel account of sovereign legitimacy Hobbes developed would ultimately replace divine right doctrine, not just in Europe, but around much of the world.

To enter his subject matter, Hobbes took an approach like Descartes's reductive method of taking a complex situation and breaking it down into simpler parts, meanwhile abstracting out everything not directly relevant to the question at hand. In this case, Hobbes notes that if we want to uncover the true nature of sovereignty, studying contemporary kings or the societies over which they rule does no good, since over the centuries, particular societies have developed so many diverse customs, laws, and institutions that it is impossible to know which of these are essential to civic society and its governing structures and which are mere local or historical accidents. Analyzing the true nature of sovereignty therefore requires that we strip away the trappings of civic society and consider how people must have behaved and interacted prior to its establishment. Having gotten down to the simplest units of social organization, individual people, we can start putting the pieces back together, considering how these simple units must have come together to form the more complex civic societies we inhabit today.

As noted earlier, Hobbes was an armchair theorist, preferring to ruminate on his subject matter without getting bogged down by empirical observations. In his defense, at the time he wrote, there simply *was* no science of anthropology to which he could have turned for empirical information about prehistoric social life. To study the human condition outside of civic society, therefore, Hobbes performed what we would now call a thought experiment: He asked what the world must have looked like back when people still lived in a "state of nature," prior to the emergence of civic society or any of its associated customs, laws, or institutions.

As is well known, the portrait Hobbes painted of the state of nature was not pretty. He started with the aforementioned premise that human beings are self-interested in all they do, ultimately concerned with nothing but their own survival. He went on to note that, as material creatures, people depend for their survival on such scarce resources as food and shelter. Hobbes concluded that the residents of the state of nature would have thought nothing of attacking one another, seizing the food or other material goods others had gathered, provided they had the strength, stealth, or wit to do so without being beaten to a pulp in return.

With human behavior in the state of nature therefore being subject to no limitations but the fear of counterattack, Hobbes argued that life in this primitive state must have been "a war of all against all," with no one enjoying any security except as provided by their own strength. Yet, even the strongest would have needed to rest at times, and they had no one to guard them as they slept, so everyone must have been consumed by anxiety and fear. At the same time, the inhabitants of the state of nature would have been desperately poor. No one could own any tools to aid them in their struggle with nature since these "possessions" would have just been stolen the moment they were laid down. Nor, for this same reason, could people store food for the winter. Absent the laws and institutions that would give meaning to such concepts as "ownership" or "private property," all that you owned was what you could hold in your grasp at that moment. And thus,

Hobbes famously concluded, life in the state of nature must have been "solitary, poor, nasty, brutish, and short."

The Social Contract and Rule by Consent of the Governed

If these were the conditions into which humankind was born, our own egoism driving perpetual conflict, poverty, and fear, how did we rise above this mean state to form the civic societies we now inhabit? Surprisingly enough, Hobbes argues, our self-interest prompted this. At some point, various individuals in the state of nature must have concluded that the status quo, plagued by constant violence, material deprivation, and fear, was simply intolerable. It is difficult to know how their first conversations would have gone, but eventually people must have come together and started offering proposals to the effect of, "I will promise not to attack you or take the food you have gathered if you promise to refrain from doing the same to me."

The resulting social contract, Hobbes notes, would have had two parts. As a first step, people will agree to submit to the rule of law. In the state of nature, individuals have the freedom to do whatever they want, limited only by their physical power, as compared to that of others. Given the mutual insecurity this situation produces, however, when people come together to form a compact, each will agree to place certain limits on their natural freedoms, on the condition that others agree to these same limits. First and foremost, people will pledge not to attack one another, nor to take the material goods to which others have laid claim. However formally or informally these prohibitions may get articulated, they come to serve as laws, which are thenceforth regarded as binding.

Hobbes cautioned, however, that merely submitting to the rule of law is not enough, since "Covenants, without the Sword, are but Words, and are of no strength to secure a man at all." Hobbes realized, in other words, that if people merely *promise* to observe the rule of law, then however sincere these promises may be, self-interest will lead people to renege on their commitments as soon as this seems advantageous. Granted, I may refrain from attacking my more powerful neighbor once we have established a social contract, since self-interest would have counseled this even in the state of nature. But if I stumble across my weaker neighbor, whom I could easily relieve of the food he has gathered with little worry of counterattack, why should I not break the compact, just this once, and attack him? If everyone were to behave this way—including my more powerful neighbor when he stumbles across me—none of us will have escaped from the state of nature, and we will all still face the same fear and insecurity.

What is required for the social contract to be effective, therefore, is that we not only submit to the rule of law but that we also place a member of our group in a position of power over the rest of us, granting this person both the legal authority and the physical power to enforce the rule of law on us. This person is the sovereign, to whom the rest of us are henceforth subject. Now, when I encounter my weaker neighbor, I know that if I attack him, the odds are very good that I will be struck down in return, if not by my neighbor, then by the sword of the vastly more powerful sovereign. Accordingly, I realize it is in my best interest to always observe the law, without exception. To be sure, this means I have lost some of the freedom I once enjoyed in the state of nature. But the situation is still a net gain for me, since I know my neighbors, both weak and strong, have a similar interest in always following the law, without exception. And this means that we have all finally achieved the peace and stability for which we had been longing, thereby greatly advancing our personal interests.

Hobbes had therefore answered his own question as to how socially responsible, moral behavior is possible on the assumption that human beings are self-interested in all they do. As we have seen, this sort of behavior arose not despite self-interest but out of it. Using their powers of reasoning, our ancestors must have determined it to be in their best interest to escape from the state of nature by freely submitting to the rule of law, and to the rule of a sovereign charged with enforcing the law. Once these conditions had been established, socially responsible, moral behavior was in everyone's best interest, since misbehavior was sure to incur the wrath of the sovereign. And this meant everyone could enjoy the benefits of living in a stable society in which most people, most of the time, behave in a socially responsible, moral fashion—while those who do not are quickly brought into line at the point of the sovereign's sword.

Developing a response to the Hobbesian dilemma was not, however, all Hobbes had accomplished. He also formulated a revolutionary answer to the central question of political philosophy, "Whence derives the sovereign its legitimacy?" The sovereign holds power, Hobbes had established, because his subjects have invested him with this power, not out of compulsion, but freely, because this was in their own best interest. Thus was born the distinctly modern notion that the sovereign derives its legitimacy not from God or heredity or the king's own regal nature. The sovereign, rather, derives its legitimacy from the consent of the governed. And this means the rest of us are morally obligated to respect the sovereign's authority, not because God has so commanded us, nor because we are born with a servile nature, nor because this whole hierarchical arrangement is the nature of things. Rather, we are obliged to respect the sovereign's authority for the same reason we are obligated to fulfill the conditions of any contract: because we have freely placed ourselves under this obligation.

With this basic account of sovereign legitimacy on the table, Hobbes understood the precise laws and institutions by which a sovereign governs will vary from society to society. Nevertheless, there were two closely related points on which he insisted. First, the power accorded to the sovereign must be absolute, without legal limit or countervailing authority. Second, rebellion against a ruling sovereign can never be justified, no matter how ineptly or corruptly the sovereign may be ruling. This insistence on an absolute, unchallenge-able monarch was driven by the unflattering view Hobbes took of human nature. The impulsion to serve our own inter-ests is just so strong, he believed, that if we are given the slightest free rein, we will immediately begin breaking the law and taking advantage of neighbors. Civic society will then collapse, and the resulting state of nature will be so violent and unstable that everyone will be worse off than if we had remained in civic society, no matter how repressive this may have been. Hobbes's conviction on this point was only strengthened by the events taking place as he wrote *Leviathan*. With English civic society having descended into civil war, upward of eighty-four thousand soldiers died on the battlefield, and another hundred thousand perished from disease, to say nothing of the civilian impacts of the war. So even if you had not been a fan of Charles, could life under him really have been any worse than this?

Hobbes on Natural Rights

If Hobbes therefore remained an unapologetic advocate for absolute monarchy—as conservative in this regard as he was revolutionary in others—his own account suggests no king can ever wield a power that is truly absolute. To see why, we need to consider his discussion of natural rights. The concept of natural right, as a right that cannot be *conferred* by any mundane authority, since it is something we already inherently *possess*, was first conceived by the Stoics and later explored by various scholastic theologians. In the scholastic context, not surprisingly, any such rights were understood to come from God; think about the right to rule with which God invests certain families under divine right doctrine. It is also not surprising that the scholastic conception of right had an unmistakable Aristotelian flavor to it: there exists a discrete substance, the person of the king, and the right to rule inheres within this substance just like any other property. In fact, the hereditary nature of sovereignty almost makes it sound as if the right to rule is a discrete substance in its own right, capable of being passed down from a king to his son like the crown they wear.

When Hobbes approached the concept of natural right, he came at the topic from a completely different angle than had the scholastics. For Hobbes, a right is not something we metaphysically *possess*, whether coming to us from God or anywhere else. For Hobbes, as for so many other modern philosophers, what we possess is a faculty of reason. A right, accordingly, is something we *figure out*; it is something we arrive at using our reason. Hobbes suggests we have only one right, the right to self-defense. Admittedly, this does not make for an expansive doctrine of natural rights. Nevertheless, considering how Hobbes arrived at this right will give us an idea of how he was rethinking the notion of right in a way that would give natural rights a place in the rational order of nature being revealed by the modern sciences.

In a pre-civil state, we all possess a wide variety of natural freedoms, given that no laws or rulers stand above us. These freedoms include the freedom to attack my neighbor: Nothing stops me from launching such an attack, other than my neighbor's strength to resist. That said, this is a freedom I may coherently relinquish when I enter a social contract with those around me, since our agreement passes two tests. First, it is psychologically coherent, on Hobbes's account of human psychology. It is in my own interest to give up my freedom to attack my neighbors, provided my neighbors agree to the same, since we all benefit from the increased security this non-aggression pact provides. Second, the mutual pledge to abstain from attacking one another is enforceable. Once my neighbors and I have collectively invested a sovereign with both the authority and the physical power to enforce our pledge of non-aggression, I can be confident even my strongest neighbors will generally honor this pledge, since failure to do so will trigger a devastating reprisal from our mutual sovereign. Our covenant, in other words, has a sword to back it up.

Continuing with Hobbes's argument, in the state of nature, I also possess the freedom to defend my life, should someone else attack me. Unlike the freedom to attack others, however, this freedom to resist attack is not one that I may coherently relinquish. Why not? Imagine some strange scenario in which I find it to be in my best interest to relinquish my freedom to defend myself. Therefore I enter an agreement to this effect, pledging not to defend myself, even if attacked. How could this pledge ever be enforced, even if my neighbors and I place an absolute sovereign above us? Suppose, after I have agreed not to fight back when attacked by others, the sovereign sees me getting into an altercation in which I end up struggling for my life. The sovereign may say, "Stop! Self-defense is not permitted, as you, yourself, agreed." But what could the sovereign do to enforce this command? He could send his soldiers to attack me, threatening my life. Yet it is my life I am fighting for, and if I stop fighting I will surely die, so what possible leverage could this threat have over me? Indeed, even if it is the sovereign's own soldiers who attacked me in the first place, they cannot stop me from struggling to defend myself. The worst they can do is kill me—but that is what I am struggling against. To be sure, these soldiers may well overpower me, and they may well kill me. But what they have not managed to do, nor could they possibly do, is deprive me of the freedom to defend myself unto death, using whatever strength I have.

The freedom to defend myself is therefore a freedom I cannot logically relinquish, even by voluntary agreement, since such an agreement could not meaningfully be enforced. A covenant without possible sword, this agreement would be incoherent—and hence invalid—from the beginning. Accordingly, the natural freedom to defend ourselves may be classified as a natural right, to distinguish it from other sorts of natural freedoms we *can* relinquish as we enter civic society. As noted above, this right to self-defense that Hobbes secures for us may not sound like much. Particularly if an absolute monarch is in power, it may amount to little more than my right to keep kicking and screaming as the king's soldiers drag me off to be executed. What is nonetheless significant about the novel, rational approach Hobbes took to the concept of natural right is that it dramatically expands the sphere of those to whom such rights apply.

When a right is regarded as a commodity God hands out, or even as a property God instills in certain discrete substances (persons), there is no guarantee God will distribute such rights to everyone. In fact, the right to rule, per divine right doctrine, is a right God does not confer upon one person in one thousand. Similarly, the feudal system was replete with rights that were not merely limited to the nobility, but they could be enjoyed only at the direct expense of the peasantry. Consider the *droit de seigneur*, for instance, the right a feudal lord could invoke when two of his peasants married, compelling the bride to spend her first night of marriage in his bed. As this last example suggests, moreover, even when scholastic theologians occasionally debated whether certain natural rights might be extended to all men, it went without saying that they really were discussing *all men*. The notion that a woman might possess any rights, at all, whether in relation to her feudal lord or even to her husband, was simply not up for discussion. By the same token, the "all men" who might possess certain rights were clearly Christian, European men, not the various infidels and savages European explorers were encountering on their voyages.

Shifting to the modern context, when Galileo made his study of falling bodies, his groundbreaking move was to stop viewing the objects of nature as discrete Aristotelian substances, each possessing its own distinctive set of properties. Instead, he abstracted out as many of these properties as he could, thereby reducing the diverse array of qualitatively different bodies to identical, abstract material objects. The advantage of this approach was that, when Galileo then discerned a regular pattern in the rate at which various bodies fall, he could be confident that the resulting law of nature applied to *all* falling bodies, regardless of their unique properties, thus dramatically expanding his knowledge. Analogously, when Hobbes studied human nature, he used the conjectural state of nature as a means of abstracting out all the particular qualities people might possess, including those they may have acquired as a result of living in civic society. This allowed him to confirm that the universal law determining that all human behavior is self-interest. Significant here is not so much the precise content of this natural law Hobbes was proposing as the "nature" to which he saw it applying. Specifically, Hobbes was asserting that individual human beings do not all possess their own unique natures. Rather, he was following Galileo in regarding nature as the whole field of things, governed by certain universal laws, which thereby apply to every individual who happens to occupy this field.

On this view of nature, there are simply no metaphysical grounds left by which we could assert that one individual is naturally, inherently entitled to something another person is not. Even when the social contract invests one individual with sovereign power, there is nothing metaphysically distinctive about this individual; the person has just been assigned a particular role in keeping the group organized. Accordingly, when Hobbes began reasoning about whether the inhabitants of the state of nature might possess any rights that could not possibly be taken from them, even through voluntary surrender, he had no metaphysical grounds by which to assert that any of the rights he so discovered might apply to certain people, but not to others. Thus, even if Hobbes never managed to identify anything but the bare-bones right to self-defense, this natural right was already more expansive than any of the traditional feudal rights, insofar as it applied—logically—to every human being, regardless of the station into which they were born or any other characteristics that might distinguish one person from the next.

This observation suggests a terminological refinement, which has become familiar in contemporary speech, but was by no means self-evident when Hobbes wrote. This is the distinction between rights and privileges. A privilege is, by definition, exclusive. It applies to some individuals, but not to others; this is what makes it a privilege. Accordingly, when medieval thinkers spoke of the divine right of kings, or the *droit de seigneur*, such rights would have been better referred to as privileges, since their scope was necessarily limited to specific individuals or groups. A right, in contrast—at least under the modern conception Hobbes was pioneering—is characterized by its universality. If a right is proposed that applies to some people, but not to others, it is not a right; it is a privilege.

A thesis I will be developing at various points in this book is that, prior to the eighteenth century, virtually every human society was governed by some version of what I will call "the system of privilege." Under this system, different people are accorded different levels of privilege, almost always depending on the station into which they are born. Those born near the top of the social hierarchy are granted a wide array of privileges denied to those lower down the hierarchy. In fact, those near the bottom of the social ladder are tasked with a range of duties, most designed to supply the benefits to which the privileged classes are entitled. The peasant has a duty to provide the local lord with a certain portion of his crops, for instance, not to mention offering up his bride on his wedding night.

Not surprisingly, those in the privileged classes have always argued that this highly imbalanced manner of organizing society is right and good, a reflection of the metaphysical nature of things. The system of privilege, in other words, has always been buttressed by an *ideology of privilege*, which seeks to establish that the world is constructed to render the system of differential privileges natural, the way of the world. Thus, just as celestial bodies, traveling in circular paths, are more perfect than mundane bodies, kings and lords possess a greater moral worthiness than anyone else; they are noble, not just by title, but by nature. The implication, of course, is that those in the privileged classes *deserve* all the exclusive privileges they are accorded. Indeed, given the contrast between the exalted nature of the nobleman and the rude, servile nature of his peasants, it would be an affront to the natural order of things—and to this order's creator—if the nobleman was *not* granted a slate of privileges denied to his peasants. Privileges, in other words, really are "rights" to which superior people are entitled, by virtue of their superior natures.

As modern scientists began discarding the metaphysical view that the world comprises individual substances, each bearing its own nature, in favor of the view that what exists most fundamentally is *nature*, the whole field of things, as governed by certain universal laws, the metaphysical underpinnings of the ideology of privilege began to dissolve. Hobbes helped move this process along by showing that, under the new metaphysical framework, anything we consider a natural right must be universal, thus rendering untenable the traditional slipperiness between rights and privileges. Eventually, European society would begin to move away from a political order based on the ancient system of privilege and in the direction of a political order based on the modern idea of universal rights. Before this shift could proceed very far, however, further work would be required on the theoretical front. As revolutionary as Hobbes's approach to political theory was, its internal difficulties had to be confronted.

The Limits of the Hobbesian Account

Two significant objections can be brought against Hobbes's account of the state of nature and the social contract. The first concerns the moral obligation we are under to respect the sovereign's authority. Again, Hobbes insists that this obligation arises, not because God commands it, nor because the king is inherently superior to the rest of us, having inherited a unique metaphysical nature, ultimately from Adam. Rather, we are morally obligated to respect the authority of the sovereign for the same reason we are obliged to fulfill the terms of any other contract into which we enter: because we have freely placed ourselves under this obligation. The fairly obvious rejoinder is, "*I* never signed the social contract. *I* never agreed to place myself under the sovereign's rule. I just happened to be born into this particular society, being ruled by this particular monarch. So while the threat of punishment may well induce me to stay in line, why am I *morally* obliged to respect the sovereign's authority?" This was a question for which Hobbes, quite simply, did not have a good answer.

The second major difficulty with Hobbes's account stems from his insistence on an absolute monarch. Again, because covenants without the sword are empty, Hobbes believed the sovereign must be given absolute power. Absent an all-powerful enforcer of the law, people would follow the law only when convenient; yet this would mean they had never really left the state of nature. That said, the problem with an absolute monarch is obvious. If a single person bears sole responsibility for enforcing the law, who will police the sovereign? Who will ensure, in other words, that the sovereign is ruling for the benefit of the kingdom, administering the law in even-handed fashion, as opposed to using his power to further his own interests, quite possibly at the expense of his subjects? In fact, if self-interest is the universal law of human nature, and if kings are human beings—which they are, on Hobbes's account, not metaphysically different from anyone else—how could a king *not* elevate his own interests above those of his subjects?

Foreseeing this objection, Hobbes was forced to note that even the most powerful human king must answer to a divine king, with the threat of eternal punishment being the "sword" that keeps the absolute monarch from abusing his power. Following Hobbes's dramatic moves to locate the origins of civic society in human reason, this *deus ex machina* is theoretically unsatisfying, to say the least. Nor had centuries of experience with absolute monarchs given Europeans much confidence that divine oversight would be enough to check the power of an ambitious mundane king. On the contrary, history had seemingly shown, in the words of Lord Acton, "Power tends to corrupt, and absolute power corrupts absolutely." Hobbes therefore left his successors with challenges to render fully coherent the doctrine that the sovereign derives legitimacy from the consent of the governed. One who took up this challenge was his countryman, John Locke.

Locke on the State of Nature, the Natural Law, and Natural Rights

Locke was one of the foremost exponents of empiricism, an

epistemological stance that gained traction on the British Isles, and which holds that everything we know, we learn through empirical experience. Most emphatically, Locke denied that we come preprogrammed with any of the "innate ideas" that more rationalistic philosophers on the European continent were using to ground human knowledge, or at least the most significant types of knowledge. Descartes, for instance, had argued that we find we have an idea of God in our minds. Yet, because everything we encounter in experience is finite, whereas our idea of God is precisely the idea of an infinite being, nothing in our experience could have suggested this idea to us. God must have therefore implanted this idea in our minds, like a craftsman marking his work with a seal, thereby proving God's existence. Rationalist philosophers debated what other ideas God might have placed in our minds, but it seemed certain these would include the necessary truths of logic and mathematics, as well as presumably moral truths.

Regarding this whole line of reasoning as metaphysical claptrap, Locke insisted that when we enter the world, our minds are a blank slate, to be filled with knowledge only as sensations stream in over time. Locke did not publish his monumental work of epistemology, *Essay Concerning Human Understanding*, until 1689, but he had finished writing it ten years prior, at which point he turned most of his attention to politics. The 1680s, coming about a generation after Hobbes wrote, was another turbulent decade in English political history. This one culminated in the Glorious Revolution of 1688, which saw James II deposed, followed shortly thereafter by the accession to the throne of William of Orange, a Dutch-born nobleman offered the English crown on the condition that he observe a more limited form of constitutional monarchy. Locke published his *Two Treatises of Government* in 1689 in explicit support of William III, as the new king came to be known. In the first treatise, Locke offers a thorough refutation of Filmer's divine right of kings theory. In the second treatise, he lays out his own version of contract theory, which rejects Hobbes's insistence on an absolute monarch and instead provides the theoretical underpinnings for just the sort of limited monarchy William had promised.

Following Hobbes's lead, Locke begins his account of the social contract by considering human life in the state of nature. The Lockean state of nature, however, is not nearly as bleak as the Hobbesian version, for Locke did not believe the natural human condition was to be at war with one another. Locke rather draws a distinction between the state of nature and the state of war. In a state of war, no laws are observed beyond the law of force, with participants having openly declared their hostility to one another. Hobbes had believed people to be so self-interested that, absent an absolute sovereign hovering over them, they will be at war with one another. Locke counters that *because* people are self-interested, the state of nature will *not* be characterized by warfare. Far from constantly attacking one another, that is, the inhabitants of the state of nature will tend to leave one another alone, or even band together in informal communities, since this will reduce the likelihood of triggering violent reprisals.

Locke goes even further, however, to argue that the inhabitants of the state of nature are bound by a natural law.

This law has two provisions. The first is that, "No one ought to harm one another in his life, health, liberty, or possessions," and indeed a person ought, "As much as he can, to preserve the rest of mankind." The second provision of the natural law is that if anyone should violate the first, then anyone else— not just the victim—is entitled to exact retribution on the offender. Thus, if someone should steal a bundle of food from my neighbor, my neighbor may rightfully track him down and punish him. But I am entitled to do the same, merely having witnessed a violation of natural law, even though I suffered no injury myself.

What is the origin of the natural law? What *is* the natural law, metaphysically speaking? Unfortunately, Locke is not clear on this point. At times, he makes it sound as if the natural law is something God has handed down to us, as to Moses on the mountain. At other points in the *Second Treatise of Government*, the natural law sounds like it is fully human in origin. Most likely, Locke did not take care to distinguish between these two positions because he did not see a contradiction between them. Like most European philosophers of the seventeenth and eighteenth centuries, Locke continued to believe that God exists, and that God created the world along the lines of the Genesis account, mainly because anyone had yet to suggest a better explanation of where the world comes from. Increasingly, however, whereas scholastic theologians had been content to concede that the ways of God are inscrutable, modern philosophers had begun to emphasize that a perfect God who creates a rational world must himself be perfectly rational. This rationality of both God and the world implies any laws we might discover through our own powers of reasoning will be identical to the laws God decrees, whether he ever reveals these laws to us or just leaves them for us to discover on our own. In any case, we learn far more about the natural law when we think through how the inhabitants of the state of nature would have come to recognize it on their own, as opposed to simply accepting it as divine decree. This naturalistic approach, moreover, accords far better with Locke's broader stance of empiricism than the appeal to divine command, so this is the approach we will take in working through Locke's account of the natural law.

Based on their daily experiences, the inhabitants of the state of nature would have inductively formulated such general factual assertions as, "The sun will rise every morning." In the same way, experience would have taught them such prudential rules as, "Do not eat raw pork (unless you want to get sick)." Experience must have further shown the inhabitants of the state of nature that if you attempt to kill or enslave other people, or if you take the material goods to which they have already laid claim, this just invites retaliation. Hence, just as people in the state of nature will naturally come to view eating raw pork as taboo, they will start making it a general rule not to harm others in their "life, liberty, health, or possessions." People will further learn from experience that acts violating this rule tend to cause discord in those loose communities that have emerged. And even in the state of nature, people will understand that living in a peaceful, stable community is preferable to either isolation or warfare. Accordingly, they will make it a general rule to exact retribution on violators of the natural law, even when not personally victimized, to punish the offender for threatening the community and to deter future offenses.

Beyond arguing that people will observe a natural law even before they enter civic society, Locke asserts that people enjoy certain natural rights in the state of nature. He most often speaks of the right to one's "property," although he uses this term to refer, not just to material possessions, but to life and liberty. What is a natural right, on Locke's account? In one sense, natural rights are simply the flip side of the natural law. According to the natural law, I may not indiscriminately kill, enslave, or steal from others, so when I observe the natural law, I recognize others as having a right to life, liberty, and material possessions. Still, Locke seems to mean something more when he refers to natural rights. Indeed, he appears to follow Hobbes in believing rights to be those freedoms we enjoy in the state of nature, of which we cannot logically be deprived, nor may we coherently relinquish them, even when freely entering a social contract with others. This becomes clear as we work through Locke's arguments for various specific rights.

Hobbes had already shown why the right to defend my life is an inalienable right. To make me stop fighting for my life, the worst another person can do is threaten me with death, yet this threat carries no weight, since death is what I already struggle against. Nor may I coherently contract this right away, since I can only be held to my side of the bargain through the threat of death—which holds no sway when my life is already in jeopardy. Locke extends this argument to show that the right to defend one's liberty is similarly an inalienable natural right. When I am enslaved, my life is in my master's hands. Should he decide to kill me, I lack the physical means to resist. Yet, I have an inalienable right to defend my life, so I likewise have a natural right to use whatever force I can muster to avoid enslavement, or to free myself once enslaved. This means I cannot reasonably contract away my liberty, even through a free act of will. Accordingly, even if events compel me to sign a contract selling myself into slavery, I am not bound by this agreement, for once enslaved, I find myself in a condition where my life is threatened by the absolute power my master has over me. And since my master can threaten me with nothing worse than death, he cannot compel me to abide by my renunciation of freedom. Granted, my master can forestall any attempts of escape or rebellion through the threat of immediate death, or perhaps torture. But he can do nothing to stop me from biding my time and attempting to free myself when the moment is favorable. My original commitment to give up all claim to liberty therefore being unenforceable, the contract I signed was invalid from the beginning.

The same argument can be extended to justify the natural right to claim possession of material goods. As human beings, we depend on a steady supply of material goods to keep ourselves alive. Such goods can be found in nature, but they are of little use to us until we somehow modify them through our labor—plucking an apple from a tree, if nothing else, so we can eat it. The state of nature has no formal property laws, but Locke suggests that when I modify a natural object through my labor, I essentially take possession of it: I signal to others that it is mine, and that I intend to use it for my upkeep. Were I unable to take possession of material goods and consume them as I saw fit, I would quickly die of starvation or exposure. Assume, however, some powerful person tells me I may no longer appropriate goods for myself; rather, I may only eat when he deigns to feed me. If this other person is powerful enough, he may well force this arrangement upon me. But he cannot force me to accept this condition. On the contrary, I always retain my right to resist this form of slavery, for just as no one can take away my right to defend my life, neither can anyone take away my right to appropriate and consume those goods that are necessary for my survival. Indeed, I cannot even freely give up my right to hold possessions, for this would equate to selling myself into slavery: I would lose the power to ensure the conditions of my survival. That is not to say I cannot reasonably give up certain of my possessions. I may trade some goods I hold for others, or even give away various possessions out of goodwill. I may further agree not to take possession of certain *types* of objects, assuming such objects are not indispensable for my survival. But I cannot coherently pledge to refrain from taking possession of any objects whatsoever since I could be held to this pledge only through the threat of death, whereas this threat will be empty if I already stand on the brink of starvation.

Locke on Social Contract and the Nature of the Sovereign

Thus, even if the state of nature is governed by no written laws or established leaders, its inhabitants will generally observe the natural law of their own accord, and they will recognize one another as possessing certain natural rights. As a result, the state of nature, on Locke's account, will be far less warlike than what Hobbes had imagined. Nevertheless, even the Lockean state of nature must contain a good deal of violence and fear. For one thing, if the more intelligent inhabitants of the state of nature will understand that abiding by the natural law is in their own long-term best interest, there is no guarantee everyone will be far-sighted enough to grasp this fact or, in any case, to act upon it consistently. Indeed, if one person should happen to grow considerably stronger than his neighbors, it may turn out that it *is* in his best interest to exploit others, natural rights be damned. Thus, in the state of nature, violations of the natural law will inevitably occur. And when attempts are then made to uphold the law through acts of retribution, further conflicts will arise. Although anyone may punish a violator of the natural law, in most cases the victim, or someone close to the victim, will be inspired to take action. This means someone with a vested interest in the case is responsible for deciding exactly what provisions of the natural law have been broken, who broke them, and what punishment should result. One individual, in other words, is serving as legislator, judge, and enforcer of the law, moreover doing so in a case in which the person has a strong personal stake and emotional bias. Not even the most reasonable and well-meaning individual can judge fairly under such circumstances, so punishments meted out in the state of nature will often violate the natural law just as badly as the original offenses, thereby inviting further retribution. Hence, while the rule of law in the state of nature is real and meaningful, it cannot be very strict, and it is sure to be dogged by all the irregularities and biases that accompany vigilante justice.

Thus there must come a time, as Hobbes observed, when violence and anxiety drive the inhabitants of the state of nature to form a compact with one another and enter civic society. In so doing, everyone agrees to give up certain freedoms they enjoyed in the state of nature, instead submitting to the formal rule of law. For Locke, those freedoms relinquished primarily relate to actions that violate the natural law, anyway. But whereas in the state of nature individuals must enforce the natural law themselves, the sovereign is now vested, by common consent, with the power of making and enforcing laws. Indeed, the one "right" people have in the state of nature that they must yield upon entering civic society—not giving it up completely but transferring its exercise to the state—is the right to exact retribution on violators of the law. If someone attacks me in civic society, I may still defend myself, the right to self-defense being inalienable. But if I survive the attack, I may not hunt my assailant down and punish him myself. I must leave it to the designated authorities to apprehend the offender, judge him according to the established laws, and carry out any punishments deemed appropriate. Perhaps this retribution will not be as harsh as what I would have exacted. But I am biased, having been the victim of the attack, and it is precisely to escape the uncertainty and prejudice inherent in vigilante justice that we all agree to turn law enforcement over to the state.

If entering civic society therefore entails giving up certain natural freedoms, as well as transferring the right of retribution to the state, Locke stresses that people cannot coherently give up their natural rights to life, liberty, or material property, these rights being inalienable. The conclusion he draws is what truly distances him from Hobbes: While allowing that the social contract must invest the sovereign with adequate power to make and enforce laws, Locke insists that the compact cannot grant any person or group absolute power. To do so would effectively place the life, liberty, and possessions of every other member of society in the hands of the absolute ruler. Yet since no one may reasonably contract away the inalienable right they have to their essential "property," even if a social contract was signed to institute an absolute ruler, it would be incoherent, and hence invalid. Hence, whereas Hobbes had argued that civic society requires an absolute ruler, Locke establishes that an absolute ruler can never be legitimate.

Because civic society requires a sovereign, yet the sovereign cannot be absolute, the biggest challenge people drafting a social contract face is structuring the sovereign authority such that it may govern effectively, yet without becoming absolutistic. Locke's primary strategy for accomplishing this relies on a principle that was already being explored by the English political system, with its twin institutions of Parliament and the monarchy: the separation of powers. As noted earlier, the main problem with the administration of justice in the state of nature is that the same person serves as legislator, judge, and executioner, doing so in cases in which the person has a vested interest. When the sovereign's power is absolute, he or his representatives serve as legislator, judge, and executive in every case arising among his subjects. And because the absolute ruler lays ultimate claim to all the property within the state, he has a vested interest in every case on which he rules. To remedy this situation, Locke suggests that the sovereign be divided into three different bodies invested, respectively, with legislative, executive, and federative powers.

Since it makes the laws, the legislative body is the state's supreme governing power. The executive is then charged with enforcing these laws. By "federative" powers, Locke means the authority to deal with foreign states. He acknowledges that executive and federative powers will often be in the same person, the head of state. But this is not a problem, since carrying out domestic and foreign policy will rarely lead to a conflict of interest. Locke even approves of the executive playing some role in the legislature, as was the case under the English system of mixed government, which made the Crown responsible for convening and dissolving Parliament while allowing it to introduce some bills. Locke stresses, however, that the executive cannot *be* the legislating entity. The bulk of legislative powers must reside in some person or group distinct from the person functioning as chief executive, to prevent the executive from passing laws directed more toward personal gain than the good of the state. Locke does not include the judiciary as one of the three primary branches of government, as would later become standard, but he does insist on an independent judiciary, to ensure that neither lawmakers nor the executive can exempt themselves from the laws they establish and enforce.

When a government is set up according to some such plan, different people make, enforce, and interpret the laws. This allows for effective governance while preventing any one person or group from accumulating too much power over the others. And thus Locke had resolved one of the most significant problems with the Hobbesian version of contract theory: if people are so self-interested that they require an absolute monarch to keep order among them, what is to prevent the absolute monarch—himself a self-interested human being—from using his power simply for personal gain? Locke's response was not to deny that people are inherently self-interested; he took this premise of the Hobbesian dilemma as a given. Rather, he tried to channel this self-interest into a more sustainable dynamic, specifically by dividing the sovereign's power among multiple bodies and using the power of each to limit the power of others.

Locke on Tacit Consent and the Right to Revolution

If doing away with the need for an absolute ruler may have been Locke's most important practical advance over Hobbes, another theoretical improvement he made upon the Hobbesian account of the social contract came through his doctrine of tacit consent. As noted above, an inevitable objection to contract theory is that *I* was not there for the signing of the social contract; *I* never gave my consent to being ruled by the sovereign. So why should I be morally obligated to respect the sovereign's authority? Locke grants that few of us were around when civic society first emerged, nor even when the countries we now inhabit were founded. Accordingly, few of us have had the opportunity to give our *explicit* consent to the governing arrangements under which we find ourselves:

no one has ever asked us for it. Nevertheless, Locke argues, when I remain in the society in which I live for a significant length of time, meanwhile enjoying all the benefits that both the society and its governing order provide, I give these arrangements my *tacit* consent. If I was unhappy, after all, why did I not leave? Thus, even though I may never have had the opportunity to freely bind myself to the terms of the social contract, I have freely gone along with these terms for so long, reaping their benefits all the while, that I have essentially placed myself under the same obligation as the original signatories—namely, to abide by the law and to respect the authority of the sovereign charged with enforcing the law.

It might here be objected that, if in Locke's time the world still contained enough uninhabited regions that people could exercise their option to leave civic society, this is no longer true. Nowadays, even if I renounce my national citizenship, I can still only move to another country with an established government. And since I therefore have no way of opting out of civic society, my continued presence in one society does not indicate even a tacit acceptance of that government's authority. Even so, physically departing one's country is not the only way a person can opt out of civic society. I can also simply declare myself no longer a member of my society, unbound by its laws. Withdrawing my consent from the government, I return to the state of nature. To be sure, the state will not take my pronouncement lightly, especially if I begin breaking its laws. It will, rather, use its superior force to apprehend and punish me. I might complain, "The state has no right to punish me according to its laws since I have not consented to them." But my complaint falls flat, since I am trying to invoke my rights against the state, when I have already renounced any civil relation to it. Indeed, when I openly declare that I will defy the state, I effectively declare war on it. And since the state of war is governed only by the law of force, I have no grounds for complaint when the state uses its superior force to subdue me, in the interest of preserving itself. If I am willing to face the state's wrath, or believe I can avoid it, I may opt out of civic society. The fact that I do not implies that I give the government my tacit consent.

Drawing out the full implications of the doctrine of tacit consent, Locke notes that not just individuals but whole populations can revoke their consent to being ruled by a particular sovereign. More bluntly, Locke declares that people have not just the right but the moral imperative to revolt against a tyrannical government. This right to revolt is not a civically conferred right; no state can freely permit its people to engage in armed rebellion, since the state exists precisely to replace violence with stability. The right to revolt is rather a natural right, stemming from the right of each citizen to resist enslavement. Before revolt becomes justified, Locke cautions, the government must commit a long pattern of major abuses, and the people should exhaust all legal means of redress. When, however, a government chronically oppresses its people, it fails to uphold its end of the social contract, so the people have a right, not just to withdraw their support of the government but to enter a state of war and seek its overthrow. When revolution breaks out, neither side is bound by any rights or laws, since both are fighting for their survival. Who wins depends on who can muster the most force. The government will typically have amassed a great deal of power, especially if it has an army at its command. But the general population will always outnumber its leaders, so if a rebel movement can garner public support, it stands a chance of success. In any case, should rebels topple the government, returning to civic society will require drafting a new social contract, the old one having been torn up first by the tyrannical government and then by the revolutionaries.

It is interesting to note that when James II fled to France, Parliament was careful to specify that he had abdicated the throne, rather than having been toppled. This implied—the term "Glorious Revolution" notwithstanding—that civic society had not been dissolved, so no new social contract had to be concluded. Instead, William III could just be installed into an empty position within the established political order. A hundred years later, when a group of English colonists living across the Atlantic Ocean grew weary of the oppression they were suffering under the Crown, they felt no such squeamishness about invoking their Lockean right to revolt. Preparing to meet in 1776 to affirm their decision to withdraw themselves from British rule, they charged Thomas Jefferson with drafting a declaration of independence. He responded, in part, with the following remarkable summary of Locke's political philosophy:

> We hold these truths to be self-evident, that all men are created equal, that they are endowed by their Creator with certain unalienable Rights, that among these are Life, Liberty and the pursuit of Happiness. — That to secure these rights, Governments are insti-

tuted among Men, deriving their just powers from the consent of the governed, — That whenever any Form of Government becomes destructive of these ends, it is the Right of the People to alter or to abolish it, and to institute new Government.

When the revolt against Great Britain proved successful, the former colonists found themselves in a unique position: rather than being able to presume the existence of a social contract that had always existed, they really did need to sit down and draft a new social contract. This gave the American founders the opportunity, not just to tweak an existing regime around the edges, as England and various other European countries had been doing for some time, but to build a whole new political order from scratch. After an initial false start under the Articles of Confederation, what they came up with was the Constitution of the United States, a governing document specifically designed to establish a new society based on such Lockean principles as government by consent, respect for the rights of the individual, and the separation of powers.

To be sure, the Constitution was a flawed document, as judged by the Lockean principles that inspired it. Most egregiously, it legally sanctioned the institution of chattel slavery, flatly contradicting Locke's assertion that personal liberty is an inalienable natural right, while strangely twisting his discussion of property rights to provide for the ownership not just of material objects but of human beings. At various later points in this book, we will consider the American experiment in democracy more closely, including the moral contradictions it has embodied since the time of its founding, but also the slow, painful, incomplete, but nonetheless very real progress the country has made towards overcoming these contradictions, thereby bringing its lived reality into better alignment with its founding ideals.

The Hobbesian Legacy

Hobbes was widely reviled by his contemporaries, mostly because he took such a dim view of the human condition. Nor is there any denying that his account of the state of nature—a perpetual war of every self-interested wretch against every other—was as dismal as anything the staunchest Calvinist, obsessed with human depravity, had ever preached. There was a difference, however, between the origin story Hobbes told and the traditional Christian narrative. For Hobbes, the state of nature did not represent a fallen state, a consequence of paradise having been lost. Rather, this miserable state stood at the *beginning* of the human story. Nor was this a condition people were doomed to occupy forever, much less being condemned to sink deeper into the mire, absent divine intervention. On the contrary, for as brutish as the inhabitants of the state of nature may have been, they had one thing going for them: their powers of reasoning. And at some point, when all the instability, violence, and fear had grown unbearable, some of them must have reasoned there was another way they could live. Driven by their own self-interest, they must have figured out that if they came together and agreed to sacrifice some of the freedoms they enjoyed in the state of nature, they would all be better off. Therefore, they entered into a compact by which they all submitted to both the rule of law and rule by a sovereign, thereby transcending the state of nature through the creation of civic society. Rather than being a story of descent from a Golden Age into the depraved world of today, therefore, this was a story that begins with people living in a miserable, lonely, lawless condition, then climbing toward a contemporary state that not only better serves our collective interests but operates at a higher moral level. According to this narrative, moreover, people make this ascent not by getting transported to some radically different order through divine agency, but by using their own powers of reasoning to reshape the world around them.

As pessimistic as Hobbes may have often seemed, therefore, he was actually as optimistic as his contemporary, Descartes, at least with respect to reason's potential for improving the quality of human life. Descartes's optimism sprang from the following calculus: if the world around us is governed by immutable, rational laws, and if we can use our own rational powers to reveal these laws, we can predict how the objects around us will behave under particular circumstances. And if we can do this, we can manipulate these circumstances in such a way that nature starts furthering our human ends rather than frustrating them. We can develop useful technologies that ease human suffering and make life more pleasant and rewarding.

Hobbes realized that, for human beings, the most significant objects in our world are other human beings. And while philosophers and theologians had long worried that if we are somehow objectively determined in our actions, civically responsible, moral behavior will be impossible. Hobbes countered that it is precisely *because* we have a lawful predictability to our actions that a moral order can arise. This predictability is what allows us to design social structures that channel our natural self-interest into actions that benefit not just ourselves but also one another. Civic society, in other words, is a technology we have collectively designed and implemented to bring our frequently conflicting personal interests into better alignment with one another. And the fact that even the unsophisticated residents of the state of nature were able to stumble across this technology gives us reason to hope we may keep improving upon it, such that our collective lives, already better now than they were in the state of nature, may tomorrow be even better than they are today.

Hobbes's legacy was felt most directly in the political realm, where he inspired or influenced the work of such later thinkers and statesmen as Locke, Montesquieu, Jean Jacques Rousseau, Jefferson, and James Madison. But civic society is not just defined by our political relations. And Hobbes also established the philosophical framework within which one of his direct descendants in the line of British moral philosophers, Adam Smith, would analyze and seek to improve upon a second social technology we have collectively devised to better align our diverse personal interests: our various modes of economic organization.

CHAPTER 4

THE GROWTH IMPETUS OF CAPITALISM: ECONOMIC PROGRESS

It may seem odd, in a book about the progressive worldview, to devote a chapter to the writings of Adam Smith. Political conservatives, after all—or in any case, fiscal conservatives in the traditional mold—tend to regard Smith as their patron saint, whereas contemporary progressives frequently decry the *laissez-faire* capitalism that has become synonymous with his name. Be that as it may, Smith fits squarely into the line of British thinkers, starting with Hobbes and Locke, who were trying to take the insights of the Scientific Revolution and apply them to areas of life beyond the hard sciences, partly to increase our understanding of these uniquely human domains but also to help us reshape these domains to better serve our human wants, needs, and aspirations. Indeed, one way to read Smith's economic analyses in *The Wealth of Nations* is as a sustained response to the Hobbesian dilemma identified in the last chapter: assuming people are guided by self-interest in all they do, as seems to be required for human beings to have a place in the rational, law-governed order of nature the modern physical sciences were revealing, how is civically responsible, moral behavior possible?

In developing his answer to this question, Smith showed how—in the context of the free market—the invisible hand of the market tends to translate self-interested strivings into socially beneficial behaviors. He further showed how the specifically capitalist mode of production contains an impetus toward economic growth unknown to previous economic systems, most of which tended toward stasis. As Smith conducted his investigations in the late eighteenth century, European capitalism was still in its nascent, pre-industrial form, yet already it had begun to produce noticeable improvements in the quality of life for many Europeans. To be sure, the shift toward capitalism also had its downsides, many of which are still with us today. Nevertheless, for a European population that had long been accustomed to living in grinding poverty, generally without any realistic hope of things getting better over the course of a lifetime, the emerging possibility of sustained economic improvement provided a more tangible sense of progress than either the abstract discoveries of the Scientific Revolution or even the prospect of a more liberal political order being suggested by the American and French Revolutions.

One note about this chapter: It will contain some mathematics, albeit of a very simple variety. This is by design. Smith did not invent capitalism, nor any of the other modes of economic activity that led up to its development. He was, rather, one of the first major modern economists to apply the methods and tools of the modern physical sciences—including mathematical analysis—to a whole range of exchange relationships. The intuitive, quantitative clarity of Smith's analyses helped convince many of his early readers that material progress was not only possible in a market economy but could be further encouraged through the appropriate policies. For Smith and many of his late eighteenth-century readers, therefore, the very mathematics of capitalism painted a hopeful vision of the future.

The Theory of Moral Sentiments

The Wealth of Nations was the second book Smith published. The first was a work of moral psychology titled *The Theory of Moral Sentiments*, of interest to us here because it was even more explicit about addressing the Hobbesian dilemma of how human beings, apparently self-interested in all they do, can engage in socially responsible behaviors that sometimes appear to be disinterested or even downright altruistic. One of Smith's teachers, Francis Hutcheson, had already worked out the basic logic of this response to the Hobbesian dilemma.

Just as we have sense organs that present us with sights, sounds, and smells that can delight or repulse us, Hutcheson suggests, we are also born with a moral sense that causes us to experience certain moral sentiments under particular circumstances. When I witness someone in pain, for instance, I do not just register this fact disinterestedly. Rather, viewing the other's pain causes me to feel discomfort, much like touching a hot stove causes me to feel not just the hardness of the iron but also a painful burning sensation. Similarly, when I see someone showing signs of happiness, I am infused with a pleasant feeling, much as when biting into a piece of rich chocolate. Hutcheson's strategy for explaining supposedly "disinterested" moral behavior, even on the assumption of inveterate self-interest, is thus clear. Suppose I am alone in a room with a child who holds a delicious-looking chocolate bar. Nothing would stop me from ripping the chocolate from the child's hands and eating it myself—the course of action self-interest would seem to dictate. As Hutcheson observes, however, most of us would not do this. While allowing the child to keep the chocolate means I must sacrifice the pleasure of eating it myself, it does give me the pleasure of watching the child munch on the chocolate delightedly. Even more importantly, I know that if I were to deprive the child of the chocolate, I would have to endure the discomfort of seeing the child crying in despair. Seeking to maximize my own net pleasure, therefore, or pursuing my own self-interest, I perform the socially responsible act of allowing the child to keep the chocolate.

If the moral sense thus gives us a self-interested reason to act in morally laudable ways, the obvious question for Hutcheson is where we get this moral sense, which so conveniently makes morally good actions feel good and morally bad actions feel bad. Hutcheson's answer was straightforward: God endows us with the moral sense, engineering us so that we will naturally feel inclined to do the right thing. Setting aside the question of why, then, so many people frequently *fail* to behave in a moral fashion, Smith accepted the basic logic of Hutcheson's response to the Hobbesian moral dilemma, yet sought to reformulate sentiment theory in a way that would render it more naturalistic and less reliant on divine action. Abandoning the moral sense per se—in the sense of an independent sense faculty—Smith suggests that when I see someone in pain, this triggers certain associations in my mind, taking me back to times when I have been in pain. These memories that have been stirred up, Smith argues, cause me to feel a certain amount of distress. These echoes of pain are not as intense as the pain I originally felt, but they are real and manifestly unpleasant, and thus they give me a positive incentive to help the other person: If I can lessen her pain, this promises to diminish the secondary pain I feel upon witnessing her condition.

Over the course of *The Theory of Moral Sentiments*, Smith develops a range of similar explanations for such experiences as the righteous indignation we feel upon seeing a stronger person forcibly taking something from a weaker person, thereby leading us to the more general judgment that stealing is unjust. Without going into the detail of these arguments, Smith's general approach remains consistent: particular social situations trigger associations in our minds that are either pleasurable or painful, and these positive or negative associations drive our moral thinking, giving us self-interested reasons to act in ways that are socially beneficial while avoiding socially harmful behaviors.

Smith's work on moral theory aroused some academic interest at the time, as did an even more elaborate psychological account of human behavior developed by his friend, colleague, and fellow Scotsman David Hume. Outside of intellectual circles, however, moral sentiment theory never had much impact, likely for two reasons. First, while Smith, in particular, made a conscious effort to fit the study of moral behavior within the larger framework of Newtonian science, it would be nearly two centuries before neuroscientists and cognitive psychologists had developed the technical means to empirically detect or measure any phenomena resembling moral sentiments. Lacking an empirical basis, therefore, the theories of Hutcheson, Smith, and Hume remained mere hypotheses, without there being an objective means of determining which, if any, was correct. Second, while everyday experience does suggest that people can act in ways that appear to be disinterested or even altruistic, experience also tells us that most people, most of the time, behave in ways that are more straightforwardly self-interested. It follows that if your overarching goal is more practical than academic—that is, getting people to behave in a socially beneficial fashion on a large scale—the most effective approaches will be those, like contract theory, that take human self-interest as a given, but then try to establish social structures that channel this self-interest in prosocial directions. This, in fact, is the approach Smith took in *The Wealth of Nations*, although rather than focusing on the political relations Hobbes and Locke had studied, Smith turned his attention to economic relations.

The Rise of the Market Economy

Taking a step back for a moment, the feudal economy—like two other medieval institutions we have considered, the scholastic study of nature and the political system of absolute monarchy—was characterized by stasis. Year after year, life proceeded as it always had, with peasants scratching out a subsistence living through a combination of farming and herding, while the local lord or baron then claimed a percentage of this already meager yield in feudal dues. In theory, the lord compensated his peasants for this tribute by providing for their defense, but this was not an example of exchange relations. The feudal relationship, for one thing, was manifestly one-sided, with the lord living in luxury—at least by the standards of the time—even as his peasants barely scraped by. Moreover, feudal relations were entirely compulsory, with the lord using his power as local executive, legislator, and judge to keep his vassals in a state of servility and destitution.

In any case, the resulting arrangement was characterized by economic stasis because under it, no one had an incentive to increase their production, whether by working harder, improving established methods of production, or otherwise innovating. Had the peasants increased their agricultural output, the resulting surplus would have just been confiscated by the lord, so they were better off saving their energy once they had produced enough to live on. And once the lord had extracted enough in taxes to build his castle and stock his table, he had little use for additional output, since any additional crops he commandeered would just rot before they could be consumed. Thus, if drought and plague could be avoided, everyone would do as well as they could expect in this life, with nothing really changing over the generations and any hopes for material improvement being pushed off to the next life.

Around the time of the Renaissance, a merchant class did appear in Europe, and this began to shake up the entrenched feudal order. Not only did merchants live outside the hereditary classes of lord and peasant, earning a living by a means other than agriculture or taxes on agriculture, but—traveling around to buy goods in one place and sell them in another—they were more dynamic in temperament than either of the two feudal classes tied to the land. Indeed, success in trade required that merchants be constantly sniffing out new markets, new products with which to tempt their customers, and new strategies by which to outfox their competitors. Perhaps even more significantly, however, merchants discovered that they had a positive incentive to increase their wealth beyond simply living in greater luxury—an incentive limited by the amount any one family can consume. If a merchant, purchasing stocks in one place and selling them in another, can turn a healthy profit, he can then use the surplus wealth he acquires to buy another, larger stock of goods and sell them at an even greater profit. With the resulting returns, he can buy another stock of goods, or perhaps a ship on which to transport his goods, or one day a whole fleet of ships. Trade, in other words, raises the possibility of sustained economic gain, and thus it opened the door to an economic landscape in which dynamism, rather than stasis, would become the norm.

By the time Smith wrote *The Wealth of Nations* in the latter part of the eighteenth century, the European economy, led by England and the Netherlands, was well on its way toward shedding its feudal roots and developing market structures. For several centuries, the English enclosure movement had been fencing off lands on which semi-emancipated peasants had once been able to raise subsistence crops. With this land now being converted to private sheep ranching, many farmers were forced into non-agricultural work in the northern part of the country, where small-scale workshop production was just beginning, most notably of textiles made from wool produced in the south. This growing urban population, meanwhile, gave those farmers who managed to retain some land an incentive to increase their agricultural output, since they were now growing cash crops to sell to hungry city dwellers. The forced urbanization and the other social changes associated with the enclosure movement were doubtless traumatic for many individuals. In the broader picture, however, the emerging market economy was spurring not only greater social mobility but also an uptick in standards of living, with both more goods and more types of goods becoming available to a public that was now earning cash wages with which to purchase these goods.

To Smith's chagrin, few of the policymakers of his time realized that the free exchange of goods was primarily responsible for these gains. Ever since the conquest of the New World, European governments had been forcibly extracting gold and other forms of wealth from their colonies, much as lords had traditionally extracted taxes from their peasants. Gold bullion was used, first and foremost, to fund the navies that were required to defend one's colonies against encroachment by other imperial powers. Gold, in other words, was used to defend the nation's access to gold. Accordingly, when imperial powers engaged in trade with one another, the standard policy they enacted was one of mercantilism, according to which the overt goal of international trade was to establish a positive balance of payments—that is, to ensure that more gold was pouring into the country than was flowing out. To this end, governments enacted tariffs and other protectionist measures in accord with something like the following logic.

England was now producing enough textiles, for instance, that it could not only clothe its own population but also sell some textiles abroad. The country's cool climate, however, forced English subjects to purchase citrus fruits from Spain. England could therefore impose a duty on the import of citrus. Beyond providing the English government with some tax monies, this tariff would—in theory—shift the balance of payments in favor of England. English textile producers, after all, could still expect to sell the same amount of woolen goods to Spanish consumers as before, thereby bringing a certain amount of gold into the country. English consumers, meanwhile, would purchase fewer Spanish citrus fruits than before, given their tariff-induced higher price. And thus, with more gold entering the country than leaving, England should increase its net holdings of gold, thereby giving the Royal Navy an advantage over the Spanish Armada.

For those of us who have grown up in the era of global capitalism, the flaw in this strategy is obvious. If the Spanish government had not already been contemplating a tariff on English woolen goods, it would certainly enact one when England imposes its duty on Spanish citrus. Yet, this puts both countries in a position where they are worse off than they were before the trade war. On the English side, the Spanish tariff on English woolen goods draws England's balance of payments back down to breaking even, so the country has gained nothing in this regard. Individual English producers, meanwhile, are now selling fewer woolen goods than before, which not only lowers their own incomes but reduces the amount of raw wool and other domestic goods they can purchase, thereby depressing the entire economy. English consumers, meanwhile, are purchasing fewer citrus fruits than they would like, while paying more than they are accustomed for the oranges they do purchase, so they are net losers. All in all, therefore, a policy that was intended to promote England's self-interest has just ended up hurting it, with the same being true on the Spanish side.

Given this predictable result, what was needed was an entirely new approach to trade, one that would remove barriers to free exchange rather than imposing them. When people or nations are allowed to trade freely, Smith argued in *The Wealth of Nations*, the surprising result is that their self-interested actions end up benefiting one another and thus increasing the well-being of everyone involved. To make this case, Smith plunged into one of the world's first comprehensive, quantitative studies of the workings of the market economy. We will here touch on only a few of his key analyses, focusing on the market dynamics that characterize three increasingly sophisticated levels of economic development. Confusingly, Smith does little to notify his readers that he is jumping around between these three levels, so for the sake of clarity, we will here distinguish them as the exchange economy, the marketplace economy, and the capitalist economy.

The Exchange Economy

To sort through the workings of the exchange economy, Smith imagined a primitive setting not unlike the Lockean state of nature. With social relations being as yet undeveloped, people needed to be self-sufficient, so they tended to be jacks of all trades, doing some farming and some hunting, building their own huts, crafting their own tools, and so forth. Suppose, however, that living under these conditions, I develop a knack for some particular task—say, building bows. Enjoying this craft at which I excel, I make a few extra bows in my spare time. I cannot really use more than one bow, however, so when I amass some extras, I do the only thing that makes sense: I give one to someone who could use it, perhaps a member of my extended family who particularly excels at hunting. Utilizing my high-quality bow, my cousin is now even more adept at hunting than before. And because he now has more time to spend hunting—not needing to make his own bows—he starts returning from the hunt with even more meat than he can eat. Not wanting this meat to spoil, and appreciative of my gift to him, he returns my favor with a gift of meat, indeed, more meat than I could have obtained on my own, given my weaker hunting skills. Notice what has happened here. Neither my cousin nor I entered into this transaction with any foresight or planning. We both just spent a bit of extra time pursuing crafts at which we happen to excel. Nevertheless, in performing this labor, then informally exchanging the products of our work, we have both ended up with more and better goods than we could have secured, had we remained isolated jacks of all trades.

Remaining in this same scenario, as I continue with my bow-making, the circle of people to whom I give bows will naturally widen over time. Yet, because I am no longer just giving bows to family members, with whom I already share a bond of affection, I will eventually become unwilling to part with my bows in the vague hope of receiving a reciprocal gift in the future. I will, rather, start demanding certain items that I need now, whether meat or other goods, in exchange for one of my bows. For trade to proceed in this fashion, however, it requires a rate of exchange: How many bows should be traded for how many pounds of meat? The axiomatic answer is that equal values should be traded for equal values. Yet, what determines value? At this most primitive level of exchange, no formal exchange rates will be set. People will simply make offers and counteroffers, and deals will either be struck or walked away from. Nevertheless, if—as outside observers—we analyze the deals agreed to, we will find they share a similar baseline determination of value: the labor going into a commodity's production.

To explain, recall Locke's observation that nature makes certain goods available to us, yet these products are useful to us only if we first mix some of our labor with them, such as by picking an apple off the tree. The labor required to make an object usable can be quantified, first and foremost by the amount of time it requires. And thus, labor time will come to serve as the basis for the first, loosely determined exchange rates. For a more detailed idea of how this works, we can borrow Smith's favorite example of trade in the exchange economy, that between a hunter and a trapper.

Assume I am an early jack of all trades, but with a particular penchant for hunting. Out on my hunt one day, I stumble across a trapper who is carrying some beaver pelts. I had been wanting 4 pelts with which to make some hats, and I happen to have a few extra deerskins with me that I believe the trapper might like. The question is, how many skins should I offer for those 4 pelts? From my own experience, I know it takes me an average of 6 hours to take down a deer and prepare a skin. I also know that, with my relatively weak trapping skills, pelts cost me 4 hours of labor apiece, which means I would need to work 16 hours to come up with 4 pelts on my own. It would make no sense, therefore, for me to offer 3 skins in exchange for 4 pelts, since this would essentially cost me 18 hours of hunting labor to save 16 hours of trapping labor. So perhaps I offer the trapper 1 skin. She has not told me how long it takes her to trap a beaver or take down a deer, but she knows: With her own particular skill set, it takes her about 3 hours to secure a pelt, but 8 hours to obtain a deerskin. The offer of 1 skin for 4 pelts will therefore not be attractive to her, since this would cost her 12 hours of trapping labor in order to save 8 hours of hunting labor. So she will likely reject my proposal. Perhaps, however, she will counter with a proposal of 2 skins for 4 pelts. To an outside observer, this is finally a "fair" offer in the sense that that it involves an exchange of 12 hours of hunting labor for 12 hours of trapping labor. For the trapper and myself, we do not worry about such abstract considerations as fairness. Each of us just knows that the proposed deal is good for us. From my perspective, I give up the product of 12 hours of hunting labor to procure pelts that would have cost me 16 hours of trapping labor to obtain. The trapper, meanwhile, trades away the product of 12 hours of trapping labor in exchange for skins that would have cost her 16 hours of hunting labor.

The deal being mutually attractive, we shake hands and make our exchange.

With this first rudimentary instance of exchange, we are in a position—again as outside observers—to quantify just how much the trapper and I have benefitted by specializing in our labor, then trading the products of this labor, as opposed to remaining jacks of all trades and producing our own goods. Clearly enough, we are both getting the mix of goods we want, while saving 4 hours of labor by trading away what it takes us 12 hours to produce, in exchange for what would have cost us 16 hours of labor. Alternately formulated, if we assume the trapper and I both typically work a 12-hour day, then 1 day of labor has yielded us 33% more material goods than we could have produced by working on our own. And the striking thing about this result is that, when I encountered the trapper, I had no intention of helping her out, just as she had no intention of aiding me. We both merely sought to promote our own self-interest, but in so doing, we collectively produced a situation in which each of us is better off than before.

This is the first appearance of the invisible hand in the *Wealth of Nations*. Although this term is widely associated with Smith's economic theory, it is a phrase he uses only twice in his writings, and only once in *The Wealth of Nations*. It refers to the fact that, when exchange is allowed to proceed freely, things generally work out to produce results that are mutually beneficial, even though neither party meant to help the other, but instead only sought to promote their own interests. Emphatically, the invisible hand is *not* some supernatural force that secretly manipulates markets as people engage in trade. It is rather just a metaphor: when self-interested economic activity leads to mutual benefit, the result is so counterintuitive that it seems *as if* an invisible hand must have been quietly directing people's behaviors. In fact, however, the mutual gains are easy to explain, at least on the simple level of exchange we have been observing.

When we specialize in our labor, each of us develops certain skills, tools, and tricks of the trade that allow us to produce our chosen good more efficiently than we could have as non-specialists. Each of us can therefore produce more goods over the course of a day than before, not to mention that these goods will often be of higher quality. Of course, specializing in one particular type of good leaves us without the time or skill we would need to produce all of the other goods we require for our maintenance. But since we now end up with more of our specialized product than we need, we can trade away our surplus to those who specialize in making other products, leaving us all with the mix of goods we desire. And with all these goods having been produced with the efficiency and skill of a specialist, we all finish the day better off than when we stuck to ourselves, having obtained more and better goods than we could have produced on our own.

The Marketplace Economy

If trade likely started through chance encounters of the sort we have just observed between the hunter and trapper, at some point groups of people must have agreed it would be worthwhile to gather at certain fixed times and places to trade, not just for this or that good, but for all the goods they required. At such a marketplace, the introduction of money helps trade proceed more efficiently. For one thing, money promotes circular exchange. If I am a hunter with a deerskin to sell and I need a beaver pelt, I need not worry about whether the trapper at the market will, coincidentally, be looking for a skin that day, as opposed to, say, a water jug. I can instead sell my deerskin to the potter for money, then use this money to buy a pelt from the trapper, who, in turn, will use this money to purchase a water jug from the potter. Money lubricates trade by allowing for prices to be set using a common measure of value. Rather than determining that a deerskin is worth 2 pelts or 1.5 water jugs, for instance, we can simply say a deerskin is worth $6, a pelt $3, and a water jug $4. How are these prices set? Addressing this question takes us to the real workings of the marketplace economy.

The marketplace economy is most clearly distinguished from the exchange economy by the presence of multiple buyers and sellers—not just different types of producers offering different sorts of goods, but multiple hunters and multiple trappers. This introduces an element of competition into trade relations. To explain how prices are set when sellers start competing with one another for business, Smith introduces a technical distinction between a good's real price and nominal price. A product's real price is a measure of the labor time going into the product. Smith further discusses how a product's real cost can be modified by such factors as the relative difficulty of the labor involved, but we can ignore these nuances here. We already know that taking down a deer and preparing the skin for market takes a professional hunter 6 hours. If the skin retails for $6, and if a beaver pelt that takes a professional trapper 3 hours to bring to market, the pelt can be expected to sell for $3. Who tells trappers to set the price of pelts at this level? No one. But if a trapper charges $2 per pelt, she might do a brisk business, but she would just end up hurting herself, since she would have to sell 3 pelts (requiring 9 hours to trap) to buy 1 deerskin, which she could have obtained through 8 hours of her own non-expert hunting labor. If, conversely, trappers were to start charging $6 per pelt, they could not hope to sell many pelts, since all of the hunters at the marketplace would be better off trapping their own pelts (requiring 4 hours of non-expert trapping labor apiece), as opposed to buying pelts at a price equal to 6 hours of hunting labor. The price of pelts will therefore gravitate towards $3 per pelt, since at this level, both hunters and trappers will feel that they are getting a reasonable return on their labor. To be sure, the individual trapper may try to get ahead by selling her pelts for, say, $4 apiece. But the presence of other trappers at the market selling their pelts for $3 will quickly bring her back into line, since at $4 she could not be expected to sell any pelts, given that the same product is available for a cheaper price just a few stalls away.

If the determination of a pelt's real price is therefore straightforward, $3 may not be the price for which pelts actually sell at the market. To see how a product's nominal price—or what we would now call its market price—might vary from its real price, let us assume a case of plague sweeps through the local beaver population. Suddenly, we notice the price of beaver pelts rising to, say, $5 apiece. In part, this price increase may reflect the additional labor time it now requires trappers to find beavers, since the number of beavers has diminished. But it also indicates some buyers' willingness to pay more than others in a marketplace where there are no longer enough beaver pelts to go around. Not just multiple sellers show up at the marketplace, but also multiple buyers, and buyers compete with one another just as much as sellers.

To illustrate, suppose an individual trapper has more customers gathering around her stall than she has pelts to offer. These customers might begin shouting out offers of what they are willing to pay for a pelt. A hunter, for instance, might offer $4, since he knows it would now—beavers having become scarce—take him even more than 4 hours to trap a beaver with his non-expert trapping labor. Yet, suppose an elderly potter is standing next to the hunter who simply does not have the physical means to go out and do any trapping himself. Really wanting a pelt and knowing supplies are limited, this potter may offer $5. The potter may well need to spend more time at his wheel crafting water jugs to earn this $5 than the trapper requires to produce a single pelt, so in a sense, the potter is getting a bad deal. But the potter also knows that the alternative is to get no pelts, so he throws out his offer. If similar scenarios are playing themselves out at the booths of other trappers at the marketplace, the nominal price of beaver pelts will settle somewhere around $5, and all the trappers at the marketplace should just be able to sell out their stock of pelts.

Once again, we see the invisible hand has been at work. In this case, it has helped to set the market price of beaver pelts at its optimal level—namely, the level at which there are just enough pelts on the market to supply everyone who wants one at that price, but no more. At the same time, those buyers who most wanted beaver pelts have obtained them, whereas buyers who may have fancied a pelt at a lower price, yet had other priorities as the price of pelts went up, have gone without. To achieve this result, the market's organizers did not have to hire a team of researchers to interview all the market participants to determine how long it takes various sellers to produce their goods, how badly different buyers want various products, and so forth. Rather, this optimal pricing has simply worked itself out through what Smith calls the "higgling of the market," without any central direction.

Nor is this all the invisible hand does at the marketplace. Perhaps the greatest social benefit to arise from individual market participants acting on their own behalf is the allocative efficiency of the marketplace: the market will tend to produce exactly that mix of goods that the community most wants. To see how this works, consider a change, not in supply, but in demand. Specifically, let us assume the local beaver population has been restored, such that the market price of pelts has returned to $3. To the dismay of trappers, however, beaver hats now go out of fashion, while deerskin coats come into vogue. Based purely on labor time, the real price of beaver pelts remains $3, while that of deerskins stays at $6. But fewer people are now buying pelts, so trappers find they need to drop the price of a pelt to, say, $2 to sell out their stocks. Hunters, meanwhile, find they can raise the price of deerskins to $8 and still sell out, simply because buyers are crawling over each other to obtain a deerskin coat. The hunter is therefore quite happy, but how will the individual trapper respond to this situation?

Assuming a trapper procures 12 beaver pelts per week,

it takes her a total of 36 hours to bring these pelts to market. In normal times, she could sell these pelts for $3 apiece, for a total of $36, with which she could purchase 6 deerskins at $6 apiece. Now, however, in selling her dozen pelts for $2 apiece, she makes only $24 for the week. And with deerskins having gone up to $8, she can purchase only 3 of these with the proceeds from her pelt sales. This effectively means she is now doing the same amount of work as before but getting only half the reward. Given this change in outcome, at some point the trapper may decide to start doing her own hunting. With her amateur hunting skills, it may take her 24 hours to procure 6 deerskins, as compared to the 18 hours it would take a professional hunter. Still, she would now have to spend 40 hours trapping to earn the money to buy these same 3 deerskins, so being a do-it-yourselfer has suddenly become more attractive. Indeed, if consumer tastes do not soon shift again and the pelt market does not recover, there may come a time when the trapper decides to switch to being a professional hunter. Switching careers is difficult and costly, so not every trapper will make this decision, nor will they all make it at the same time. With the market being what it is, however, some trappers will eventually start to make the switch. Every time one does, a few less pelts come onto the market, as compared to a few more deerskins. This change in supply will start pushing the price of pelts back up, while reducing the price of skins. This dynamic will continue as more and more trappers switch careers, until finally the price of pelts climbs back to $3 and that of deerskins settles back down to \$6, thus accurately reflecting the labor time going into the production of these two goods.

At this point, the market is in equilibrium, so there is no further pressure on anyone to switch careers. But notice what has happened. The marketplace now has far fewer trappers in the labor force bringing pelts to market, and more hunters bringing deerskins. But with beaver hats being out of fashion and deerskin coats in vogue, this is exactly what the community wanted! Again, the marketplace has had no central director telling people what to produce, nor how much of it. Each participant has simply pursued their own interests. Nevertheless, the pressures of supply and demand have quietly nudged individual producers in one direction or the other until the community is producing the optimal mix of goods, or the mix the community itself most desires. Hence, just as the division of labor increased the quantity and quality of goods available to the exchange economy, the marketplace economy uses the forces of supply and demand to steer collective production toward the types and quantities of products that consumers most desire, even while setting their prices at the optimal levels—further evidence of the market's invisible hand.

The Capitalist Economy

If the marketplace economy was well established in Europe at the time Smith wrote, the third level of economic development he describes, the capitalist economy, was just beginning to emerge. What makes a market specifically capitalist in nature? As the marketplace economy matures and comes to be dominated by such craftspeople as potters, blacksmiths, spinners, and weavers, economic activity is typified by the following flow of goods and money: the individual craftsperson buys up raw materials, adds a certain amount of value to these materials through labor, then sells the finished product for a higher price. A tailor, for instance, may go to the marketplace and purchase deerskins for $6, spend 3 hours apiece sewing them into coats, then return to the marketplace to offer the coats for $9 apiece. All other factors being equal, the difference between the price of the raw materials and that of the finished product should reflect the value of the labor put into it, possibly as modified by the forces of supply and demand.

As commerce develops even further, a new flow of goods and money will start to emerge. Some industrious merchants may begin acquiring more raw materials than they can work themselves. Having extra cash on hand from past sales, they will start doing the only thing that makes sense: hire other people to work their surplus raw materials. Historically, this is what happened in Europe in the fifteenth and sixteenth centuries when merchants began sending piecework out to farmers and their wives, who might shape a hat or sew a coat in their spare time, then send the finished product back to the merchant, earning a small fee for every piece so produced. Gradually, however, as the demand for finished goods grew, while enclosure pressures kept pushing farmers off their land, merchants began gathering small groups of workers in workshops, who now started working together to manufacture finished goods in a cooperative fashion.

Two key points must be noted about this shift to workshop production. First, workshop production is dramatically more efficient than production by individual artisans working alone. Smith illustrates this point by describing a pin factory he once visited. Pin making, Smith observes, requires some fifteen different steps. At one time, a single artisan performed all these steps, slowly moving from one task to the next, each time setting down one tool and picking up another. In the pin factory, conversely, each step is assigned to a single worker, who performs his task, then passes a batch of partially completed pins on to another worker who performs the next step, and so on, until all of the pins have been fully assembled. With this degree of specialization, each worker becomes an expert at his one particular task, learning all of the skills and subtle tricks needed to perfect it. The worker, moreover, is not constantly having to set down one tool to pick up another but rather can keep using the same tool all day. The result, Smith writes, is that the workers collaboratively produce 4,800 pins each day, whereas they could not have produced 20 pins between them, had each been working separately.

The second point to note about workshop production is the new pattern by which money and goods are now flowing. Previously, a craftsman purchased stocks, worked them, and sold the resulting finished goods at a higher price, such that the entire monetary surplus—what Smith calls "the product of labor"—flowed back to the craftsman. Now, however, multiple parties are involved in the production process: the worker applies his labor to stocks that were purchased by a merchant, in a workshop typically owned by a third party, the landlord. For this arrangement to be mutually agreeable, certain "deductions" need to be made from the product of labor before it flows back to the worker who supplied the labor. For one thing, the landowner must be paid a rent. Smith's younger contemporary, David Ricardo, would develop a comprehensive theory of rents, but Smith's own interest lay more in the merchant who similarly claims a deduction from the product of labor, in the form of profit.

Indeed, this merchant—whom we may now call "the capitalist"—must be accorded this profit, or he would have no incentive to purchase raw materials for the worker to finish in the first place. To some extent, this profit may compensate the capitalist for his managerial labor. Profit rates, however, must be set higher than the capitalist's investment of time would apply, for if a managerial wage were all the capitalist could hope to earn, he would be better off hiring himself out as a manager to someone else, rather than taking the risks associated with purchasing stocks upon himself. Nor, speaking of risk, can the capitalist's profit simply equal the losses he expects to accrue over the course of doing business. Why go to all the time and effort of setting up a business, after all, if you just hope to break even in the end? Hence, the profit the capitalist can reasonably expect must exceed both his own time investment and the foreseen risk, thereby giving the capitalist an incentive to roll the dice. How great must this profit be? Smith does not say, nor can there be an exact formula, since numerous factors will influence profit levels. In general, the marketplace will establish certain "normal profits," or typical profit rates, within particular industries. Given competitive pressures, the individual capitalist cannot hope to earn much more of a profit than this industry standard would dictate without raising his prices or skimping on production costs, either of which could cost him customers. But if the normal profit capitalists find they can earn in a particular industry starts dropping much below that of other industries, this will eventually push some capitalists to switch industries—thereby pushing profit rates back up for those capitalists who remain in the original industry.

With rents and profits therefore having been deducted, the remainder of the product of labor flows back to the worker, in the form of wages. How exactly are wages determined? We can approach this question from one of two directions. We can ask how the wage rates for different jobs are determined, relative to one another. And since labor is typically compensated on an hourly basis, different sorts of work will be assigned different hourly rates, based on such factors as their physical difficulty and the training they require. Market forces can then further influence wage rates; a shortage of mechanics on the labor market, for instance, may push up mechanics' wages as compared to those of potters or weavers. Yet, when workers advocate for higher wages, perhaps by staging a work stoppage, they are not generally competing with other workers for a fixed wage pot. Rather, they are pressing their employers for a larger share of the total product of labor; they are arguing that the percentage of the total returns devoted to wages should grow, as opposed to the percentages devoted to rents and profits. Smith notes that particular industries will develop their own "normal wages," or the percentage of the product of labor typically reserved for workers. At the upper limit, the normal wage must still leave room for rents and profits, or else capitalists and landlords would have no reason to open the workshop doors. At the lower limit, the normal wage must be enough for workers to house and feed their families, or the labor pool will shrink, workers being unable to sustain themselves. Between these two limits, wages are determined by market forces and negotiation. Smith acknowledges that, in wage negotiations, capitalists will typically have the upper hand, since they can hold out longer during strikes than workers living paycheck to paycheck. Conversely, if a capitalist economy is young and growing, aspiring capitalists will compete to hire the limited supply of workers. And with the strong demand for labor therefore driving up wages, workers may start to see real improvements in their standards of living.

In fact, when a capitalist economy is in growth mode, profits, rents, and wages tend to rise, such that capitalists, landlords, and workers may all see improvements in their material conditions. And the remarkable thing about a capitalist economy is that, while downturns can certainly occur, growth is a capitalist economy's natural condition—an entirely novel development in economic history. We have already seen one reason why stasis was the norm in feudal society: Whether you were a prince or a peasant, once you had met your basic needs, why produce anything more? Particularly when wealth was mostly held in agricultural form, surplus production would just rot before it could be consumed. We have also seen what gave the market economy its initial impetus toward growth: certain enterprising merchants figured out something to do with surplus wealth, namely, invest it to generate even more wealth. This investment took on a specifically capitalist character when certain enterprising merchants stopped merely transporting goods from place to place and instead started purchasing stocks of raw materials, hiring workers to finish these raw materials in workshops owned by landlords, then selling the finished goods at a profit. This allowed the budding capitalist to purchase even more stocks, earning even greater profits, and so on through the cycle. To complete this account of capitalism's natural impetus toward growth, however, we need to consider one more distinction between feudalism and capitalism, that between zero-sum and non-zero-sum scenarios.

By and large, the feudal economy was a zero-sum game: with the supply of material goods being essentially fixed, one person's gain could only come at another person's loss. If I was a feudal lord, for instance, I could increase my wealth by taxing my peasants more heavily, or perhaps by going to war with the neighboring lord and capturing some of his lands and peasants. In either case, however, the total quantity of material goods in the economy has not increased; their distribution has just shifted. If I am a successful capitalist, conversely, my success is likely to ripple. With capitalist production requiring that I rent a workshop and hire laborers, the more profits I earn, the more production I can finance, and thus the more land I will rent and the more workers I will hire. To be sure, there are still zero-sum relationships within this larger cooperative system. Capitalists compete with one another for business, just as landlords compete for tenants and workers compete for jobs. The precise distribution of profits, rents, and wages, moreover, can be a zero-sum competition to divide up a fixed product of labor—and we have already seen that capitalists enjoy a natural advantage in this competition, particularly over workers. Even so, when capitalists across the economy are doing well, the increased demand for land and workers will drive up rents and wages, such that all three major groups stand to improve their lot. Thus, the capitalist economy turns out to be less a zero-sum game than an expanding pie, in which a larger slice of pie for one participant need not necessarily come at the expense of others, but may sometimes drive an increase in size of the whole pie, thereby enlarging the slices everyone receives. This is generalized economic growth, or an increase in the size of the economy as a whole, as opposed to a mere redistribution of fixed resources. And all three major players in the capitalist economy have a strong interest in working hard to help drive this growth.

Nor is the growth impetus of capitalism merely limited to rising incomes. For capitalists, landlords, and workers are not just producers, earning money for the contributions they make to the production process. Rather, all three groups are also consumers, using the money they earn in their respective industries to purchase the whole range of products they require for everyday living. And with multiple capitalists competing for consumers in every market niche, they are almost compelled to innovate, such that more goods, more types of goods, and higher-quality goods can be expected to flow onto the market all the time. At the same time, as capitalists strive to increase their profits by improving production efficiency, many goods will trend downward in price. Hence, even if workers typically saw the smallest income gains as the economic pie expanded, with ever more low-cost consumer goods coming on the market, even such modest gains could translate into significant improvements in standard of living. Eventually, even many European workers could afford products that had once been luxuries—or may not even have been dreamed of by medieval kings and lords.

This final observation helps us loop back to the end of the chapter on the Scientific Revolution: with the growing hope that the rapid advances being made in the natural sciences would spur technological advances that might, in turn, improve the quality of human life. No doubt, the theoretical work performed by such modern scientists as Galileo, Boyle, and Newton was a necessary precursor to applied disciplines such as mechanical engineering, metallurgy, and industrial chemistry that began appearing in the eighteenth century. Nevertheless, few kings or governments were funding scientific research on anything near the scale Bacon had once recommended, and they were certainly not assembling teams of engineers to develop and refine new technologies. Rather, it was capitalists in search of a profit who inspired and funded such eighteenth-century innovations that revolutionized the textile industry as the flying shuttle, the spinning jenny, and the power loom—inventions that brought clothing of decent quality within reach even of workers, a true novelty for many of these. Similarly, James Watt received support from several industrialists as he tinkered with steam engines, the game-changing innovation that would eventually drive the massive industrialization of the nineteenth century. Even by the eighteenth century, however, it was becoming clear it would be a partnership between science and industry that would begin to realize Descartes's dream of helping humankind achieve a degree of mastery over nature by developing and implementing new technologies. And with capitalism having a growth impetus inherent to it, business would become the real driver of technological innovations, with new technologies then spurring further economic growth, in a cycle that continues to this day.

Capitalism and the Progressive Worldview

This chapter, focused on Adam Smith's economic analyses of the late eighteenth century, has painted a sunny picture of capitalism and of the free market more generally. By the middle of the nineteenth century, with the advent of full-scale factory production, it became increasingly clear that capitalism has a dark side. And as conditions on the factory floor and in worker tenements grew ever more Dickensian, many observers with progressive leanings began to gravitate to the side of workers, coming to view the capitalists who were trying to squeeze every last drop of productivity out of the working class as the enemy. This growing wariness of the market is an important chapter in the story of the progressive worldview, and it is one to which we will return. But for early progressives like Smith, the free market was a source of what we have seen to be the essential ingredient for any worldview with a trajectory that points forward and upward: the realistic hope that things can change for the better, within a human lifetime and within this world.

It is obvious why the rising capitalist order offered hope to those enterprising dreamers who had the educational, social, and financial resources to bring some new product to market, or perhaps to deliver some familiar product to market in a more efficient fashion: they stood to grow rich. But as Smith saw it, this emerging form of economic organization offered just as much hope to those near the bottom of the social ladder, who had traditionally not just been poor but who had long been locked into the lowly station into which they were born, with no realistic hope of improving either their social status or their material condition, nor really of changing the conditions under which they lived in any way. To be sure, rags-to-riches tales remained a rarity in the budding capitalist economies of Europe and North America. But they were possible. And more generally, the market system allowed for a degree of social mobility that was completely unprecedented under feudalism or other traditional economic systems. Yet, even for those who did not climb the social ladder, the generalized growth toward which a capitalist economy will tend, combined with the non-zero-sum nature of this growth, meant that even the lowest-ranking workers could increasingly expect to see meaningful improvements in their standard of living over the course of a single lifetime, or in any case, they had good reason to hope their hard work would at least set their children up for a better life.

On more of a theoretical note, in revealing the workings of the invisible hand on three different levels of economic development—increased productivity through specialization in the exchange economy, the allocative efficiency of the marketplace, and the growth impetus of capitalism—Smith had provided another answer to the Hobbesian question of how socially beneficial, moral action is possible on the assumption that people are self-interested in all they do. Smith's general response was like that of contract theory, in that Smith did not dispute the premise that human beings are self-interested but, rather, he identified and sought to improve a social mechanism that promised to channel the self-interested strivings of individuals into behaviors that benefited other individuals and ultimately society. In fact, in many ways, the liberal political order Locke described and the liberal economic order Smith championed complement one another. While a simple exchange economy may be able to function in something resembling the state of nature, by the time a market economy has begun to shift to capitalist production, it requires a stable social order governed by the rule of law, including strong protections for property rights and the legal means of enforcing contracts. A market economy, meanwhile, lends support to Locke's project of getting away from the need for an absolute monarch or other forms of governance so domineering as to crush individual rights and freedoms. Hobbes, again, had believed an absolute monarch was necessary to keep self-interested individuals from tearing their neighbors apart, even once they had entered civic society. But if my society features a free market, my neighbors may be my customers—or my boss, or my landlord, or my employees—in which case my own self-interest dictates, not merely that I refrain from attacking them but that I work hard to meet their needs. Under these circumstances, we will still need a government above us to maintain basic order and ensure that no one cheats in their economic dealings. But if these economic dealings promote a baseline social behavior that is more cooperative than combative, basic order can be maintained through a form of governance far less heavy-handed than Hobbes had imagined possible—and thus far more likely to meaningfully reflect the consent of the governed.

Most readers will have noticed that the foregoing two chapters have focused almost entirely on seventeenth and eighteenth-century political and economic thinking emanating from the British Isles, with a nod to where England's North American colonies took some of this thought. This emphasis on the Anglo-American tradition has been partly due to this book's focus on American progressivism, but also to the tremendous influence the combined theories of Hobbes, Locke, and Smith ended up having, not just in Great Britain and the United States but throughout Europe and eventually throughout much of the world. Certainly, the institutions they spawned of liberal democracy and a liberal market economy have done more to shape the modern world than any others, except possibly for the modern approach to the study of the natural world that helped inspire them both. But this emphasis on English-speaking thinkers should not be taken to imply that philosophers, scientists, and statesmen on the European continent were not actively considering these same topics. Notably, in France, Jean-Jacques Rousseau developed his own account of the state of nature and the social contract that differed in significant ways from the accounts of Hobbes and Locke, and may well have helped steer the French Revolution onto the very different path it took from the American Revolution. It would be tempting to dive into a comparison between the British and continental approaches to political and economic theory, but in the interest of keeping our story of the emerging progressive worldview moving forward, the next chapter will revisit an even broader topic on which British and continental think-ers differed considerably: the workings of the human mind. The next two chapters will highlight the efforts of German philosopher Immanuel Kant to transcend the mechanistic account of thinking Hobbes and his British successors had assumed, supplanting it with an account of the human mind dynamic enough to explain how such a radical intellectual event as the Scientific Revolution ever could have occurred but also adequate to the demands for intellectual and moral autonomy being voiced across Europe and North America as the Age of Enlightenment flowered.

CHAPTER 5

KANT AND THE ENLIGHTENMENT CONCEPTION OF MIND: PHILOSOPHICAL PROGRESS

In 1784, the German philosopher Immanuel Kant published a short essay titled *Answering the Question: What is Enlightenment?* Addressing this question, Kant characterizes Enlightenment as "Man's release from his self-incurred tutelage," and he suggests the motto of the Enlightenment should be "Sapere aude," or, "Dare to know." Dare, in other words, to strike out on your own, trusting your ability to navigate the world using your own powers of reasoning rather than clinging to tradition and authority like a dog who yearns for the comfort of its master's leash.

Historians have long debated the precise dates of the Enlightenment. Some push its inception as far back as 1650, when Descartes and Hobbes were still active. More often, the start of the Enlightenment is pegged to such early eighteenth-century events as the death of the French King Louis XIV in 1715. In any case, the Enlightenment's timeframe will likely always remain fluid, for it was never anything so formal as a "school of thought." The Enlightenment was more an *attitude* shared by a diverse group of thinkers hailing from many different countries and spanning several generations. Specifically, it was an intellectual excitement, a sense of possibility, inspired first and foremost by the dramatic advances in learning that resulted from the Scientific Revolution. We have already mentioned several key Enlightenment figures, including Montesquieu, Rousseau, Smith, and Jefferson. Other names commonly associated with the Enlightenment are Cesare Beccaria, Voltaire, Denis Diderot, Jean le Rond d'Alembert, David Hume, and Kant. Their interests were diverse: Beccaria pioneered the modern study of criminal law, Diderot and d'Alembert published the world's first comprehensive encyclopedia, and Hume followed in Locke's footsteps as the next great British empiricist. Nevertheless, Enlightenment thought circled a common set of themes, including:

1. *Distrust of authority.* We have already seen how seventeenth-century scientists came to view the scholastic practice of appealing to such authorities as Aristotle as more likely to result in self-perpetuating errors than knowledge. The seventeenth century further witnessed an erosion in the respect once automatically granted to political authorities, as evidenced by the English willingness to depose two kings in a century. In the eighteenth century, Enlightenment thinkers turned a particularly distrustful eye toward ecclesiastical authorities, whom they viewed as being more concerned with

clinging to their waning temporal power than with caring for people's souls.

2. *Rejection of superstition.* For most Enlightenment thinkers, the rejection of superstition did not equate to atheism. Many were Deists, believing in a watchmaker God who sets the world ticking, then leaves it to operate in accord with the laws of nature. These thinkers sneered at attempts to explain day-to-day events through constant appeals to an interventionist God, while lamenting how political and ecclesiastical authorities often stoked popular fears of eternal damnation as a means of preserving their own power.

3. *Reverence for reason.* Few of the prominent Enlightenment thinkers were themselves practicing scientists, but they were deeply impressed with the results of the Scientific Revolution and convinced that ongoing rational inquiry in both the natural and human sciences would lead to ongoing improvements in the quality of human life. From this perspective, "listening to reason" was as much a moral as an intellectual demand.

4. *Autonomy.* The concept of autonomy implies freedom, though not the lawless freedom of the state of nature. Autonomy is, rather, a freedom whereby we govern ourselves rationally, in accord with laws of our own giving, as opposed to having our actions dictated by outside forces. The thinkers of the Enlightenment believed humankind had come of age, to the point that people could be trusted to govern themselves

responsibly, rather than needing to be kept in line by a wrath-ful God, an absolute monarch, or the strictures of tradition.

5. *Belief in Progress.* The Enlightenment is usually regarded as the time when the concept of Progress got its capital "P"—in written English, at least—gaining sufficient philosophical stature to be represented by a proper noun. Other European languages have different conventions regarding capitalization, but the sentiment was widely shared, with progress becoming a frequent and central topic for numerous writers across Europe and North America. Granted, several seventeenth-century philosophers, like Descartes, had waxed hopefully about the possibilities of progress. Others had described particular forms of progress, such as Hobbes and Locke detailing the transition from the state of nature to civic society. In broad terms, however, we could say the thinkers of the seventeenth century were so busy *making* progress within their own fields of study that they had little opportunity to step back and consider the concept of progress in itself. That task of reflection was left to the eighteenth century when the thinkers of the Enlightenment began to consider progress as a topic in its own right, thus helping draw many of the forward-looking ideas that had been floating in the air into a complete and coherent worldview. When they did so, they overwhelmingly understood progress to be a human phenom-enon, rooted in the capacity of human reason to discern the laws governing the rational world around it and to then use this knowledge to reshape the world to better accord with human ends.

For reasons of space, we cannot here consider the contributions all the major Enlightenment figures made to the emerging progressive worldview. We will, however, take a close look at Kant's philosophy over the next two chapters, since in many ways this represents the culmination of Enlightenment thought. Indeed, we could say Kant was to the Enlightenment what Newton was to the Scientific Revolution: the great systematic thinker coming at the end of an intellectual movement who was able to pull that movement's various strands together, not so much to complete its work as to consolidate its insights into a new paradigm that future generations could use as a platform on which to take their own steps forward.

Kant divided his own thought into theoretical and practical philosophy, and we will follow his lead by considering his theoretical philosophy in the current chapter before turning to his practical or moral philosophy in the next. Theoretical philosophy, for Kant and most other philosophers since the early seventeenth century, centered on the question of how the human mind works. In developing his own account of the mind, Kant had two overriding goals. The first was to establish—in the face of a recent skeptical challenge—that the mind can attain objective knowledge of the rational order around it, particularly of the sort exemplified in Newton's *Principia Mathematica*. Kant's second goal was to demonstrate that the mind is free from the mechanical determinism that gives the rest of nature its rational predictability. As Kant came to appreciate, this second goal was instrumental to the first: showing the mind to be capable of spontaneous thought is crucial to explaining how we can attain any objective knowledge, and particularly the sort of knowledge that was flowing out of the Scientific Revolution. And as we will see in the following chapter, spontaneity of thought is equally crucial to human beings attaining the Enlightenment ideal of autonomy, which is why even Kant argued that the greatest achievement of his theoretical philosophy was to set the stage for his moral philosophy.

Kant's Rude Awakening

Kant was a late bloomer who spent most of his professional life as a well-liked but obscure professor of science and mathematics at the University of Konigsberg in eastern Prussia. A systematic thinker by nature, he frequently organized his thoughts into elegant charts and tables, and it is said his neighbors could set their clocks by his departure to walk to the university each morning. Philosophically, Kant was a follower of the rationalist philosopher Gottfried Wilhelm Leibniz until around age fifty when he stumbled across the empiricist writings of David Hume. Upon reading Hume, Kant was, by his own account, "shaken from his dogmatic slumber." It took Kant the better part of a decade to figure out how exactly to respond to Hume, but the ultimate result was *The Critique of Pure Reason*, initially published in 1781.

The *First Critique*, as it is often called—Kant would write two more *Critiques*—is an immensely challenging work, written in notoriously impenetrable prose, featuring run-on sentences that frequently stretch half a page or more. Readers had such a hard time understanding the *Critique of Pure Reason* that Kant felt compelled to issue a second, highly revised edition six years later, although the existence of two editions probably just added to the confusion. Scholars have been debating the twists and turns of Kant's theoretical philosophy ever since, proposing some sharply differing interpretations of his thought. We will not go down all these alleyways here. I will simply present my own reading of Kant, saving its rigorous defense for another occasion.

Why was reading Hume such a rude awakening for Kant? By the time Kant entered academia, European philosophy had split itself into the competing epistemological schools of empiricism, based in the British Isles, and rationalism, with advocates scattered across the European continent. As a German-speaking Prussian, a self-professed Leibnizian, and an obsessive systematizer, there was no doubt into which camp young Professor Kant fell. Rationalism, as mentioned in a prior chapter, was defined by the claim that we are born possessing certain innate ideas, and these inborn ideas ground all our knowledge—or at least the most important varieties of knowledge—with the necessary truths of mathematics providing rationalist philosophers with their paradigmatic example. None of us has ever encountered a physical triangle with perfectly straight sides and perfectly regular angles. How, then, do we have absolutely certain, mathematically precise knowledge of the properties of triangles? It must be, the rationalists concluded, that we have the idea of a perfect triangle in our minds, thereby granting us intuitive access to this idea. Plato, of course, had argued that Forms or Ideas exist in some transcendent realm, of which the mind can catch only the briefest of glimpses. Scholastic theologians then moved these Ideas into the equally transcendent, and equally opaque, mind of God. But with advances in modern mathematics dramatically expanding the truths available to us that would appear to be both absolutely certain and intuitively clear, rationalist philosophers concluded that God must have placed these ideas in our own minds when he created us, thus opening the door to a wide swath of knowledge we can achieve through the use of pure reason alone, without having to look to the empirical order around us.

Although rationalism began as an epistemological stance—addressing questions of what we can know and how we know it—its practitioners did not hesitate to veer into sweeping metaphysical claims. Descartes's proof of God's existence provides a good example. Having used his skeptical method to doubt away everything in the world of which he could not be absolutely certain, Descartes was left knowing only that he existed and that—given the stream of ideas he witnessed going by—he existed as a thinking thing. Noting that one of the ideas he had in his mind was the idea of an infinite God, while reasoning that a finite mind could never produce the idea of infinity on its own, Descartes concluded that God must have placed this idea in his mind when creating him; hence, God must exist beyond the mind. Descartes then used God's transcendent existence to establish that real material objects must likewise exist beyond the mind. While conceding he could be intuitively certain only that he had various *ideas* of extended bodies, and that we can never step beyond our ideas to see what might lie behind them, Descartes noted that bodies certainly *seem to* exist beyond us; we never think, in any case, to question their reality in everyday life. Accordingly, if bodies did *not* exist in a real extended realm beyond us, yet God created us believing they do, God would be guilty of deceiving us. Yet, on pain of contradiction, an infinite, perfectly wise, powerful, and benevolent God cannot be a deceiver; hence, real bodies must exist beyond the mind.

Writing a generation after Descartes and attempting to impose some discipline on Descartes's rather freewheeling approach to theorizing, Baruch Spinoza argued that all philosophy should be conducted in the manner of one of Euclid's geometric proofs. Spinoza then used his geometric method to demonstrate that the entire extended realm is nothing but a vast idea in God's mind, with our own minds being specific modes of God's thinking. This metaphysical doctrine, among other things, allowed Spinoza to resolve the mind-body problem Descartes left to his successors. Having divided the world into two distinct types of substance, thinking things and extended things, Descartes was never able to explain how these two substances interact, as would appear to be necessary for the mind to receive sensations or to exert control over its physical organism. Spinoza dissolved this difficulty by arguing that only one substance exists in the world, God, and this infinite mind interacts with extended bodies the one way we can conceive of unextended minds and extended bodies interacting: God *thinks* bodies, with God's thinking of a particular human organism being what we typically understand as an individual human mind. Spinoza went on to note that God is perfectly rational, so as he develops his ideas, these thoughts proceed with the same inevitability as a mathematician carrying out a geometric proof. And that is why, Spinoza concluded, both the mental and physical realms develop in accord with the universal laws of nature, which Spinoza took to be just as necessary as the laws of mathematics.

Rejecting Spinoza's pantheism but not his speculative approach to metaphysics, Spinoza's younger contemporary Leibniz argued that God creates innumerable minds beyond himself, all of them conceiving the idea of a physical realm, on the model of Spinoza's God. As finite, however, each of these minds—or "monads," as Leibniz calls them—can picture the physical realm only from one limited perspective. God then turns these monads loose to develop their ideas of the physical realm in lawful fashion, as if each isolated monad were being shown a movie, the physical order featured in this movie operating in accord with the laws of physics. And because every monad starts out picturing the same physical order (correcting for perspective), while they all represent nature as developing according to the same natural laws, the movies they watch maintain a preestablished harmony with one another. This makes it *seem* as if we are interacting with real, physical objects beyond us—and by extension, with other minds. In reality, however, each of us remains forever locked within the sphere of our own thoughts. In this extreme version of rationalism, therefore, not just our abstract, theoretical knowledge derives from innate ideas. Even our empirical knowledge of the physical realm arises through the unfolding of a complex idea contained within us since the moment of our creation.

Clearly, Spinoza and Leibniz had to take some major speculative leaps to make their rationalistic accounts of human knowledge work. Responding with English practicality, Locke introduced the humbler premise of empiricism: The mind starts life as a blank slate, and everything it learns comes to it through sensation. Although Locke made a conscious effort to stick to epistemology and avoid the metaphysical flights of fancy his rationalist counterparts were taking, he did stake out a clear metaphysical position. Specifically, if Spinoza and Leibniz avoided Cartesian dualism by arguing that minds are metaphysically primary, with bodies having their only existence as the ideas minds have of them, Locke presumed that material nature is primary, with the mind somehow arising through the physical operation of the body. In this materialistic view, the mind-body chasm again disappears, in this case because sensation comes down to nothing more than external bodies acting mechanically on the physical components of the brain. And this mechanical action, Locke argued, is enough to explain all our knowledge, including our knowledge of particular empirical states of affairs, such as, "My desk now sits before me," but also the use we make of such abstract concepts as substance, causality, the self, and the external world. These concepts had long been cherished by philosophers, leading rationalist philosophers to classify them as innate ideas, but in *An Essay Concerning Human Understanding*, Locke sought to reveal the psychological mechanisms by which these concepts could arise through empirical experience.

As Locke's most prominent successor in the empiricist tradition, Hume developed his own psychological account of how sense experience leads us to formulate such abstract concepts as substance, causality, the self, and the external world. Locke and Hume, however, drew very different implications from their work. Locke viewed the investigation of the human mind as a branch of modern science, whereby empirical evidence is amassed to draw objective conclusions about how nature works. Admittedly, in the late seventeenth century, Locke had little reliable psychological data upon which to draw, leaving his theory of how the mind operates largely conjectural. But Locke at least approached his work in the spirit of modern science, which is to say, in the spirit of furthering our objective knowledge of the world. Hume, conversely, used empiricism as a platform from which to launch a skeptical attack on the very notion of objective knowledge. While agreeing with Locke that we can identify a series of psychological mechanisms that lead the mind to form such concepts as substance, causality, the self, and the exterior world, Hume took the fact that the mind, itself, generates these concepts to imply that these concepts *do not* reflect objective reality. These concepts are rather subjective constructs, or really just fictions, perhaps indicating something about how the mind works, but telling us nothing about the objective world we believe our thoughts represent.

We can therefore understand why reading Hume was such a rude awakening for Kant. Hume's scathing skeptical attacks made clear that the metaphysical systems philosophers had long been constructing based on certain abstract ideas are little more than castles made of sand. That, in itself, would have forced Kant to reconsider his Leibnizian commitments. But Hume's critiques cut even deeper. In arguing that the most basic concepts we utilize, not just in philosophy but in everyday life, are nothing more than subjective constructs, Hume was denying that we can have any objective knowledge at all. And this was a threat, not just to traditional metaphysics, but also to modern science, the whole purpose of which is to reveal the objective workings of nature. The concept of causality, in particular, had come to play an essential role in modern science, although the traditional concept of substance—that which remains the same even as accidental properties change—had also been revived as modern scientists began searching for various conservation laws. Yet, if Hume was right and concepts like substance and causality are mere subjectively generated fictions, the entire project of modern science would appear to stand on foundations no more secure than Leibniz's monadology.

This, however, was something Kant was unwilling to concede. Persuasive as Hume's arguments were, Kant had spent much of his early career teaching mathematics and physics, and he was convinced the Newtonian model of the universe is essentially *right*. No doubt, scientists still had plenty of work remaining to fill in the details of how nature operates. Nevertheless, the tremendous progress they had already made in this regard, together with the fact that their findings were driving the development of new technologies that actually *worked*, seemed to demonstrate that modern scientific knowledge has *something* objective to it; modern science could not all be subjective fictions. Again, it took Kant nearly a decade to identify where Hume had gone wrong and to construct his own positive account of objective knowledge. To retrace this journey, we first need to consider Hume's critiques in greater detail.

Hume on the Concepts of Substance,

Causality, the External World, and the Mind

Let us start with the concept of substance. In everyday life, I take for granted that the desk at which I sit is the same desk I sat before yesterday, and if I close my eyes, this same desk will still be there when I reopen my eyes. Aristotle used this commonsense view of things as the foundation for his metaphysics, arguing that the world is fundamentally composed of discrete substances with properties. More specifically, Aristotelian substances are characterized as follows. (1) A substance has an essential unity to it; it is *one* substance. (2) A substance has certain essential properties that determine its identity; it is *this* substance. (3) A substance maintains its identity over time, even as it acquires or loses accidental properties; it *remains* this substance. Hume conceded that the Aristotelian account of substance reflects our everyday understanding of the world and of the objects we encounter within it. But, he asked, how do we know any of it to be true?

When I look before me, Hume notes, all that enters my mind is the color brown, arranged in a rectangular shape with four protrusions coming down from it. I do not see the concept "desk" anywhere before me, much less the concept "substance." And I certainly do not see any of the supposedly self-evident truths philosophers have long ascribed to substances, such as, "A thing is the same as itself," or, "A thing is inseparable from its essential properties." All that I immediately experience is the visual pattern of a brown rectangle with four protrusions, perhaps accompanied by a tactile sensation of hardness. Anything else I attribute to the desk must come from somewhere else.

In fact, Hume argues, what happens when I view my desk is thus. The visual pattern with which I am presented resembles a visual pattern I have experienced on numerous prior occasions. My current sensations therefore trigger memories I have of these prior visual sensations. They may also trigger the memory of a tactile hardness I have experienced when, upon seeing this visual pattern, I have reached out my hand and touched it (or more precisely, when I have reached out the pattern of shapes and colors I have come to regard as my hand until they touch the brown rectangle). In any case, now that I am associating all these sensations with one another—brown, rectangle with protrusions, hard—for convenience I begin lumping these sensations together under the label "my desk."

Such acts of association, Hume notes, are quite useful for navigating everyday life. They allow me, for instance, to assert, "My desk was here last night; it is still here before me right now; and the desk will probably be here when I return to work in the morning." So this is helpful information, but do I *know* this same desk will still be here tomorrow morning? Do I *know* the desk remains there when I close my eyes? Do I know my desk is even a "thing"—a substance—with some sort of enduring metaphysical existence beyond me, when all I experience is a series of visual and tactile sensations that I associate with one another? Absolutely not, Hume replies. All that I have are the sensations. Nowhere in this process do I see, feel, or otherwise experience the concept of "substance." This gives me no justification for asserting this same substance will still exist tomorrow, much less for grounding an entire metaphysics on a notion that actually springs from the mind, itself, and not from any of the objects the mind supposedly encounters in the world.

If this attack on the Aristotelian concept of substance was withering, what probably rattled Kant even more was when Hume trained his fire on the concept of causality, given the prominent role this concept had taken on in modern science. Philosophers had long maintained that such axioms as, "Nothing happens without a cause," and, "There is no cause without an effect," provide us with some of the most certain, foundational knowledge we have. Aristotle identified four types of cause—formal, efficient, material, and final—and in medieval philosophy, the principle of efficient causality (one object pushing another from behind) was used, for instance, to prove God's existence: the order of nature is so intricately complex that it could not possibly have arisen by chance, and thus some intelligent being must have created it. When modern scientists began taking their decidedly non-Aristotelian approach to nature, they nonetheless retained efficient causality as a foundational concept, positing that nothing in nature happens by chance, but rather the motion of every body is determined by its prior collisions with other moving bodies.

Yet, for all the use both ancient and modern thinkers had made of the concept of causality, Hume wondered, had anyone ever seen a cause? I watch my cat extend its paw and strike the pile of notes on my desk; the papers fall to the floor. Without a second thought, I assert that the cat caused my notes to fall, using this as a justification for evicting the perpetrator from my study. And yet, the only sense data I received is a pair of events, one following the other. I did not experience any sensations, nor did I encounter any objects, that would correspond to "cause." Indeed, I do not even know what such a thing would look like.

What we experience, Hume contends, are sequences of events that frequently occur in similar order. When a particular sequence arises often enough—when I witness event A several times, and it is consistently followed by event B—the resulting memories begin to trigger certain associations in my mind, such that when I witness event A, the idea of event B now comes to my mind, even before this event has had a chance to recur in the world. With my ideas proceeding in this fashion, idea A inevitably leading to idea B, it begins to *feel* as if there is a necessary connection between A and B. This feeling conjoining two ideas, something manifestly in my mind, has led philosophers to assert *event A* causes *event B*—in the world—with the resulting "cause" being elevated to the highest ranks of metaphysical principles. Yet, in making these grandiose claims, Hume argues, philosophers have overstepped what they can possibly know, for causes are not objects we experience. All we experience, again, is the regular succession of events, not any sort of necessary link between them. The more limited form of knowledge we do acquire is perfectly adequate for navigating the world. If I see my cat preparing to strike the papers on my desk, I can still chase her away, thereby saving my notes. But this does not change the fact that the "objective" knowledge philosophers and scientists have long claimed to have of causes and effects is little more than a subjectively generated fiction.

This purportedly objective knowledge, in other words, does not correspond to any actual objects in our world.

Yet, neither did this final phrase, "in our world," escape Hume's skeptical critique. The question of whether an external world exists beyond our thoughts had been standard fare for modern philosophers since Descartes. Hume offers his own take on the reality of the external world in a fashion that is by now familiar to us. He notes that, for all the sense impressions we receive, "externality" is not among them. To be sure, the brown rectangle with four protrusions *comes* to me. I do not just make this idea up, at least not consciously, which is why I am tempted to say the idea comes from beyond. Yet, the image is simply *there*, floating before my gaze. It does not bear any marks that would indicate a second object, lying somewhere behind the visual sensation. Even if I come to associate a feeling of hardness with this visual sensation, hardness is likewise just another sensation, immanent to the stream of thought; it does not point to anything lying beyond or behind this stream.

Hume's elder contemporary, George Berkeley—an Anglican Bishop—had utilized a similar line of reasoning to argue that material bodies do not, in fact, exist. All that exists in the world are minds, Berkeley proclaims, with bodies being nothing more than the ideas minds have of bodies. When I close my eyes, therefore, my desk really *does* disappear from the world until I reopen my eyes (unless, perhaps, the ever-vigilant God keeps an idea of my desk in his mind). Yet, even Berkeley's denial of the physical world's reality was asserting too much for Hume. For one thing, if our sensations do not point to any sort of "real" objects lying behind them, neither does sensation tell us such objects do *not* exist. All we have are the sensations; we simply cannot know what may or may not lie behind them. Berkeley, moreover, built an entire metaphysical system around the claim that minds are the one true substance in the world—in this regard sounding more like a rationalist than the empiricist he claimed to be. Yet, we have already seen what Hume thought about the concept of substance. Indeed, when Hume took his skeptical knife more specifically to the concept of the mind, it survived no better than any of the other fundamental concepts we have been considering.

When Descartes engaged in his skeptical exercise, doubting away everything of which he could not be certain, the one claim he found he could not doubt was, "I think, therefore I am." Even if I try to doubt this claim, there is still an "I" there doing the doubting, so I must exist. And since doubting is a form of thinking, I must exist as a thinking thing. Yet, what is this "I", Hume asked, whose existence Descartes claimed to prove? Reflecting on our mental life, we observe a steady stream of thoughts going by: sensations, feelings, beliefs, opinions, doubts. Nowhere in this stream, however, do we encounter the mind itself. True, the faculty of association leads us to bundle certain sensations into discrete packets, labeling one packet "my desk," another "that tree." None of these sensations, however, even hint at the existence of an object we would label "I." When we use this pronoun, therefore, we cannot be referring to any particular object of experience, of which we might have objective knowledge. Rather, we are simply bundling the entire stream of thoughts together, perhaps highlighting certain ideas we have regarding one particular body (my physical organism). Only philosophers and theologians then try to claim more, insisting that these thoughts must be contained in some sort of repository: the self or mind. This repository, however, is not something we see, feel, hear, or otherwise experience. Hence, the mind is not something about which we can know anything. Accordingly, any claims we do make about the mind, even claims as sparse as Descartes's "I exist as a thinking thing," are little more than subjectively generated fictions, perhaps useful for helping us organize our experience, but lacking any correspondence to objective reality.

Kant's Response to Hume

Although it took Kant some time to figure out how to respond to Hume's account of human thought, the basic objection he arrived at was straightforward: Hume claimed to demonstrate that such traditional philosophical concepts as substance and causality are nothing more than subjectively generated fictions, yet his own account of thought assumes the objective functioning of these concepts from start to finish. This is seen most clearly in the case of causality. Hume explained the origin of this concept, again, through the psychological mechanism of association. We frequently observe event A being followed by event B, and this leads us to associate the two events together. Moving forward, when we observe event A, this prompts us to think event B, with the resulting feeling that A must be followed by B then leading us to claim event A causes event B. As Hume points out, this leap from an association between two ideas (in the mind) to the claim that one event causes another (in the world) is invalid. But when Hume then concludes that the concept of causality is a fiction, having no objective basis, he forgets that his own account of how we arrive at this concept depends entirely on idea A causing idea B to arise. Given empiricism's underlying materialism, moreover, Hume assumes this mental act of association occurs as the result of a physical stimulus mechanically triggering certain memories that have been physically stored in the brain. In denying the objective meaning of causality, therefore, Hume was cutting the legs out from under his own account of human thought, including his explanation of how we generate the concept of causality.

Though somewhat more subtly, Hume's account of thought likewise depends on the concept of substance. In fact, as Kant came to realize, the entire debate between rationalism and empiricism depends on this concept. After all, the question guiding this debate—Where do our ideas come from?—presupposes that ideas must come from *somewhere*, as opposed to, say, the mind just making them up. And this, in turn, suggests ideas are a sort of object, on the order of rocks and trees, bound by such substance-based principles as, "Something cannot come from nothing." This line of reasoning is perhaps most obvious in Descartes's proof of God's existence, when he claims the presence of the idea of infinity in our minds proves the existence of an infinite being who places this idea in our minds, since a finite mind could never generate the idea of infinity on its own. Locke and Hume rejected this argument, along with the broader rationalist claim that we are born with any number of innate ideas pre-loaded into our minds. Yet, in countering that all our ideas must therefore come from sense experience, the empiricists were similarly asserting that our ideas must come from *somewhere*, thus implying they have a substantial character, or in any case they are subject to some sort of "principle of the conservation of ideas." With the debate between rationalism and empiricism therefore coming down to the question of whether the ultimate source of our ideas is God (before we are born) or sense experience (after we are born), neither camp entertained the notion that the human mind might generate certain ideas on its own.

As Kant reflected on the use his predecessors made of the concepts of substance and causality, the larger point he began to discern is that both rationalism and empiricism offer accounts of human thought that are highly mechanistic: certain ideas come to mind, these ideas interact with other ideas already there, and this produces further ideas in predictable fashion. For the empiricists, with their materialistic metaphysics, the crucial mechanism of association could be traced back to the physical interaction of incoming sensations and stored memories. On the rationalist account, rooted in an idealistic metaphysics, the mechanical nature of thought is a bit harder to visualize. Think back, however, to Spinoza's invocation of the geometric proof as the exemplar of rational thought. As we work through a demonstration, the mind is led ineluctably from one idea to the next, such that once we have accepted the starting axioms, the path our thought must follow is determined. And since the world, for Spinoza, is nothing but God rationally developing his ideas, everything in the world is ultimately a result of this predetermined mental action. Leibniz departed from Spinoza in allowing finite minds to exist beyond God, but he argued in analogous fashion that once a monad is created conceiving the idea of a physical realm, it will develop this idea in a fashion so mechanical that its thoughts remain perfectly synchronized with those of every other monad, even though these isolated minds never interact.

As we look back on early modern philosophy, we can readily understand why philosophers on both sides of the English Channel would have proposed these various mechanistic accounts of thought: they were following the same impulse that inspired Hobbes as he considered what motivates human action. The Scientific Revolution had demonstrated that nature is a rational system, composed of bodies interacting in mechanical, lawfully predictable fashion. And almost nobody was satisfied with Descartes's mind-body dualism, seemingly the only avenue by which minds might be undetermined in their thoughts, even as bodies are subject to the laws of nature. Accordingly, it appeared that if human beings are to be given a place in the rational order of nature, our thoughts must proceed in a fashion at least analogous to the mechanical operation of bodies. This could be, as the empiricists argued, because thought really is a function of the physical workings of the brain. Or it could be, as the rationalists maintained, that minds are metaphysically primary, with the mechanical operation of bodies being a byproduct of the lawful fashion in which minds conceive bodies. What Kant came to realize, however, is that while both the rationalist and the empiricist accounts of human thought were inspired by the Scientific Revolution, *neither account was adequate to explain the Scientific Revolution itself.* Both rationalism and empiricism, in other words, represented attempts to use modern scientific thinking to explain the workings of the human mind, but neither of these mechanistic accounts of thought could explain the particular acts of mind upon which the modern scientific method had come to depend.

To unpack this claim, let us think back to the chapter on the Scientific Revolution and its discussion of the two traditional forms of logical judgment: deduction and induction. Deduction, again, moves from the general to the particular, or from "All men are mortal" to "Socrates is mortal," typically by means of a syllogism. The advantage of deductive judgments is that they are absolutely certain; if a syllogism's premises are true, so too must be its conclusion. The downside of deductive logic is that, because it merely involves taking ideas we already possess and drawing out their contents, it never tells us anything we did not already know, at least implicitly. To draw a loose analogy, we might say the various rationalist accounts of thought are deductive in character. To be sure, when thinkers like Descartes and Spinoza proposed that mathematics replace formal logic as a paradigmatic example of rational thought, they were opening the door to a mode of reasoning that allows for discovery of novel truths: whereas a logician can deduce nothing about triangles beyond the three sides and three angles that went into their definition, a geometer drawing a triangle on a piece of paper may be able to discover certain novel facts about the triangle, such as that its interior angles will always add up to two right angles. That said, when we perform a geometric proof, there is a sense in which its conclusion is already determined even before we start the demonstration, with each step of the proof proceeding to the next with an ineluctable mathematical necessity. The various rationalist accounts of thought all suggest a similar determinacy, where we begin with certain innate ideas already in mind—in the mind of God, for Spinoza, or within individual monads, for Leibniz—and thought then proceeds as the necessary unfolding of these initial ideas.

If the various rationalist accounts of thought are therefore roughly deductive in character, the empiricist account draws heavily on induction, the form of judgment that moves from the particular to the general, or from "This crow is black and that crow is black" to "All crows are black." Inductive judgments do allow for some expansion of knowledge, insofar as they move from observing a few crows to drawing conclusions about all crows, including some crows that no human observer may have ever seen. Yet, this also points to induction's major drawback: its uncertainty. For all I know, the next crow I observe may be white, thereby falsifying the general conclusion I have just drawn. Induction is limited, moreover, in how far it can extend our knowledge: while I can draw conclusions about particular individuals I have never seen, I can generalize only about the *types* of individuals I have observed. Granted, even this limited, provisional information can be useful, both for navigating everyday life and doing science. But as we saw in Chapter 2, if the modern scientific method makes important use of both deduction and induction, its most important step—the step that can generate truly novel knowledge—cannot be reduced to either of these classic forms of judgment.

Thinking back to Galileo, it is true that, having observed

many steel balls rolling down inclined planes at a rate such that total distance traveled was proportional to the square of the time the body had been traveling, Galileo drew the inductive conclusion that all bodies fall at this accelerating rate. Once he had proposed this general law, moreover, Galileo probably tried to deduce certain consequences that should follow from his hypothesis, such as that *this* steel ball should travel 12 feet in 3 seconds, before conducting experiments to test his prediction. That said, Galileo's truly groundbreaking move came prior to either of these inductive or deductive acts. Before it could have even occurred to Galileo to measure the time and distance a body is falling, he must have suspected something that is not directly observable—nor was it a generalization from multiple observations, nor a claim Galileo might have derived from certain concepts he already possessed, such as the concept of earthen bodies. Galileo must have somehow struck upon the notion that a body's fall can be represented by something taking a completely different form, an algebraic equation. Proceeding to test this notion, Galileo may well have tried out any number of different equations, discarding those that did not fit the data he began amassing, until finally he struck upon an equation that matched this data in instance after instance. It was only then—having completely reformulated the sense data he was receiving into numbers and algebraic symbols—that Galileo hazarded the inductive judgment that all bodies fall at an accelerating rate such that $s = xt^2$.

We earlier identified this creative act of putting forward a rule intended to capture an observed pattern as a third form of logical judgment, abduction. Abductive judgments are unique in that they do not depend on any sort of principle of the conservation of ideas. They do not involve the manipulation of ideas already given, whether by drawing out the contents of a general idea or by lumping many particular ideas together to form a general idea. Judging abductively rather involves taking a stab in the dark: tossing out a new idea in the hope of better grasping a given subject matter. It follows from the underived nature of abductive judgments that they will often be wrong. Think, for instance, of Ptolemy trying to account for the observed retrograde motion of planets by proposing that the crystalline spheres that carry planets around the earth have smaller crystalline spheres, or epicycles, embedded within them. This possibility for error is the reason why the testing of hypotheses came to be a second vital step in the modern hypothetico-deductive scientific method: without error correction, abduction slips into mere fictionalizing. As modern scientists began to discern, however, the risk of error inherent in abductive judgments is outweighed by the potential for gain, since abduction is the only form of judgment capable of generating knowledge claims that are truly novel. This novelty springs from the fact that, while abductive judgments may well be *informed* by prior ideas—and they should be if they are not just to be random guesses—abductive judgments are not the *product* of prior ideas. Abductive judgments are instead the product of a creative mind taking a creative leap as it attempts to discern order amid disorder.

To be clear, Kant never uses the word "abduction." As noted in Chapter 2, this term was not coined until a hundred years after Kant wrote, by the American philosopher Charles

Sanders Pierce—although Pierce is said to have made a discipline of reading *Critique of Pure Reason* for an hour each morning when developing his own thought. A related term Kant does employ is "synthesis": the act of holding a manifold mental content together in a single mental act, thereby giving a complex subject matter the unity of a common intuition or concept. This is what happens when I view the three lines and three angles on the page before me as a single geometric figure, or when I hold this particular geometric figure together with other three-sided, three-angled figures I have observed under the concept of a triangle. Kant viewed synthesis as the central act of human thought. In fact, though Kant was loath to speculate about anything as nebulous as "human nature," if the mind he portrays has an inborn nature, it is to be constantly striving to synthesize the manifold, or to be constantly striving to hold its variegated mental content together by means of unifying mental acts. As we will see shortly, this is the role such foundational concepts as substance and causality play in Kant's account of thought: they are among the most powerful tools the mind discovers for gaining a handle on the manifold content playing out before it. And the mental act of synthesizing the manifold by means of concepts, I would suggest, presupposes the groping, grasping act of abduction. Thinking conceptually requires that the mind first come up with the concepts it will use, and that the mind then take chances, trying out certain concepts to see whether they fit for their subject matter, building on those that do and discarding those that do not. In this experimental fashion, the mind gradually builds up what we call "experience"—which, Kant sought to establish, is not mere fictionalizing, but rather objective experience by its very nature.

The Transcendental Turn

When Kant developed his own positive account of what we can know and how we know it, he sided with the empiricists in arguing that the starting point for our epistemological investigations must be the everyday experience we have of the world. He objected, however, to empiricists' characterization of this starting point. When Locke asserted the basic premise of empiricism—all knowledge comes through sensation—he was effectively equating "experience" with sense experience, or the stream of sensations we receive. This saddled him with the task of showing that any knowledge claims we would like to maintain must be the product of particular sensations. Accordingly, when Hume observed that we do not, in fact, receive any sensations that would correspond to such concepts as substance, causality, the self, or the world, the basic premise of empiricism forced him to conclude that these concepts lack objectivity. Kant, however, rejected the Lockean premise that all our knowledge must come through sensation, on the grounds that the "experience" that serves as the starting point of our knowledge is not exhausted by the sensations we receive. Even in daily life, Kant noted, we do not merely experience such sensations as brownness, hardness, loudness, or sourness. Rather, our experience is of desks and chairs, of cats and dogs, of other people. Our experience is of *things*—of unified, enduring objects. And even in daily life, we experience these objects as interacting with one another in regular fashion, with one event predictably following another. One of the objects we experience, moreover, is ourselves, which we uniquely experience from the inside, thereby distinguishing ourselves from the larger world of causally interacting objects that exist beyond us. Whether we are philosophers, shopkeepers, or uneducated laborers, it is *all of this*, not just the flow of sensations, that comprises "experience" in our everyday, pre-reflective sense of the term.

With our starting point therefore being not raw sensation but the rich variety of experience we actually have, the task of theoretical philosophy, as Kant saw it, is to determine how this experience is possible. What, in other words, are the conditions necessary for experience? Kant labeled his approach "transcendental philosophy," insofar as its subject matter transcends empirical experience. We must be careful here, however, to follow Kant's precise use of language. Kant was not suggesting that the concepts that ground our knowledge lie *transcendent* to experience, perhaps on the model of Platonic Forms. But neither did Kant believe these concepts can be found *immanent* to experience; he accepted Hume's observation that such concepts as substance, causality, the self, and the world are not objects we encounter within our experience, like rocks or trees. Hence, these foundational concepts must be *transcendental*, meaning that they sit right on the edge of experience. These concepts are not objects of experience, that is, but it is the use of these concepts that makes experience possible. And because we *have* experience—in the rich sense of the term—and we *know* we have this experience, we can attain an objective knowledge of these concepts by inquiring into the mental acts required for experience to arise.

To elucidate this rather subtle point, it will be simplest to start considering the concept most foundational to our thought, substance. One disclaimer: in the interest of lending clarity to Kant's discussion of our most basic concepts—this was a section of the *Critique of Pure Reason* Kant rewrote almost entirely in the second edition, while still managing to confuse readers—I will approach this topic from a different angle than Kant did, drawing on some observations from contemporary developmental psychology to which Kant would not have had access. I believe that Kant and I still get to the same philosophical endpoint, but this is where a full defense of my interpretive approach will need to wait for another occasion.

Kant on Substance

Consider the newborn infant. As she enters the world, she is flooded with sensations: sights, sounds, tastes, smells, tactile feelings. At this early age, the infant does not comprehend anything that is happening around her; she is simply bathed in sensations. Nevertheless, her newborn mind is already striving to make sense of the rhapsody of sensations with which she is confronted. Stroke the infant's palm, and she will gropingly try to grasp your finger. Without any conscious intent, she is instinctively trying to get a handle on the sense content with which she is presented. The same thing happens when the infant looks around her, drinking in the visual and auditory stimuli. She is casting about for something to lock onto, perhaps her mother's face or the stuffed bear her father holds out. Just as it may take some time for the infant to develop the hand strength needed to grip your finger, the same is true of her mental powers. As a newborn, she may not register any difference between the stuffed bear, a colorful pattern on her blanket, and a shadow on the wall. At some point, however, she will start isolating discrete objects from the noisy background. Slowly, she will come to view these isolated bundles of sensations, not as sensations, but as *things*, or as objects in the full sense of the word.

Developmental psychologists have determined that if you show a baby a favorite toy, then cover it with a blanket, at three months the baby will show no signs of suspecting the toy is beneath the blanket. By about six months, however, most babies will try to look beneath the blanket, giving a smile of recognition when they see the toy again. The baby has come to recognize that the toy is not only a discrete object, distinct from the background of other sensations, but that this object continues to exist even when she is not immediately seeing or touching it. She has gained what psychologists would now call object permanence. Or in the much older language of philosophy, she has begun to utilize the concept of substance.

Yet, where did the child get this concept? The claims of rationalism notwithstanding, it does not appear the child was born having the concept of substance in her mind as an innate idea. Otherwise, why would she not be able to use it proficiently from the moment of birth? But neither, as Hume would note, is the concept of substance one of the objects the child comes to identify. She begins to discern Mommy, the stuffed bear, and her blanket as distinct objects, but nowhere in the flood of sensations does she encounter anything that would correspond to "substance." But if this concept is neither an innate idea, nor a sensation, nor an object of experience, what is it? Kant's answer, in so many words, is that this concept is a strategy the child tries out to make sense of the sensations she does encounter; it is a mode of grasping.

As the young child is bombarded with sights, sounds, and tactile feelings, she may well experiment with a number of different strategies for holding these diverse sensations together. If her parents have decorated the nursery with many blue items, for instance, she may try viewing everything blue as somehow unified. The blue sensations, however, seem to come and go without rhyme or reason, showing little apparent relation to one another. Trying to gain a handle on the visual manifold by means of color, therefore, turns out to be like when the baby tries to grasp the smoke rings from her father's pipe: with the rings dissipating in the child's fingers, she cannot latch onto them, so she finally stops trying. Grasping for her father's finger, however, the child finds she can latch onto it, so she does. And the same is true when she starts viewing the stuffed bear as a discrete, enduring object. Unlike the patterns on her blanket, which change every time the blanket is rearranged slightly, the bear remains there, solid and unchanging. As her mental powers develop, the young child may even begin to make certain predictions that utilize the concept of substance. "If I cover the bear with my blanket, the bear will still be there when I pull the blanket back." When these predictions are repeatedly borne out, the child begins making similar predictions with respect to other objects, many of which likewise pan out. And thus, like a scientist making the conscious decision to adopt a hypothesis confirmed by numerous lab experiments, the young child gropingly, pre-consciously adopts the concept of "thing," or substance, as a means of imposing order on the flood of sensations.

But does this mean the concept of substance—which the young child essentially invents as she gropes her way about the swirling sensations—is merely a useful fiction, a subjective construct rather than an objective determination? This is what Hume had argued, but Kant responds that the concept of substance is quintessentially objective, insofar as it is the most fundamental tool by means of which we cognize objects *as objects*, as opposed to mere sensations or even bundles of sensations. Again, all the mind receives are the sensations. These sensations may contain certain patterns that are suggestive of distinct objects. Still, these sensations do not divide themselves into discrete entities. The brown the child senses does not contain any marks suggesting it should be ascribed to the stuffed bear, and not to the green wall behind the bear. And the brownness certainly does not contain any marks to suggest it is the *same* brownness that was contained in the *same* stuffed bear that was around five minutes ago, and should still be around five minutes hence. Thus, to regard these particular sensations as pertaining to a discrete object that endures over time requires an act of mind. It requires, as Kant put it, that the mind impose a conceptual form onto the raw material of sensation. And because substance is the conceptual form by which the mind most fundamentally transforms its flood of sensations into objects, as opposed to mere sensations, this concept's claim to objectivity is unsurpassable. Not itself an object of experience, the concept of substance is *objectifying*, insofar as it is a strategy the mind uses to start transforming mere sensation into experience proper.

This claim to objectivity on the part of the concept of substance is only strengthened, moreover, by the fact that it is a concept we all share. The concept of substance, in other words, is not merely objective but intersubjective. Yet, how can this be true if we are not all born with the concept of substance as an innate idea—if every infant must effectively invent this concept anew as they confront the sense manifold? The answer is that the decision to latch onto this particular concept, and to continue using it for the rest of our lives, is not randomly made. On the contrary, substance is the only concept we can imagine a child struggling to make sense of her world could conceivably latch onto for an appreciable length of time. Again, she might experiment with any number of concepts, trying to gain a handle of the sensations flooding her. And perhaps different children will experiment with some different concepts. Nevertheless, every child who attains anything resembling normal mental development will eventually stumble across the concept of substance, and will begin using this concept again and again, simply because it *works* like no other, binding disparate sensations into discrete, enduring bundles that the mind can hold within its mental grasp.

Kant goes so far as to argue that the concept of substance will be shared by every rational being, whether human or not, thus driving home the point that this concept is not simply an accident of human psychology. If intelligent beings happen to exist on some distant planet, they may well have bodies that are quite different from ours, which would presumably mean they have different brains. Still, if these alien creatures do not, at some point, start to cognize the sense data they receive as *things*, as discrete objects enduring over time, it is difficult to see how they could attain anything resembling rationality. Could some strange race utilize a different base concept, perhaps "blue" or something else, upon which to ground a rich form of experience? We have no idea, although it is difficult to see how any foundational concept could be as useful as substance for carving sensation into meaning-ful, manageable bundles. In any case, should these strange creatures exist somewhere, they will have their own form of experience. It will not be "experience" as we know it, nor can we even imagine what their experience might be like, given that our own version of experience is rooted so deeply in one particular set of concepts, the most fundamental of which is substance.

Kant on Causality, the Self, and the World

If the concept of substance therefore lies at the heart of objec-tive experience, that of causality is nearly as foundational, and similar in origin. Returning to our developing child, imagine a one-year-old contemplating a tower of blocks her parents have just built. Gingerly, the child reaches out a hand. As she touches the blocks, they fall over. Her parents clap and encourage her, rebuilding the tower. This time, the child reaches out to strike the tower a bit more assertively. The family plays the game repeatedly, and each time the child strikes the blocks more confidently. What is happening here? For one thing, the child is practicing her motor skills, and thus she keeps getting faster and more accurate in reaching out her hand. But she is also practicing a new way of making sense of the stream of sensations flowing by. Having already come to view both the blocks and her hand as discrete objects, she is now groping for an effective means of holding these distinct objects and the events in which they participate in a unified thought.

Once again, the child may experiment with any number of different concepts, likely with varying degrees of success. Eventually, however, one of these concepts will be, "If event A, then event B." As Hume correctly observed, this if-then statement, or the causal link between A and B, is not something the child sees or otherwise senses. But neither is it true that the only thing taking place here is that the sight of event A mechanically causes an image of event B to pop into the child's mind. Doubtless, the act of association takes place, and doubtless it is crucial to suggesting the concept of causality to the child. Still, she does not just receive the chain of associated ideas passively. Rather, she actively links event A to event B, holding them together in a unified thought by means of the concept of causality, making use of its if-then form. Of course, this concept is not something the child can fully integrate into her thinking just by playing with blocks on a single occasion. It may take months or years of practice to become proficient with the notion of causality, learning when it may be successfully applied and when not. "Extending the hand causes the blocks to fall," is repeatedly confirmed, so this use of causality is retained and further built upon. When the child extends her hand and immediately hears a clap of thunder, she may similarly assert, "Extending the hand causes thunder." It is unlikely, however, that the child will be able to replicate this sequence of events very often, so she will probably soon abandon this causal link.

By this point, the developing child has abductively generated and tried out any number of different concepts in her attempt to gain a handle on the sense manifold. And she has found at least two, substance and causality, that are highly effective in tying multiple disparate sensations into coherent, manageable bundles, so she keeps coming back to these concepts, constantly refining their use. The child is now well on her way to "experience," in the full sense of the term. To fully achieve this, however, she still needs to make one final conceptual leap. In this case, the leap involves two novel concepts, but they are related like the twin poles of a magnet, so one cannot really arise without the other. Specifically, the child needs to learn to distinguish between herself and the larger world. For the newborn, there is no distinction between "I" and "it," or between "in here" and "out there." There is just the stream of sensations. Slowly, the young child starts to divide the streaming sensations into discrete objects and events, some of them causally related, others not. So doing, she may begin to identify herself as one of the discrete objects in the world: There is Mommy and Daddy, there is the stuffed bear, and there is Baby. It may still take Baby some time, however, to realize what a unique thing she is.

Let us now consider the young child at eighteen months old, this time playing a game of peekaboo. Her father holds a napkin over his face and asks, "Where's Daddy?" He then pulls the napkin down, exclaiming, "There's Daddy!" The child roars with laughter, her concept of object permanence having been confirmed through this reappearance of her father's face. When it is the child's turn to hide, she may fumblingly use the napkin to cover her eyes, not worrying about how well it conceals the rest of her face. When her father then asks, "Where's Baby?" this question strikes the child as quite appropriate, and in the spirit of the game, since—her eyes being closed—Baby and everything else have completely disappeared. The complex notion that a world exists beyond her, and that she has one perspective on this world, but other people have their own unique perspectives—such that the child's father might still be able to see her face even when her own eyes are closed—simply does not occur to the eighteen-month-old.

The distinction between an inner self and the outer world is not one that arises overnight, but developmental psychologists have devised clever experiments to tease out how this line gets drawn over the first few years of life. Young children may be asked to watch a puppet show, for instance, in which one puppet hides something under a rock while a second puppet has its back turned. When quizzed by an interviewer, the average two-year-old will assert that the second puppet knows what is under the rock. The child knows what is under the rock, after all, so why would the second puppet not also know? By age three, however, the child may start to realize the first puppet may know something—and she, the viewer, may know something—that the second puppet does not.

What has happened in the interim? It would appear that

the child, struggling to get a better handle on the stream of sensations, objects, and events now appearing before her, has stumbled across a new hypothesis. Specifically, she posits that she has an inner realm, populated by all manner of sensations, feelings, and thoughts that are not directly accessible to others, even as certain of the objects in her outer realm—other people—have inner realms that are likewise inaccessible to her. Developmental psychologists now call this cognitive advance Theory of Mind, which just highlights the fact that the distinction between inner self and external world—and the further distinction between inanimate external objects and external objects with their own inner realms—cannot simply be read off the sensations the child receives. Rather, these various distinctions must be put forward as a theory. As it turns out, this theory is highly effective in explaining, for instance, why merely thinking, "I am hungry," elicits no response from the child's mother, whereas crying out, "I am hungry!" gets the child quickly fed. Accordingly, the theory that she has a private inner realm, that an external world exists beyond her, and that some of the objects in this external world have their own private inner realms, it is a theory the child will eventually embrace and then rarely question again—at least, until she takes a freshman philosophy class.

Reflecting on this cognitive development in one of his later works, *Anthropology from a Pragmatic Point of View*, Kant notes that very young children will often refer to themselves in the same third-person language that others use when speaking about them, saying, for instance, "Susie wants a cookie." At some point, however, Susie will begin to say, "I want a cookie." This grammatical shift to the first person is a good indicator that Susie has begun to have experience in the full sense of the word. This is not just sense experience, but rather the experience of discrete, enduring objects that causally interact with one another, all within the context of a common world—a world of which we are a part, but which also lies beyond us, distinct from the sensations, thoughts, and feelings we might have about this world. This is the experience, not just of philosophers, but of everyday life.

The Legacy of Kant's Theoretical Philosophy

What had Kant accomplished with his account of human experience? His most immediate aim, again, was to reestablish the possibility of objective knowledge in the wake of Hume's skeptical attacks, which had reduced virtually everything we might claim to know about the world to subjectively generated fictions. In particular, Kant wanted to provide Newtonian science with a firm epistemological foundation. To fully assess whether Kant achieved this goal, we would need to consider additional topics not addressed here, notably Kant's account of space and time, which he used to justify the application of mathematics to the study of nature. We do not have time to go down that sideroad here. In any case, for as urgent as the task of "saving" Newtonian science was to Kant, inspiring and guiding the development of his theoretical philosophy, the ultimate success or failure of his epistemic project was not of great consequence for the history of science. Working scientists, after all, rarely have much concern for whether philosophers have signed off on their knowledge claims, deeming them properly grounded. The ultimate pragmatists, scientists go with what *works*, utilizing whatever approaches, concepts, or assumptions are producing results, allowing them to extend their knowledge. If philosophers then want to label these results more objective or subjective in character, that is their prerogative, but for scientists, the more interesting question is whether the results generated lead them to yet further discoveries.

From a historical perspective, therefore, the enduring significance of Kant's theoretical philosophy lay not in its epistemic details but in the portrait it painted of the human mind, and particularly in the active, groping, grasping role Kant accorded the mind in its acquisition of knowledge. By way of historical context, most ancient and medieval philosophers treated the mind as completely passive in its reception of knowledge. Real objects *exist*, in the premodern view, whether in the world before us or in some transcendent region like the realm of Platonic Forms or the mind of God. In these latter cases, especially, the observer may well need to work hard to glimpse the object of knowledge. Once the proper vantage point has been attained, however, the observer is simply bathed in the object's light; the observer simply receives the object, or in any case a copy or image of it. Crucially, the observer makes no contribution to what is learned, on pain of distorting the object of knowledge and thereby falling into error.

Early modern philosophers in both the rationalist and empiricist camps began viewing the mind as more active in its acquisition of knowledge, not merely absorbing what is given, but processing the information received in a manner that further shapes the ultimate knowledge gained. As we saw, however, both rationalism and empiricism—inspired by the mechanical approach to nature that was proving so fruitful in the physical sciences—offered highly mechanistic accounts of thought, whether locating the relevant mechanisms in the mental or material realms. Both accounts, in any case, portrayed the mind as a computing machine that receives certain inputs, crunches this data by means of established rules, then spits out a predictable result. Undoubtedly, much of our thinking *does* proceed in this quasi-mechanical fashion, so initiating a search for thought's rules was a laudable achievement in its own right—even if it would be the twentieth century before this search began to acquire a strong empirical basis. That said, if *all* the mind's operations were purely mechanical, it is difficult to see how the mind could generate novel knowledge claims, or claims that are not simply a repackaging of what was already known before. It is difficult to see, in other words, how the mind could have begun to make the tremendous advances in learning that were flowing out of the Scientific Revolution, the event that inspired the search for the laws of human thought in the first place.

As Kant developed his own positive account of how the mind works, he doubtless got numerous details wrong. We should hardly expect otherwise, given the new ground he was breaking, combined with the paucity of empirical data with which he had to work. Indeed, Kant was not trying to develop a complete psychological account of how the human mind operates. He was just trying to identify the set of concepts that any rational being will use, assuming it attains an objective experience of its world comparable to our own. Even in this regard, philosophers have debated whether Kant got everything right—whether the various lists and tables he composed of the concepts essential to rational thought are accurate and complete, and whether making such lists and tables is even useful. All of that aside, what Kant made clear to future students of the mind, whether in philosophy or psychology, is that any mind capable of attaining human reason cannot be a mere passive receiver of knowledge, nor can it be exclusively a processing machine, capable merely of accepting inputs and spitting out mechanically determined outputs. A reasoning mind must rather be, not just an active participant in shaping the knowledge it acquires, but a groping, grasping, spontaneous, creative, risk-taking participant. The human mind must be capable, in other words, of abductively proposing novel means of conceptually framing the manifold content it encounters. And it must then be capable of assessing the results of its conceptual experiments, abandoning those that do not work, before casting about for other, more effective means of grasping the manifold.

Stepping back further to consider the importance of Kant's account of the mind for the ongoing development of the progressive worldview, we have repeatedly stressed that the Enlightenment conception of progress rests on the conviction that the world is a rational place, governed by universal laws, and that if we use our powers of reasoning to discern these laws, we can not only better understand the world but start reshaping it to better suit our own ends. On this conception of progress, therefore, human reason is the driver of progress, whereas nature is the stable, rational arena within which progress takes place. Given this framework, the most obvious impact Kant's theoretical philosophy had on the progressive worldview is that it took the notion of human reason and kicked it up a notch, granting the mind a power to drive progress surpassing even what had been envisioned by such an intellectual optimist as Descartes. For Descartes and his rationalist successors, the mind is operating at the height of its rational powers when it is working through a syllogism or carrying out a geometric demonstration. From a Kantian perspective, however, what truly showcases the power of human reason is the fact that, two to three thousand years ago, certain human minds *invented* syllogisms and geometric proofs. These acts of invention did not involve the mind moving from given premises to some predetermined results. Rather, they required that the mind start viewing the objects of its experience in completely novel fashion, in this case by abstracting out their sense content and considering only their bare logical or geometric forms. For the first logicians and geometers who attempted these acts of abstraction, there was no guarantee any of this would work, or in any case prove useful. Nevertheless, their willingness to go out on a limb and experiment with new ways of viewing the world helped set human minds on a course to where we can now engage in all manner of high-level reasoning.

A second way in which Kant takes the Enlightenment conception of progress and heightens the role it accords to reason is somewhat less obvious, but equally significant. Kant showed that even the rational structure of nature is something we, as reasoning minds, impose upon it. The mind, in other words, is responsible for generating even the rational arena within which reason can make its progress. This is a strong claim, so we will need to work through it carefully. We can start by considering Galileo's famous remark that the book of the universe "is written in mathematical language, and the symbols are triangles, circles, and other geometrical figures, without whose help it is impossible to comprehend a single word of it." Clearly, Galileo was expressing his wonder that nature should behave in accord with such mathematically elegant principles as the law of falling bodies. Galileo's purple prose aside, however, it is equally clear that, in a literal sense, nature is *not* written in mathematical language. When a wolf looks up at the stars, it does not see abstract circles and triangles. When ancient peoples looked up at the heavens, they might have seen archers and bulls, but they did not see algebraic equations. Accordingly, when Kepler posited that planets travel around the sun in elliptical orbits defined by the equation $x^2/a^2 + y^2/b^2 = 1$, he was not reading this off the book of nature, fluent as he may have been in mathematics. Planets do not have equations written across them, so Kepler, himself, had to impose this mathematical structure upon the heavens.

Of course, modern scientists were not the first to try to make sense of their experience by invoking certain unifying conceptual structures that transcend anything empirically given. Ancient peoples who told stories of sun gods dying every night, only to be reborn each morning, were doing the same thing: they were trying to lend the complex, confusing realm of nature some unity and stability by viewing diverse events as repetitions of the same eternal cycle. Similarly, the authors of the ancient Hebrew narrative used a linear account of God's stewardship of the world to tie together a series of cultural events spanning centuries. Greek philosophers made the West's first attempt to gain a handle on the world's complexity by means of stories that were more rational than religious in character, in the sense that its lead characters were abstract principles rather than divine personalities. These rational stories were soon superseded, however, by another religious narrative that came to dominate Western consciousness for over a millennium and a half, this one binding global history together by giving its constituent events an ineluctable downward trajectory.

Diverse as these foundational stories have been, they all represented abductive attempts on the part of individuals and cultures to make better sense of sensations, objects, and events bombarding them. When seventeenth- and eighteenth-century scientists then began imposing a new set of conceptual structures on the world, many of them written in the language of mathematics, this began giving the world a rational appearance even stronger than what it possessed in ancient Greece. Indeed, what particularly distinguished this new way of viewing the world as rational—beyond the mathematics—was the fact that the modern scientific method began mandating that we regularly, rigorously check back with nature to determine whether the rational structures we are imposing on it are a good fit, or whether nature is instead exercising its veto power, rejecting some concept, law, or narrative we have proposed as inappropriate or false.

Ultimately, therefore, the modern scientific portrayal of nature, though a product of the human mind, is not a mere subjective fiction, on par with every other mythology people have concocted to make sense of their experience. The scientific story of the world is objectively grounded because it is vetted on an ongoing basis by the world, itself. This, in turn, gives us reasonable confidence that, when we use the ever-growing body of scientific knowledge to inform our interactions with nature, nature will respond as we predict, thus allowing us to use our powers of reasoning to start reshaping the world to better suit our human wants, needs, and aspirations. And this, finally, allows us to conclude that—although we understand we could frame our experience in terms of any number of foundational narratives—our decision to view the world through the hopeful lens of progress, binding together the diverse events of human history by giving them a trajectory that points overarchingly forward and upward, is itself objectively grounded.

This conclusion will only be strengthened in the next chapter, which will consider how, for Kant, we can use our powers of reasoning to transform not just the world around us but ourselves.

CHAPTER 6

KANT AND MORAL UNIVERSALISM: MORAL PROGRESS

Thus far, we have considered the progressive worldview from the viewpoints of history, the natural sciences, political science, economics, and the philosophy of mind. Each of these disciplines has told its own story of progress, but if a common thread has run through all these narratives—beyond the concept of progress itself—it has been the principle of universalism. Modern science first came into being when investigators like Galileo stopped viewing the world as a collection of discrete substances, each with its own individual nature, and instead began viewing nature as a unified, interconnected system governed by universal laws, or laws that apply equally to every object, in every place, at every time. Similarly, virtually every premodern system of social organization rested on the presumption that different people possess different degrees of moral worthiness, as determined largely by birth, thus making it right and good that the worthiest people should enjoy exclusive privileges at the expense of others. When modern thinkers such as

Hobbes, Locke, and Jefferson then challenged this ideology of privilege by proposing that we are all born with certain natural rights, the defining feature of these rights was their universality: if a right is not universal, it is not a right, but a privilege. Accordingly, if Kant may be viewed as the culminating figure of the Enlightenment for many reasons, foremost among them is that he took the concept of universality and placed it at the center of his moral philosophy—and at the heart of the progressive worldview, where it has remained ever since, even as the progressive worldview has otherwise evolved in some dramatic ways.

Kant himself always maintained that, for as significant as his contributions to epistemology and metaphysics were, the highest purpose his theoretical philosophy served was to set the stage for his practical or moral philosophy. In the last chapter, we saw how the *Critique of Pure Reason* did this in a general sense, by portraying the human mind as exactly the sort of spontaneous, rational agent required to fulfill the Enlightenment ideal of autonomy. One of the more technical arguments of the *First Critique* further allowed Kant to transcend a dilemma that had been guiding—but also limiting—the development of moral philosophy for over a hundred years, particularly on the British Isles: the Hobbesian dilemma. To enter our discussion of Kant's moral philosophy, let us revisit the Hobbesian dilemma to see why and then how Kant sought to move beyond this moral dilemma. This critique, not just of Hobbes but of the entire British approach to moral philosophy, will prepare us for Kant's development of his own doctrine of moral universalism.

The Limits of British Moralism

When Hobbes turned his attention to political philosophy in the mid-seventeenth century, modern scientists had already begun to show that nature is governed, not by certain vague tendencies inherent to the different types of things in the world, but by a relatively small number of immutable, universal laws of nature, such as the law of falling bodies. This means, Hobbes reasoned, that if human beings are to have a place in nature, our behavior must likewise be guided by some simple law or laws. Observation would suggest, moreover, that self-interest is the only reasonable candidate for such a law of nature that would govern the behavior, not just of human beings, but of all animals. Yet, if people are guided by self-interest in all they do, how is any sort of socially responsible, moral action possible?

As discussed in earlier chapters, Hobbes, Locke, and Smith all responded to the Hobbesian dilemma in similar fashion: they accepted that human beings are guided by self-interest in all they do, then looked for ways that socially beneficial behaviors might be in our best interest. Exploring moral sentiment theory, Smith argued that the human mind is constructed such that, sometimes, it just feels good to help other people, thus giving us a self-interested reason to perform certain "disinterested" actions. Of far greater historical significance, British thinkers sketched out two social systems—Hobbes and Locke focusing on consent-based government, Smith on the market economy—that take the self-interested strivings of individuals and channel them into behaviors that benefit other individuals, as well as the larger society. According to contract theory, each person agrees to give up certain freedoms they enjoy in the state of nature, submitting their actions to the rule of law, as enforced by a sovereign. Although this involves an initial sacrifice, it provides everyone with the security and stability of living in civic society: a net gain for all. Similarly, according to Smith's economic theory, when people specialize their labor, then exchange the products of this labor, the invisible hand of the market steers their self-interested strivings into mutually beneficial actions that increase the size of the pie from which everyone may enjoy a slice.

When Kant published *Groundwork for the Metaphysic of Morals* in 1785, followed by the *Critique of Practical Reason* in 1788, the twin institutions of consent-based government and free market capitalism were just providing the first hints of how dramatically they would come to shape the modern world. Kant nevertheless rejected the entire approach British philosophers had been taking to moral theory. Note that, as we have here discussed the work of Hobbes, Locke, and Smith, we have been using terms like "socially responsible" and "socially beneficial" synonymously with "moral." Kant, however, refused to equate these terms. He freely acknowledged that our default mode of action is to pursue our own interests, and that we are therefore wise to craft social institutions that steer self-interest toward mutually beneficial ends. That said, social arrangements of this sort will not render our actions moral if, in performing them, we are merely doing what self-interest would have counseled anyway, had we been making no attempt to behave morally. When I trade two deerskins for four beaver pelts, this helps the trapper as much as it helps me, and it benefits both of us more than if we had never traded, so my participation in this exchange can be deemed socially beneficial. But that is not why I make the trade. I would still do the same thing, even if told my actions would not help the trapper in the least (provided she would still trade with me), since this trade is what best serves my interests.

Accordingly, Kant reasoned, while there is nothing *wrong* with doing things like engaging in trades or entering contracts of various sorts—whether social contracts or business deals—there is also nothing that distinguishes such actions as *right*, in a moral sense. Even if we assume the moral sentiment theorists were correct, thereby providing a psychological explanation as to why I might sometimes help others at considerable cost to myself, performing such other-directed actions will not render my actions moral if, in performing them, I am merely trying to maximize the moral pleasure I experience. Why, after all, should indulging my natural desire to help others be morally preferable to indulging my natural desire for, say, food or sex? Or to frame this question in broader terms, if we do nothing but what our animal natures incline us to do, what is to distinguish us from the meanest of beasts? What will give us the unique moral dignity we fancy ourselves to possess as human beings?

In fact, Kant responded, even in everyday life, and even among those who have never read a word of moral philosophy, we understand there *is* a difference between self-interested behavior and moral behavior. We understand, moreover, that striving to serve one's own interests does not become moral simply because it happens to produce an outcome that benefits others. "The only thing in the world that is unconditionally good," Kant writes, "is a good will." The only thing that is morally good, in other words, is genuinely striving or willing to do the right thing or making a good-faith effort to determine our actions, not by self-interest but by the principles of morality. With the Hobbesian dilemma looming in the background, however, we must ask how this sort of moral behavior is even possible if (1) everything in nature is governed by universal laws; (2) this requires that human beings likewise be governed by certain universal laws; and (3) self-interest is the only reasonable candidate for the particular law of nature that would determine the behavior of human beings and other living creatures.

Kant's response to this quandary was to accept Hobbes's initial premise, that everything in nature is governed by universal laws, but to deny Hobbes's second claim, that human beings must therefore be determined by the laws of nature in everything they do. And this, in turn, does away with the need for Hobbes's third claim, that human beings have no choice but to act in their own perceived best interest. But how, we might press Kant, can human beings escape the laws of nature? Assuming we are not angels plunked down onto Earth, how can we exempt ourselves from the universal laws that would appear to govern everything else in the world?

Kant's more specific answer to this question has two parts. The first he labels his negative argument for freedom. By means of this argument, Kant sought to establish—contra Hobbes and the British moralists—that we need not regard human beings as being strictly determined by the laws of nature in everything we do. Reconciling human freedom with the lawfulness of nature is a question of theoretical philosophy, so for Kant's discussion of this topic, we will need to return briefly to the *Critique of Pure Reason*. With the negative argument for freedom having thus established the *possibility* of human freedom, we will be able to turn to the *Critique of Practical Reason* and Kant's other works of practical philosophy, in which he develops his own positive account of morality—an account that allows us to demonstrate the *actuality* of freedom through our moral thoughts and actions.

The Negative Argument for Freedom

To get a sense of how human freedom is even conceivable, when everything else in nature is governed by immutable, universal laws of nature, we need to recall Kant's account of how experience first arises. All our knowledge, again, starts with sensation. As thoughts stream before me, I receive nothing from beyond but the image of a brown rectangle with four protrusions, coinciding with a feeling of hardness. It is then through an act of mind that I come to regard this color, shape, and feel as forming a unified, enduring substance: my desk. Applying another fundamental concept to this object, I begin viewing the desk as causally interacting with other objects, such as the stack of papers it holds on it. Then, in a final act of mind, I regard all these objects as forming a unified world that exists beyond me—a world of which I am a part, but which is also distinct from me, external to my thoughts.

This externality that I ascribe to the world, however, is

a strange thing. For while I posit that objects such as the desk or the papers exist beyond me, my perceptions of these objects remain fully immanent to thought. The desk I see, in other words, remains the desk *I see*, a group of visual and tactile sensations that I bundle together under the concept of substance. To be sure, I am explicitly positing that the desk exists in an external world—as opposed to, say, my opinion of the desk, which I regard as being located interior to thought. Yet, the external world I posit is still the world *I perceive*. It is something like the totality of my perceptions, or the totality of all possible perceptions, all bundled together under the unified concept, "world."

Admittedly, this situation is confusing. When we posit that objects like desks exist beyond us, we would seem to be asserting that these objects have some sort of existence beyond being mere thoughts in our minds. We would seem to be asserting that these objects have some sort of existence in themselves. But what, Kant asks, is a "thing in itself"? What are its properties? What are the principles that govern it? In fact, Kant argues, these are questions we cannot answer, for we can never go beyond the sphere of our thoughts to see things as they are in themselves. Everything that we can see, hear, touch, or even imagine are appearances, or things insofar as they appear to us, not things in themselves.

As we reflect on this confusing situation and try to make sense of it, our first instinct may be to assert that things—real things—exist in themselves, in a real world lying somewhere beyond the mind. These things then act on the mind, causing certain sensations to arise within it. Perhaps the mind somehow acts upon the sense data it receives, reshaping it in a way that distorts how things in themselves appear to us. The surface of my desk, for instance, may have a coarse texture, but when light bounces off this surface and strikes my eyes, I see the object as "brown". On this model of thought, then, the mind acts as a sort of lens, modifying the sensations it receives to generate what we know as "experience." But it is still real objects in the real world that trigger these sensations, acting upon the mind in causal fashion.

This, in fact, is roughly the model of thought Locke assumed when he developed his empiricist account of experience. And yet, Kant charged, this materialistic, mechanistic model of thought oversteps the bounds of what we can possibly know since it attributes causal relations to things in themselves, whereas causality is a concept we, ourselves, dream up. We abductively generate this concept, moreover, *within* the realm of appearances, to make better sense of our appearances. Whether things in themselves, lying somewhere *beyond* the realm of appearances, act on one another by means of cause and effect—and particularly whether they act on the *mind* by cause and effect, causing the mind to receive certain sensations—is something we cannot know. Even asking whether things in themselves operate in accord with the principle of causality involves a misapplication of this principle, since causality is a concept that has meaning solely within the realm for which it was developed, the realm of appearances. What properties things in themselves possess, whether and how they interact with one another, and whether and how they form a unified world are questions we simply cannot answer, and will never be able to answer, since we will never be able to step beyond the sphere of appearances to see things as they are in themselves.

If we therefore remain locked within the realm of appearances, does this mean the only thing I can know is my own mind? This was Descartes's argument when—having skeptically doubted away everything else in the world—he determined the one proposition he could not possibly doubt was, "I think, therefore I am." And this argument would have been valid, had Descartes stopped there. But he did not. Descartes went on to assert that, because he was manifestly having thoughts, he must be a thinking *thing*—a discrete substance with a particular nature. And because a thinking substance is manifestly a different sort of thing than the extended substances filling its perceptual realm, Descartes concluded the mind must be unextended. And since a substance that is unextended cannot have any parts, the mind must be indestructible, and hence it must be immortal. And so on.

When Descartes advanced these sweeping metaphysical arguments, his error lay in taking the concept of substance—a concept we use to bind together certain of our appearances—and applying it to something that lies beyond the field of appearances, the mind. Descartes then used the logical structure of the concept of substance to deduce all sorts of metaphysical properties that must seemingly inhere in minds, given their substantiality. But this logic is invalid since Descartes misapplied the concept of substance in the first place. Substance is a concept we use to unify certain of our appearances, whereas Descartes applied this concept to a particular variety of thing in itself, the "mind in itself", of which we can have no direct knowledge, whatsoever.

Kant's critique of Descartes has at least two major implications. First, it dissolves the mind-body problem that had bedeviled modern philosophy ever since Descartes split the world into thinking things and extended things. Extended substances, again, bump into one another, thereby creating the mechanical system of nature. An unextended substance, however, has no surface area by which to contact extended substances, so how do minds and bodies interact? Empiricists tried to sweep this problem away by reducing minds to the mechanical workings of the body. Rationalists, conversely, constructed elaborate metaphysical systems that reduced bodies to nothing more than the ideas minds have of bodies. Kant showed, however, that the mind-body problem was never a metaphysical problem to begin with. In fact, the extended substances we observe, existing and causally interacting within the larger realm of nature, are appearances. Whether anything exists beyond or behind these appearances—"real" objects, things in themselves—we can have no idea. In any case, if such things in themselves do exist, we can have no idea what sort of metaphysical properties they possess, since we can never see beyond the sphere of how things appear to us. By the same token, when we reflect on ourselves, as minds, all we can see is the stream of thoughts flowing by. We cannot intuitively reflect on the mind in itself, and thus we can have no conception of how the mind is ultimately put together. Yet, because we can know nothing about the metaphysical nature of *either* things in themselves *or* the mind, we have no reason to believe their interaction should be problematic. All we know is that this interaction—should it occur—takes place in a realm completely transcendent to thought, and thus beyond the proper application of such concepts as substantiality or causality.

The second implication of the distinction Kant draws between things in themselves and appearances takes us to the heart of Kant's negative argument for freedom. Because causality is a concept the mind applies to its appearances, whereas the mind itself exists outside the realm of appearances, we simply cannot know whether the mind is bound by anything resembling the principle of causality in generating its thoughts, including its thoughts regarding potential actions. Indeed, we misuse the concept of causality when we even speculate about whether the mind's operations are "caused" by anything—whether in the sense of its sensations being caused by external bodies or in the sense of one idea causing another to arise—since this involves taking a concept that was developed for the purpose of unifying our appearances and applying it to a particular type of thing in itself, the mind.

Hobbes's intuition that the modern scientific view of nature demands a mechanical account of thought was therefore misguided, given that modern science studies nature insofar as it appears to us, whereas the mind is an unknowable thing in itself. In fact, Kant argues, just about the only thing we can know about the mind, considered as a thing in itself, is that its operation cannot be *causal* in nature, since causality is a concept that has meaning only within the realm of appearances. And thus, Kant concluded, there is no contradiction in asserting *both* that nature is fully governed by causal laws, as the modern scientific view of nature demands, *and* that the mind is free, in the sense of not being fully determined by prior causes, as presupposed by any rich notion of morality.

Does this allow us to conclude that the human mind *is* free, in its deepest metaphysical essence? Not, Kant cautions, as long as we remain within the domain of theoretical philosophy. For just as reflection cannot tell us that the mind is bound by causal laws, neither can reflection tell us that the mind is *not* bound by such laws or essentially free. With respect to what the mind is in itself, we simply cannot know *anything* through mere reflection. If we want to go beyond Kant's negative argument for freedom, therefore, which merely establishes the possibility of human freedom, and instead assert the actuality of freedom, we must ask the mind to provide us with a positive demonstration of its freedom. It must provide this demonstration, moreover, in the one place we can observe it, the realm of appearances. And this requires that we turn from theoretical philosophy to practical philosophy.

Inclinations, Interests, and Morality: Laying the Groundwork for Moral Action

Let us take stock of where things now stand. At this point, Kant's negative argument for freedom has set aside the Hobbesian dilemma by showing that we need not regard people as being fully determined by the law of self-interest, or any other causal law, in everything we do. This negative argument says nothing, however, about how we *do* determine our actions, nor about the role self-interest may play in this determination, other than that we need not regard self-interest as the sole determinant of our actions. This does not mean, however, that we do not have interests. Kant was well aware that we are living organisms, such that we have a natural interest in remaining alive. And while our consideration of the inner life of the mind has thus far highlighted such knowledge-oriented mental content as sensations and concepts, the briefest inward glance reveals another type of content that fills and colors our mental stream: desires, aversions, appetites, lusts, disgusts, and cravings of all sorts, which Kant collectively refers to as "inclinations."

Even before the infant has begun to mentally grasp any of the objects surrounding her using such concepts as substance or causality, she is crying out for food, instinctively giving outer expression to the hunger she feels within. As we grow older, we never lose the inclination to eat when hungry, nor any of the countless other inclinations that would appear to stem from our bodily condition. Finding ourselves cold, we feel the inclination to warm up; experiencing pain, we are inclined to seek relief; feeling lust, we are inclined to gratify our sexual urges. It is true that some inclinations, such as the desire to be loved, to defend our social status, or to avoid boredom, may seem to be housed more in the mind than the body. The precise location of these inclinations, however, is a question more for empirical psychology than moral philosophy. To the extent that our urges and aversions impose themselves on us, having apparently been triggered by specific states of affairs in the material world—which may well include physical states of the brain—we can lump these ideas together as inclinations.

Further reflection tells us we do not just have a handful of inclinations; rather, they are legion. Reflection also reveals the most basic fact about our inclinations: we like it when they are fulfilled, and we dislike it when they are not. Feeling hunger, I may not always eat. Food may be unavailable to me, or I may choose to fast in light of some overriding consideration. Everything else being equal, however, when I feel hunger, I would *prefer* to eat; this is the very definition of an inclination. If we bundle all our inclinations together, moreover, and imagine what it would be like to have them all fulfilled, this gives us the notion—admittedly rather vague— of "happiness." It goes without saying that I would prefer to be happy than unhappy. I do not need to justify this preference through any sort of philosophical argument. This preference simply *is*; it presents itself to me as a basic fact of my existence.

With inclinations therefore coming with a value attached to them, it follows that, if I am not giving any further thought to my actions, I will typically do whatever appears to be most likely to satisfy my strongest inclinations. Otherwise stated, I will do whatever appears to best serve my interests. Even if it is not a law of nature that I *must* pursue self-interest in everything I do, absent any other considerations, this will presumably be my default mode of action, with my overriding interest being to attain happiness by fulfilling as many of my inclinations as possible.

Nor is it merely inner reflection that convinces us the pursuit of self-interest, as guided by the inclinations, is the default mode of voluntary action. When we look around at other people, other animals, or even puppets in puppet shows, we naturally try to make sense of their actions; we seek out some unifying principle that ties all their actions together into a coherent package. As young children, we may try out any number of theories to explain the actions of others, such as, "Everyone acts so as to gratify *my* desires." Frustratingly, this hypothesis is quickly refuted by empirical experience, so all but the most spoiled of children will quickly give it up. What proves more successful in explaining the actions of others is the proposition that, "Everyone strives to fulfill *their own* interests," or equivalently, "Everyone tries to be happy."

Thus, it was not Thomas Hobbes who first came up with the notion that human beings, and indeed sentient creatures of all types, pursue self-interest as a matter of course. This is what we all assume in everyday life. Hobbes merely gave high-level expression to this proposition, proclaiming it to be a universal law of nature that does not admit to possible exception. Even when we are not engaging in philosophical speculation, however, our default mode for explaining voluntary actions—whether our own actions or those of others—will be that these actions are directed toward fulfilling self-interest. Naturally, we realize that people must sometimes pit one inclination against another, or they must weigh an inclination's short-term gratification against its long-term fulfillment. Accordingly, when we observe that, "Immanuel does X," the precise explanation for why Immanuel chooses to do X, as opposed to Y, may not be obvious. Nevertheless, our presumption will be, "Immanuel perceived X to be in his best interest," and if we wish to pursue the matter further, we will try to determine why X looked better to Immanuel than Y, typically appealing to some inclination we would expect Immanuel to feel.

Even in everyday life, however, a tension can arise, since we sometimes observe people doing things that do not appear to serve their interests and may even appear to contradict their interests. The young child, for instance, may be puzzled to see her older brother cleaning his room since she knows he would rather be outside playing with his friends. Her first reaction will likely be to dig deeper—to seek out a self-interested reason her brother may have for pursuing this course of action. And indeed, upon asking her mother, the child may be told her brother is cleaning his room to get his allowance, or because he wants to avoid being punished. But the child's mother may also tell her, "He's doing it because he should; that's one of his duties." And this will likely satisfy the child. For as long as she can remember, her parents have been telling her, "You should do X," and, "You should not do Y"—or more directly, "Do X, but do not do Y." Sometimes, the issuance of these commands is accompanied by a direct appeal to the child's interests, as in, "Eat your vegetables if you want dessert," or, "Do not break your crayons if you do not want me to take them away." But sometimes, when the child asks, "Why can't I do Y?" the answer simply comes back, "Because you should not; it's not allowed." It is made clear to the child, in other words, that there are certain things we should do and other things we should not do, not because this will best serve our interests, but simply because this is the way things are; this is our duty.

Yet, what is this "should"? Where does it come from,

and why should we use it to guide our actions? In fact, not just children, but all of us are constantly bombarded with "shoulds." Some of them come in the form of direct commands some authority figure issues, be it a parent, boss, police officer, or king. Other times, the directives we encounter are standing rules that govern the institutions in which we participate: the rules at home or school, the norms of public behavior, the laws of our society. Typically, such rules are accompanied by rewards and punishments that follow from compliance or non-compliance—you get a gold star if you behave in class, but you must sit in the corner if you talk to your neighbor. Such rewards and punishments may well help us decide, based on self-interest, what we will do. Indeed, a well-crafted system of rewards and punishments can be highly effective in steering both children and adults toward the sorts of socially responsible behaviors in which we would like to see people engaging.

That said, the existence of a system of rewards and punishments is not sufficient to tell us what we *should* be doing. For one thing, we may find ourselves enmeshed in any number of systems of rewards and punishments, and they may give us conflicting directives. If a bank robber abducts me, for instance, and tells me he will break my knee-caps unless I help him rob the next bank, this will certainly explain my actions, should I choose to help the robber. But we would not want to conclude that bank robbery is therefore morally right, or something I *should* do, just because it is encouraged by a particular system of incentives. Experience tells us, moreover, that for as much praise as we heap on children who rack up large numbers of gold stars, we esteem it even more when people do what they should, not because this promises to bring them some reward, but simply because this is their duty. We esteem it, in other words, when people do what they should *because* they should.

This is where Kant made his break with the British moralists. Hobbes, Locke, and Smith were all convinced human behavior would have to be self-interested to find a place in the modern scientific world, and thus they tried to "save" morality by showing how self-interest can be channeled into socially beneficial behaviors. The negative argument for freedom having relieved Kant of this theoretical burden, he could acknowledge what he sometimes refers to as our "everyday moral understanding": the intuition that our behavior is genuinely moral only when we are *not* using self-interest to guide our actions, but rather we are doing what we should because we should. This is not to suggest Kant thought our actions must contradict our interests to be moral. What we should do, morally, may well coincide with what we should do, prudentially. In fact, what we should do, morally, will often align with behaviors encouraged by the various systems of rewards and punishments our society has established. Even in such cases, however, our actions will not be moral, properly speaking, unless we perform them *because* we should, and not merely because they bring us some benefit.

It follows, moreover—and this was Kant's most significant insight—that if we do not deliberately, earnestly, open-mindedly confront the question of what we should be doing, morally, we will have no way of knowing which systems of rewards and punishments may be encouraging moral behavior, and which systems of incentives are more like the commands of the kidnapping bank robber, inclining us toward actions that are prudential but morally wrong. We must therefore directly pose the question of what we should be doing, morally. This is by no means an easy question, but the way Kant goes about answering will take us to the heart of his moral philosophy.

The Moral Law

Kant faced two questions at this juncture. First, where does the "should" underlying moral behavior come from? Second, what sorts of actions does this "should" prescribe, permit, or forbid? Starting with the first question, we have already seen that, for our actions to be moral, they must somehow be distinguished from self-interested behavior. More specifically, what must be distinguished is the motive guiding our actions. It is always possible that self-interest and morality will align, directing us toward the same action. But even when we perform such dually prescribed actions, this does not automatically render our actions moral. The question is whether we are acting solely out of self-interest, or whether we are rather guiding our actions by some other principle, which would render our actions moral. Yet, what would this other principle be?

For one thing, Kant notes, the principle underlying moral action must *be* a principle. For actions to be moral, in other words, they cannot simply be random. How, after all, could my behavior be considered right or moral if I could have just as well done something else? Indeed, truly random behavior is something of which we can scarcely conceive, given the mind's innate urge to discern order in the manifold it encounters. Perhaps, since the negative argument for freedom has shown that the human mind need not be governed by the laws of nature, there is a certain abstract sense in which we can imagine a person acting completely at random. In practice, however, because our minds are always striving to make sense of things, we will always be looking for some pattern or law that holds the diverse actions we observe together. So, if we observe a person who claims to be acting randomly, we will naturally suspect that some inclination is guiding her actions. Perhaps this inclination is so subtle as to fall below the threshold of consciousness, such that the other person truly believes she is acting randomly. But unless we, as observers, are given some reason to believe otherwise, we will almost certainly revert to our default mode of explanation, which is to assume the other person is slipping back into the default mode of human action: pursuing self-interest, as determined by the inclinations.

Again, however, if moral action must be guided by some principle, as opposed to being random, yet this principle cannot be self-interest, what could this other principle be? Kant's answer to this question is deceptively simple: If we want to act morally, our actions must accord with the moral law. "Well, of course," we might be tempted to respond, "Of course, if we are acting morally, of course our actions will accord with the moral law. What other law would they follow?" Yet, Kant's assertion is not as tautological as it might sound. It actually contains two separate claims. The first is that, for an action to be moral, it must accord with the *moral* law. We have already discussed this assertion at length, in the context of Kant's rejection of British moralism. For an action to be moral, it must be distinguishable from what we would have done anyway, had we not tried to be moral. Hence, our actions cannot merely be prescribed by the law of self-interest, nor any other law of nature. They must rather be prescribed by some different law, which—for the want of a better term—Kant calls the moral law. At the same time, however, Kant is asserting that, for our actions to be moral, they must be determined by the moral *law*. If our actions are to be guided by some sort of principle, that is, rather than being random, they must have some common rule binding them together. Nor can this rule just be a rule of thumb, applicable at some times, but not others. Rather, for our actions to accord with the moral law, they must have the *form* of law. And as modern science had made abundantly clear, a law is only a law if it is universal. What is perhaps rather surprising is that the moral law's universal form goes a long way toward answering the second key moral question of, "What does the moral law tell us we should be doing?"

Kant here introduces the signature concept of his moral philosophy, the categorical imperative. An imperative is an instruction that tells us what we should or should not do. When the child's parents tell her, "Do not break your crayons," this is an imperative. Most of the imperatives we encounter in everyday life are not, in fact, categorical but rather hypothetical: they tell us what we should or should not do *if* we want to achieve a certain end. "If you want a nice dinner, you should walk down the street to the new kebab house." Nothing here is said about whether the purpose or end of walking down the street—getting a nice dinner—is good or bad. At issue is merely what I should do, assuming I make this my end. Given the large number of inclinations we experience as living organisms, nature provides us with a huge number of ends to pursue: my hunger suggests I should look for something to eat, my chilliness suggests I should find a coat, and so forth. Navigating everyday life therefore consists largely of prioritizing the ends nature hands us, then determining the best means by which to realize as many of these ends as possible, or at least the most important of them. Much of life, in other words, consists of discerning the hypothetical imperatives that will best steer us toward our overriding natural end of happiness.

If making use of hypothetical imperatives as just described is therefore quite reasonable, and indeed an inevitable part of life, this does not render our actions moral. For our actions to be moral, again, they must accord with the moral law. Yet, for an action to accord with the moral law, the imperative determining it must, at the very minimum, have the *form* of law. And laws, by their very nature, are universal, applying in every instance, at every place, and at every time. This means the imperative guiding our actions must not apply merely when we want to achieve some end. The imperative guiding our actions must be universal, applying in every case, without exception. This imperative must, in other words, be categorical.

To begin fleshing out this rather abstract argument, Kant offers several formulations of the categorical imperative. The first and most fundamental is, "Act always such that the maxim of your action could at the same time be a universal law." A maxim, as Kant uses this term, is the general rule we cite for why we take a particular action. I might make it a general rule, for instance, that if I am hungry, I should find something to eat. If one of my friends then encounters me walking down the street and asks what I am doing, this is the rule I will invoke to explain myself: "I was hungry, so I'm walking down the street to the new kebab house to find something to eat." This particular maxim, of course, has the form of a hypothetical imperative; it directs me to act a certain way, assuming I want to achieve the particular end of satisfying my hunger. For an action to fall under the categorical imperative, the maxim guiding it must hold in every case; it must be capable of being formulated as a universal law. To show how this works, Kant presents a series of examples, the most straightforward of which addresses the question of whether I may, in good conscience, renege on a promise I have made.

Let us say I borrow a hundred dollars from my neighbor, promising to pay him back when I receive my next paycheck. I spend the money, but then, just after I receive my next paycheck, a friend invites me to join her for dinner at the new kebab house. The restaurant is pricey, so I know I can afford to eat there only if I forego repaying my neighbor. Being hungry—and a kebab lover to boot—I have no doubt as to which course of action my stomach is inclining me toward. But I also pride myself on being morally upstanding, so I would like to know whether going back on my promise is morally permissible. Invoking the test of the categorical imperative, I must first formulate a more general maxim for the action I am proposing, such as, "I may break a promise whenever this is more convenient than keeping it." I must then ask whether this maxim could be formulated as a universal law. Put into universal form, this maxim would apply, not just to me, on the particular occasion of desiring a kebab dinner. It would have to apply to everyone, everywhere, always; we would all be permitted to break our promises whenever this was more convenient than keeping them.

Clearly enough, this outcome contradicts the very notion of a promise. If I did not wish to make a firm commitment to my neighbor, I could have always told him, "I will pay you back when I get paid—assuming nothing else comes up that I would rather spend the money on." In this case, however, I am not really promising anything—nor is my neighbor likely to lend me the money. But if I tell my neighbor, "I promise to pay you back," then by the definition of a promise, I am telling him, "I *will* pay you back at the specified time, period." Accordingly, when I try to imagine a maxim that permits the breaking of promises as a universal law, I find I cannot do so, since such a law would contain a contradiction within it; the attempted law would amount to something like, "Promises, which must be kept in every case, may be broken when convenient." Practically speaking, if we were to run a social experiment in which we told everyone they could break their promises whenever they liked, we would see promising, itself, soon disappear. No one would take promises at face value, knowing they could be broken at any time, so people would stop even trying to make promises; the institution of promising would collapse under the weight of its own contradictions. The "breakable promise" therefore turns out to be inconceivable as a universal law. Accordingly, I may conclude that breaking my promise to my neighbor merely because this serves my immediate interests is not morally permissible. I can still choose to break the promise, but doing so will be morally wrong.

What has this exercise told us? It has not told us whether we should or should not make promises. Nor has it told us whether we have an interest in keeping our promises, once made. Had we approached this scenario through the lens of self-interest, a strong case still could have been made for keeping my promise: I can reasonably predict that if I break my promise to my neighbor, not only will this neighbor stop lending me money, but rumors of my untrustworthiness will spread, and soon no one will take my word on anything. The categorical imperative, however, is blind to such considerations of interest. What the test of the categorical imperative tells us is that, if I make a promise, I *should* keep it, period. If I fail to keep a promise, I may suffer repercussions for my actions, or I may not. But I cannot reasonably claim I have acted morally in this situation, for in fact, I will have done something that is not just morally neutral, but wrong.

Kant's Abductive Approach to Ethics

Stepping back from the particular question of whether promises should be kept, this example illustrates more generally how Kantian ethics works. Notably, Kant does not present us with a complete moral system, in the sense of spelling out some fifty or a hundred actions that we must perform, may perform, or must not perform. This has frustrated some of Kant's critics, who have complained that his moral theory lacks content. "What," these critics want to know, "Does the moral law tell me I should *do*?" As Kant saw it, however, the task of moral philosophy is not to provide us with a fixed list of moral prescriptions. Where, after all, would we obtain such a list? And given that many different moral prescriptions are possible, how will we know when we have the right list? Indeed, as Kant saw it, this latter question points to the real task of moral philosophy: evaluating those moral prescriptions that do get proposed, by whatever means, so that we may know which of these prescriptions to accept and which to discard.

To contrast this approach to ethics with some of the other standard approaches that had been taken over the centuries—and to tie Kant's account of moral reasoning back to his broader account of how the human mind operates, as discussed in the last chapter—we can note that most traditional approaches to ethics are either deductive or inductive in character. Starting with the former, a deductive approach to ethics is one that begins with certain accepted moral axioms, then uses these general principles to determine what specific actions are morally required, permitted, or forbidden. In the traditional Christian story, for instance, God hands Moses a set of ten commandments intended to serve as the basis of the Hebrew law. God then inspires a series of biblical authors to memorialize his revealed Word in the books of the Old and New Testaments. Some of these books, such as Leviticus, explicitly include detailed legal codes. Other books, such as the gospels, are more exemplary in nature, providing a model of godly behavior we can emulate in our own lives. With all these moral sources being combined within the Bible, if we want to determine how to behave in any particular instance, we need to figure out which biblical passages are most relevant to our particular situation, then deduce how these passages indicate we should behave. The required deductive judgment may not be quite as straightforward as working through a syllogism, but the basic movement is still from general principles to particular prescriptions for action.

The deductive approach to ethics may yield a rich normative system, especially when backed up by such a trove of moral insights as the Bible. Nevertheless, any such approach will inevitably run into at least two major problems. First, deduction is useful only if we have indisputable moral axioms from which to set out, and upon which we will all presumably agree. In practice, however, we find that not only do different cultures have strikingly different ideas about moral behavior, but even within such relatively unified traditions as Christianity, different theologians have articulated very different conceptions of the foundational moral axioms. Accordingly, if we do not have some means of judging between the various moral principles that may get proposed as the starting point for morality, any subsequent acts of deduction will do little more than elucidate the customs of a particular moral tradition, without telling us whether this tradition has gotten its moral customs right.

Second, even if we grant the Christian premise that God has established certain absolute moral principles, and he has revealed these principles in univocal fashion—such that we can all agree on what they are—this still does not tell us what makes these particular principles right or good. In Plato's dialogue, *Euthyphro*, Socrates raises the question of whether certain things are good because the gods love them, or whether the gods love these things because they are good.

Without getting into Socrates's thoughts on what has come to be known as the Euthyphro dilemma, Kant clearly took the view that, just because God issues a decree, this does not render it good. Why, after all, would a particular decree be good if God could have just as well decreed something else? What this suggests is that, if God does establish certain moral principles and reveal them to us—a notion Kant, no atheist, was open to—there must nonetheless be a reason why God has issued these particular moral guidelines, as opposed to some others. And this is a reason that we, as rational creatures, should be able to figure out. Deduction, however, will not be the mode of reasoning that helps us in this case, since deduction can only move from established general principles to particular instances, whereas the question now before us is how anyone—whether human or divine—can determine which general ethical principles we should set out from to determine more detailed moral prescriptions.

Switching over to a possible inductive approach to ethics, let us think back to Locke's account of how moral reasoning first arises in the state of nature. Locke had already accepted the Hobbesian premise that people are self-interested in all they do—itself an inductive judgment drawn from observation. Rejecting the Hobbesian conclusion, however, that the state of nature will therefore be a constant war of all against all, Locke observes that we often have no time to calculate which action will best serve our interests. Accordingly, we rely on experience to formulate certain rules of thumb regarding which sorts of actions are most likely to yield the best results. Even in the state of nature, for instance, experience will teach that stealing usually leads to more trouble than it is worth, whether by provoking a direct conflict or making it more likely that my own things will get stolen. Thus, even in a state of nature, Locke suggests, people will informally adopt such general rules as, "You should not take things to which others have laid claim." To reinforce such inductively generated rules, communities then impose penalties on the individuals who violate them, whether through the vigilante justice of the state of nature or through the more formal laws and judicial processes of civic society. This threat of punishment has the effect of reinforcing the rule of thumb first discovered in the state of nature. Now, stealing is *definitely* likely to lead to more trouble than it is worth—thereby explaining why, in civic society, most people refrain from stealing most of the time.

Kant never denies that civic society requires a wide range of laws, including laws against stealing, together with formal mechanisms for enforcing these laws. Nor does Kant dispute that most laws probably began as the sort of hypothetical imperatives the Lockean account suggests, on the order of, "If you do not wish to invite retribution or have your own property stolen, you should not take material goods to which others have laid claim." As we have already seen in Kant's broader critique of British moralism, however, the problem with this inductive approach to ethics is that it cannot establish rules such as the prohibition against stealing as *moral* rules. If I refrain from stealing merely because experience tells me a general policy of respect for the property of others best serves my own long-term interests, that is fine. But this is not a moral judgment, in any meaningful sense. It is a calculation of self-interest.

Thus, the basic problem with both deductive and inductive approaches to moral theory is the same. Whether we start with general axioms and move to specific prescriptions, or we begin with particular experiences and move to generalized rules, neither approach gives us the means to determine whether we are setting out from the proper starting point. As a result, we have no means of determining whether the moral conclusions we are drawing are *right*. Begin, after all, with a biblical passage suggesting God condones thievery, or produce an empirical study demonstrating that the benefits of theft tend to outweigh the risks, and you will conclude stealing is right and good. In the theoretical realm, we saw that Kant transcended the limits inherent to deductive and inductive judgments by invoking a third form of judgment, abduction, a spontaneous act of mind that does not just manipulate previously given ideas but rather goes out on a limb and proposes new ideas. To highlight the similar, abductive character of Kant's approach to ethics, let us work through a second demonstration of the categorical imperative in action, this time paying particular attention to the acts of mind involved.

For the sake of variety, let us consider whether Kant can provide a moral justification for the ban on stealing that most societies have adopted in one form or another. Locke's empirical observations suggest that such bans are wise, given that everyone benefits from the material security they provide. But to determine whether stealing is also morally wrong, let us provisionally assert a prescription implying the opposite—namely, "Stealing is permissible." Before we go any further, note how we are entering into this moral exercise. We are not starting with a general axiom that is purported to be written in metaphysical stone. Nor are we studying how large numbers of people behave before inductively proposing a rule that describes how they generally act, or how they should act if they want to achieve some agreed-upon end. Rather, we are abductively throwing out a possible moral prescription, in this case, "Stealing is permissible." Admittedly, we did not pull this prescription completely out of the blue. It was suggested to us, rather, by the fact that almost every society we know of has instituted some version of the opposite prescription, namely, "Stealing is *not* permissible." Nevertheless, proposing that stealing be permitted—a condition we almost never witness empirically—requires a spontaneous, creative act of mind, not unlike that of a scientist who, having scanned the initial data, casts about for a theory or hypothesis to explain this data, then abductively throws something out there.

As we are well aware by now, scientific theories proposed in abductive fashion lack the certainty of deductive judgments. That is why a crucial step in the modern scientific method involves going back and testing proposed theories against the empirical data to see whether they hold up. On the Kantian approach to ethics, moral prescriptions have a similar abductive origin, with similar implications: before we can accept any proposed prescriptions as morally binding, we must put them to the test. In this case, however, empirical observation does not help us, since we are not seeking to determine the way things *are*, but rather the way things *ought to be*. Accordingly, we must test proposed prescriptions for their adherence to the moral law. This, in turn, requires determining whether the proposed prescriptions have the form of law. And since the basic form of law is universality, to evaluate a proposed moral prescription, we must test it for universalizability; we must put it to the test of the categorical imperative.

By this point, we can predict how the test for permissible stealing will turn out. I must first formulate the prescription in question as a general maxim that would guide my specific actions, such as, "I may take the personal property of others whenever this is convenient for me." When I then attempt to universalize this maxim, I find it contradicts itself just as much as the maxim that allows promises to be broken. The problem here is not merely that a maxim permitting theft, when applied to other people, would put my own property at risk—although this is also true. The bigger problem is that a blanket authorization of theft contradicts the institution of private property itself, which is the institution that makes theft possible in the first place. To be sure, a particular community need not recognize private property. In the Hobbesian state of nature, nothing guarantees possession beyond the strength of the possessor, so there is no "theft" in this scenario—just forcible taking. In a communal society, meanwhile, all goods are held in common, so there is again no way I can take something that belongs to someone else. It is with the introduction of private property that stealing first becomes possible. Once private property is on the table, however, whether as an informal principle in the state of nature or as a legal mandate in civic society, stealing can never be deemed morally permissible, since this would contradict the very institution giving rise to its possibility. Accordingly, for a society that recognizes private property, banning theft is morally permissible, and indeed morally obligatory since the converse situation—theft being allowed—is logically incoherent.

And this is how Kantian ethics works. Again, Kant's approach to ethics does not provide us with a predetermined list of the things we must do, may do, and may not do. Rather, we must supply any moral order in which we participate with its content. To do so, we simply have to make some suggestions, abductively proposing possible moral prescriptions. These prescriptions can address anything from how we behave as individuals to the laws and institutions by which we collectively organize and govern ourselves. In any case, once we have made our proposals, Kantian ethics directs us to submit these proposals to the test of the categorical imperative, or the test for universalizability. Those actions, norms, laws, or institutions that can be universalized are retained; those that cannot are discarded.

Putting Moral Philosophy to Use

Admittedly, the characterization offered here of Kantian ethics makes it sound as if the job of the moral philosopher is to sit behind a desk all day and dream up novel moral codes, optimized for universalizability. Certainly, we *can* engage in utopian exercises of this sort, using our creative powers to propose social, political, and moral arrangements the world has never yet seen, then weighing them against one another based on their universalizability. Most of the time, however, such abstract discussions will not resonate very far beyond the walls of the academy or salon. Far more likely to be of social relevance is if we apply the test of the categorical imperative to the social, political, and moral arrangements under which we currently find ourselves living. At some point, after all, *someone* must have proposed the moral prescriptions we find ourselves following. And testing these prescriptions does not require that I be the one who first proposed them, any more than scientists are barred from empirically testing hypotheses they did not generate. In fact, scientific progress is driven by precisely the opposite dynamic, where distinct members of the scientific community, often separated by generations, test one another's hypotheses. In similar fashion, I can take the moral prescriptions I find operative today and submit them to the test of the categorical imperative, whether these prescriptions were first proposed thousands of years ago by some wise philosopher or statesman, they were cobbled together over the generations by countless nameless individuals, or they just got proposed yesterday. In any case, for prescriptions that pass this test, such as the widespread ban on stealing, I can accept them and move on. But if I encounter some existing norm, law, or institution that does not pass the test of universalizability— slavery quickly comes to mind in the context of the late eighteenth century—I can advocate that it be reformed or eliminated, in the interest of bringing both my own actions and the practices of my society into better accord with the moral law.

If much of the moral philosopher's work, therefore, consists of *critique*—critically examining existing social, political, and moral arrangements for adherence to the moral law—Kant stressed that philosophers are not the only people capable of engaging in this sort of critical moral reflection. In fact, he denied that he was trying to invent any sort of new morality. He felt rather that his practical philosophy merely lent clarity and precision to a form of moral reasoning that had been in use, however informally, for as long as people had been organizing and governing themselves in accord with the idea of law—which is to say, in the language of contract theory, for as long as civic society had been in existence.

Writing in the late eighteenth century, Kant had little more empirical knowledge of the origins of civic society than did Hobbes or Locke. But Kant never found the narrative of contract theory compelling, finding it unbelievable that the inhabitants of the state of nature ever would have gotten together and signed a contract, submitting themselves to the rule of law and appointing one among their number as sovereign. Far more likely was that the first rulers were simply stronger, more assertive, or more cunning than their neighbors, using a combination of strength and charisma to claim power over those around them.

Presumably, the earliest of these leaders ruled through direct command, telling individual subjects exactly what they should be doing at each moment. At some point, however, as societies grew larger, this approach must have grown unwieldy: the leader would have acquired too many subjects to direct their every move. And thus it was that some wise ruler struck upon the idea of the law. Perhaps this was Moses, handing the law down to the Hebrew people—possibly with divine assistance. Or maybe it was Hammurabi, the ancient Mesopotamian king who inscribed one of the first known law codes on a stone pillar for all his subjects to see, or the Athenian legislator, Solon, who authored one of the first Greek legal codes. Laws, in any case, are distinguished from commands by the fact that commands are issued to particular individuals under particular circumstances, whereas a law applies to everyone, at all times. "Do not eat of the tree of life" was a command God issued to Adam and Eve when he placed them in the Garden of Eden. "Thou shalt not steal" is a law, binding upon all the people of Israel, no matter what their precise circumstances, once it had been handed down.

For those early lawgivers who were not divinely inspired, how did they decide which laws to give their peoples? Presumably, their first instinct would have been to draw on their society's collective wisdom and experience in something of the manner Locke described. People would have long since learned, for instance, that appropriating the material goods to which others have laid claim invites conflict and further theft, so a general disapproval of stealing would have already been customary, as reinforced through vigilante justice. This taboo against stealing would have strongly suggested to early lawgivers that a formal ban on theft should be among the first laws they enact. That said, the new law would still need to go through a vetting process, in the mind of the lawgiver, if nowhere else. Ruminating on one of his more troublesome underlings, for instance, Hammurabi might have first drafted a law proclaiming, "Erok may not steal from the granaries." The slightest reflection, however, makes clear that this pronouncement has the character of a command, not of a law, in virtue of its scope: it applies to just a single individual, in one particular circumstance. "Thou shalt not steal," conversely, applies to everyone, in all cases, and thus it has the universality of law. Neither Moses, Hammurabi, nor Solon had the categorical imperative to assist them in carefully distinguishing moral prescriptions that have the form of universality from those that do not. Nevertheless, they must have possessed at least an intuitive ability to draw this distinction, as evidenced by the fact that they mostly handed down, not direct commands, but laws.

What Had Kant Accomplished?

At this point, we may reasonably stop and ask how much Kant had accomplished as a moral thinker, given that he did not give us a comprehensive moral system, in the sense of a long list of the things we should and should not be doing. Instead, he merely gave us a test by which to evaluate possible moral prescriptions that we, ourselves, must supply—whether novel moral prescriptions that we have abductively generated ourselves or established customs and practices that we wish to submit to critical reflection. This was a test, moreover, and indeed a whole approach to moral reasoning, that Kant insisted he had not invented but simply provided with clarity and precision after thousands of years of more informal use.

Kant's modesty aside, his moral philosophy occupies a crucial place in the history of the progressive worldview, insofar as Kant clearly articulated a proposition earlier progressive thinkers had only danced around: that the cardinal moral value of progressivism is universalism. To appreciate the significance of this development, let us set aside the question of how the test of the categorical imperative might guide our personal ethical decisions, such as whether to keep our promises, and consider what happens when we apply this test to the political question of how we ought to organize and govern ourselves.

It was just noted that such early lawgivers as Moses, Hammurabi, and Solon gave Western society the idea of law, which contains within it the implication that laws are only laws if they apply to everyone, in every situation, always, as contrasted with commands, which are directives issued to specific individuals under specific circumstances. Having innovated the idea of law, most of these early lawgivers then took back most of what they had given by exempting themselves from the same laws they had just handed down. The first lawgivers, in other words, took a first stab at articulating the principle of universalism by proposing, in so many words, that everyone is equal before the king. This was a novel moral proposition, given that we are manifestly unequal in any number of ways, whether in terms of such intrinsic characteristics as physical strength and intelligence or such extrinsic traits as wealth and social status. But if the giving of the law—and along with it the abductive positing of the idea of law—was therefore a crucial moral development, administering it in accord with the principle of "equal before the king" fails to fully capture the idea of law since it makes abundantly clear that the king is *not* equal to his subjects, and he is *not* bound by the laws to which he binds his subjects. And this had inevitable consequences for how kings and other sorts of premodern leaders have traditionally ruled.

Granted, over the course of history, a handful of kings have probably been genuinely benevolent patriarchs, governing solely for the benefit of their subjects. Self-interest being what it is, however, even the most fair-minded of kings have typically used their disproportionate power to claim certain privileges they denied to others. Why be a king, after all, if you cannot enjoy the finest cut of meat at the banquet or get your first choice of wives? Kings have families, moreover, whom they not only love but rely on for political support. Accordingly, kings have typically extended certain privileges to their families and broader clans. As their realms grew larger, moreover—thus prompting the shift from rule by direct command to rule by law—most kings discovered they needed even more help than family could provide to administer their realms and maintain order among their subjects. Accordingly, they began spreading various privileges around to an even wider circle of retainers in exchange for loyal service, with most of these privileges amounting to legal permission to extract taxes, labor, or other forms of tribute from those beneath them in the social hierarchy.

Over time, therefore, a whole array of ranks emerged, with each level of the hierarchy having certain privileges and duties assigned to it. Those near the top of the hierarchy were accorded a wide array of privileges, while their primary duty was to enforce the rule of law upon those below them. This helped maintain general social order, but also kept a steady stream of material benefits flowing up the social ladder to fund all the privileges the king had doled out. Those near the bottom of the social order, conversely, enjoyed few privileges. They were rather saddled with a wide range of duties, most of them directed toward providing their superiors with a variety of material benefits. In practice, therefore, the law was never enforced with the universality the idea of law implies. What began as the king exempting himself from certain laws he applied to his subjects ended up producing a situation in which entirely different laws were applied to different levels of the social hierarchy, with the benefits stemming from these laws flowing up the social ladder, while their costs were thrust upon those farther down.

Thus was born the system of privilege upon which virtually every political order prior to Kant's time had rested. The system of privilege, moreover, was typically accompanied by an ideology of privilege. With those near the top of the hierarchy maintaining control over the priestly caste and other educated groups, that is, they used their power to ensure that their society's foundational narrative justified the existing hierarchical arrangement. This foundational story might be more mythical, religious, or philosophical in character, and it might be strongly colored by local conditions or the accidents of history. Regardless, because the story-telling classes owed their livelihood and protection to the upper classes, the stories they transmitted—perhaps with a few minor variations each generation—inevitably came to suggest that the prevailing social hierarchy reflected the natural order of things, thus making it right and good. Different individuals and groups, according to these foundational stories, are born with different degrees of inherent moral worth, so it is only natural that those born into the ranks of nobility should rule and enjoy certain material benefits, whereas those less exalted by nature should serve.

With their discussions regarding the social contract and natural rights, Hobbes, Locke, Jefferson, and various other early modern and Enlightenment thinkers had already made important advances against the ideology of privilege. Notably, Hobbes and Locke had re-framed the scholastic conception of natural right to suggest that there are certain rights people will possess—as a matter of logic—even in a state of nature, and that we cannot reasonably give up these rights when we enter civic society. Such rights are distinguished from privileges by their universality, whereas privileges are necessarily exclusive in scope. Locke's discussion of natural rights, in particular, was of tremendous historical significance, in that it helped Madison and the other American founders devise a new form of government that expressly limited the power accorded to the sovereign, in large part by specifying certain individual rights that the government was constitutionally prohibited from abridging. This crucial advance notwithstanding, it may be remembered from Chapter 3 that the arguments Hobbes and Locke used to logically establish the concept of natural right were fairly strained, ultimately resting on Hobbes's assertion that we cannot reasonably forfeit our right to self-defense, given that this forfeiture could never be enforced: someone can try to prevent me from defending myself only by threatening my life, but if I am fighting for my life, this threat will carry no weight. This argument has a logic to it, but the logic is so abstruse that it hardly generates a sense of moral urgency.

With the test of the categorical imperative, Kant opened

up a much cleaner line of attack on the ideology of privilege than contract theory had managed. Kantian ethics makes clear that if we want to distinguish ourselves as moral actors, as opposed to being governed solely by self-interest, we must behave in accord with the idea of law. This holds true no matter whether we are considering how we conduct ourselves as individuals or as whole societies. And because—as modern science makes abundantly clear—the idea of law implies universality, if the societies in which we live are to justify themselves as morally upright, the social practices, laws, and institutions upon which they rest must have the form of universality; their social, political, and legal structures must apply equally to every individual, in all cases, always. This exposes the contradiction that had been inherent to virtually every political system instituted up to Kant's time, dating back to the earliest lawgivers. Most premodern political systems claimed to ground themselves on the idea of law, yet the specific laws they instituted were not universal in scope. At a minimum, such laws contained massive exceptions for the leader, his family, and entire ruling classes. Over time, moreover, premodern political systems came to apply dramatically different laws to different social classes, with class membership being determined mostly by the accident of birth, thereby contradicting the very idea of law.

Kant's great achievement in the moral sphere was thus to expose the contradiction inherent to virtually every premodern system of governance while providing a relatively straightforward test to determine what modes of governance truly embody the idea of law, which is to say, what modes of governance possess the form of universality. Modern scientists like Galileo paved the way for this ideological shift by discrediting the Aristotelian metaphysics of discrete substances bearing properties—a metaphysics well-suited to justifying a social order that treats different classes of people differently, based on their distinctive inborn natures. With modern science turning its attention to universal laws that hold true across all of nature, Newton made particularly clear that, in the modern scientific context, we have no metaphysical grounds for asserting that the moon is any more exalted than an apple, since celestial and mundane bodies are equally subject to the principle of universal gravitation. When Hobbes made room for human beings in the modern conception of nature—accomplished through the abstractive act of considering how people must have behaved in a pre-civic state of nature—he established that human beings possess a similar natural equality, at least in the negative sense that nothing metaphysically distinguishes different individuals from one another in terms of their inherent moral worth. This explains why everyone has an equal say going into the negotiations that produce the social contract and why the sovereign can only derive its legitimacy from the consent of all those whom it governs. Hobbes and Locke then developed the notion of universality further through their discussion of natural rights, which can only be rights, as opposed to privileges, if they are universal. Finally, Kant pulled all of this together by establishing the metaphysical possibility of human freedom within a law-bound natural realm while giving us a relatively simple test to determine whether we are using our freedom to behave in moral fashion, whether as individuals or societies: Can the maxim of your action—or can the maxim shaping some particular social norm, law, or institution—at the same time serve as a universal law? Those principles, practices, and governing structures that can be universalized may be retained. Those that cannot must be modified or abandoned, at least if our goal is to render both our individual and our collective behaviors morally justified in a sense that withstands rational scrutiny.

It must be acknowledged that Kant himself did not push the method of moral critique he pioneered all the way to its logical conclusion. For one thing, he never wavered in his support for the institution of the monarchy, believing more democratic forms of government would necessarily lead to mob rule—a fear he saw being confirmed by the horror into which the French Revolution plunged over the 1790s. If Kant therefore believed, in principle, that humankind had come of age, to the point that people could start taking responsibility for their own actions, in practice, he was convinced the uneducated masses lacked the rational capacity needed to achieve moral autonomy; they were still moral children who required the care of a benevolent patriarch. Reflecting a similar mentality, Kant's scattered comments on women and such non-Europeans as Native Americans and Africans suggest it never occurred to him to include these traditionally marginalized groups as full-fledged members of the community of rational beings who might govern themselves in accord with the idea of universal law. Presumably, again, this was because Kant took it as a given that such non-male and non-white lack the rationality required for moral autonomy.

These prejudices on Kant's part are significant, and they

should not be glossed over, since they represent a failure to properly apply his own foundational concept of universality to various specific moral judgments he offered. At the same time, however, these failings highlight the advantage of Kant's approach to ethics, which was not to put forward a fixed body of moral prescriptions but rather to develop a method of critique. Had Kant given us a list of the fifty or a hundred things we should or should not be doing, anyone who wanted to be a Kantian today would be stuck with that same list—just as many Christians feel compelled to live by a moral code the authors of Leviticus spelled out nearly three thousand years ago. As it is, those of us who come after Kant are perfectly justified in applying the test of the categorical imperative to the specific moral prescriptions Kant did put forward, using the perspicacity we have gained through time and experience to critique those moral judgments we find to have been wrong.

In a broader sense, Kant's critical approach to ethics set the stage for a continual progress in the moral realm not unlike that found in the modern sciences, where Galileo made his key advances by critiquing Aristotle, just as Einstein would later take physics a step further by critiquing Newton. In the case of ethics, particularly as applied to the socio-political realm, the progress we have witnessed since the eighteenth century has been a slow, uneven, often bloody, but nonetheless discernible progress in the direction of greater universalism. More specifically, such progress has typically involved some traditionally marginalized group being drawn more within the social mainstream, often by granting its members some supposedly universal right or other form of equal treatment they had long been theoretically promised but were practically denied. Such changes are generally preceded by a period of critique, during which a relatively small number of activists, intellectuals, or ordinary citizens argue that the broader society is failing to live up to its own universalistic standards by permitting, or even promoting, certain traditional privileges, rather than treating all its members as equals; as Kant wrapped up his career, a handful of American abolitionists were just starting to make this case against slavery.

To be sure, even when some particular injustice does get diminished or eliminated, this usually just reveals more instances of privilege that had been so firmly ensconced in the culture that no one had yet thought to question them. This makes moral progress feel like a never-ending task—which it is. But that is the nature of progress, always more of a journey than a destination. And Kantian critique gives us a means by which to engage in an ongoing journey of social, political, and moral progress that is perhaps even more consequential to human well-being than the stupendous progress we have witnessed in the scientific and technological realms.

Why Be Moral?

Before we move on from Kant, we need to consider one final question that has been lurking in the background ever since Kant broke with the Hobbesian position that even moral actions must be self-interested. That question is: Why be moral? Granting that the test of the categorical imperative establishes, for instance, that we should keep our promises, why should we bind ourselves to the results of this test? Would I not be smarter to break my promise just this once, when I know I can get away with it and the results will benefit me greatly? Or shifting to the context of how we organize and govern ourselves, if I happen to occupy a social position where I enjoy a degree of power and privilege over others, why should I risk losing these benefits by advocating for a more universalistic social order?

To put a finer point on these questions, let us return briefly to Hobbes, who had the crucial moral insight that we can be morally bound to uphold only those laws or institutions to which we have freely bound ourselves. Should some aggressive, powerful leader take control of my community, I may choose to obey his commands as a matter of self-interest, but I have no moral obligation to respect his authority. I never consented to this governing arrangement, so this self-appointed sovereign enjoys no moral legitimacy. A sovereign's rule is only legitimate—and hence his subjects are morally bound to respect his authority—only when these subjects have collectively agreed to submit themselves to both the rule of law and the rule of the sovereign. In similar fashion, Kant argues that the moral law is binding upon us only because we freely chose to submit our actions to this law. Indeed, this is how we positively demonstrate our freedom and thereby gain moral autonomy: by governing ourselves, not at random, nor merely in accord with our interests—and thus as dictated by the laws of nature—but rather in accord with a law of our own giving, the moral law. But this prompts the question: why bind ourselves to the moral law, even in those cases where doing so may be contrary to our interests?

Why should we even *want* to be moral, in the universalistic sense Kant describes?

Given the rigor of Kant's approach, he makes this question very difficult to answer. In the Hobbesian context, the answer to the question of why the inhabitants of the state of nature should freely submit themselves to the rule of law and the sovereign's authority is straightforward: this is in their best interest. Even if relinquishing the freedoms enjoyed in the state of nature involves a sacrifice, this is more than offset by the peace, stability, and greater prosperity promised by civic society. In the Kantian context, when we raise the question of why we should be moral, we may similarly be tempted to ask *what interest* we have in being moral. And as noted already, we often *do* have an interest in behaving morally. If I refrain from attacking other people, I am less likely to be attacked; if I keep my promises as a matter of course, it is more likely other people will believe me when I need them to trust me. As Hobbes established, moreover, we all have a strong interest in belonging to a society that encourages and enforces socially responsible behavior. So, again, morality and self-interest will often coincide. This is fortuitous, in that it greatly increases the odds that most people, most of the time, will behave in morally permissible fashion. But we already know that, for Kant, if our actions are to be genuinely moral, we cannot be acting merely out of self-interest. On the contrary, morality requires that the guiding motive of our action be *distinguishable* from self-interest. Specifically, we must be acting for the sake of morality itself.

Yet, if we cannot answer the question, "Why be moral?" with some sort of interest we have in morality, what reason *can* we cite for acting morally, particularly in those inevitable instances where doing the right thing will conflict with our interests? This is a challenging question, but Kant attempts one direct answer to it. His answer still invokes an interest, although an interest of a different sort than usual. Most interests, for Kant, arise from inclinations: I feel hunger, or the inclination to eat, and this gives me an interest in finding food. Inclinations, in turn, generally arise from a physical cause: it is because my body is lacking nutrients that I feel hunger in the first place. Kant notes, however, that thinking and acting morally responds to a different sort of interest, namely, an "interest of reason."

To explain, recall the observation from the previous chapter that if the human mind possesses an inborn nature for Kant, it is to be constantly synthesizing, or constantly striving to unify the manifold mental content with which it is presented. This synthetic groping is what leads us to abductively posit such concepts as substance and causality as means of grasping particular objects and events within the sense manifold. Ultimately, this synthetic urge leads us to bind the entire sense manifold together under the concept of a unified world. With this innate striving to unify the manifold therefore giving the mind its innermost vocation, moral thinking and acting can help to advance this vocation in at least two ways.

First, we sometimes witness other people engaging in behaviors that appear to be altruistic, and thus are difficult to explain on the assumption that human beings can only guide themselves by self-interest. To be sure, we can dig deeper and try to discern the underlying interest a person may have in pursuing an apparently self-denying course. We might look for a social structure, for instance, that incentivizes an otherwise unrewarding behavior. Alternatively, we could posit a moral sense—updated with the latest neurophysiological knowledge—that shows why making a particular sacrifice might actually feel good. Such approaches may sometimes yield valuable insights into human behavior, but a more straightforward approach is to posit that the person we are observing is doing the right thing, simply because they should. Granted, the moral law is not a comprehensive moral system that tells us exactly what we should be doing at every moment—an arrangement that would give our diverse moral actions the strict unity of being derived from a single moral axiom. Nevertheless, the moral law does give us a common test to apply to all the actions we might propose, to see whether they fall within the bounds of morality. Accordingly, when a person invokes this test and uses it to guide their actions, we need not ask which of the hundreds of naturally-occurring inclinations may have determined their choice of actions. We can rather understand their behavior based on a single, unified principle: They have determined their actions through reference to the moral law.

Nor does this possibility of lending unity to the manifold apply only when I am considering the actions of others. In the case of my own actions, which I do not just observe but determine and perform, the moral law can lend a unity to my life that is lacking when I do nothing but pursue self-interest. Serving our interests, once again, requires responding to our inclinations, and our bodies impose countless inclinations on us. Some of these inclinations are obvious, but others are more subtle, making it difficult to discern which inclinations are determining any particular behavior. Some of our inclinations, moreover, directly conflict with one another: my inclination to drink wine tonight conflicts with my inclination to avoid a headache in the morning. To best serve our interests, therefore—or to maximize our happiness—we can engage in what utilitarian philosophers would later call a "eudemonistic calculus." We can try, in other words, to consider every possible interest we might have, weigh them against one another, then settle on the course of action that promises to yield the greatest net satisfaction. In practice, of course, no one has yet figured out how to perform such calculations with any degree of precision. Yet, even if we could manage the math, governing ourselves in this fashion means that our actions are being determined by any of the hundreds of inclinations that may be striking us at a particular moment, with no guarantee that an inclination guiding us today will not be overridden by a stronger inclination that arises tomorrow.

To be clear: binding ourselves to the moral law will not free us from these inclinations. My mind will still be flooded with inclinations that originate in the body, and to the extent that gratifying these bodily inclinations is permitted, or even required, by the moral law—I have a duty, for instance, not to let myself starve to death—I will still need to sort through my diverse inclinations and prioritize them, deciding which to indulge and which to deny. Nevertheless, because the overarching determinant of my actions will not be the multitude of inclinations swirling around my body and brain, but rather the question of whether my proposed actions accord with the moral law, my life is likely to be far more orderly and structured than that of the hedonist. Living a disciplined life of this sort may not give me the highest score on the eudemonistic scale. Indeed, to the hedonist, such a life may appear quite boring; the image of Kant walking to the university at the same time every day comes to mind. (Although, to be fair, Kant is said to have been quite cheerful and sociable.) In any case, the unity of purpose the moral law can bestow on our lives answers to the ultimate "interest" the mind has in holding its world together as a coherent, unified whole, thereby giving us a positive incentive—albeit of a unique variety—to engage in moral thinking and acting.

Whether or not this argument is particularly compelling, Kant's own approach to morality continues to stipulate that the morality of our actions cannot be derived from any of our interests, whether our natural, bodily-based interests or the more nebulous interest of reason. For our actions to be truly moral, we must perform them simply for the sake of acting morally; we must make morality an end in itself. But then, once again, why be moral? Ultimately, the only answer Kant can give to this question is that acting morally is the only way we can realize our autonomy. Binding ourselves to the moral law, in other words, is the only way we can realize our freedom in positive fashion. Kant's negative argument for freedom merely establishes that there is no contradiction in asserting both that nature is governed by universal laws and that human beings are free. Yet, because we cannot observe the human mind as it exists in itself, we cannot simply reflect on our thoughts to determine whether or not we are actually free. If we want to observe human freedom in action—if we want to empirically confirm that freedom is not just possible, but actual—we must demonstrate our freedom in the realm of appearances. And we can only do this through our physically manifested actions, specifically by acting in accord, not with the laws of material nature, but with the moral law.

To elucidate this point, Kant draws a technical distinction between autonomy and heteronomy. Heteronomy implies that we are not in control of our own actions, but rather we are controlled by some outside force, as when a slave has no reasonable choice but to do his master's bidding. As previously discussed, the condition contrary to heteronomy—autonomy—does not amount to living lawlessly. Granted, it may *feel* like I am manifesting my autonomy when I adopt an attitude of, "Eat, drink, and make merry." Having no cares for tomorrow, I freely indulge whatever inclinations happen to strike me at the moment. Yet, this just reveals the state of bondage I am in, precisely to my inclinations. For no matter how much I eat today, I will again be hungry tomorrow. In fact, the more I gorge myself on rich foods now, the stronger my future cravings will be, preventing me from feeling satisfied, or even thinking about anything else, until I have eaten further. To be sure, cravings of this sort are "mine," rather than being imposed upon me by some external agent. Nevertheless, these inclinations continually force their way into my consciousness, as if from beyond; they refuse to obey my command, instead making their own demands on me. And thus, when I use self-interest as the ultimate determinant of my actions—and particularly the undisciplined self-interest of the hedonist—I end up in a state of heteronomy just as strict as if I were enslaved by an external master.

It is important to note, moreover, that I can end up in this state of bondage even if I am king, or even if I occupy some other position of power and privilege in my society. Indeed, when I use my elevated social rank to better serve my own interests, then almost by definition, I am failing to govern myself in accord with the moral law, since if I were, I would recognize that my practice of demanding exclusive privileges at the expense of others is not universalizable. Absent any guidance from the moral law, I am likely to remain a slave to my own inclinations and interests. That is not to suggest we should pity the privileged of the world, as if their condition of moral heteronomy was just as lamentable as the material heteronomy under which they force others to live. The privileged, after all, can make themselves feel better by gratifying their inclinations; that is what privilege buys you. But the Kantian account of autonomy suggests that even the privileged of the world have an interest in submitting themselves to the moral law, notwithstanding that this may require a sacrifice of certain privileges. The "interest" thereby served is not the garden variety material interest, nor even an interest of reason. It is rather what we might call an "existential interest."

When I bind myself to the moral law, I place limits on my actions, including limits on how I indulge my appetites, but also on how I treat others. When I do this, I am—for once—fully in control of my actions. It is not that I have freed myself from my inclinations, achieving an interest-free state of being that many ascetics have dreamed of but few have achieved. Given my human condition, desires and aversions will continue to strike me, crowding into my mind as if from beyond. Nevertheless, when I bind myself to the moral law, these inclinations are not determinative for me. What determines my actions is the law to which I have freely committed myself. Subjecting my proposed actions to the test of the categorical imperative and abstaining from actions that fail this test, I am behaving in a fashion that does not violate the laws of nature, yet it is also not fully determined by natural laws, whether the law of self-interest or any other. And thus, through my actions, I begin to transcend the order of nature, not by acting in completely lawless fashion, but by governing myself in accord with a higher law of my own giving. This is moral autonomy.

Why, then, seek autonomy? Perhaps this question is best answered by posing yet another. Some half century after Kant wrote, the utilitarian philosopher John Stuart Mill asked: Is it better to be a happy pig, or Socrates unhappy? If we remain on the level of the pig—the level of nature, the level of inclinations and interests—this question almost answers itself. Given that, by Kant's definition, happiness is nothing but the abstract idea of fulfilling every inclination and interest we have, happiness is necessarily our highest interest, or that end which is to be preferred over all others. If we choose, we can remain on this level of nature: we can dedicate ourselves to gratifying our natural appetites and inclinations. And if we are fortunate—particularly if we happen to occupy a position of privilege in an affluent society—we may win some degree of happiness. Doing so, however, we are acting no differently than a pig wallowing in the mud. Perhaps we can use our superior brainpower to serve our interests more effectively than the pig, whether by winning a greater quantity of happiness or some more refined variety of happiness. But if achieving happiness is our final purpose, we remain chained to our inclinations and interests just as much as the lowest beast.

It is only by governing ourselves in accord with the moral law that we raise ourselves above the level of material nature and thereby invest ourselves with the unique dignity we fancy ourselves to possess as human beings. And this, ultimately, is the "existential interest" we have in being moral. We find ourselves existing, but we realize this is only for a finite span of time. Facing eventual death, we want our lives to have some meaning larger than ourselves. No doubt, the possibility of happiness provides our lives with considerable meaning, and Kant went so far as to suggest that unnecessarily forfeiting possible happiness amounts to a sin against life. Nevertheless, a life dedicated *only* to securing happiness fails to give us moral dignity, and dignity is an end worth pursuing in itself.

Ask a pig if it would trade its muddy happiness for the dignity of being a moral agent, and it will stare at you blankly: morality has no meaning to those who are limited, or who limit themselves, to existing on the plane of nature. The moral order only arises when we bring it into existence, first by abductively positing the concept of the moral law, then by giving this law an objective reality by using it to determine our actions in the world. Given the "unnatural" character of the moral order, it is only once we have glimpsed its possibility that we can understand why anyone should want to dedicate their lives to living morally. But ask Socrates if he would trade his moral dignity for the happiness of the pig, and he will not hesitate in his answer.

Looking Forward

And thus, as the eighteenth century ended, Kant had not only managed to capture the spirit of Progress that was born of the Scientific Revolution and thematized by the Enlightenment, but he had taken it several steps forward. Already with Descartes and Bacon, the conviction had arisen that nature is a rational order, and that human beings are rational creatures, suggesting that human beings can use their powers of reasoning both to better understand their world and to reshape it to better accord with their unique ends. Kant's theoretical philosophy only bolstered this conviction, first by confirming that nature is a rational, law-governed system, and second, by making clear just how dynamic and powerful human reason is. In this latter regard, Kant's theoretical philosophy showed that the human mind is not a mere calculator or mechanical processor of information, but rather a groping, grasping, creative risk-taker, constantly striving to synthesize the manifold content before it by proposing and testing novel modes of conceptualizing its subject matter. This experimental, abductive variety of thinking is what made the Scientific Revolution possible in the first place, and it gives us the capacity for ongoing intellectual progress—which, in turn, allows us to continue devising new and better means of serving our interests, whether in the physical realm, through the development of new technologies, or in the social, political, or economic realms, where we can use our growing knowledge of human nature to craft modes of social organization and governance that are more stable, cooperative, and productive.

Yet, if reason is therefore instrumental to the human quest to better serve those ends with which nature has bequeathed us, the mind's abductive capacity further allows us to propose novel ends of our own devising, including the end in itself of generating a whole new order of being: the moral order. This novel moral order does not contradict the laws of nature but rather transcends them by operating in accord with its own law, the moral law. As we have seen, the moral law is defined by the principle of universalism, with more specific prescriptions qualifying as moral only if they can be applied equally to everyone, in contrast to the traditional practice of applying different rules to different types of people, depending mostly on the station into which they are born.

To be sure, as the nineteenth century approached, the ideal of universalism was far from being realized to any great extent anywhere in the world. Even in the United States, the world's first nation to be founded on the proposition that all people are created equal, sharp contrasts in material and legal condition could still be found between masters and slaves, European Americans and Native Americans, men and women, wealthy and poor. Nevertheless, the American and French revolutions had demonstrated that socio-political orders that had seemingly been cast in stone could be challenged, overthrown, and rebuilt along new lines. And if a movement in the direction of greater universalism—no matter how halting and incomplete—was possible in these instances, further movement in this same direction could surely be achieved.

CHAPTER 7

WORLD IN MOTION: RUMBLINGS IN GEOLOGY

If the eighteenth century was the Age of Enlightenment, the nineteenth century was the Age of Industrialization. As the steam engine came into use on an industrial scale, it gave rise to many of the century's iconic images: massive machines of iron and steel belching out smoke, fireboxes glowing red with burning coal, factories full of clacking looms churning out textiles, "iron horses" roaring across the countryside on newly laid rails. Industrialization drew together many different streams of progress that we have been tracing over the seventeenth and eighteenth centuries. It was made physically possible by advances in such basic sciences as mechanics, thermodynamics, and chemistry, which in turn drove developments in technologies related to minerals extraction, metallurgy, and mechanical engineering. Economically, the rise of the factory system in Europe and the United States helped usher in the sort of full-scale capitalism that Adam Smith had foreseen, under which factory owners, materials suppliers, landlords, and workers do not just play separate roles in the production process but occupy completely different social classes. The extreme division of labor characteristic of factory production dramatically increased productivity, which kept average standards of living gradually rising throughout Europe and North America, the utter destitution of rural serfdom having been largely eliminated. That said, the fruits of industrialization were by no means equally divided, and the overworked laborers who now crowded into European cities began to pressure for more representative forms of government—pressures that occasionally burst into violent revolution, as with the widespread uprisings of 1848.

In the United States, the original "democratic experiment" was getting enduring legs beneath it. At the same time, however, industrialization was pushing the country's most blatant moral conflict to a head. On one hand, power looms in northern cities and England were driving a strong demand for cotton, thus giving slavery on southern plantations a second wind. On the other hand, the nation's expanding wage economy was making slavery ever more of an economic anachronism, and by the middle of the nineteenth century, crusading abolitionists were finally starting to convince some mainstream political leaders that a nation founded on the ideal of universal, inalienable rights simply could not force a significant portion of its population to live in chains. It took a devastating Civil War to eliminate the institution of slavery from the United States, and even this did little to correct the massive racial inequalities that had built up over hundreds of years of bondage. Nevertheless, Abraham Lincoln's signing of the Emancipation Proclamation in 1862 represented a significant—if overdue—step in the direction away from the privileged-based forms of government that had been the way of the world for so long, featuring one group that legally and morally dominates another, and in the direction of emerging regime of rights-based universalism.

Although "progressive" was not a label many people yet applied to themselves, the nineteenth century did see the rise of various intellectual, social, and political movements that we would now identify as progressive. In Germany, biblical scholars began to apply rigorous methods of historical research to the Bible, thereby putting its stories into historical context and calling their literal truth into question. Suffragists in many countries began advocating for an extension of the legal franchise to more groups, notably women. In the United States, social workers such as Sarah Hull sought to provide better living conditions for the urban poor, even as the first workers' movements began protesting for better pay and more humane working conditions, with an early focus on limiting the workday to ten hours. And while the avoidance of alcohol is not typically associated with the political Left, the temperance movement that ultimately led to Prohibition drew much of its support from nineteenth-century liberals, motivated by a desire to protect women from the violence frequently committed by their alcoholic husbands.

Still, for all the bustling action in the nineteenth century's economic, political, and social realms, we must return to the natural sciences for the events that would most dramatically impact the ongoing development of the progressive worldview. Indeed, the turn of the nineteenth century marks an inflection point in the evolution of the progressive worldview. As I will here describe it, developments in a variety of sciences over the nineteenth century occasioned a shift from the first major iteration of the progressive worldview to its second.

As we know well by now, the concept of progress first entered European thought with the Scientific Revolution of the seventeenth century, when a new approach to the study of nature began to produce stunning advances in learning. This sudden intellectual progress led Enlightenment thinkers of the eighteenth century to articulate a whole new worldview that regards history, not as going around in circles nor sliding ever downward, but rather as moving *forward* and *upward*. According to this Enlightenment view of progress—which I will start referring to as the first iteration of the progressive worldview—human reason is the primary driver of the world's progress, while the rational order of nature forms the stable, predictable arena within which progress can occur.

This precise conception of progress came into question as nineteenth-century scientists began making their own progress toward uncovering the workings of nature. Specifically, researchers in a variety of fields began to discern that human reason is not the only force that has been driving progress forward, nor does reason operate within the context of a static natural order. On the contrary, the world itself has been in motion—and for far longer than anyone had previously imagined—while human reason has not so much been the driver of this global progress as representing one of its most notable products.

The notion that human reason had its genesis in time, as a result of natural processes, would get a colossal boost toward the middle of the nineteenth century when Charles Darwin introduced his theory of evolution. Darwin's theoretical leap will be the focus of our next chapter. Laying the groundwork for this revolution in biology, however—both scientifically and philosophically—was less headline-grabbing work done earlier in the nineteenth the century in a discipline closely tied to rising industrialization: geology. The study of rocks is not typically associated with the progressive worldview, and our consideration of this topic in the present chapter will be correspondingly brief. Nevertheless, nineteenth-century geology deserves at least a mention in this history of the progressive worldview, for it was the first in a series of sciences over the nineteenth and twentieth centuries to challenge the Newtonian conception of nature, and by extension the first iteration of the progressive worldview. Geology issued this challenge less explicitly than some later sciences would, but nineteenth-century geology still stands as the first modern science to cast doubt on the Enlightenment premise that nature is the static container within which progress can take place, as opposed to being in constant motion, itself, even in its most fundamental architecture.

The Changing Conception of Nature: Static versus Dynamic

To expand on this last point, as the nineteenth century dawned, Newton's *Principia Mathematica* continued to serve as the archetype for the modern scientific conception of nature. Describing a universe governed by a relatively small set of mathematically formulated laws, the *Principia* portrays nature as a coherent, interwoven system in which every body stands in some determinate relation to every other. To be sure, Newton's motion laws allow for local movement within the system of nature—picture a diagram of the planets orbiting the sun—but the system itself remains augustly unchanging in its governing structures. Indeed, this constancy of nature is what made the Enlightenment conception of progress possible: it is only because nature is so regular in its behavior that scientists can not only discern the laws of nature but also use these laws to predict how nature will behave under certain circumstances, ultimately allowing inventors and engineers to modify these circumstances so as to produce outcomes that make life better for human beings.

This bedrock constancy of the world around us is what geologists called into question as they began to realize the earth is literally moving beneath our feet. Granted, some centuries earlier, Copernicus had already challenged the common-sense belief that the earth stands immobile beneath us. The notion that we instead live on a round orb that is constantly racing around the sun was unsettling to many of Copernicus's contemporaries, partly because it contradicts our everyday experience of a stationary earth, but also because it raises questions about the biblical story of creation, which implies that the earth and its human masters stand at the literal center of creation. Over the centuries, European society slowly came to accept the counterintuitive Copernican model, to the point that, by the early nineteenth century, only a few "flat-earthers" continued to hold out for geocentrism. Nevertheless, even among most scientists of the seventeenth and eighteenth centuries, the Genesis story of creation remained the default account of the world's origin, at least in its broad outlines—the heavens and the earth were created some six thousand years ago, and they have remained in essentially the same physical state ever since—for the simple reason that no one had yet suggested a more likely alternative.

Granted, the Newtonian model of the universe does not even require that the world has a beginning or end; Newton's universally applicable equations can extend backward into an infinite past just as well as they can project forward into an endless future. For most eighteenth-century Europeans who gave the matter any thought, however, the notion that the universe has always existed seemed implausible. Why, for instance, would human historical records stretch back only a few thousand years if the world had been around forever? And if our world was not created at some point in time by a wise and powerful designer, where did it get all the complexity, sophistication, and beauty it now has?

As the Scientific Revolution played out over the seventeenth and eighteenth centuries and a handful of scientists began turning their attention to the earth itself, some puzzles about our planet's history did start to arise. Ever since antiquity, seashells had been discovered in such unlikely places as mountaintops, far from any bodies of water. As long as such discoveries remained isolated, they could be attributed to some early traveler dropping a seashell while climbing the mountain, or perhaps a large bird depositing the shell at its present location. As mining began to grow in commercial importance, however, the vertical shafts being dug clearly revealed that the earth is composed of multiple strata of rock.

Many of these layers, moreover, were proving to contain fossils, including some suggesting marine life, even though their location was far from any contemporary bodies of water. Although such discoveries undoubtedly caused some head scratching, the biblical account does contain one ready explanation: just a few chapters after the creation story, Genesis tells of a Deluge that covered the Earth, sparing only Noah, his family, and the pairs of animals he managed to cram into his ark. Already by late in the seventeenth century, therefore, William Whiston was arguing in *A New Theory of the Earth* that the planet's stratified geology could be explained by the Great Flood sweeping across the earth, laying down its current layers of rock, along with the fossilized remains of any creatures swept up in the flood.

As geology matured into a full-fledged science over the late eighteenth and early nineteenth centuries, it had no Newtons or Kants: monumental figures whose work would come to define an entire intellectual era. Geology rather moved forward slowly and incrementally, gaining particular impetus from a series of interrelated debates that ran from roughly the 1870s through the middle of the nineteenth century. The first round of debate featured a pair of colorfully named protagonists, the Neptunists and the Plutonists. Following in the tradition of Whiston, while drawing on a growing understanding of the chemical processes involved in rock formation, Neptunists like Abraham Werner argued that minerals such as granite and basalt were formed when precipitants settled out of a great ocean that must have once covered the earth. Presumably, the precipitating event was the Great Flood, which is why the Neptunist position also came to be known as Diluvianism. Plutonists like James Hutton responded that volcanism, not flooding, was the key dynamic shaping the earth's geology. Pointing to the observable behavior of such volcanos as Vesuvius, outside of Pompeii, where eighteenth-century tourists could climb down into the crater and probe the molten lava with their walking sticks, Hutton proposed that most contemporary rocks began as molten masses that slowly cooled to their present temperature and solidity.

It should be noted that when Hutton formulated his Anti-Diluvian position, he was not simply expressing a personal preference for fire over water. On a more philosophical level, he objected to the Diluvian claim that the early earth was shaped by dynamics that differ radically from those we observe at work today. At the heart of Newtonian physics lies the assumption that the laws of nature are universal, working in the same way in all places, always. Diluvianism, Hutton felt, violated the spirit of modern science by arguing that the forces shaping the early earth were different in kind from those we observe today, and indeed, that these early forces arose only through divine action, rather than through the ordinary workings of nature.

As this debate moved into the nineteenth century, Hutton's broader position came to be dubbed uniformitarianism, in that it posits a uniformity over time to the geological forces at work on our planet. This position also implies the closely related stance of gradualism: given that the geological forces we observe today, such as volcanism and erosion, work very slowly, uniformitarianism suggests that the earth's current geology had a long, slow, relatively continuous development. Lively debate continuing, the opposing stance came to be known as "catastrophism," with advocates arguing that present-day geological features were shaped by a series of abrupt, catastrophic events that occurred at some point in the not-too-distant past. Originally, the goal of catastrophism was to reconcile the biblical story of the Flood with the growing body of empirical geological evidence. By the 1820s, however, the sheer number of diverse rock strata being discovered forced even catastrophists such as Adam Sedgwick to concede that there must have been numerous floods over time, some of them more localized than the Great Flood.

In 1830, Charles Lyell made a strong pitch for both uniformitarianism and gradualism in his widely circulated *Principles of Geology.* Lyell's book did not break significant new ground, mostly being a compendium of prior research. Nevertheless, its popularity among both professional and general readers made it the closest thing to a standard reference in mid-nineteenth century geology, thus helping tilt the overall scientific consensus in favor of uniformitarianism, where it has remained—with some caveats—ever since.

Scientific Implications of the Great Geological Debates

Looking back on the geological controversies of the nineteenth century from our contemporary perspective, we can regard them in a couple of ways. We can view them as a series of confrontations between, on one side, traditionalists whose first commitment was to preserve an ancient religious story, and on the other, forward-looking scientists committed to following the empirical evidence wherever it led, with the empirical approach—as in other fields—slowly winning out through its sheer explanatory success. More charitably, however, we can view these debates as a productive exercise conducted within the framework of modern science, given that all the different positions represented eventually proved to have some degree of empirical truth. Geologists came to agree, for instance, that Earth's crust is composed of three different types of rock. And if igneous rocks have their origins in the fires of volcanism, water is crucial to the formation of sedimentary rocks, thereby vindicating both the Plutonist and the Neptunist positions. (Composite rocks, pressed together by intense pressures beneath the earth's surface, form the third class of rock.) Similarly, as geologists continued to use empirical evidence to refine the story of the earth's geological history, they eventually agreed that, if this story has been dominated by long stretches of slow, gradual change, the quiet periods have been punctuated by catastrophic events ranging from floods to volcanic eruptions to meteor strikes, all of which have left their mark on present-day landscapes.

Because the science of geology itself had a gradual development, its protracted debates did not grab the popular attention that biology later would. Nevertheless, the conclusions toward which most geologists began moving challenged long-standing beliefs, most acutely for those with a religious orientation, but also for practicing scientists. Returning to the fossilized seashells that kept turning up on mountaintops, even as theoretical geologists engaged in their sweeping debates regarding the nature and cause of geological change, empirical researchers within the sub-discipline of stratigraphy—the study of rock layers—were quietly amassing ever more data. The first practitioners of stratigraphy had determined that the presence of fossils in rock strata is not just a curiosity but a key investigative tool, since the type and quantity of fossils found in each stratum give it a particular signature that distinguishes it from the strata above and below. And as researchers began to compare the stratigraphic results from various sites, a few key findings stood out.

First, similar patterns of layers were often found at remote locations, thus suggesting these distinct landscapes were formed by the same series of geological events. Second, many rock layers proved to contain marine fossils. These marine layers, moreover, were typically interspersed with layers containing evidence of land-based plants and animals, thereby ruling out the possibility that a single Deluge was responsible for shaping all our present geology. Third, and perhaps most striking, was the fact that, while the rock strata in some locations might lay flat, in more mountainous regions, these same strata could be found pointing upward at harsh angles, thereby strongly suggesting a violent uplift. The inevitable conclusion geologists began to draw is that the marine fossils now found on mountaintops had not been deposited when some flood swept over the Earth. Rather, these mountaintops were seabeds when the fossils were deposited, but then these seabeds were pushed up to their present altitude—often being knocked askew—by some tremendous force from below, whether volcanic or otherwise. Nor did all this happen in a single catastrophic event. Because the typical excavation revealed many different strata containing marine fossils, often interspersed with layers containing land-based fossils, the typical patch of the earth must have risen and fallen, not just once, but many times over the course of its history.

Even for the scientifically minded, this result was jarring, for several reasons. For one thing, it is difficult to imagine any mundane forces powerful enough to move mountains. The Copernican Revolution notwithstanding, if anything in our world is stable and steady, it would seem to be the earth beneath our feet. The evidence was showing, however, that the earth is in constant motion, even if—most of the time— this motion is unnoticeably slow. While this imperceptible movement may not have much impact on everyday life, it does give rise to a philosophical question: If natural forces are capable of elevating a seabed thousands of feet above sea level, later dragging this same mountaintop back down beneath the waves, not just once but numerous times, is our world really as stable in its superstructure as the idealized graphs and equations of Newton's *Principia* would suggest? Does nature really provide us with the solid, predictable platform upon which to exercise our powers of reasoning that the Newtonian model of the universe implies?

Second, as both uniformitarians and catastrophists were well aware, six thousand years is not nearly enough time for a river to carve a canyon out of solid rock, much less for a mountain to claw its way out of the ocean. Catastrophists, wedded to the traditional biblical timeline, took this as an argument for their position: they argued that there simply had not been enough time since our planet's creation for it to have changed as much as it has *other than* by means of a few quick, violent catastrophes, presumably occasioned by the world's creator. Uniformitarians found such religious arguments uncompelling. Convinced the physical evidence was indicating a much longer natural history of the earth, they suggested the Genesis account of creation must be non-literal in its truth, at best. Yet, even for these scientifically minded thinkers, unhindered by religious preconceptions, contemplating the new global timeline that was emerging must have been staggering.

Already in the mid-eighteenth century, George-Louis Leclerc had performed experiments with cooling globes to mimic what he believed were the conditions of the early earth. He interpreted his results as showing that, if the earth had cooled to its present temperature from molten magma, this cooling process must have taken at least 75,000 years. A few decades later, Lyell declined to offer precise estimates of the earth's age, but he suspected the planet must be much older, on the order of hundreds of millions of years. Bolstering this position, in 1862 one of the pioneers of nineteenth-century thermodynamics, William Thomson (Lord Kelvin) used analytical techniques more sophisticated than Leclerc's to show that a cooling of the earth from molten magma could have taken up to 400 million years. For perspective, this particular calculation suggests our planet is more than 60,000 times older than virtually everyone in Europe had long assumed.

Of course, if these numbers may have given even practicing scientists in the early nineteenth century some vertigo, for those whose first commitment was traditional Christianity, this dramatic pushing back of earth's origin was downright threatening. From a biblical perspective, the obvious question such an extended global timeline prompts is: Where do Adam and Eve fit into this ponderous story? And when did God create the other living creatures over whom he gave Adam and Eve dominion? Nor were other empirical discoveries in geology making the biblical literalist's job any easier over the first half of the nineteenth century. As stratigraphers continued to use fossil evidence to differentiate rock strata, some noteworthy patterns within the fossils themselves began to emerge. For one thing, although many fossils pointed to plants or animals that were familiar enough, others suggested odd variations on present-day organisms, while still others indicated creatures, the likes of which had never been seen. As a rule, moreover, the deeper investigators dug, the more unfamiliar the fossils became. Common sense dictates that the shallowest strata must have been laid down most recently, on top of accumulated older layers. With the most unfamiliar fossils therefore being concentrated in the oldest rock strata, this suggests such fossils were created by plants or animals which have since gone extinct. And because mid-level strata often feature fossils that are less bizarre, yet still noticeably different from the plants and animals we observe today, this suggests the characteristic features of these species have undergone significant changes over time.

All this conflicts, of course, with the biblical claim that God created all the plants and animals at the same time, "each after its kind," and that these species have remained fixed ever since. Faced with this troubling fossil evidence, some Diluvians argued that extinct species were the ones who failed to secure passage on Noah's ark. But since many of the strangest and oldest fossils indicated marine life—

presumably capable of surviving a flood—this argument was not persuasive among researchers who were fascinated by these new fossils that kept turning up. Among this latter group was a young English naturalist who became a protégé of Lyell before devoting most of his attention to biology, and eventually changing the world.

If the geologists of the early nineteenth century raised an initial challenge to the first iteration of the progressive worldview by calling into question the notion that nature is the stable, unchanging arena within which human reason can make its progress, the second iteration of the progressive worldview would not come into its own until Darwin had shown that human reason is not so much the primary driver of global progress as one of its products. Accordingly, we will reserve a more complete discussion of the second iteration of the progressive worldview for the end of the next chapter. To close out the current chapter, however, we can sum up the place nineteenth-century geology occupies in the history of the progressive worldview by suggesting an analogy to a prior development we have already considered in the history of worldviews.

Geology and the Progressive Worldview

At the beginning of this book, we saw that virtually all of the earliest human myths and religious narratives were cyclical in character. Drawing from the observable cycles of nature, and most particularly from the regular circles the sun, planets, and stars trace across the sky, these stories suggest that even as the world undergoes its regular cyclical change, the cosmos remains unchanged and essentially timeless in its fundamental structure. The Hebrew narrative first contested this cyclical, essentially static view of nature by introducing a linear conception of time in which events take place that permanently change the world, rendering "the time after" irrevocably different from "the time before." As we saw, the unilinear events of Hebrew narrative do not possess a single, overriding trajectory. The Tanakh, rather, portrays the people of Israel as undergoing a series of ups and downs, with periods of cultural glory being punctuated by times of dissipation and bondage. Nevertheless, the linear Hebrew story, with its conception of real and permanent change, set the stage for a pair of later foundational narratives that *would* give time a determinate vector, namely, the declinist narrative of traditional Christianity and the much later story of progress that the scientists and philosophers of the seventeenth and eighteenth centuries would eventually begin to tell.

This having been said, even as Newton was helping cement the progressive worldview's upward trajectory by showing that nature possesses a rational structure that human beings can discern and ultimately manipulate through the use of their reason—thus making real and meaningful progress possible in the human realm—Newtonian physics suggests a broader universe that allows for local motion, now exemplified by the cyclical motion of the earth and the other planets around the sun, yet this universe remains fixed and unchanging in its underlying architecture. Accordingly, when the geologists of the early nineteenth century proposed that even the ground beneath our feet is constantly moving, this put the timeless character of the Newtonian universe on notice. To be sure, the terrestrial changes geologists began studying do not possess a single, consistent trajectory. The rise and fall of mountaintops over the ages echoes the repeated rise and fall of the fortunes of the Hebrew people. Nevertheless, the dynamic natural history of the earth that geologists began to uncover in the early nineteenth century prepared the way for a series of later scientific advances that would give, not just the human world, but time itself an irreducible arrow, and one that points unmistakably forward and upward—albeit with some crucial qualifications.

CHAPTER 8

THE EVOLVING WORLD: DARWIN'S REVOLUTION IN BIOLOGY

———

Charles Darwin's personal story is well known. His father was a well-to-do physician who hoped his son would either follow him into medicine or become an Anglican priest, but Charles preferred to spend his time wandering the countryside, searching for interesting rocks and beetles. Knowing of this passion, one of Darwin's Cambridge University professors arranged to have him serve as the (unpaid) naturalist on the *Beagle*, a surveying ship that was scheduled to make a two-year voyage mapping the coast of South America. Charged with collecting and documenting noteworthy geological and biological specimens, Darwin was handed a copy of the newly released first volume of Lyell's *Principles of Geology* just before he sailed. Reading the book shipboard, Darwin was deeply impressed by Lyell's uniformitarian arguments for a gradually changing landscape, and for the dramatic results this could produce once the global timeline was extended into the millions of years.

When the *Beagle* made its first landfall on Saint Iago in

the Cape Verde Islands, Darwin used what he had learned in the *Principles* to think through how the island might have formed, later writing, "This showed me clearly the wonderful superiority of Lyell's manner of treating geology." Reaching the coast of South America, Darwin stumbled across a pair of relatively shallow fossil troves that included the bones of giant sloths and armadillos. Whether or not the young Darwin had yet begun pondering how these ancient, presumably now-extinct creatures might be related to their smaller contemporary cousins, the fossils bolstered his conviction that the extended geological timeline Lyell had assigned to the earth must be essentially correct. Much later in the *Beagle's* journey, which ended up lasting five years and including a sweep through the South Pacific, Darwin developed a theory of the formation of coral atolls. He sent a copy of his paper to Lyell, who was impressed enough to arrange a meeting upon Darwin's return, and thus began what would be a long professional collaboration and personal friendship.

The Galapagos Islands

Darwin's interest in geology notwithstanding, it was, of course, in biology that he would make his lasting mark. As the *Beagle* mapped a stretch of coast, Darwin would be dropped ashore, where he would spend weeks at a time exploring the local flora and fauna, taking copious notes and gathering specimens, which he carefully preserved and crated for shipment back to England. His most famous observations came during a tour of the Galapagos Islands, off the coast of Ecuador.

The first thing Darwin noted about these islands is that, while the Galapagos all form part of the same volcanic archipelago, each island has a subtly different landscape. Some of the islands are low and wind-swept, while others feature craggy hills. Some of the islands are almost completely barren, while others are more vegetated. What drew Darwin's attention next was the birds. Though bearing some resemblance to one another, the birds on the different islands each had their own distinctive features, varying most noticeably in the size and shape of their beaks. This observation is sometimes portrayed as the "eureka moment" in Darwin's thinking on adaptation, but in fact, Darwin did not pay as much attention to the distribution of distinctive beaks across the various islands as he later wished he had. It was only in reflecting on these observations much later that he began to realize that these variations were not random, but rather that each group of birds had a beak that perfectly suited it to the environment of its home island, and specifically to the primary food source available on that island.

To fictionalize slightly for purposes of illustration, on an island where the primary food source was small crabs or other shellfish, Darwin found that the birds had short, stout beaks, which they could use for cracking shells. On the next island over, where shellfish were lacking but insects were plentiful, the birds might have longer, thinner beaks, better suited to poking down into the rocks to root out grubs and insects. (Actually, what Darwin observed is that the birds of the Galapagos mostly dine on different varieties of cacti, each requiring a different beak shape to safely access, but such differences are a bit difficult to visualize, so in the discussion that follows, we will stick with our fictitious crab-eaters and insect-eaters.)

Darwin was not, of course, the first naturalist to note a frequent affinity between living creatures and the environments they inhabit. And with the religious training he had received while still thinking he might become a minister, he would have known the traditional theological explanation for this fortuitous alignment: when God created the earth and all of the creatures that would inhabit it, he created each animal "after its kind," giving each species the physiology that would best prepare it for the environment into which it was to be placed. Bass and cod, for instance, were given fins and tails so they could swim. Iguanas and rabbits were given legs on which to walk. And God gave the birds of the Galapagos not just wings to fly, but beaks specifically tailored to the environments of their home islands. And because God is a master craftsman who gets things right the first time, the argument ran, species do not significantly change over time. This would imply that the birds now inhabiting the various islands of the Galapagos are direct descendants of the birds God first placed there, having essentially the same physical characteristics as their divinely created forebears.

While this argument is straightforward enough, Darwin increasingly began to question it. As a general matter, he was sufficiently imbued with the spirit of modern science to resist appealing directly to God to explain every last detail of our world, without first looking for more natural causes. In this particular instance, moreover, as Darwin began thinking in terms of the extended geological timeframe that Lyell and others had proposed, the traditional account of species that remain fixed from the moment of their creation through the present day began to seem ever more unlikely. While the Galapagos Islands are sufficiently far apart from one another that birds cannot simply hop from one island to the next, they are not so distant that a bird could never make this crossing, particularly if blown by a strong storm. Perhaps if the world had just been around for 6,000 years, we could believe that each group of birds had stuck to its home island for this entire time. But if the islands have been around for millions of years, is it conceivable that each variety of bird would have remained right where it was created for this entire time, without occasionally venturing out and intermingling with its neighbors? And if many of the earth's landmasses have served as both seabeds and mountaintops many times over, rising and falling multiple times over the eons, how can we know these volcanic islands even existed at the time of creation for God to place its resident population of birds upon?

A New Theory Coming Together

Darwin may have mused on questions such as this as the *Beagle* made its way around the globe, but the real jolt in his thinking came when he returned to England and asked the noted ornithologist, John Gould, to examine the avian specimens he had brought back from the Galapagos. Having performed his dissections, Gould informed Darwin that the birds from the different islands were not members of different species, as Darwin had assumed, given the diversity of their traits. Rather, most were finches, or members of the same species. What exactly constitutes a "species" was already a matter of some debate among biologists, but the general rule they had begun to observe was, if two animals can successfully procreate, they are members of the same species. Obviously, Gould could not try breeding Darwin's preserved specimens to determine their mating possibilities. Nevertheless, his dissections made clear that these birds shared enough traits that it was unrealistic to think they did not come from the same species, whose ancestors were not merely capable of intermingling, but had once formed the same stock.

Other observations had already been leading Darwin to question the traditional belief that species are completely fixed and unchanging, or even that they can always be cleanly delineated from one another. Armed with what Gould had told him about the Galapagos finches, he began speculating that this larger population must have originated in a single flock, but then, as its members scattered across the various islands, each sub-group must have evolved certain unique traits to better adapt itself to the environment of its home island. By the middle decades of the nineteenth century, the notion that species might evolve over time was not something Darwin had to invent. His own grandfather, Erasmus Darwin, had been a physician and natural philosopher, and in 1794 Erasmus published a book titled *Zoonomia* in which he argued that the species are not fixed, but rather the individuals composing them tend to grow stronger and more vigorous over time. Erasmus's explanation for this phenomenon was simple. The strongest and most vigorous members of any population will be the most likely to breed—just think about two rams butting heads over the right to mate with a choice ewe. Accordingly, these individuals will pass their own virility down to their offspring. The weaker members of the population, conversely, will often be shut out of the mating game. Dying without procreating, their weakness will not get passed down. Given this twin dynamic of the strong reproducing and the weaker dying childless, the strength and vigor of the population can be expected to increase over the course of generations.

This "survival of the fittest" argument doubtless provided Charles with food for thought as he considered the Galapagos finches, but he later complained that his grandfather had done very little empirical research to back up his speculations. And although his grandfather's theory might explain how birds could grow *stronger* over time, it did not provide an obvious explanation as to how their beaks might get longer or stouter to better procure the food available to them. Another author who had addressed precisely this sort of question was the French naturalist Jean-Baptiste Lamarck. Over the first two decades of the nineteenth century, Lamarck laid out what was probably the first comprehensive theory of evolutionary change, which he grounded on two fundamental concepts: acquired characteristics and heritable change. According to Lamarck, an individual can subtly alter its morphology over the course of its life through the activities in which it engages. Giraffes, for instance, may have once had shorter necks, but as individual giraffes strained to reach the leaves from ever taller trees, each giraffe would have stretched its own neck just slightly. This claim was debatable, but not completely unreasonable; it was the second half of Lamarck's theory that was more controversial. When two giraffes that had stretched their own necks mated, Lamarck argued, they would pass this acquired characteristic down to their offspring. Each generation of giraffe would therefore start out with a slightly longer neck, with these individual giraffes then stretching their own necks even further through their continual straining. And thus, over the course of many generations, the whole species would have developed the long necks giraffes now have.

Although Darwin had been familiar with Lamarck's theory since his early student days, he never found it convincing. For one thing, while a giraffe might conceivably stretch its neck by straining for leaves, could a finch rooting around for insects, or amid the spines of a cactus, really strain hard enough to extend the length of its beak? More to the point, even if individuals may be able to acquire certain physical characteristics over the course of a lifetime, nothing we know about the reproductive process even remotely suggests acquired characteristics are capable of being passed down to the next generation. Indeed, a breakthrough in Darwin's own thinking came when he realized we have mountains of evidence concerning the relationship between reproduction and species change, and that a researcher need not travel to the Galapagos to study this evidence. Ordinary people, after all, have not only been observing species change for thousands of years but actively promoting it.

Ever since the first farmers began domesticating livestock, they have been breeding animals to better suit their own needs, whether this means individuals that produce more milk or wool, provide tastier meat, or better resist disease. Relying on common sense and experience, breeders the world over have all gravitated towards the same general practice: if you want to breed sheep that produce more wool, allow your woolliest rams and ewes to mature and mate, while eating your more scraggly lambs for dinner. As every breeder knows, pairing two wooly sheep will not always produce a wooly offspring. Sometimes, a scraggly lamb will result, and on very rare occasions, a lamb with some bizarre trait such as a third eye will be born. These cases on the margins notwithstanding, long experience has shown that, on balance, two wooly parents will tend to produce offspring that are at least as wooly, if not more so, than their parents. By pairing the most desirable adults, therefore, then again selecting among their offspring for further breeding, while culling out those individuals that do not possess the desired trait, the breeder can alter the average traits of an entire herd over time, accentuating those traits that are desirable, while suppressing those that are not.

With the mutability of species therefore being a surprisingly commonplace fact, at least when guided by the mechanism Darwin came to label "artificial selection," he still faced the question of how similar changes might occur in nature, where conditions differ from the controlled setting of the breeding ground in at least two ways. First, whereas a breeder can select for certain traits by determining who mates with whom, nature does not appear to have such a breeder in charge, regulating mating opportunities. Second, whereas the changes a domestic species undergoes are typically designed to benefit its human breeders—tastier meat, for instance—the changes that occur in nature generally seem to help the members of the changing species itself, as in the case of a beak shape that helps individual birds better exploit the food sources available to them.

Pondering these distinctions, Darwin's second breakthrough came when he encountered the writings of Thomas Malthus, an English economist whose theories helped to earn economics its sobriquet "the dismal science." Noting that most animals are capable of producing multiple offspring, Malthus argued that a typical population will grow exponentially: If two rabbits mate to produce four rabbits (a very conservative estimate for rabbits), their offspring will produce eight rabbits, which will produce sixteen rabbits, then thirty-two, and so forth. This exponential population growth notwithstanding, an animal's food source will typically grow only linearly: The carrots in a field may spread, but they will not multiply as quickly as the rabbits. Left unchecked, therefore, an exploding population will soon outstrip its food supply, thus leading to mass starvation, which will violently drag the population size back down to a manageable level— at which point its surviving members will mate again. To be sure, nature will sometimes provide a check on this exponential population growth, as with the foxes who hunt rabbits. Malthus warned, however, that because human beings had managed to defeat most of our natural enemies, we should soon expect to see a population crisis of apocalyptic proportions. Certainly this was a dismal enough prediction.

Whether or not Darwin shared Malthus's pessimism regarding the fate of humanity, what struck him was the more general point that the frequent scarcity of resources in nature implies that survival will often be a fierce competition. And this—combined with his grandfather's observation that the opportunity to mate generally falls to the victor—led Darwin to his fundamental insight. If life is a heartless competition for survival, those less equipped for the competition will typically perish, often before they have had a chance to reproduce. The winners, on the other hand, will be those individuals who survive for at least long enough to procreate, thereby passing their traits down to their offspring. And thus, without a breeder around to select among individuals for the most desirable traits, it is rather nature, and more specifically the natural competition to survive, that selects which animals will live long enough to breed. As a rule, it will be the fittest individuals who win this existential competition—not necessarily the "fittest" in the sense of being the strongest or most physically fit, as Erasmus Darwin had speculated, but rather those individuals whose attributes are the best fit for the environment in which they live. These attributes having been selected for through the success of their bearers, they will tend to grow more accentuated over time, whereas those traits that are disadvantageous will tend to die off, along with the individuals who happen to be born with them.

Darwin labeled this process of selecting for advantageous characteristics "natural selection," to contrast it with the artificial selection practiced by breeders. Most readers are probably familiar with how natural selection works, but for a simple example, we can return to our slightly fictionalized Galapagos. Let us suppose that, at some point in the distant past, a tremendous storm blows a flock of nearly identical finches from mainland South America to one of the islands of the Galapagos. Fortunately, the flock happens to land on an island with no other birds, but ample food of many different varieties. In this mini-Eden, the finches will continue to mate with one another, thereby producing offspring very similar to themselves. Minor variations will appear here and there—one chick may have a slightly longer beak than its siblings, another a beak that is shorter and stouter—but these differences will tend to cancel out over time, since any sort of beak will serve its bearer equally well on this well-provisioned island. Absent any competition for the plentiful resources available, the species simply does not have an impetus to change.

Paradise cannot last, however. Over time, other storms arise and blow small groups of these finches to other islands. As we know, the islands of the Galapagos feature different environments, most of them quite harsh. On one island, the only food available to finches might be grubs and insects tucked into the rocks. Under such conditions, those individuals that happen to hatch with longer, more slender beaks will have the easiest time obtaining food, whereas those individuals with beaks that are shorter and stubbier will struggle digging down into the rocks. And because, on this desolate island, even insects are in short supply, a finch that cannot efficiently root for insects stands a real chance of starving to death before it reaches reproductive age. With long-beaked finches therefore having a better chance of surviving, mating, and passing their traits on than their shorter-beaked counterparts, the next generation of finches on this island can be expected to have a slightly longer average beak length.

On the neighboring island, meanwhile, where the primary food available is small crabs, a contrary dynamic may start moving beak size in the opposite direction. When you need to crack open crab shells to eat, having a long, slender beak is disadvantageous, or even dangerous—your beak may break before the shell. On this island, therefore, those finches that hatch with longer beaks are more likely to perish before they reproduce, whereas those who inherit shorter, stubbier beaks will thrive, making them more likely to mate and pass this characteristic down to their offspring.

Stepping back to view these two groups of finches over the course of a very long time, the changes in beak size that occur each generation may be quite subtle. Over hundreds of generations, however, these modifications will compound themselves to the point that the birds on the two islands look very different from one another, each having adapted its physiology to the conditions of its environment. At some point, these changes may progress to a point that, should another storm blow the two populations back to the same island, they will not intermingle and produce joint offspring. Perhaps the members of the two groups will simply decline to mate with one another, each finding the other sexually unattractive, with their ugly beaks. Or if the two populations have been separated for an extremely long time, and the differences in their morphologies have become even more pronounced than what Darwin observed among the Galapagos finches, the two groups may find themselves physically unable to couple, or unable to produce viable offspring if they do. When this happens, naturalists will conclude the original species has diverged into two distinct species. To be sure, we are dealing with some murky gray areas here, not the nice, clean lines that had traditionally divided species. Yet, as Darwin saw it, the messiness creeping into his account of speciation was not an argument against it. Rather, it provided confirmation for his rising conviction that species are not fixed, discrete, metaphysically real categories, but rather fluid and sometimes arbitrary groupings that are constantly being transformed by slow and subtle changes over time.

With Darwin now having the basic principles of natural selection on the table, he had little trouble recognizing that the Malthusian competition for scarce resources will not just occur between individual members of the same species. It will also play out between species. Imagine, for instance, that our long-beaked finches get blown to an island already inhabited by a lizard that uses its long tongue to dig insects from between the rocks. Perhaps this island originally contained enough insects to support its resident lizard population, but now that birds are competing for this same resource, scarcity sets in. Which species will fare better in the resulting competition? The short answer is whichever species can grub insects more efficiently. If a beak turns out to be better for digging among the rocks than a tongue, the island's new bird population will start gobbling up most of the insects, thus leaving the lizards that once ruled the island starving. If the lizards are unable to adapt, perhaps by switching to an alternate food source not fancied by birds, their numbers will likely diminish over time, until—unable to compete with the flourishing bird population—the species goes extinct. Or if a lizard tongue turns out to be a better means of digging out insects than a long beak, it may be the finches that go extinct.

Looking back over the hundreds of millions of years that plants and animals had been living, dying, and leaving behind fossilized remains, Darwin could see that this same dynamic must have played out innumerable times over the course of the world's history, thereby explaining the fossils of extinct species geologists had long been encountering. In the case of shallower fossils bearing a resemblance to present-day creatures, such as the giant sloths and armadillos Darwin had seen in South America, some environmental pressure must have begun selecting for individuals more like the contemporary versions of these animals. Perhaps shrinking food supplies, for instance, had given smaller sloths and armadillos—requiring less nourishment—an advantage over their larger compatriots, thereby leading to a gradual diminishment in the average sizes of these two species. In the case of those fossils that are more deeply buried and give evidence of creatures that are wholly unrecognizable today, they must represent species that went completely extinct—essentially the end of the line for certain experiments nature ran, which may have been successful for a time, but which ultimately collapsed as the species encountered new competitors or other environmental challenges it could not overcome.

As the various pieces of Darwin's theory of evolutionary change fell into place, he repeatedly held off on publishing his results. His hesitation was partly due to scientific scruples; he wanted to be certain all the details of the theory were not just correct but supported by overwhelming empirical evidence before he went public. Yet, his tentativeness likely also sprang from another source. The more evidence he accumulated, the more convinced Darwin became that species had, in fact, evolved over time. But he also knew this flatly contradicted the biblical doctrine of fixed species, and he worried about the anguish his theory would cause among those of a more traditional mindset—including, not least, his beloved and highly devout wife Emma. Indeed, even Darwin's onetime mentor and close friend, Charles Lyell, admitted he had difficulty accepting that species are as pliable as the earth's crust, capable of gradually transforming themselves over time. So, if the theory of evolution was going to be a hard sell to Lyell, how would it go over with the public?

Having delayed for nearly twenty years, Darwin was startled in 1858 to receive an academic paper from a younger colleague, Alfred Russel Wallace, who was in the middle of an eight-year research expedition to the Dutch East Indies. The paper was only a few pages long, and thus it did not include any of the detailed evidence Darwin had been amassing, but it unmistakably identified natural selection as the mechanism by which species evolve over time, even using this same label. Unwilling to concede priority to Wallace, yet also not wanting to behave unfairly toward a sharp-witted young colleague who had reached out to him in good faith, Darwin turned to Lyell for advice. Lyell's misgivings about the whole notion of evolution notwithstanding, he judiciously arranged for a joint reading of papers by Darwin and Wallace before the Linnean Society. The event, as it turns out, attracted little notice. A year later, however, Darwin followed up with the publication of his full manuscript, *On the Origin of Species*, and a firestorm erupted that still simmers to this day.

The Theory of Evolution Goes Public

By the second half of the nineteenth century, most travelers in European and American intellectual circles were ready to concede that the traditional story of Adam and Eve in the Garden of Eden probably contained more figurative than literal truth. *On the Origin of Species*, however, was not just suggesting some minor revisions to the long-accepted story of life on earth. It was proposing a complete re-writing of this story. As Darwin now told it, in the beginning—whenever that might be, with Darwin guessing around 300 million years ago—there were no finches, armadillos, or other modern species. In the beginning, rather, the earth was devoid of life. Then at some point in the very distant past, some exceedingly small and simple life forms somehow came together. Darwin did not pretend to know how this happened, but he speculated it may have occurred in some wet and sheltered environment like a tide pool, where just the right mix of chemicals got jolted into a state of higher organization by some external energy source, perhaps a lightning strike. In any case, however these first proto-organisms originally came about, once they existed, and particularly once they had developed the means of reproducing themselves, the competition was on. Life, as it turned out, was a perpetual competition for the scarce resources needed to stay alive, for at least long enough to reproduce and pass one's own essential traits down to the next generation.

As Darwin realized, the world's first tiny, single-celled organisms would have reproduced asexually, basically just splitting in half to create two identical copies of the parent cell. Even in this case, however, nature can make mistakes, and an offspring can result that is slightly different from its parent. As soon as such differentiation occurs, the competition for survival begins to hinge on more than just the grit of the individual participants. Rather, those organisms that happen to come into existence with the traits best suited to the local environment will be the most likely to survive and pass their traits to the next generation, while less-advantaged individuals are likely to die before reproducing. Through this process of natural selection, the typical characteristics of the whole species may begin to change in subtle ways that are advantageous to its members. Yet, because the earth is large and contains many different environments, an adaptation that works well in one place may prove disastrous in another. Hence, as life began spreading around the globe, it would have branched out, with primitive organisms that possess one trait thriving and reproducing here, those possessing another trait doing better over there. At some point, one or more of these groups must have stumbled into sexual reproduction as a means of passing down their traits, which just increased the possibilities for differentiation among the younger generation and thereby quickened the pace of change, both within species and in terms of their branching out into distinct species. So, by this point, the competition was *really* on.

Once multiple species are present within an environment, and particularly once they have branched into the distinct classes of predator and prey, the struggle for survival becomes not just a competition among the individuals within a particular species but a competition between species. Those species that are best able to obtain food and perform the other tasks necessary for survival—including not becoming food themselves—are most likely to survive as species, whereas those that cannot compete go extinct. Yet environments, themselves, change over time, so even a species that thrives one day may be overtaken by some upstart species the next, whether because this younger species already happens to be better suited to the new environment, or because it is better able to adapt to the changing conditions. As a rule, the more sophisticated a creature is—whether in terms of its morphology, metabolism, sensory capabilities, powers of locomotion, intelligence, or any number of other factors—the better equipped it will be to exploit its current environment, and the more capable it will be of adapting to changing circumstances. Accordingly, over the eons, the story of life on earth has involved a gradual movement from the relative simplicity of the first proto-organisms in the direction of greater complexity and sophistication. The leading characters of this story, as Darwin now told it, were not God, Adam, and Eve, but rather first the amoeba-like creatures swimming around in tide pools, later to be joined by larger fish, then amphibians, then much later such relatively sophisticated land-based animals as reptiles, birds, and finally mammals.

When Darwin wrote *On the Origin of Species*, he was careful to avoid any mention of the place human beings occupy in the story of life he was now telling, foreseeing how much angst and moral outrage this would cause. Even his opponents, however, could easily see where the story was headed. If every other living creature is descended from some single-cell organism swimming around in a tide pool, can we expect that human beings will be any different? As Darwin's earliest critics liked to frame the most shocking charge they leveled against him: Charles Darwin believes human beings are the descendants of apes. This charge was not completely accurate. When Darwin did finally address the topic of human evolution toward the end of his life with the publication of *The Descent of Man*, he argued, not that humans are descended from modern-day apes but rather that the two species share a common ancestor, some earlier, now-extinct species of primate. The technical distinction was lost on Darwin's opponents, for it did not alter the fact that Darwin was denying human beings are created in God's image, set atop the hierarchy of the created world. Darwin was rather asserting that human beings are no different from any other beast that clawed its way out of the swamp, a product of random chance, blind evolutionary forces, and the cutthroat struggle for existence.

Indeed, to take a step back farther, Darwin's evolutionary theory did not just threaten to rob human beings of their God-given dignity but seemed poised to write God right out of the larger global narrative. Over the seventeenth and eighteenth centuries, as we have stressed numerous times, even most scientists continued to assume that God not only created the world at a particular point in time but had designed it with the care of a master architect, the elegance of the Newtonian universe reflecting God's own supreme rationality. And while it is true that Newton's laws were allowing scientists to provide naturalistic explanations for many diverse phenomena once ascribed to divine intervention, it still seemed that the phenomenon of life, and particularly human life, is so complex and purposively ordered that it simply could not have arisen through the blind workings of nature. Life must have rather had an intelligent creator. And yet here was Darwin claiming that the existence, not just of lizards, birds, and fish, but even human beings, can be explained through natural causes alone. All you need is a reproductive capacity with some potential for variation, a competition for scarce resources, and an enormous stretch of time, and the simplest protozoa will eventually transform itself into Dante, Galileo, or Mozart. If nature can do this on its own, who needs God?

Darwin and the Progressive Worldview

Unsettling as Darwin's theory may have been for many, particularly those of a more traditional religious bent, the mechanism of natural selection was so simple and intuitively clear that, within just a few decades, it had won almost universal acceptance among biologists. Darwin's theory similarly came to be embraced by many non-scientists who leaned in a progressive direction, given that it took a concept they already championed, the Enlightenment notion of progress, and developed upon it in novel fashion.

As noted in the previous chapter, the conception of progress that had developed over the seventeenth and eighteenth centuries—the first iteration of the progressive worldview—rested on the Newtonian premise that the universe is a stable, rational order that allows for local motion, even as it remains majestically unmoved in its broader structures. This stability, in fact, is what gives nature its lawful predictability. And as modern scientists made progress in discerning the laws by which nature operates, this knowledge allowed people to start reshaping the world to better serve their own, uniquely human ends, whether in the realms of technology, politics, economics, or morality. For the thinkers of the Enlightenment, therefore, we could say progress was one of the varieties of local motion that the broadly unchanging Newtonian universe could accommodate, while human reason was the primary driver of this forward and upward motion.

By around the turn of the nineteenth century, geologists had begun to realize the larger world is not as static as everyone had once believed. On the contrary, even the earth beneath our feet is in constant motion. Granted, this geological movement is typically very slow and gradual, which explains why we rarely perceive it. Yet, the account of the earth's history that nineteenth-century geologists began to relate also pushed the global timeline back much farther than anyone had previously imagined, at least into the hundreds of millions of years. This challenge to the traditional biblical timeline, in itself, doubtless caught the attention of many who were progressively minded. Still, geological change has little clear directionality to it. Noteworthy as it may be when a seabed becomes a mountaintop or vice versa, it is difficult to regard such change as *progress* when it does not appear to be headed in any particular direction; hence the comparison to the ancient Hebrew narrative, a linear, unidirectional story that features plenty of action, yet contains so many ups and downs that the plotline lacks an overriding vector.

Things were different with the biological story Darwin began to tell. Like his colleagues in geology, Darwin was proposing that one of the world's most fundamental structures, long assumed to be rigid and unchanging, is actually quite fluid. In this case, the structure was the division of living creatures into distinct species. The change these creatures have been undergoing, however—while still quite slow and gradual—is unambiguously linear in character, at least in the sense of being unidirectional. Featuring a cast that includes, in order of appearance, bacteria, fish, amphibians, mammals, primates, and human beings, the drama cannot begin with humans, then work its way back to bacteria, nor can it skip or rearrange any of its various scenes. The evolutionary story must rather start with single-cell organisms and move forward from there. Indeed, the plotline of evolutionary history features a consistent, unmistakable trajectory: forward and upward. However one chooses to define "progress," the evolution of species is clearly, unquestionably an example of it. Any rational observer will agree that human beings are more sophisticated than monkeys, just as monkeys are more sophisticated than fish, just as fish are larger, more complex, and capable of more elaborate behaviors than bacteria.

What was perhaps most striking about the story Darwin and his fellow biologists began to tell, however, clearly moving it beyond the first iteration of the progressive worldview, is that the story does not involve human beings using their powers of reasoning to make progress within a static world. Rather, evolutionary theory portrays the world, itself, as changing over time, with human reason serving not as the primary driver of this progress, but rather as one of its most distinguished outcomes. To be sure, this new manner of conceiving progress did not completely displace the Enlightenment view of progress. The world Darwin describes is still a rational order, with the evolution of species having a logic all its own—namely, the logic of natural selection. Human reason, moreover, still makes its appearance in Darwin's portrayal of nature, and thus it still allows people to pursue all the uniquely human varieties of progress Enlightenment thinkers had envisioned. Nineteenth-century science, however, began to set the story of human progress against the backdrop of a much larger, longer story of global progress. The suggestion began to percolate up that progress may not just be a form of local motion, set within the world's static architecture. Perhaps progress itself is one of the world's defining structures—albeit a dynamic structure, ever building on its past accomplishments.

We can therefore understand why Darwin's theory struck such a chord among readers who were already progressively inclined. Indeed, for as much as Darwin worried about the social and moral implications of his theory, when we view evolutionary theory through a progressive lens, it turns out not to drag human beings down to the level of apes, much less to that of lungfish or protozoa. On the contrary, there is a real sense in which the evolutionary story accentuates the traditional human role at the apex of the natural order. To be sure, nature itself does not ascribe any particular value or significance to the human species on the Darwinian account.

Evolution is undirected, so we cannot pretend that other creatures have been evolving over the course of millions of years simply to produce us. Nor can we even guess whether human beings are the highest lifeform nature will ever produce. Perhaps in some distant future, a new species will evolve that transcends our capabilities. Or perhaps on some distant planet, nature has already produced a creature more sophisticated than ourselves. Regardless, in the world relevant to us, here on planet Earth, human beings are the most sophisticated, most intelligent, most adaptable type of creature that has yet emerged, the product of an evolutionary process that has been working itself out for an unimaginably long time. And while this does not invest us with any sort of metaphysically prefabricated moral virtue, evolution *has* equipped us with the powers of reasoning we require, not just to survive and thrive in the natural order but also to transcend the natural order by constructing a law-governed moral order, thereby fashioning a unique moral dignity for ourselves.

And thus, as the nineteenth century entered its final decades, Western society had begun to view the world's trajectory in two starkly different ways. Religious conservatives still clung to the traditional declinist narrative of humankind's fall from grace and subsequent downward slide, with growing secularism in Europe and North America just seeming to bolster the case that the world was fast approaching its final plunge into the abyss. Among secularists and the growing class of religious liberals, conversely, the mood was increasingly one of giddy optimism. Sharing with their Enlightenment forebears the conviction that, after nearly two thousand years of political and ecclesiastical authorities holding human reason in chains, thought had once again been freed, liberals of all stripes welcomed the sudden and remarkable progress that was being made in realms ranging from science and technology to politics and social policy. Now that Darwin's theory was on the table, moreover, there was a growing sense that this progress was not just a human phenomenon but was rather an instance of a much larger global evolution that had been taking place since long before human beings came on the scene. According to this second major iteration of the progressive worldview, it was becoming clear that nature itself has a bias in favor of progress, taking the form of a steady increase in the observable degrees of order, complexity, and sophistication.

This optimism notwithstanding, storm clouds were looming. The biggest tempests, of a sort that would consume nearly all Western society and much of the world beyond, would not erupt until the early decades of the twentieth century. Nevertheless, the underlying tensions were already building in the final decades of the nineteenth century. We could certainly consider some of the more specific conflicts that were brewing in the social, political, or economic realms. In keeping with our thesis, however, that as the progressive worldview has developed, the single most important force driving and shaping its evolution has been the concurrent advance of the modern natural sciences, to get a sense of the headwinds the progressive worldview was just starting to experience, we must turn next to the relatively obscure science of thermodynamics.

CHAPTER 9

THE HEADWINDS AGAINST PROGRESS: THE SECOND LAW OF THERMODYNAMICS

———

At the end of the last chapter, it was noted that the story of evolution is irreversible: single-cell organisms may eventually evolve into people, but the story cannot run in the opposite direction, starting out with people who evolve into single-cell organisms. And this posed a challenge to Newtonian science, since one of its hallmarks is reversibility. Using the equations of *Principia Mathematica*, you can describe the path by which Earth travels around the sun with great precision. It is a matter of complete indifference to these equations, however, whether Earth is moving clockwise or counterclockwise. It follows that if you were shown a film of Earth orbiting the sun and you had no prior empirical knowledge of our solar system, you would have no idea whether the film was running forward or backward. Indeed, this reversibility helped give the Newtonian model of the universe its timeless quality. Although local motion is possible in Newton's world, what actually *happens*—how events start and how they end—fades into obscurity as the rational structure of the whole is what persists.

We know from everyday life, however, that some stories *cannot* be told backward. Setting evolution aside for the moment, imagine watching a time-lapse video of an ancient temple crumbling from its original glory to its present ruined state. It will be obvious whether the film is running forward or backward. Indeed, if you were shown the film backward, you would quickly object that something is wrong with the movie, since we know from experience that temples may erode, but they do not spontaneously spring from piles of ruins. By the same token, eggs may break, but broken shells do not knit themselves together. Or place a drop of black dye in a glass of water, and the drop will slowly disperse until the entire glass is pale gray. Watch the colored water for as long as you like, but the dispersed particles of black dye will never reconvene at the center of the glass to form a concentrated drop.

Newton's laws notwithstanding, therefore, it appears some changes in nature are simply not reversible. Some events appear to have a flow that is not just linear, but unidirectional, where A can lead to B, but B will never be followed by A. The examples just cited make clear, moreover, what many of these irreversible changes have in common: They involve a movement from greater order to lesser order. Without getting bogged down by a technical definition of "order", it is obvious that, on the day the ancient temple was completed, when every stone was in its proper place, the temple was more ordered than it is now, as the stones from its collapsed walls lie strewn about the ground. It took scientists most of the nineteenth century to determine that this tendency of nature to move from order to disorder is a universal law, but this has since come to be viewed as one of the most foundational, most certainly known laws of nature. Going by the imposing title of the second law of thermodynamics, this law is what gives time its arrow, ensuring not only that the events of our world play out in linear fashion, but that a film taken of any significant portion of these events will have a distinguishable "forward" and "backward."

Nature's universal tendency to move from order toward disorder is a puzzling phenomenon, however, not least because it appears to contradict virtually every phenomenon we have studied up to this point in this book. Most obviously, we just spent a chapter considering evolutionary development, and while this type of change is linear and irreversible, it appears to be a movement in the *opposite* direction of what the second law would dictate, with minimally ordered protozoa transforming themselves into highly ordered human beings. But earlier chapters featured their own transformations from lesser to greater order, albeit most of them in the human realm. In the Hobbesian state of nature, warring individuals came together to form larger, more peaceful, and increasingly more sophisticated civic societies. On Smith's account of the state of nature, isolated jacks-of-all-trades began specializing their labor and trading with one another, ultimately leading to interwoven market economies and ever more complicated modes of factory production. Even in the moral realm, Kant showed how the anarchy of the inclinations can be countered by giving one's actions the unity of the moral law. Indeed, it was precisely such examples of movement from lesser order to greater order that was driving the rise and development of the progressive worldview, giving people a sense that the world is not merely *capable* of getting better over time, but that it *has* been getting better over time—indeed, since long before we were around—with "better" appearing to be at least closely linked to "more highly ordered." Yet, how can we square this progressive view of a world growing more ordered over time with the second law of thermodynamics?

This is a question to which we will return at the end of this chapter, once we have gained a greater understanding of how the second law works. The route scientists took to identifying this law was circuitous, so this will be a long chapter, spending much of its time a long way from the philosophical implications of the second law. The effort will be worth our while, however, for it will reveal the physical underpinnings for a fact of life with which any mature conception of the progressive worldview must come to grips, namely, that progress is hard. Progress will always be hard. But it is nonetheless possible.

To work our way up to this lesson, we must first return to the beginning of the nineteenth century, when the scientists doing the research that would lead to the discovery of the second law had no idea they were studying order and disorder, much less that their work would end up challenging both Newtonian physics and the progressive worldview. They were just trying to build a better steam engine.

The Quest for Mechanical Efficiency

As the nineteenth century dawned, industrialization was ramping up in Europe and North America, and the steam engine was its driving force. The workshops of earlier centuries had relied mostly on human power, sometimes supplemented by a horse turning a wheel—hence the term "horsepower" as a measure of power. Later in the eighteenth century, as factory production began, the first factories began springing up next to streams so that waterwheels could be used to turn their shaft-driven equipment. This led to dramatic increases in productivity, but waterpower has certain limitations. Most significantly, the power available to any factory is limited by the size of the stream on which it sits. Furthermore, the mere fact that the factory's location is dictated by geography—rather than, say, proximity to suppliers, workers, or customers—is a restriction in itself. These limitations were transcended by the steam engine, since industrialists could always purchase more or larger engines if they wanted to increase their output, and they could locate their factories wherever they pleased, including in the middle of urban centers.

The shift to steam power thus spurred even greater increases in productivity, yet steam engines come with costs of their own. Not only is there the initial expense of purchasing an engine, but for an engine to do its work, it must be fed large amounts of fuel. The first steam engines burned wood, but by the nineteenth century, coal was the fuel of choice. And while steam power was helping make coal mining more efficient, with some of the first steam engines being used to pump water out of mines, mining was still expensive. This meant that every ton of coal getting shoveled into an engine's firebox was cutting into the industrialist's profits. Accordingly, both factory owners and the engineers they employed had a keen interest in building more efficient engines, or engines that would generate greater output, using less coal. The research in this field led to the development of a new science, which one of its originators dubbed thermodynamics: the study of the flow of heat.

Contemporary thermodynamics recognizes four laws, but only the first two of these are relevant to our discussion here. The first law of thermodynamics, better known as the principle of conservation of energy, was not formally proposed until around 1850, but various scientists were working their way up to its articulation over the first half of the nineteenth century. In fact, there is a sense in which students of nature had been searching for this principle since the early days of the Scientific Revolution, if not since antiquity.

The Search for Conservation Laws

When the earliest Greek philosophers began trying to give a rational account of nature, as opposed to invoking mythical or religious narratives, they focused on the question of what the world is made of, or of what constitutes matter. Thales, usually considered the first Western philosopher, argued that everything in the world is water. Though unintuitive, this claim reflects the crucial insight that, if the world is to behave in regular, predictable fashion, something must remain constant, even as the objects we observe undergo constant change. Drawing on the fact that water can transform itself into solid, liquid, or vaporous forms, yet remain water, Thales concluded that water is the best candidate for such a principle of constancy. Other pre-Socratic philosophers offered their own theories of matter, holding that the world is composed of fire; of Love and Hate; of innumerable seeds; or of a mix of earth, air, fire, and water. While differing in their details, all these claims were meant to provide the most reasonable explanation of what remains constant throughout the process of physical change.

Although the pre-Socratic approach suggested a unified, rational order of nature, it did not offer much predictive power as long as it remained nothing but a qualitative account of what composes the world. And when Aristotle then argued that what remains constant over time is, in fact, unified substances bearing their own inner natures, this split nature into a conglomeration of discrete objects, and the search for a common term binding everything together was put on hold for over two thousand years. The search was only revived in the seventeenth century, when the Scientific Revolution was spurred by a pair of insights: nature is governed by certain universal laws, and these laws take a quantitative form. With the modern approach doing away with discrete Aristotelian substances, it could no longer be argued that bodies travel through space by straining in some direction of their own accord—heavy bodies, for instance, straining downward. Rather, the modern, mechanistic view of nature demanded that all motion be instigated by a push from behind. A key question therefore became: When one body bumps another, thereby transferring some of its motion to that other body, what is the term that is conserved throughout this interaction? What is the quantity that remains constant, even as one body comes to rest and another starts into motion?

Descartes took the first real stab at answering this question. Keeping in mind that Descartes held a geometric view of nature, he argued that bodies are nothing more than their extension in space. He further proposed that when two bodies collide, what gets conserved is their total "quantity of motion," as measured by their extensive size multiplied by their speed. Accordingly, when a cue ball travels across a billiards table, to determine its quantity of motion, you multiply its size—its geometric volume—by the speed at which it travels. The prediction is that, when a cue ball strikes an 8-ball and then comes to rest, the 8-ball will acquire the same quantity of motion the cue ball originally had, as measured by the 8-ball's own size multiplied by its speed. As noted already, Descartes never did much empirical testing of his theories, and while this prediction turns out to hold true in the special case of two objects that are virtually identical, like billiard balls, it breaks down as soon as some other scenarios are introduced. Assume, for instance, that the 8-ball is not a typical billiard ball, but rather it is a similarly-sized whiffle ball, or alternately, a cannon ball. Quantity of motion being nothing but geometric size multiplied by speed, Descartes's theory predicts that, when the cue ball strikes any of these balls, they will start moving at exactly the same speed—a prediction that fails even the test of common sense.

As other seventeenth-century scientists, such as Christian Huygens, took up the question of what gets conserved in mechanical interactions, they realized they should be measuring a body's mass rather than its geometric size, and not merely the speed at which it travels through space, but its velocity—a measure of speed that accounts for the direction in which the body is moving. A debate raged for years as to whether the conserved term should be measured as mv, mass times velocity, or mv^2, mass times velocity squared. Without going into the details of this dispute, by century's end Newton had provided the most general measure of mechanical force with his famous equation $f=ma$, or force equals mass times acceleration. Equations aside, the central point everyone agreed on is that, when a heavy body travels through space, it possesses a certain quantity of force in virtue of its heft and motion. When it then strikes another body, it may lose some of its motion, or it may change its course. The motion of the second body will likewise change, but when you combine the force vectors of these two bodies, the total force present in the system will be unchanged. This gives scientists a great deal of predictive power, since if they know the force present in a system prior to a collision, they can predict the collision's outcome with high precision.

Excited by these results, many seventeenth-century scientists were optimistic that everything in nature could be explained through the mechanical action of heavy bodies bumping into one another. Even before century's end, however, it was becoming clear that not all motions can be traced back to one body pushing another from behind. Suppose, for instance, I take a cue ball, but rather than putting it into horizontal motion across a pool table, I throw it vertically into the air. The cue ball will gradually decelerate until it stops—evidently without having transferred any force to neighboring bodies. Then the cue ball will start back into motion, this time without any apparent push from behind, until finally it strikes my hand, indeed, with the same force my hand imparted to the ball a few seconds prior, albeit pointed in the opposite direction. Alternately, if I compress a spring, then lock it into this compressed position, the spring may sit idly for years. When the lock is released, however, the spring will fly back to its uncompressed position, even though no other moving bodies have pushed it from behind.

Phenomena such as this made clear that, if nature conserves mechanical force, not every force can be tied to a heavy body in motion. For one thing, it appears even mechanical force can be stored in any number of ways, as Leibniz sought to establish when he argued that force can take two different forms, "living force" or "dead force." Living force, or *vis viva*, is the force a heavy object has in virtue of its motion; this is what get conserved in mechanical interactions. Dead force, in contrast, involves a certain straining toward motion, as when a heavy body strains to move earthward, or a compressed spring strains to re-extend itself. Although this straining does not itself involve motion, it gets translated into motion as soon as conditions allow, which is to say, as soon as the countervailing forces holding it in check are released. When this happens, the dead force begins converting itself into living force. Indeed, these two forms of force can flow smoothly into one another, as illustrated by a swinging pendulum. When a pendulum blade is at the bottom of its arc, it is travelling with its maximum velocity, and thus it would strike any object in its path with maximum living force. As the blade climbs in its arc, it gradually loses velocity—and hence living force—until both become zero. At this point, the blade's motion momentarily ceases. But we know the blade must have stored up a great deal of dead force, since it now starts back into motion of its own accord, this time descending through its arc at an accelerating rate, with the blade gradually reacquiring all the living force it had lost, until this is again maximized at the bottom of its arc. Throughout this process, dead and living forces have been flowing back and forth into one another, yet the sum of the two together, or the total force present in the system, has been conserved.

This distinction between living and dead forces was helpful in that it extended the range of phenomena scientists could explain using the principle of conservation of force. Other phenomena remained, however, that defied explanation even in these extended mechanical terms. Consider what happens, for instance, when a fireman shovels coal into a locomotive's firebox, then the locomotive begins to move down the track. Or consider the analogous situation when I shovel a plateful of food into my mouth, then I get up from the table and walk to the kitchen. In both cases, a heavy body starts into motion, but to all appearances, this is *not* through the action of any external bodies pushing it from behind. Rather, in both scenarios, a fuel is added to the system, then some sort of combustion takes place—the fuel is burned—and this initiates the motion. To expand on the example of the steam locomotive, coal is burned in the locomotive's firebox, heating the firebox. Some of this heat is transferred to a chamber partially filled with water. This heats the water, turning it to steam and causing it to expand dramatically. The steam then rushes into a second chamber, with a back wall formed by the back side of a piston. With the pressurized steam driving the piston out, this causes the locomotive's drive wheel to turn. The drive wheel is connected to the drive shaft, itself connected to the locomotive's wheels, so the wheels begin to turn, and the train starts down the track.

As even this brief summary makes clear, if various mechanical interactions are indispensable to the workings of a steam engine, a complete account of its operation would require the integration of two further terms: heat and work. The notion of heat seems straightforward enough: burn coal and the firebox heats up, as you can feel by reaching out a hand. Work, meanwhile, can be described as the tangible result—the change in the world—brought about by the action of a machine. In the case of the engine we just considered, the work it performs might be measured by the distance it propels a train down the track, multiplied by the train's mass. Alternately, if the engine is being used to drive a mine pump, work performed could be measured by the height to which it raises a certain mass of water. Determining the best way to measure both heat and work would require further investigation, but as the nineteenth century dawned, the more general question rising to the fore was: If the operation of a steam engine involves both heat and work, how exactly are these two terms related?

In fact, an answer to this question had already been suggested by the armaments industry. To build a cannon shaft that fires true, you start with a solid brass cylinder, attach one end to a spindle, then press the other end into a stationary abrasive bit. As the spindle turns, this bores out the center of the cylinder, creating a perfectly symmetrical hollow tube. One obvious side effect of this operation is that both the brass cylinder and the drill bit get very hot. The cause of this heat is not a mystery, given that you can generate the same effect by rubbing your hands together vigorously. To study the phenomenon of friction more closely, in 1798 Benjamin Thompson (Count Rumford) had a cannon shaft bored in a vat of water, using a drill bit that was intentionally left dull to generate as much friction as possible. Rumford found that, although the water in the vat started out cold, after two and a half hours of boring, the water was boiling.

Rumford ended his investigation here, but it was not difficult for later researchers to extrapolate further from his results. Using a dull bit, Rumford's experiment had generated a great deal of heat, while the work of boring the cannon shaft proceeded slowly. Had Rumford used a sharper bit, we can surmise more work would have been performed in a given timeframe, while generating less heat. This inverse relationship between the quantity of heat generated and the amount of work performed—more work means less heat, more heat means less work—strongly suggests that heat and work are two different manifestations of the same stuff, perhaps capable of flowing back and forth into one another like living force and dead force. Lavoisier had already shown in the 1770s that in chemical reactions, mass is conserved, thus setting the stage for a more general principle of the conservation of matter. Might heat be a unique variety of matter that flows through a steam engine's various chambers before flowing into the work, itself, perhaps undergoing some sort of phase transition at this point, like liquid water turning to steam? The image was suggestive, but what was the common term linking heat and work that would allow them to flow back and forth into one another?

The First Law of Thermodynamics

In 1820, Sadi Carnot published *Reflections on the Motive Power of Fire*, widely recognized to be the work that inaugurated the modern science of thermodynamics. In this treatise, Carnot argues that an engine is essentially a device for converting heat into "useful effect," or work. As it turns out, Carnot completely misunderstood the nature of heat. Like many other scientists of his day, he assumed heat to be an invisible, liquid-like substance—commonly known as "caloric"—that can flow through solid objects but still have tangible effects. Indeed, on Carnot's account of the steam engine, caloric flows through an engine and turns its drive wheel almost like water turning a water wheel. Carnot's successors would later determine that caloric does not exist, and more generally that heat is not a *type* of matter, but a *property* of matter. Still, this mischaracterization of heat did not significantly impact Carnot's groundbreaking analysis of the flow of heat through engines. Nor did it prevent his work from inspiring the next generation of thermodynamical researchers to conclude that the term for what nature ultimately conserves—along with matter—is energy, with heat and work being two different manifestations of energy. Over the 1840s, Julius Robert Mayer, James Joule, Rudolf Clausius, and William Thomson (Lord Kelvin) all proposed slightly different articulations of the principle of conservation of energy, which also came to be known as the first law of thermodynamics—once thermodynamics had a second law with which to pair it.

To briefly summarize the import of this discovery, we have already seen that burning coal in a steam engine's firebox can ultimately lead to such useful results as water being pumped out of a mine. This particular result clearly involves both living and dead forces. As the water is being drawn upward, it is given living force in virtue of its motion. At the same time, the ascending water acquires ever more dead force, as evidenced by the fact that, if we release the pumped water into a stream running downhill, the water can turn a waterwheel and thereby perform further useful work. With the principle of the conservation of energy on the table, scientists were able to rebrand dead force as potential energy and living force as kinetic energy, thereby emphasizing their interconvertibility and ultimate unity. At the same time, the umbrella concept of energy was wide enough to consider whether it might cover any number of other phenomena, including some not directly tied to the location or motion of heavy bodies in space. This included the interweaving forces of electricity and magnetism, whose study James Maxwell pioneered in the 1860s, as well as the chemical energy somehow stored in a lump of coal, even if the precise mechanism by which this storage takes place would remain a mystery until the twentieth century.

The first law of thermodynamics, in any case, holds that the total quantity of energy present within a closed system will always remain constant, even as this energy may adopt different forms. Articulating this broad principle still left scientists with plenty of work to do. They still had to determine, first, how best to measure the various forms of energy, and second, how to convert these different types of energy into one another, whether physically or in the language of mathematics. In principle, however, the first law gave scientists and engineers a precise, quantitative means of predicting the outcome of a wide variety of physical interactions. If you could determine, for instance, how much potential energy a ton of coal contains, this should allow you to determine how many gallons of water you can pump from a particular mine when you feed this coal into the steam engine driving the mine's pump.

In a sense, the discovery of the first law may have been a disappointment for industrialists, since it confirmed they would need to keep buying coal to fuel their factories. Since ancient times, innovators had dreamed of building a perpetual motion machine that would, once set into motion, continue running indefinitely of its own accord, ideally performing some sort of useful work as it moved. The first law made clear, however, that perpetual motion machines are a pipe dream. Perhaps, in an ideal world devoid of friction and other factors that would cause a machine to run down, a machine could be built that would keep running forever, without any further pushes from behind. But if this machine were to perform any useful work, this would divert energy into the work, thus no longer leaving the machine with enough energy to keep moving of its own accord. Of course, the good news for industrialists is that steam engines are not closed systems, so it is always possible to keep shoveling more coal into their fireboxes, thereby keeping the machines they power in operation. But the upshot of the first law is that the work these machines perform must be funded by a continual input of fuel, or embodied energy. And while the market price of coal may go up or down, the price that nature charges for performing work remains constant: you must pour *at least* as much energy into the production process as you want the final product to embody, *plus* whatever energy might get lost during production.

To this last point, there were probably not many nineteenth-century industrialists who still entertained the realistic expectation of building a perpetual motion machine; most had come to accept that any work done in their factories would need to be paid for through a continuous input of fuel. Nevertheless, industrialists quite reasonably hoped the engines they installed would be as efficient as possible, such that they could minimize their purchases of coal, while generating maximum output. As we can now refine the concept of mechanical efficiency: in an ideal case, an engine will capture all the heat energy the coal burning in its firebox releases and convert this heat energy into useful work. Even before the formal study of thermodynamics began, however, it was obvious the steam engines of the early nineteenth century were operating at nowhere close to 100% efficiency. Indeed, this is what first launched Carnot on his study of engines. Even Carnot was shocked to discover, however, that the typical engine of his day had an efficiency of no more than 5% or 10%. In physical terms, this meant less than a tenth of the heat the burning coal produced was getting converted into useful work. In monetary terms, it meant more than nine out of ten dollars industrialists were spending on coal was simply disappearing. Carnot's analyses of engines would eventually help engineers make some modest improvements in the efficiency of steam engines. More significant for our purposes, his exploration of *inefficiency* would set the stage for his successors to discern, not just the first law of thermodynamics, but also the second law.

Carnot and the Heat Engine

If energy is never lost from a closed system, yet the steam engines of Carnot's day were operating with no more than 10% efficiency, where was all the lost energy going? Carnot realized, of course, that when machines run in the real world, their moving parts generate friction, such that no machine will ever operate with 100% efficiency. But he also knew that friction, alone, could not account for the 90% energy loss engines were typically experiencing, or engines would seize up before they ever started running, if they did not melt. Friction, moreover, was a practical problem engineers could, and did, address through such practical measures as machining parts with greater precision and developing better lubricants. Carnot suspected, however, that not even the most successful of these measures would allow engines to function with anything close to 100% efficiency. To investigate why, he designed an engine that utilized the same basic principles as the steam engines of his day yet differed in its precise construction so as to make the flow of heat through the engine more intuitive. Engineers have since built functioning "heat engines" or "Carnot engines," but Carnot did all his own work on paper. A simplified version of his design is shown below.

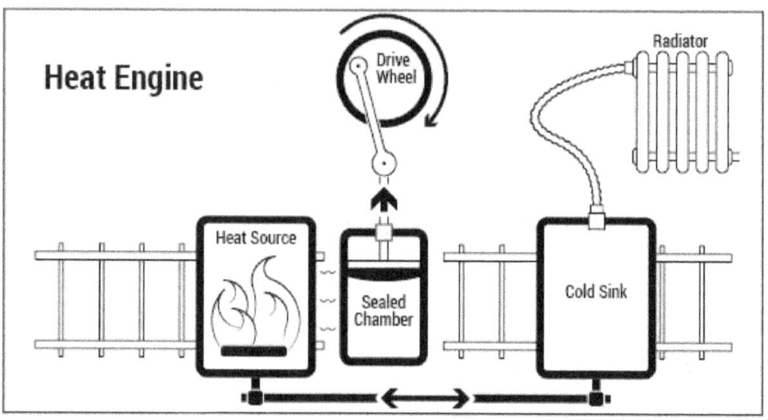

As the diagram suggests, the heat engine is built around a gas-filled chamber, the back wall of which is formed by the back end of a piston. In a typical steam engine, hot steam would be pumped into this chamber to drive the piston out. In a heat engine, however, the gas-filled chamber remains sealed. The engine also features a heat source located outside the chamber. The precise nature of the heat source is unimportant, but to make clear that some sort of energy input is required, we will imagine the heat source to be a small firebox. Let us further assume the firebox is mounted on a set of rails that allows it to move left and right in our picture.

To start the engine running, we shovel some coal into the firebox to generate the necessary heat. We then slide the heat source to the right until it touches the lefthand wall of the sealed chamber. This warms the gas inside the chamber, causing it to expand. When Carnot published *The Motive Power of Fire*, no one knew exactly *why* hot gasses expand, but the phenomenon was well known; indeed, this is the driving force behind every steam engine. In any case, the gas in the sealed chamber trying to expand further makes room for itself the only way it can—by driving the piston out. This turns the drive wheel attached to the other end of the piston, thereby turning the driveshaft at its center. Some other machine can now be hooked onto the spinning driveshaft and used to perform useful work. To illustrate, let us assume the machine is a mine pump, such that with every turn of the driveshaft, the pump lifts a certain mass of water a few inches higher.

Now, however, comes the problem. We have taken energy stored in the coal, released it as heat, and successfully converted this heat into the first bit of useful work. But we do not want to stop here; we want to continue pumping the water higher. An engine, after all, is not like a cannon. A cannon operates in much the same way as the engine just described, with explosively burning powder causing a rapid expansion of the gas trapped in the shaft behind the cannonball, thus violently driving the shot from the open end of the shaft. But the cannon's work is done at this point, at least until it is manually reloaded, whereas the whole point of an engine is for it to run continuously, without any need for constant intervention on the part of an operator. And yet, with the engine's piston now fully extended, it will not be able to turn the drive wheel any further until the piston is retracted and a new burst of heat can push it out again.

To an extent, the drive wheel can accomplish this task itself, especially if it is very heavy. Acting as a flywheel, the drive wheel will want to keep turning in virtue of its rotational momentum, and thus it will start pushing the piston back into the sealed chamber. The gas in the chamber is still hot, however, so it will want to remain expanded. Granted, even a hot gas can be compressed, but this takes work. In fact, because the force of the expanding gas is what drove the piston to its extended position, the drive wheel would have to exert an equal amount of force to compress the hot gas back to its original volume, as required to get the piston fully retracted. At this point, with the drive wheel continuing to turn, the hot gas could again start pushing the piston out, thus starting the cycle over. Yet, to keep the engine running in this fashion would do us no good, since the drive wheel must expend so much energy retracting the piston that it cannot afford to do any other useful work. If any of the energy flowing to the drive wheel is tapped off to pump water, the engine will seize up, unable to get the piston fully retracted. So, what do we do? How do we make the engine work for more than one cycle?

Since the hot gas in the sealed chamber provides the resistance against which the drive wheel must struggle, to reduce this resistance, we need to cool the gas. Another key feature of the heat engine is therefore the cold sink. In our diagram, this is located to the right of the sealed chamber. Let us further stipulate that the cold sink is mounted on the same rails as the heat source and tied to the heat source by a well-insulated bar, such that the two move in tandem. Now, when the piston has reached its full extension, the cold sink is pressed up against the sealed chamber, which simultaneously pushes the heat source away from the chamber. The effect produced is like holding an ice cube against a hot mug of tea, with the colder object drawing heat away from the hotter. As some of the heat from the sealed chamber therefore dumps into the cold sink, the gas cools, and thus it begins to contract. Pushing the piston back has now gotten much easier, allowing the drive wheel to accomplish this task with little work. This means virtually all the force the piston first generated by thrusting outward can be dedicated to the work of running the pump. What is more, the piston is now back in its retracted position, and thus it is primed to run through this cycle again, which is accomplished by withdrawing the cold sink, while simultaneously pressing the heat source back against the sealed chamber.

This is progress, but unfortunately we still do not have a fully functioning engine. Although the current setup may allow us to run the engine for a few cycles, every time the cold sink presses up against the sealed chamber, some of the chamber's heat dumps into the cold sink. Eventually, therefore, the sink will "fill up" with heat. The cold sink will warm up, in other words, until it is the same temperature as the heated gas, by which point it can no longer function as a cold sink. And with the engine no longer being able to cool the gas in its sealed chamber, it will seize up. Luckily, the solution is straightforward. Since our problem involves the cold sink filling up with heat, we just need to give it a "drain." We need to devise a means, that is, of drawing heat away from cold sink so that it can always remain cooler than the sealed chamber. In practice, this generally involves attaching the cold sink to a radiator that will dissipate the heat it acquires into the surrounding air.

At this point, the industrialist looking over Carnot's

shoulder might get dollar signs in his eyes and propose an ingenious method of saving energy, and hence coal. We have seen how the cold sink must continually be emptied to keep the engine running. Yet, because we also need to keep pouring more heat into sealed chamber, typically by burning more coal in the heat source, why not run a hose from the cold sink's drain back to the heat source, thereby dumping the excess heat back into the engine and thereby driving the work it does? To explain to the disappointed industrialist why this proposal would not work, Carnot might sketch of a type of engine that is even easier to grasp on an intuitive level: a waterwheel.

With a waterwheel, water is diverted from a downward-flowing stream into a sluice located above the wheel. The sluice dumps water into the buckets on the front side of the waterwheel, pulling them downward and thereby turning the wheel's driveshaft, which can be hooked up to some machine. By the time a bucket reaches the bottom of the wheel's rotation, however, it must be emptied, or the buckets on the back side of the wheel would weigh just as much as those on its front and the wheel would stop turning. As the water dumps out, moreover, it must be channeled back into the stream and allowed to run its natural course down the hillside, or else a lake would form and engulf the waterwheel, stopping it from turning.

Of course, nobody worries about how much water gets "wasted" by dumping it down the hillside, since the stream continuously brings new water to keep the waterwheel turning. Yet, what if a tight-fisted industrialist simply could not bear to see the potential energy of this water flowing away, so he commands his engineer to re-use the water being dumped at the base of the wheel to keep the wheel turning? The engineer might run a pipe from the base of the wheel back to top, with the idea of capturing the discharged water and re-running it through the wheel. But this scheme obviously would not work, for the simple reason that water does not flow uphill; the water will not travel up the pipe of its own accord. Seeking to appease the industrialist, the engineer might hook a pump to the pipe, pumping the discharged water back to the top of the waterwheel, where it can be re-used. Such a setup could, of course, be constructed. It would be useless, however, since pumping water to a higher elevation takes work, and indeed—given that the waterwheel generates power by allowing water to travel naturally to a lower elevation—it would require at least as much energy to pump the water uphill as the waterwheel generates by allowing the water to fall back down, with no energy left over to perform useful work. For the waterwheel to serve any purpose, therefore, water flowing downhill that has already been exploited once must simply be allowed to continue down the hill, forever lost to this factory, at least, for purposes of performing useful work.

And thus it is with the heat engine, or in fact, any sort of engine. On Carnot's understanding of the nature of heat, again, caloric is an invisible fluid that can pass through the walls of the sealed engine chamber, but it otherwise behaves like water, particularly in the sense that it always flows "downhill." In the case of caloric, however, it does not flow from higher to lower elevations, but rather from hotter to colder locations. Heat from the raging firebox therefore pours into the moderate climate of the sealed chamber, before emptying into the cold sink and getting discharged through the radiator, always flowing from warmer to cooler locations. Yet, while this unidirectional flow of heat is what drives the engine, it is also what prevents us from capturing the heat discharged from the cold sink and routing it back to the engine's heat source. Hooking up a hose to connect the cold sink and heat source would be like running a pipe from the discharge pool at the base of a waterwheel back up to the sluice. Given the direction in which heat flows, no heat would travel "up" the hose from the cold sink to the heat source. If anything, heat from the firebox would run directly down to the cold sink and heat it up still further. To be sure, we could devise a heat pump that forces the excess heat back to the firebox. But pumping heat takes just as much work as pumping water, so running this pump would require at least as much energy as it might recapture, meaning the whole arrangement would serve no purpose.

And that is why, Carnot concluded, an engine can never be built that runs with 100% efficiency, converting all the heat generated by a burning fuel into useful work. In fact, Carnot calculated—taking into account several steps in the "Carnot cycle" that we ignored for the sake of brevity—even if all the heat lost due to friction is eliminated through perfectly machined parts or frictionless lubricants, an engine can still never function with any more than 40-50% efficiency. Much of the heat generated in the firebox must simply be allowed to flow through the engine and into the cold sink, ultimately getting dissipated by the radiator, to keep the engine running. Perhaps this dissipated heat can still be put to some secondary use, such as heating the factory in winter. But for purposes of running the factory's machinery, the industrialist must simply accept that over half the heat produced by burning the coal he purchases must be squandered for the remaining heat to do any useful work. In an economic sense, this loss is just a cost of doing business. And likewise in the economy of nature, it is simply a fact to be accepted that, if the total energy present in any closed system will always remain constant, converting this energy into useful work will always involve some waste, in the sense that a portion of this energy will be lost from future use, without ever having performed any useful work.

The Second Law of Thermodynamics: Initial Interpretations

If Carnot's work would eventually help to inspire the discovery of the second law of thermodynamics, Carnot did not make this discovery, himself. It was not until the 1850s, when the first law of thermodynamics had already been articulated, that the debate began in earnest as to how exactly the second law should be formulated. Drawing on Carnot's results, Kelvin proposed that the fact that no engine can be 100% efficient should itself stand as the second law. Rudolf Clausius did not doubt this fact about engines, but Kelvin's formulation struck him as an odd candidate for a "law of nature." Would nature really govern itself in accord with a law that apparently could not take effect until a certain intelligent mammal had invented engines? Was it not more likely that the limited efficiency of engines is an effect of some deeper, more fundamental law of nature?

Suspecting the latter, Clausius initially argued that the law Carnot had stumbled across was the fact that heat flows from hotter to colder locations, but not vice versa, much as water only flows downhill. Again, however, while this characterization of heat's flow was undoubtedly correct, Clausius began to wonder whether it is truly the most fundamental law at work here. For one thing, if we continue playing on the analogy between heat and water, "Water flows downhill" is not a law of nature. The underlying law here is rather Newton's principle of universal gravitation, which decrees that any two bodies will be attracted to one another in proportion to their mass. This translates into the phenomenon of water flowing downhill only when a relatively small quantity of water happens to be located on the surface of a much larger body such as Earth. By analogy, might there be some deeper principle underlying the fact that heat tends to travel from hotter to colder locations? By the 1850s, however, the whole analogy between heat and water was beginning to fall apart. For a variety of theoretical and experimental reasons, Kelvin and Clausius both came to reject the view that heat is any sort of substance. But this leaves the question as to what heat is and why it flows from hotter to colder locations. Perhaps, Clausius suspected, gaining a better understanding of the nature of heat would reveal a more fundamental formulation of the second law.

In 1857, Clausius proposed an account of heat that did not just reject the caloric model but challenged the entire prevailing view of how material nature is composed. Since antiquity, a debate had raged over whether matter is a continuous stuff, or rather it comprises discrete, unbreakable atoms. Aristotle had maintained that matter is continuous, so this was the position scholastic philosophers took. And while a handful of seventeenth-century thinkers had advocated for atomism, notably Boyle and Hobbes, the continuity of matter was one Aristotelian doctrine that survived the Scientific Revolution more or less intact, in the absence of any compelling evidence to the contrary.

Clausius noted, however, that if we conceive of matter as composed of molecules that move about the void and bounce off one another, this allows us to conceive of heat as the average kinetic energy a group of molecules possesses: the hotter a lump of matter, the more vigorously its constituent molecules move about and crash into one other. This explains, among other things, how heat can pass through such solid bodies as the iron walls of a heat engine and why heated gasses expand. To illustrate, let us review the heat engine's operation, this time construed in terms of Clausius's atomic account of matter. When coal is burned in the engine's firebox, this releases a tremendous amount of potential energy stored within the coal. Infused with newly released kinetic energy, air and coal molecules inside the firebox begin violently bouncing off one another. Some of these molecules will inevitably crash into to firebox's iron walls, thus raising the average kinetic energy of its constituent molecules. When the firebox wall is then touched to the wall of the engine's sealed chamber, kinetic energy is again transferred, first to the molecules comprising the chamber walls, then to the gas molecules within the chamber. Having gained kinetic energy, these gas molecules start bouncing off one another more vigorously, and the gas strives to occupy a larger volume: its pressure rises. This increased pressure is not strong enough to move the fixed walls of the sealed chamber, but since the piston is not fixed, as the hot gas molecules strike the back of the piston with greater force than before, the piston travels out. And with the piston then turning the drive wheel and drive shaft, itself tied to a pump or other machine, we now have a complete explanation of how heat energy first generated in the firebox ultimately gets converted into useful work.

At the same time as he was formulating this new account of heat, Clausius was rethinking the second law of thermodynamics in terms of a wholly novel pair of concepts: order and disorder. These concepts do not bear an obvious relation to the phenomena of heat or work, but to highlight the connection he suspected must be there, Clausius coined a new term meant to sound like "energy"—namely, "entropy." Combining the Greek word *en* (meaning "in") with *trope* ("transition or turn"), Clausius defined entropy as the disorder present within a system. Time has shown that this linguistic juggling did little to help Clausius explain what he meant by the concept of entropy. Nevertheless, the terminology did allow him to propose a new, concise articulation of the second law: the entropy within a closed system will never decrease over time, but only increase. To see how Clausius arrived at this claim, and to see how it relates relate back to the phenomena of heat and energy, let us trace through the operation of the heat engine one more time, but this time peering through the lens of order and disorder.

Before a heat engine is fired up, we start with a pile of coal, which has potential energy stored up within it. As noted already, in the 1850's, no one knew exactly *how* matter stores energy, but when coal is burned, it releases so much heat that we must assume its potential energy had been stored in some compact, organized fashion, presumably reflecting a high degree of order among its constituent molecules. When the coal is then burned, energy is released. One glance inside the firebox tells us, moreover, this energy is now flying around in all different directions, completely disordered. In such a disordered state, heat energy is not useful for doing much more than warming us on a cold day. The heat engine, however, is specifically designed to channel this raging energy into useful work. As kinetic energy migrates into the sealed chamber, its gas molecules begin banging against the chamber walls ever more vigorously. This energy is still disordered, yet because the back end of the piston is the only wall in the chamber that has any give to it, as the piston extends in straight line, it translates the random, disordered motion of the gas molecules into a more highly ordered recti-linear motion. This turns the drive wheel, thereby further channeling the energy present in the system into a circular motion ordered enough to perform some sort of useful work. The product of this work—say, a bolt of colorfully pattered cloth emerging from a power loom—contains more order than did its constituent materials, back when they were just spools of thread. This increase in order is useful; in fact, it was the whole point of setting up the steam engine and power loom. Clausius stressed, however, that this increase in order can only come at a cost, in the form of even greater disorder emerging somewhere else in the process. And indeed, we can see that the lumps of coal that were once highly ordered have been reduced to disordered piles of ash, now completely useless for purposes of running an engine. Thus, while Clausius never developed a precise means of quantifying order and disorder, he was confident the total amount of order present within the system had decreased over the course of the engine's operation, meaning the system's net disorder, or entropy, had increased, per his formulation of the second law of thermodynamics.

If Clausius could therefore explain the operation of a heat engine *either* in terms of his atomic account of matter *or* in terms of the second law—formulated in terms of the tendency for entropy to increase—he never managed to tie these two accounts together in satisfying fashion. This meant, among other things, that Clausius could not explain *why* disorder tends to increase over time. This final step in the development of the second law would be left to Ludwig Boltzmann, a brilliant but troubled Austrian physicist working at the end of the nineteenth century. Boltzmann battled through periodic bouts of depression to develop the interpretation of the second law physicists still used today.

The Second Law of Thermodynamics: Boltzmann's Statistical Interpretation

Why does entropy increase over time? Of course, this natural law could just be one of the defining facts of our universe, much as it appears simply to be a fact of our universe that any two heavy bodies will attract one another. But Boltzmann did not think so. It took him years to sort through the precise nature of entropy, and to tie this to the atomic account of matter Clausius had suggested, but we can cut straight to Boltzmann's fundamental insight: the second law of thermodynamics is not a free-standing law of nature that compels everything in the world to behave in a particular fashion. Rather, it is a statistical phenomenon, boiling down to the laws of probability.

To illustrate, let us consider a very simple system, a 6x6 grid, with 4 of its 36 available slots occupied by colored circles, the rest occupied by clear circles. This system could take on numerous different states, as defined by the locations of the colored circles; three such possible states are shown below.

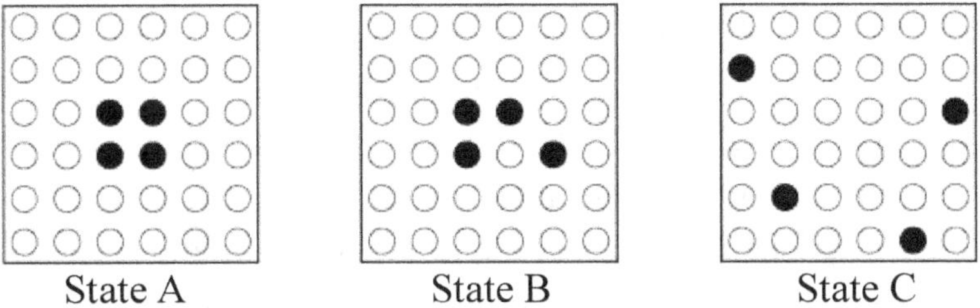

State A   State B   State C

Even without giving a precise definition of "order," we can see that State A is the most highly ordered of the three. "Everything is in its place," we might say about State A, as compared to State B, where one colored circle appears to be out of place, or State C, where the colored circles seem to be scattered about randomly, having no proper places. The second law of thermodynamics, as Clausius came to formulate it using the concept of entropy, tells us that nature will tend to move from scenarios like State A toward scenarios like State C. Nature will *not*, conversely, spontaneously move in the opposite direction, from State C to State A. This sounds reasonable enough, but why should it be true?

To begin developing Boltzmann's answer to the question, we need to do a few things. First, let us move the scenario just described off the page and into the real world, specifically into a world in which matter is composed of tiny molecules. The precise physical composition of these molecules is unimportant, so for the sake of simplicity, let us assume them to be solid spheres. Some of these spheres are clear, as represented by the empty circles in the figures above; others are black, as indicated by the colored circles. Accordingly, State A may be considered a vessel of clear water with a coherent drop of black dye at its center. In State B, this drop of dye has begun to dissipate, whereas in State C, the black molecules are fully dispersed.

Next, to see how these molecules might spontaneously move from one state to another, let us invoke Clausius's kinetic theory of heat, but kick it up a notch. Clausius, again, had proposed that heat is a measure of the average kinetic energy of the molecules in a given system. This would turn out to be correct, so far as it goes, but it still does not tell us where these molecules get their kinetic energy in the first place. In classical mechanics, billiard balls of any size will gain kinetic energy only when struck from behind by other solid bodies. Yet, if this is how we regard the molecules in our example, and we assume that the system is at rest when it begins in State A, the liquid will never move into another state unless agitated by some external force, such as a spoon stirring it. Boltzmann suggested, however, that molecules are never truly at rest. Rather, they naturally vibrate. The more energy a molecule contains, the more vigorously it vibrates, with a system's temperature therefore being determined by the average vibrational intensity of the molecules comprising it.

Finally, to finish setting up our example, let us assume the vibrating molecules in this simple system are packed together tightly enough that, when their timing is just right, two adjacent, vibrating molecules will bump into one another, perhaps knocking each other into different spaces on the grid, and thereby pushing the previous occupants of these spaces into other spaces, and so forth.

Now that we have put the system we are studying into motion, why will it tend to move from State A to State C, but not vice versa? The answer Boltzmann arrived at comes down to counting the different possible configurations the system's constituent molecules could adopt. To illustrate, let us first consider an even simpler system, a 2x2 grid containing 3 molecules of clear water and 1 molecule of black dye. The possible states this system could adopt are shown below.

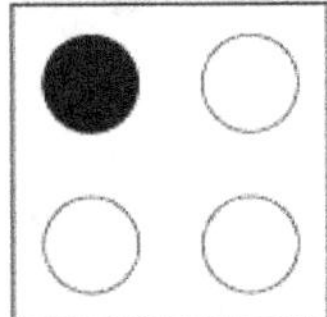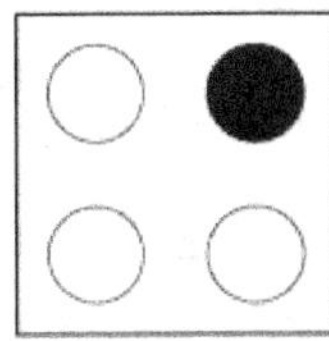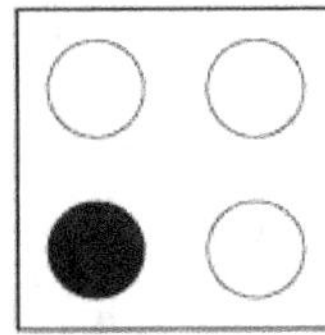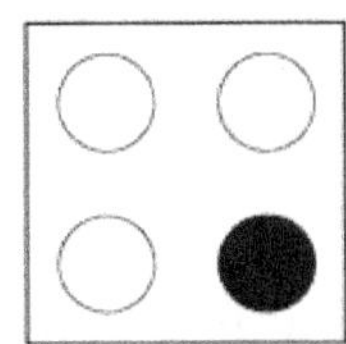

Clearly enough, there are 4 spaces here, and 1 black molecule, so this black molecule could occupy any one of the 4 spaces, thereby exhausting the total possible states. If we add a second black molecule, the number of possible states rises to 6:

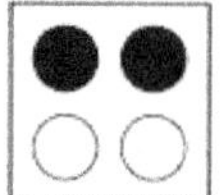 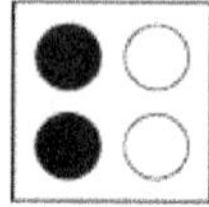 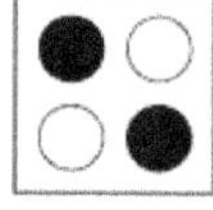 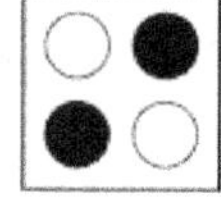 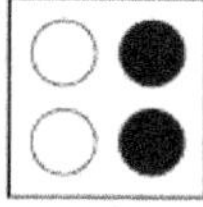 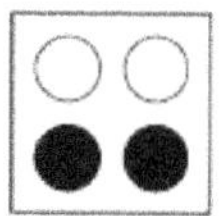

In these extremely simple systems, we have no grounds for saying one of these possible states is more or less ordered than the others. This will change, however, if we consider larger systems. Increasing a system's size, moreover, will dramatically increase the number of possible states it can occupy.

Without getting bogged down by the math used to calculate the total number of possible states a system can occupy, if we design a system containing 16 total molecules arranged in a 4x4 grid, while stipulating that 2 of these molecules are black, the system could adopt a total of 120 different configurations. We cannot show all the different possibilities here, but a couple of examples are shown below, at left.

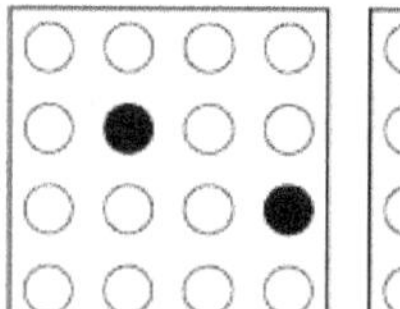 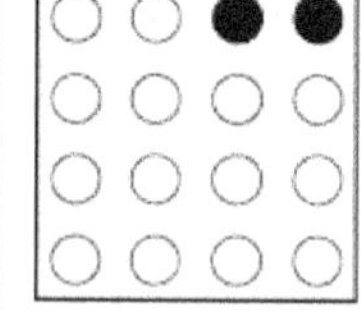 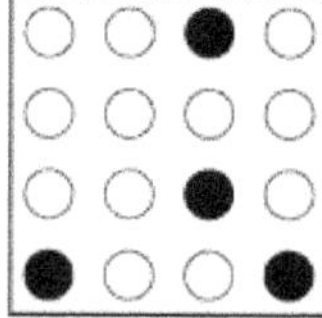 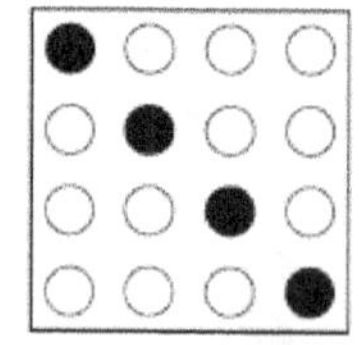

Now, if we stick with the 4x4 grid but doubling the number of black molecules to 4—as shown above, at right—this drives the number of different possible configurations up to 1,820. By the time we build our system back up to the 6x6 grid containing 4 black molecules that we used to portray States A through C, above, the total number of possible states this system could adopt has risen to 58,905. All of these numbers are doubtless starting to blur together, but the upshot is that if you were to throw 36 molecules, 4 of them black, into a vessel that divides into a square grid, there is a 1 in 58,905 chance the molecules will fall into exactly the arrangement portrayed as State A. It is hardly surprising, therefore, that if the molecules jiggle around randomly, they are not going to end up in State A very often. To be sure, this outcome is not impossible, and given enough time, State A may occasionally recur. It is just highly unlikely that, *at any given moment*, the system will find itself in State A. That is why, Boltzmann concluded, it is the general tendency of nature to move *away* from highly ordered states like State A, rather than toward them.

Yet, we might object, is it not true that the configuration of molecules found in State C is just as unique at that found in State A? And does this not mean that, at any given moment, there is a 1 in 58,905 chance that the system will fall into disordered State C, which is to say, the same odds of the system falling into the highly ordered State A? This is true, but…

This "but" is the key to Boltzmann's interpretation of the second law of thermodynamics. For while it is true that the *precise* configuration of molecules found in State C is unique, such that the odds of the system falling into this exactly this state at any given moment are quite small, we could say State C is *functionally* equivalent to any of the other disordered states shown on the next page.

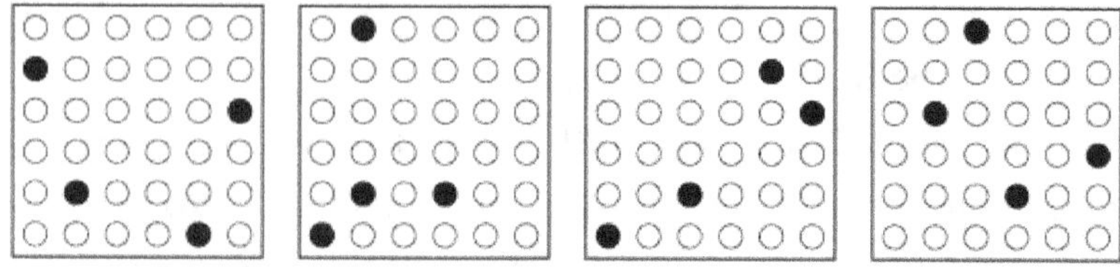

Cleary, the four configurations of black molecules shown here are quite different from one another. But who cares? In a highly-ordered configuration like State A, where every molecule has its place, it *does* matter if even one molecule happens to get jostled over a space or two; then it is no longer true that everything is in its place. But in disordered configurations like States C through F, where nothing really has a place to start with, there is no practical significance to their differing arrangements. In all four cases, the system is just disordered.

Here is the key point: Given the sheer number of configurations 4 black molecules can occupy in a 6x6 grid, the system has far more disordered states than ordered states into which it can fall. What we earlier labeled State A is not the only highly-ordered configuration of molecules possible. Our coherent drop of black ink, comprising 4 molecules bunched together at the center of the vessel, could move around to some other location within the vessel, or perhaps the 4 black molecules could arrange themselves in a straight line or some other discernible pattern. Yet, even if we are generous and stipulate that there are 100 possible highly-ordered configurations this system could take on, plus 10 times as many possible configurations that, like State B, are moderately ordered, this still means that, at any given time, there is only a 1 in 59 chance that the system will be in even a moderately ordered state, while there is a 58 in 59 chance the system will be completely disordered. The explanation, again, for these steeply slanted odds is the fact that there are so many more ways to be disordered than ordered.

At this point, we are well on our way to developing Boltzmann's interpretation of the second law of thermodynamics. Yet, it still does not feel like we are closing in on a *law* of nature. Granted, if we begin our observations at State A, with a coherent drop of black dye at the center of the vessel, then we come back later to check on things, the odds are very good that the black molecules will now be in a state of greater disorder. But this does not *have* to be the case. We could come back and find the system in a highly ordered state, possibly even State A. In fact, if we set up a computer simulation of this scenario and program it so that the molecules randomly jostle one another into different positions once every second, we would expect to see a state of at least moderate order arising approximately once per minute. And once every 58,905 seconds or so—or about once every 16 hours—we would expect to see the molecules stumbling into precisely the arrangement with which they began, State A. So, if we can actually predict that, sometimes, a system will spontaneously move from a state of complete disorder to one of greater order, can the second law really be a *law*?

This was an objection Boltzmann faced from many of his contemporaries, who had been born and raised on the Newtonian tenet that for a law of nature to be a law, it must be universal; it must operate in every place, at every time, without exception. Yet, here was Boltzmann, proposing a law that seemed to hold mostly true, most of the time—except when it did not. It was almost as if Boltzmann was reviving the Aristotelian notion of chance, which suggests that sometimes things just depart from their usual course, without there being any further explanation. And in fact, Boltzmann *was* arguing that chance should once again be granted a foundational role in physics. The reason he could nonetheless argue that the second law has a law-like character is that, while uncommon events can indeed happen "just by chance," most of the time they do not, especially when the odds against their occurrence get to be very, very steep. And this is precisely what happens when the systems we investigate get much larger than the very simple systems we have been considering thus far.

Returning to our 6x6 grid of molecules, 4 of them black, we saw that a computer simulation updating their positions once per second would be expected to return to State A about once every 16 hours. If we enlarge the system to make it an 8x8 grid, again starting out with a drop of black dye containing 4 molecules at its center, the average time we would have to wait for a recurrence of State A climbs to more than 7 days. But now let us make this system more realistic by making it three-dimensional: a 6x6x6 cubic grid of molecules, now starting out with a 2x2x2 cube of black dye at its center. Suddenly, the average wait time for a recurrence of this highly ordered starting state jumps to above 3 million years. Expand it to an 8x8x8 cubic grid, and it will return to its ordered starting point once every 3.5 billion years. With the odds against highly ordered states spontaneously arising thus climbing exponentially every time we add a just few more rows to our grid, by the time we get up to a modestly-sized system formed by a 12x12x12 cubic grid, we must expect to wait more than 4,000 times what we now know to be the current age of the universe to see a 2x2x2 drop of black dye spontaneously reconstitute itself at the center of the vessel.

These numbers are dizzying, but think about what would happen if Clausius and Boltzmann were right in their conjecture about the atomic nature of matter—as it turns out they were. In this case, as scientists have since calculated, an actual drop of dye will contain *trillions* of molecules. As these vibrating molecules begin bumping into one another, they are bound to knock each other into an increasingly disordered state, given the relatively few states they could occupy that would still count as an ordered drop of black dye, as compared to gazillions of possible disordered configurations they could slip into—the numbers here get too large to calculate. So, while it is technically "possible" that, at some point in the future, these trillions of molecules could spontaneously reconstitute themselves as an ordered drop of dye, we would likely have to wait many trillion times the current age of the universe to see this happen. Hence, in any sort of relevant timeframe, the movement from greater order to lesser order that the second law of thermodynamics predicts will hold true. With some scant possibility for exceptions remaining, this law is perhaps not "universal" in the strictest sense of the word. But it may just as well be, since it holds true just as often as Newton's principle of universal gravitation—or actually, as we will see in the next chapter, more often.

Coming Full Circle

With Boltzmann's statistical interpretation of the second law of thermodynamics on the table, we are able to address some of the questions that have been lingering throughout this chapter—and were lingering for much of the nineteenth century. Starting on a general level, we can now appreciate why an abandoned temple will have a ruined appearance, never again to achieve its original state of order unless manually reconstructed. When the temple was built, its stones could have occupied only a handful of configurations that would have allowed its builders to walk away from the job, confident every stone was in its place. As the temple fell into neglect, however, inclement weather, earth tremors, and vandals began randomly moving stones about. And because there are countless possible configurations into which the stones might shift that would give the temple more of a disordered, derelict appearance, by the time we encounter the temple thousands of years later, the odds of further random displacements restoring the temple to its original, ordered state are so astronomically small as to be non-existent. Ditto for the smashed egg: there are so many more ways for an egg to be broken than for it to be whole that we cannot expect a broken egg to knit itself back together within any sort of a realistic timeframe. In fact, with the second law of thermodynamics forever at work, quietly driving the decay of anything in the universe that possesses any order, the eggshells will rot into their own constituent molecules long before they have chanced to reconstitute themselves as a complete egg.

But this is not to say the Second Law is a wholly destructive force. Indeed, we can now understand why heat flows from hotter to colder locations—the phenomenon that drives steam engines, even if at something less than 100% efficiency. To work our way up to this explanation, let us first modify our example, stipulating that our vessel begins, not with a drop of black dye at its center, but with clear molecules on its left side and black molecules on its right. Calling this starting condition State A, we can already predict what States B and C will look like:

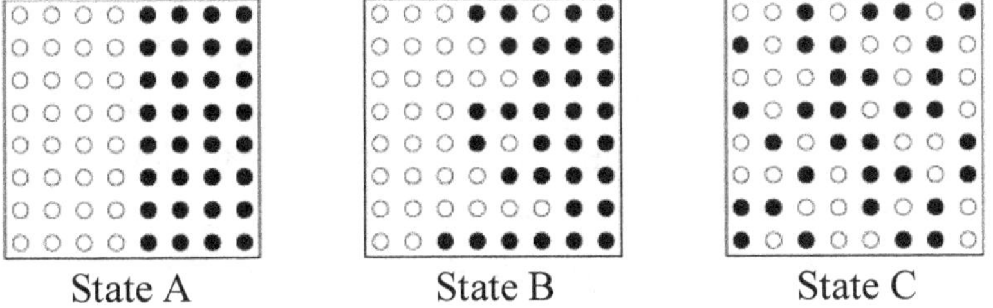

State A   State B   State C

As the molecules in the vessel vibrate and bump into one another, some of the differently colored molecules will begin trading places with one another, and the system will slip into something resembling State B. And because there is only one possible state in which all of the clear molecules are on the left side of the vessel and all of the black molecules are on the right, whereas there are an enormous number of possible states in which all of the molecules are jumbled together randomly, it is inevitable that the vessel will eventually settle into a disordered, mixed condition resembling State C, thus making the liquid appear a uniform grey from a distance. Will dumb luck ever push the various molecules back into the ordered condition of State A? With the 64 molecules portrayed here, this might happen, though rarely. With the trillions of molecules that fill an actual vessel, such a dramatic increase in order will not occur in the lifetime of our universe.

Now, however, let us stipulate that these molecules are not clear or black, but rather hot or cold. As Boltzmann (more or less) correctly surmised, this means the hotter molecules are vibrating vigorously, whereas the colder molecules vibrate more languidly. With all the molecules vibrating to some degree, collisions are inevitable, so the two types of molecules will begin to mix, as we just observed with clear and black molecules. And because temperature is a measure of the *average* kinetic energy among a group of molecules, as the intermingling continues, temperatures on the left side of the vessel—initially hotter—will drop, just as the average kinetic energy on the right side of the vessel will rise. In the case of temperature, however, this levelling out will proceed even faster, since the vibrational energy of an individual molecule is not fixed. When a hot molecule collides with a cold molecule, the precise kinetic energy each molecule takes away from their collision will largely be a matter of chance, depending on exactly how the two molecules strike one another. But since because hotter molecules have more energy to lose, on average, the hotter molecule will a portion of its vibrational energy to the colder molecule. And with this same set of odds playing out across the vessel, broader measurements of temperature taken across the vessel will tend to equalize over time, creating the effect of heat having flowed from the left side of the vessel to the right.

This latter method of heat transfer, incidentally, explains how heat manages to flow even when the molecules in question cannot trade places with one another, as when a heat engine's firebox is placed against its sealed chamber. The molecules composing their iron walls do not jump from one body to the next. Rather, as the two objects are brought into contact with one another, their constituent molecules vibrate against one another. Again, the results of any jostling will be a matter of chance, but on average, vibrational energy will tend to move from hotter molecules to colder molecules, meaning the firebox will cool down as the sealed chamber heats up. Viewed macroscopically, it will appear as if heat is flowing from the hotter body to the colder body, much like a liquid. And because this statistically driven flow can only occur in one direction, periodically cooling the heat engine's sealed chamber will require dissipating its excess heat into the environment, rather than trying to "pour" it back into the hotter firebox. So here the Second Law, given a statistical interpretation bolstered by an atomic theory of matter, cuts two ways. It explains why an engine must squander much of the heat energy poured into it. But it also explains the unidirectional flow of energy that drives the engine in the first place, allowing it to accomplish far more work than any horse or human ever could, left to their own devices.

Sadly, Boltzmann's theories were not widely accepted in his lifetime. He was challenging the established Newtonian orthodoxy on too many fronts. Newtonian science, again, is founded on the proposition that nature is governed by laws that hold true with ironclad universality, whereas Boltzmann was discussing statistical probabilities. To many of his contemporaries, therefore, it appeared that he was not even studying the laws of nature. All of Newton's laws, moreover, are reversible, meaning the events they describe can run backward just as well as forward. This was not true of the types of events Boltzmann was studying. Granted, everyone could agree that ancient temples will not rebuild themselves, nor will drops of black dye spontaneously reconstitute themselves. But most physicists at the close of the nineteenth century viewed such phenomena as curious artefacts of living in our current highly ordered state, not matters of fundamental physics. Still, probably the most significant factor driving the skepticism with which Boltzmann's theories were met was the atomic theory of matter his interpretation of the Second Law presupposed. Indeed, the real testament to Boltzmann's genius is that when he picked up Clausius's atomic theory and developed its implications all the way to the end, he was doing so in the absence of any compelling empirical evidence, one way or the other, regarding the microscopic composition of matter. He was just trusting his intuitions, while pursuing questions of order and disorder few other scientists of his day found interesting.

Increasingly hobbled by depression and despairing that his life's work was being ignored, Boltzmann took his own life in 1906. In accord with his will, his headstone was inscribed with nothing but his name, dates of birth and death, and the equation he had developed to measure entropy, $s = K \log W$. When he died, Boltzmann was unaware that, a year before, a Swiss patent clerk named Albert Einstein had published a paper empirically confirming that matter is composed of tiny, vibrating atoms.

Thermodynamics and
the Progressive Worldview

This has been a long chapter, but it has brought us to a point where we can consider some of the more philosophical implications the nineteenth-century science of thermodynamics had for the evolving progressive worldview. Most significantly, the discovery of the second law of thermodynamics gave time an arrow, at the deepest levels of physics. We saw something similar happen once before, when the ancient Hebrews supplanted the older cyclical mythologies with a linear narrative featuring a series of one-time events occurring in a determinate, irreversible order. Christianity then emphasized this story's unidirectional character by giving it a consistent trajectory: we were born into paradise, but things have been going downhill ever since. In many ways, modern science reversed this declinist trajectory by establishing that nature is a stable, rational order within which human beings can make steady progress, improving both themselves and the world around them, primarily using reason. In another sense, however, the Newtonian universe was *so* rational as to be almost timeless: it is a fixed arena governed by unchanging laws, whose permanence is best exemplified by the perpetual transit of planets around the sun. Nineteenth-century geologists and biologists began challenging this view by showing that the world is not a static structure, but rather it is constantly changing—and it has been changing for a very long time—with there being substantive differences between past, present, and future. It was research in thermodynamics, however, that revealed just how deeply time's unidirectional flow is embedded in our world. And by century's end, Boltzmann was able to explain this unidirectionality: time's arrow comes down to order and disorder, with the world's ineluctable tendency to move from greater order to lesser order itself being a function of the fact that there are so many disordered states into which the world can slip, as compared to the relatively few ordered states it must work to achieve and maintain.

But herein lies the quandary the second law of thermodynamics posed for the progressive worldview. If the Second Law is what gives time its unidirectional flow, this principle would seem to be pointing the universe, not in the direction of progress, but of decline. Again, all the examples of progress cited thus far in the book have involved a movement from lesser to greater order. The second law of thermodynamics decrees, however, that nature's tendency is to move in the opposite direction. This would seem to imply—contra what progressives were celebrating—that our scientific knowledge should be growing less sophisticated over time, civil society should be crumbling into a state of nature, the world's economies should be growing ever more depressed, and moral theory should be moving away from the inclusive doctrine of universalism, in the direction of a more fragmented tribalism. And in fact, some advocates of the traditional Christian worldview have pointed to the Second Law as proof that the Genesis account of creation must be correct. Given that nature tends to move from greater to lesser order, and given the high degree of order human being possess, we cannot possibly have evolved from monkeys, amoebas, or tide pools filled with mud. We must have been created fully formed, already possessing a high degree of order, and if anything, we have grown more dissipated since.

The short answer to this argument, and to the broader concerns the previous paragraph raised, is that both the First and Second Laws of Thermodynamics *do* allow order to increase; the ancient temple did, after all, get built at some point. The crucial point to note here is that both thermodynamical laws refer to closed systems. According to the first law, the total quantity of energy in a closed system will always remain constant, with the Second Law stipulating that the entropy of a closed system can never decrease, but only increase. Most systems we encounter in the world, however, are open, meaning energy can flow into and out of them. This is why the steam engine can keep running: the fireman keeps shoveling coal, brimming with potential energy, into its firebox. And this, in turn, is what allows the engine to keep adding order to the world—driving a power loom, for instance, which turns out bolt after bolt of intricately patterned cloth. Hence, the laws of thermodynamics do prevent order from ever increasing. They just stipulate that any increase in order must be paid for, indeed, in two ways.

First, because the world naturally tends toward disorder, any increase in order will take work. Work, in turn, requires energy—or more precisely, work *is* energy, in one of its forms. According to the first law, energy can never be created or destroyed. And therefore the work of building order world must always be paid for through some input of energy, whether this takes the form of the food we ingest, the coal being shoveled into an engine's firebox, or the gigawatts of solar energy that flood our planet at every moment.

Second, because the Second Law decrees that the total order in the universe—the ultimate closed system—can never increase, but only decrease, when order does increase in one location, this must be paid for through at least as great an increase in disorder somewhere else. Indeed, this is what we observe when a power loom turns out a bolt of cloth. With the cloth being more highly ordered than the individual spools of thread supplying the loom, this order is paid for by reducing the highly ordered chunks of coal in the engine's firebox to a disordered heap of ash. Or conceived slightly differently, if the energy this coal releases gets translated into the highly ordered, highly useful rectilinear motion the piston uses to drive the power loom, this ordered motion can sustained only by dissipating at least as much of the coal's heat energy into a useless, disordered form through the radiator.

In Volume III of *The Progressive Worldview*, we will explore the interplay between order, work, and progress in greater detail, drawing on more recent science to develop a crucial distinction between simple order and complex order. We can close out the current chapter, however, and our survey of nineteenth-century science with a few remarks on the implications of the laws of thermodynamics for the concept of progress, itself. Most emphatically, these laws ensure that progress will always be hard. Any increase in order takes work, and work is a form of energy that must be paid for through further inputs of energy. So whether we consider Galileo patiently rolling his steel balls down inclined planes in search of a unifying explanation, the inhabitants of the state of nature struggling to create a social arrangement giving them greater security and stability, the trapper adjusting her labor to changing economic and environmental conditions, or the abolitionist fighting to end slavery in a country founded on the proposition that all people are created equal, all of this is work—hard work. In fact, given the tendency of everything in the world to degrade over time, from ancient temples to the societies that build them, to the individual human beings that comprise these societies, even maintaining our current condition takes work. The second law of thermodynamics is therefore the modern equivalent to God condemning us to scratch the ground for our subsistence: given the laws of physics, merely surviving and reproducing requires incredible effort, with any progress made beyond that requiring even more work.

Somewhat more subtly, but just as significantly, the Second Law guarantees that progress will always be wasteful. Just as an engine can never be 100% efficient, neither can progress. In fact, we have been finding a link between messiness and progress throughout this book. If we go back to scholastic philosophy, this approach to nature relied heavily on deductive logic, which is an extremely safe form of reasoning, in the sense of its utter certainty. We also saw, however, that because deduction merely involves to unpacking premises that have already been given, it cannot produce any novel knowledge. And for this reason, among others, the scholastic approach to nature was characterized by a distinct lack of progress. The abductive mode of reasoning that modern scientists like Kepler and Galileo began to use is far messier than deduction, insofar as it requires making a stab in the dark, throwing a hypothesis out there, before coming back and testing the proposed theory against the empirical evidence. On this approach, Boltzmann could tell us, more incorrect theories will be proposed than correct ones, simply because there are more ways to be wrong than right. And this can translate, not just into experiments that fail to produce any lasting results, but whole careers getting spent chasing down blind alleys. How many nineteenth-century chemists dedicated their professional lives to the search for caloric? We have no idea; we have never heard their names. Such failures may be heartrending for the individual scientist, but they must be taken philosophically, for they are the price the Second Law demands for the occasional, enduring advance. And it has only because modern scientists have been willing to pay this price, trading the certainty of deductive logic for the messiness of abductive reasoning, that modern science has been able to make such stunning progress.

The profligate nature of progress is seen even more vividly in Darwin's account of natural selection. Nature, on this account, is not just "red in tooth and claw" because some of its inhabitants happen to prey upon others, as Tennyson's memorable phrase suggests. Beyond this, Darwin portrays nature as abductively trying out a variation in a heritable trait here and there, in the off chance one of these random changes will provide its bearer with an advantage over its neighbors. When such a helpful variation is struck upon, this renders its bearer more likely to survive and reproduce, and thus to pass the new trait down to its offspring, while those traits that are advantageous enough may spread throughout the entire species in this fashion, thereby improving its fitness. For every such helpful variation that takes hold, however, there will be countless disastrous variations that kill their bearers long before they can reproduce. These failed attempts can be viewed the price the second law of thermodynamics demands for the progress made to a higher level of fitness on the part of the species. But this triumph will be cold comfort to those individuals dealt the unlucky hand of an unhelpful adaptation, who perish without sharing in the gains they have helped to purchase. Indeed, this points to the tragic underside of progress: not only does progress often come at great cost, up to and including individual deaths, but neither the costs nor the benefits of progress are typically shared equally among the individuals involved. As Boltzmann showed, order and disorder are statistical phenomena, having meaning only across large groups. Thus, to the extent that progress is associated with increases in order, nothing guarantees some individuals will not get left behind or sacrificed, even as average conditions improve.

As the nineteenth century ended, however, few progressives were dwelling on the downsides of progress. In fact, the turn of the twentieth century is a time when many Western countries made a push toward universal public education, partly guided by a belief that education is a universal right that should be shared by all, but also by the conviction that, once everyone had acquired the rational capacity to discern the interest they had in working together, rather than against one another, hatred, strife, and poverty would wither away. So, with confidence in both reason and progress brimming over, even as Boltzmann's work was not yet widely known or accepted, the notion that progress will typically be a story of "two steps forward, one step back" was nowhere in the public discourse. Accordingly, with the global economy starting to lurch forward again, having clawed its way out of the depression earlier in the 1890s, the first skyscrapers springing up in cities like Chicago and New York, and gasoline-powered automobiles starting to chug their way down the road, few progressives—or anyone else—foresaw the turmoil that was coming.

CHAPTER 10

THE EXPANDING UNIVERSE: TWENTIETH-CENTURY PHYSICS AND COSMOLOGY

———

At risk of cliché, the twentieth century was the best and worst of times for the progressive worldview. The century began on the same optimistic note on which the previous century had ended. Markets were expanding, and new technologies kept rolling out every year. The United States had largely stitched itself back together following the Civil War, and the frequency of conflict between major European powers had tapered to its lowest level in centuries. The Enlightenment conception of Progress was taking hold among many political and intellectual leaders in the United States and Europe. Secularism had already come to dominate the academy, and religion was increasingly losing its traditional influence over public affairs. To those who subscribed to the progressive worldview, therefore, it seemed that the West was finally starting to move toward a more peaceful, rational, prosperous mode of existence, perhaps only limited by the entrenched power of the upper classes.

In the United States, progressivism got a particular boost in 1912 with the founding of the Progressive Party, even if the party's birth was largely accidental. Teddy Roosevelt had served as a Republican President from 1901 to 1909, taking a broadly progressive line. Concerned that such "robber barons" of the late 1800s as John D. Rockefeller, J.P. Morgan, and the Vanderbilt family had not only grown obscenely wealthy but were gaining undue political influence, Roosevelt's administration took a number of steps to combat the power of big business, including breaking up several huge corporations or trusts, increasing regulation of the railroads, and beginning to oversee the safety of the American food and drug supply. An enthusiastic outdoorsman who wanted to democratize access to America's natural treasures, Roosevelt further established the National Park Service. Nearing the end of his second term, Roosevelt hand-picked his Republican successor, William Howard Taft, but when President Taft then began enacting increasingly conservative policies, Roosevelt decided to run for a third term in 1912. Losing the Republican nomination to Taft, Roosevelt helped launch a new party, joined by associates who shared his affinity for the working class. The Progressive Party's official platform in 1912 called for many measures that would still be recognized as progressive today, including limits on campaign contributions, an inheritance tax, the right of trade unions to strike, an eight-hour workday, and women's suffrage. Roosevelt lost the general election to Woodrow Wilson—a loss from which the Progressive Party would not recover, collapsing by 1918—but Roosevelt received more votes than Taft in the best showing an American third-party presidential candidate has ever made.

Of course, any dreams progressives had of the world entering onto a permanently more peaceful course were crushed in 1914 by the outbreak of the First World War. The world, having become more globally connected, saw an assassination in Sarajevo spark a war that drew in all the world's major powers, with new technologies such as the machine gun, tanks, and barbed wire making warfare both deadlier and more protracted than ever before. A staggering 18 million soldiers and civilians died in the Great War, immediately to be followed by a worldwide influenza pandemic that claimed another 50 to 100 million lives. Devastating as the First World War was, progressively leaning President Wilson could still be optimistic enough to borrow a phrase from writer H.G. Wells and predict that this would be "the war to end all wars." Specifically, Wilson believed that, by crushing the spirit of German militarism, the war would set the stage for the development of a new cooperative global order, which he tried to promote by spearheading the foundation of the League of Nations.

As it turned out, the harsh reparations imposed on Germany at the end of the war set the stage for a second round of German militarism that would culminate in the rise to power of Adolf Hitler. Meanwhile, over the 1920s and 1930s, the Soviet revolution—which had begun with the hopeful Marxist goal of establishing an egalitarian worker's state—descended into totalitarianism, with Stalin's purges claiming somewhere around 17 million lives. Then came the

Second World War, with its unprecedented 50-80 million war dead, including roughly 6 million Jews and others sent to die in Hitler's concentration camps. The war was followed by a Marxist takeover in China, which—together with the subsequent Cultural Revolution—claimed another several million lives. By the 1950s, moreover, the United States and the Soviet Union had descended into a Cold War that threatened the entire planet with nuclear annihilation.

Still, for all the horrors the twentieth century produced, the century also witnessed many dramatic steps being taken in a progressive direction, as measured against what had become the progressive moral yardstick of universalism. Early in the century, women in many Western countries began winning greater rights, including the right to vote; American women were awarded the franchise in 1920. The longstanding Western institution of colonialism largely collapsed over the course of the twentieth century, with independence being won—sometimes peacefully, sometimes through revolution—by such large countries as India, Egypt, and Iraq, as well as a host of smaller countries across Africa, Asia, the Middle East, and Latin America. Many of these newly freed countries adopted more or less democratic forms of governance, as did a majority of the former Soviet Bloc members when the Soviet Union collapsed in 1989, thus leaving democracy far more widespread at the close of the twentieth century than it had been at the beginning.

Zeroing in on the United States, oppressive Jim Crow laws and endemic racism had long frustrated African-American hopes for equal treatment following the Civil War, but the Civil Rights movement of the 1950s and 1960s led to major gains for America's Black community, if still not complete equality. During this struggle, Dr. Martin Luther King Jr. emerged as perhaps the most compelling expositor of the progressive worldview in history, with his monumental "I Have a Dream Speech" laying out the progressive vision of a more inclusive future in which the rights, dignity, and basic humanity of all people are recognized equally. By the late 1960s, the Civil Rights Movement had helped inspire the rise of a Women's Rights movement that sought to secure—with varying degrees of success—equal rights, economic opportunities, and personal freedoms for women. This was followed over the next few decades by activist movements advocating for the rights of such traditionally marginalized groups as indigenous peoples, the disabled, immigrants, gays and lesbians, and even animals. This period also witnessed the birth of the modern environmental movement, driven by the argument—among others—that we have a responsibility to protect the right of future generations to enjoy the only planet we all have.

In the scientific realm, the pace of learning only accelerated over the course of the twentieth century. In geology, the development of plate tectonics—a theory holding that continents float upon massive subterranean seas of lava, typically drifting a few inches per year and occasionally crashing into one another—finally explained how seabeds could be pushed up to form mountaintops. The emergence of the science of genetics over the opening decades of the twentieth century provided a physical mechanism for the inheritance of traits, something Darwin recognized his own theory was lacking. Further light was then shed on the transmission of genetic information when Rosalind Franklin, James Watson, and Francis Crick identified the double-helix structure of DNA in 1953. Of note later in the century was the invention and rapid development of digital computers, representing both an impressive result of scientific learning and a powerful new tool scientists quickly began using to drive research forward at an even more frenetic pace.

For all of the scientific advances taking place over the course of the twentieth century, however, the century's truly revolutionary achievements came close to its start. We have already seen how a handful of nineteenth-century scientists, including Darwin and Boltzmann, had begun challenging key assumptions of Newtonian science. Early in the twentieth century, two novel theories in physics blew the Newtonian model of the universe completely out of the water: relativity theory and quantum theory. While the practical implications of these two theories have touched every aspect of modern life—making possible, for instance, cell phones—their most immediate impact of these theories on the ongoing development of the progressive worldview was that, between them, they allowed astrophysicists to weave a cosmic narrative showing our universe to have been progressively developing—and indeed expanding—ever since its genesis nearly 14 billion years ago.

Thus, if the nineteenth century gave the progressive worldview the notion of a world in motion, "the world" for such nineteenth-century scientists as Lyell and Darwin was literally the planet Earth. Twentieth-century physics, in contrast, expanded the picture of a progressively developing world to include the entire universe, which turned out to be much larger—and older—than anyone had ever imagined. And one of the most remarkable facts about the twin revolutions in physics that ultimately produced this expanded worldview is that both were spurred by a series of five papers published in 1905 by a single scientist, twenty-six-year-old Albert Einstein.

The Theory of Special Relativity

Beginning with relativity theory, Einstein actually developed this theory in two phases, with two of his seminal papers of 1905 addressing the theory of special relativity; this would be followed in 1915 by his publication of the broader theory of general relativity. By his own account, Einstein had already started down the path that would lead him to relativity theory by the age of sixteen when he began musing on a thought experiment of his own devising.

What would you see, the young Einstein wondered, if you were to chase a light beam? At the time he formulated this question toward the end of the nineteenth century, light was well understood to travel in waves. Newton had proposed a corpuscular theory of light, arguing that light is emitted from a source like tiny pellets streaming from a gun, but in 1801, Thomas Young performed a "double slit" experiment that clearly showed light to have a wave-like character. Cutting two very thin slits in a sheet of opaque material, Young placed the sheet before a screen and directed a bright light at the slits. If light comprised particles traveling in straight lines, as Newton maintained, Young should have seen two distinct lines appearing on the screen, directly behind the slits. What Young observed, however, was a series of brighter and dimmer lines spreading out horizontally across the screen.

This was unmistakably an interference pattern, characteristic of what happens when two waves meet, as when the wakes generated by two boats collide: where the high or low points of the two waves coincide, they reinforce one another and acquire an even stronger amplitude, but where the crest of one wave meets the trough of another, the two waves cancel one another out and the surface of the water remains level. The fact that light behaves in exactly this same way made clear that light must be a wave, much like sound. This suggested, moreover, that the frequency of a light wave must determine its color, much as the frequency of a sound wave determines its pitch. And just as a sound requires air or some other medium for its propagation—sound is just a shock wave rattling the air it passes through—it seemed light must have some medium to oscillate as it travels. This medium could not just be air, however, since it had already been determined that light will pass through a vacuum chamber from which all the air has been evacuated. Thus, many scientists had long suspected that all of nature is permeated by an ether even finer than air, which functions as the medium for the transmission of light waves.

To return, in any case, to Einstein's thought experiment, what would you see if you were to pursue a light beam, traveling alongside the beam at the same speed as the waves composing it? Glancing over at the light beam, you might see, for instance, the crest of one particular wave. Keeping your eye trained in this same direction as both you and the wave travel forward, your gaze will remain fixed on this same crest. Yet, this means the light wave is no longer oscillating for you; it instead remains frozen at one particular point in its cycle. Yet, if light *is* nothing but a wave, movement back and forth, what is left to see once the oscillation has stopped? What color will the light beam appear to be if it no longer oscillates at a particular frequency?

More interested in pondering questions of this sort than in the rote learning required of students at the turn of the twentieth century, Einstein failed to impress many of his teachers and professors. He did not, as legend has it, suffer from a learning disability, nor did he ever flunk a math class. Nevertheless, his failure to focus on what the rest of the class was studying—combined with an intellectual cockiness to which he later admitted—rubbed enough professors the wrong way that, even once he had received his degree in physics, he found himself unable to secure an academic position. Taking a job as a patent clerk to pay the bills, he found himself with enough downtime to start thinking his way more carefully through the light beam paradox, as well as various other difficulties besetting the physics of his day. Amid these ruminations, Einstein took an abductive leap that almost defies imagination. Within five weeks of his initial burst of inspiration, as he later recalled, he had worked out the theory of special relativity, thereby turning the Newtonian model of the universe on its head.

Einstein understood—like the nineteenth-century pioneers of thermodynamics, Newton, and indeed the pre-Socratic philosophers who first posited that the world is composed entirely of water, or fire, or love and hate—that if nature is to behave lawfully, certain terms must remain constant, even as other aspects of nature change. Newton had quite reasonably assumed that space and time are two of the aspects of nature that remain most constant. Space, as Newton conceived it, is a rigid, unchanging vessel, filled with bodies that engage in local motion, but itself standing augustly outside the flux of nature, unaffected by either the presence or the behavior of the bodies it contains. Time is a bit harder to visualize, but Newton similarly conceived of time as a rigid sort of *thing*, ticking away forever at a constant rate and identical for everyone in the universe.

The Newtonian view of space and time is intuitive enough, but it led to the paradox—among other problems—that a light wave will no longer appear to be a light wave when viewed by an observer traveling alongside it at the speed of light. Astronomers had already clocked the speed of light at close to 300,000 kilometers per second. Puzzling observational data had recently emerged, moreover, suggesting that light has this same speed, no matter whether it had been cast by an object moving in the same direction as the light beam or away from it. This is odd, as we would expect a light beam to travel more slowly if cast by a body moving backward, much as a baseball you throw will have less net forward motion if you throw it while backpedaling. Some physicists had begun trying to explain this anomaly away, but Einstein went in precisely the opposite direction, embracing its implications.

Einstein's crucial burst of inspiration was to take the peculiar behavior of light at face value, positing that one of the things that always remains constant in nature is the speed of light, and—here is the extraordinary leap—that this speed remains constant *no matter what perspective the light is viewed from.* This means, going back to young Einstein's thought experiment, that you *cannot* catch a light beam, pulling up alongside it. For even if you are traveling at very close to the speed of light, say, 290,000 kilometers per second—relative to some fixed point—the light beam will *still* be shooting away from you at 300,000 kilometers per second, oscillating as it goes. Even more bizarrely, if you were to whiz by another observer as you pursue the light beam—with this person standing at the fixed point—this observer would agree with you, and *also* see the light beam receding at 300,000 kilometers per second, the stark difference between your own relative motions notwithstanding. Of course, the math would seem to completely blow up here, given our usual views of space and time. But this just means, Einstein concluded, that if nature has decided to keep the speed of light constant, what must be pliable is the shape of space and time.

To get some idea of how time and space bend at high speeds, we can loosely borrow from Einstein's own favorite illustration of special relativity, which features a train traveling at uniform speed down a straight track. Imagine this train passing a station at 50 kilometers per hour. To the stationmaster, it appears that the train is moving at 50 kilometers per hour, yet to the passengers in the dining car, the train does not move; it is rather the station whips by at 50 kilometers per hour. Who is right? Both are, relative to their own frames of reference. This illustrates the relativity of motion, although in a very garden variety sense that even Galileo had recognized: All motion is relative to some frame of reference, none of which is particularly privileged over any other. Different frames of reference, moreover, can move relative to one another. To illustrate, let us assume the train's porter tosses a mailbag off the back of the caboose just as it passes the station. Heaving the bag directly backward, the porter manages to give the mailbag a velocity of 5 kilometers per hour, relative to her own fixed position on the caboose's deck. As the stationmaster watches the mailbag trace an arc through the air, he sees it moving forward at 45 kilometers per hour, at least until it crashes into the ground. All of this is straightforward enough: the mailbag was put into motion relative to both frames of reference we are considering, but we were able to translate its motion from one frame of reference to the next using nothing more than addition and subtraction.

Now, however, let us assume the train is moving at 100,000 kilometers per second, or one-third the speed of light. This speed is too fast to discharge a mailbag without destroying it, so this time the porter waits until the train has traveled a short distance down the track, then she flashes a signal light back toward the station. The speed of light being constant, the porter will view the light as receding at 300,000 kilometers per second. If she counts off the seconds, glancing at her highly accurate pocket watch and raising a finger for each second counted, she will just be raising her third finger when she sees the light reach the station. Admittedly, in the real world, she would not be able to "see" this happen at the station until the light beam had bounced back, taking more time, but for purposes of illustration, we will grant both her and the stationmaster god's-eye views of the universe, allowing them to see everything at once.

Switching now to the stationmaster's perspective, as he watches the train recede into the distance, he soon perceives a light heading toward him, and since light always travels at 300,000 kilometers per second, this is the speed at which he will see the light approaching him. This is puzzling, since he just saw the train whiz by at 100,000 kilometers per second, so it would seem the light should be moving at 200,000 kilometers per second, having "lost" 100,000 kilometers per second due to the motion of the train. But still, the light comes in at its usual speed. To make some sense of this situation, the stationmaster (using his god's-eye view) likewise begins counting off the seconds that the light has been traveling. He also has a very accurate pocket watch, so each time he raises a finger, it is truly one second that has passed by. He is therefore surprised to see that, as the light reaches the station and the porter is just raising her third finger, he has already begun to raise his fourth finger.

What has happened here? This is where our powers of visualization begin to be challenged. Seemingly, the light should have been moving more slowly through space for the stationmaster, given the motion in the opposite direction of the source emitting it. And yet the speed at which light moves *through space* can never slow down. Accordingly, to make all of the events taking place fit together within the same universe, it must be that the light's motion *through time* sped up. As the light traversed the same distance from the perspective of the porter and the stationmaster, time moved faster for the porter, and thus more seconds ticked by on his pocket watch. Alternatively stated, if we take the station to be a fixed point, as the train accelerated to its current velocity at one-third the speed of light, time began to slow down for the porter and everyone else on the train, causing their pocket watches to move more slowly than the stationmaster's. It is not that they noticed any difference. Time still *feels* like it is moving at the same pace, whether the porter counts in her head or looks at her watch. But if she compares her watch to that of the stationmaster, they are ticking at different rates, each of them perfectly accurate for their respective frames of reference.

Time, however, is not all that grows fluid when you are dealing with high speeds. So too does space, as Einstein showed in his 1905 paper, in a way that is only slightly easier to visualize than time's dilation. One way to think about space's compression is as follows. With the train rolling along at a third the speed of light, we know that time is moving somewhat more slowly for those aboard the train than it is for the stationmaster. With their god's-eye views, however, both the train's porter and the stationmaster can see that the train is eating up the same number of kilometers. Thus, with time flowing more sluggishly for the porter, if she is to perceive the train as covering the same number of kilometers as the stationmaster, then what it means to be a kilometer must shrink for her. Again, she will not notice any immediate difference. If she uses her meter stick to measure the caboose before the journey begins and finds it to be 6 meters long, then she re-measures the moving car with this same meter stick, she will still get the same numerical result. But as the stationmaster uses his god's-eye view to watch the train speeding away, he will see everything on the train—caboose, porter, meter stick, and all—as being somewhat compressed in the direction of its travel.

Actually, at one-third the speed of light, the compression of space will still be minor enough as to be scarcely noticeable unless one is really looking for it. As bodies move faster, they do not compress at a linear rate. Rather, they start compressing quite slowly, with the compression then increasing exponentially as the body approaches the speed of light. That is why, at the speeds trains normally travel, their compression is so minute as to be undetectable. Newtonian physics therefore works quite well at these speeds, or even at the speeds at which the Apollo rockets traveled to the moon. For all practical purposes, space and time *are* rigid at these slower speeds, with the minor changes that do occur falling well below any conceivable margin of error. Indeed, even if our fictitious train were to increase its speed to 90% the speed of light, its length would still only compress by about 13%. As it continues to speed up, however, the changes in size will become increasingly pronounced, to the point that, if the train could somehow reach the speed of light, its length would be zero. This is why, Einstein realized, nothing in the universe can exceed the speed of light: this would require a body to have a negative length, which is impossible. In fact, massive bodies such as trains cannot even reach this speed, since they require some extension to house their mass; light can only reach this limiting speed because, as we will learn shortly, it has no mass.

In any case, once Einstein had published his revolutionary paper on special relativity, he noticed an odd side effect of his theory, so he followed up with another short paper, still in 1905. Only three pages long, this paper introduced the world to the most famous equation in history, $E=mc^2$. According to this equation, energy (E) equals mass (m) times the speed of light (c) squared. How did Einstein get here? We cannot go into detail, but we already know from Newtonian physics that every massive body possesses an inertia, or a resistance to changes in motion. Indeed, this inertial force *is* the body's mass, which is why more massive bodies are harder to start or stop. We also know that the faster a body travels, the more kinetic energy it acquires, kinetic energy essentially being mass in motion. What Einstein realized is that, as a massive object approaches the speed of light and the space containing it becomes ever more compressed, this concentrates its kinetic energy. At the speed of light, with the body having shrunk to an extensionless point, the energy it contains would be infinite. Infinite energy is not available, however, which gives us one more reason why a massive body can never truly reach the speed of light.

With a clear link between mass and energy having therefore been revealed, and their meeting point coming at the speed of light, it turns out mass and energy are equivalent to one another, or two different versions of the same basic stuff. This is surprising, of course, since it had seemed that the age-old search for nature's most fundamental conservation principles had been wrapped up in the mid-nineteenth century when Clausius and his colleagues articulated the principle of conservation of energy, adding it to the conservation of matter Lavoisier had already established in 1785. Einstein realized, however, that these two conservation principles need to be combined, since energy and mass are ultimately the same thing, with their sum total being what nature conserves. This further suggests that it should be possible to convert energy and mass into one another, just as potential and kinetic energy morph into one another as a pendulum swings. And the fact that energy equals mass multiplied, not just by the speed of light—a large enough number in itself—but by the speed of light *squared* suggests that even the smallest chunk of matter should be capable of releasing enormous amounts of energy. As researchers began to learn over the course of the twentieth century, wringing energy out of mass is not quite as easy as swinging a pendulum. Nevertheless, under extraordinary circumstances, such as when a star burns fuel at its core or you detonate an atomic bomb, a small portion of the matter originally present really does disappear, having been replaced by a tremendous blast of energy.

The Theory of General Relativity

Although the results just summarized would seem to be impressive enough, Einstein was concerned that his papers of 1905 had managed to describe only a relatively small subset of the motions we encounter in nature, namely, uniform, straight-line motion, such as the motion of our train going down a straight track at a constant speed. Under such conditions, the passengers will not feel like they are moving, which is why we could assert that considering the station to be at rest, or the train to be at rest, provide equally valid frames of reference. If the conductor were to slam on the train's brakes, however, or take the train around a sharp curve, the train passengers would all lurch to one side of the car, whereas the stationmaster would feel nothing, thus allowing us to conclude that it was the train that had changed its motion, not the station. The train passengers are here feeling the effects of acceleration, which happens any time a body changes either the speed or direction of its motion. Having worked out the relativistic effects of one special type of motion—non-accelerated motion—Einstein wanted to develop a more general theory of relativity which would cover all motions, including acceleration. This turned out to be a tougher nut to crack, taking Einstein a full decade to work out. And if the mathematics of special relativity is daunting, that of general relativity was so difficult even Einstein had to seek help. Nevertheless, the broad implications of general relativity are not hard to grasp, so we will skip the math and jump straight to the punch line.

Einstein was interested in studying accelerated motion not just for the sake of completeness, but also because he sensed this might help unravel the longstanding mystery of gravity. Back when Newton first proposed the principle of universal gravitation, his equations could beautifully describe the fall of an apple or the orbit of a planet around the sun. Newton was the first to admit, however, that he had no idea what gravity *is*. According to the mechanical philosophy, bodies can act on one another only when they collide, so the notion of a force working at a distance seemed like a contradiction in terms. Accordingly, some of Newton's contemporaries tried to develop mechanical accounts of gravity, the most prominent of which was vortex theory. Assuming space to be permeated by an invisible ether, this ether must spin around heavy bodies, drawing smaller bodies in toward them, much as the water spinning down a bathtub drain pulls the rubber ducky down with it. From Newton's perspective, such clumsy attempts to explain *how* gravity works merely ruined the elegant simplicity of the equations describing how bodies do, in fact, behave under its influence, so he was content simply to describe this behavior, without attempting a more fundamental explanation.

Two hundred years later, Einstein was less modest in his ambitions. His first key insight was that gravity and acceleration are equivalent to one another; indeed, gravity is merely one form of acceleration. To elucidate this point in a book he later wrote to explain relativity theory to a general audience, Einstein asks us to imagine a large, closed box with a hook on top, floating in space. If you were inside this box, you would likewise float weightlessly. But now imagine some unknown being grabbing the hook and starting to pull the box faster and faster, at a constant rate of acceleration. The force this acceleration imparts would pin you to the floor of the box, just as you can be pinned to the seat of an accelerating sports car. Asked what was happening—assuming you cannot see outside of the box—you might guess someone had flipped a gravity switch, such that the force of gravity is now pulling you down to the floor of the box and holding you there. And in fact, Einstein writes, you would be perfectly justified in this conclusion: the effects of gravity and acceleration are indistinguishable, so they may be regarded as the same force.

Einstein's second key insight was less intuitive. The special theory of relativity had already established that space is flexible, that bodies contain a certain energy merely in virtue of their mass, and that massive bodies moving through space can bend space. Moving on to general relativity, Einstein further proposed that, even when a massive body is sitting motionless in the middle of space, it will bend the space around it. The image most often used to illustrate this phenomenon is a trampoline. When you set a heavy object like a bowling ball on a trampoline, this deflects the surface of the trampoline, giving it a downwards curvature. Accordingly, if you then place a smaller body, such as a golf ball, on the trampoline, it will begin rolling toward the bowling ball until it "lands" on this larger object, coming to rest against its surface. Alternatively, if you roll a golf ball past the bowling ball, the golf ball will, in virtue of its own momentum, try to continue moving forward in a straight line, yet its path will bend because the surface on which it pursues this straight-line course is curved. Roll the golf ball at just the right speed, and it will begin traveling in an ellipse around the bowling ball, effectively entering into orbit around the heavy object.

This, Einstein argued, is what happens when planets revolve around the sun, with space being a three-dimensional version of the trampoline surface. When a space is empty, it is perfectly "flat," governed by the laws of Euclidean geometry. Place an object as massive as the sun in the middle of it, however, and space itself will bend into a curved, non-Euclidean shape. When a smaller body like the earth then tries to fly by, attempting to stick to its straight-line course, this "straight" line is bent around into an ellipse, the space housing it having been so thoroughly warped by the mass of the sun. What is noteworthy about this explanation of gravity is that it does not depend on any sort of mechanical interaction between bodies. Gravity, instead, turns out to be a form of acceleration, as Einstein had suspected: as the earth tries to fly by the sun, maintaining its uniform, straight-line motion, the sun changes the earth's course, or imparts an acceleration on it, having used its own tremendous mass to bend space.

Strange as this notion of curved space must have sounded when Einstein published his theory of general relativity in 1915, an opportunity to test the theory arose just a few years later, when a total solar eclipse was predicted. By this time, it had been determined that light is devoid of mass. Accordingly, if our universe is Newtonian in character—meaning that space is perfectly flat and objects attract one another in proportion to their masses—we would not expect to see light rays traveling in anything but straight lines, these massless objects being incapable of feeling the mutual tug of gravity. But if Einstein was right, and heavy objects like the sun bend the space around them, we would expect even light rays to be deflected as they travel in "straight" lines through this warped region of space. Fortuitously, distant stars emit light rays that travel close by our sun, although the sun's own light is usually so bright as to drown out this starlight. The sun's light is dimmed only during a total eclipse, which is what made the coming eclipse such a prime opportunity to test Einstein's theory.

In early 1919, a team led by British astronomer Arthur Eddington spent months tracking the position of a particular star cluster so they could predict exactly what its "true" location should be on May 29, when the eclipse occurred. Eddington then traveled to New Guinea to observe the eclipse, sending a backup team to Brazil in case his view was obscured by clouds. As it turned out, both teams had clear skies, and they confirmed that, during the middle of the eclipse, the cluster's position next to the sun was slightly different from what one would have expected, had the light been traveling in a straight line. A massless light beam having been deflected by a heavy object, the theory of general relativity was empirically confirmed, and the tousle-haired Einstein became an instant sensation, not just within the scientific community, but among the public.

From the perspective of the ongoing development of the progressive worldview, the effects of Einstein's triumph in the realm of relativity were at least twofold. First, relativity theory put the final nail in the coffin of the Newtonian notion that nature, in its most fundamental structures, is rigid and unchanging: the timeless arena within which progress can occur, but itself exempt from change. The nineteenth century had already shown that two of the natural structures that appear most stable—the Earth beneath our feet and the biological species that inhabit Earth—are in states of constant flux. Einstein's work showed that the very fabric of space-time is pliable, depending on its precise shape on the objects and events passing through it. (And this is without even getting into a further unintuitive implication of relativity theory: that space and time are not completely different types of things, but rather complementary aspects of a four-dimensional space-time.) Second, whereas Darwin's theory of evolution had shown that, within the biological realm, nature has been progressively developing for at least hundreds of millions of years, Einstein's theory of relativity set the stage for a further series of discoveries that would push the start of the progressive story back by many billions of years, while extending this story to the broader universe. Before we can fully appreciate these discoveries, however, we need to consider the second revolution in twentieth-century physics Einstein helped launch with his 1905 publications, the quantum revolution.

Einstein and the Atomic Theory of Matter

If Einstein crafted relativity theory almost single-handedly, the development of quantum theory was far more of a group effort. Nevertheless, it was Einstein who set the ball rolling, starting with the three papers he published in 1905 that did not address relativity theory. Two of the papers spoke directly to the existence of atoms or molecules. Recall from the last chapter that when Boltzmann first introduced his statistical account of the second law of thermodynamics in the 1870s, he encountered serious resistance on two fronts. The first was that his account relied on matter being divided into discrete, indivisible particles that vibrate in proportion to their energy. At the time, Boltzmann was simply trusting his intuitions in taking this stance, since there was little empirical evidence to support it. His atomic theory flew in the face, moreover, of the long-standing conventional wisdom that matter is continuous, capable of being broken into ever smaller parts. By the end of the nineteenth century, most physicists had begun to incline toward an atomic view of matter, particularly once J.J. Thomson managed to isolate electrons in 1897. Nevertheless, the question of whether atoms even exist had still not been definitively settled by 1905. In any case, Boltzmann still faced the second major objection to his work: that his statistical account of the second law of thermodynamics dealt in mere probabilities, whereas any true laws of nature must be absolutely determinate, holding true in every case, and not just with a certain degree of probability.

The first of Einstein's papers to address the question of atomism used Boltzmann's statistical analyses to provide a method for measuring molecular size. The success of Einstein's method not only provided indirect evidence for the existence of molecules, but it demonstrated the value of Boltzmann's statistical approach to uncovering determinate facts of nature. The second paper along these lines addressed the phenomenon of Brownian motion. In 1827, botanist Robert Brown had been using a microscope to study tiny particles of pollen suspended in water when he noticed that these particles jiggle incessantly—a movement he could not explain through any known biological principles. Other scientists noted a similar jiggling among tiny dust or smoke particles suspended in the air. This phenomenon remained a mystery until Einstein's paper of 1905 provided a detailed explanation of how the jiggling of smoke particles is caused by random movements on the part of the air molecules in which the smoke is suspended. Three years later, Jean Perrin experimentally verified Einstein's account, thereby vindicating Boltzmann and definitively resolving the 2,500-year-old debate regarding the nature of matter in favor of atomism.

The significance of Einstein's two papers supporting the atomic theory notwithstanding, these papers were not completely groundbreaking, in the sense that momentum had already been building in the direction of atomism. More revolutionary was Einstein's 1905 paper on the photoelectric effect, in which he established that not just matter, but also light, comes in discrete packets. Keep in mind that, for everything else Einstein did to upend the Newtonian model of the universe, light corpuscles were something Newton had championed. Early in the nineteenth century, however, Young's double-split experiment clearly showed that light is a wave. And when, later in the century, James Clerk Maxwell unified the phenomena of electricity and magnetism under an elegant set of four electromagnetic equations, at the same time showing that visible light is a form of electromagnetic radiation, his equations treated all these forms of radiation as waves. Maxwell's equations had been empirically confirmed in numerous ways, including through such practical innovations as the electric motor. Nevertheless, by the end of the nineteenth century, it was becoming clear that Maxwell's equations could not explain a handful of phenomena—or they predicted results that were either empirically unfounded or logically impossible.

One of these troubling phenomena was "blackbody radiation," the tendency of some materials to glow when heated. An iron poker placed into a fire, for instance, will first start to glow red, then white. Waves being continuous in nature, Maxwell's equations predict that glowing bodies should emit electromagnetic radiation of every possible frequency, and hence give off light of every different color. As the glowing poker illustrates, however, heated objects tend to glow with just one color at a time. Even more inconveniently, Maxwell's equations predicted that, at higher frequencies, the amount of radiation a blackbody emits will be infinite.

In 1900, German physicist Max Planck was considering the problem of blackbody radiation when he began playing around with the mathematics of Maxwell's equations. He realized that if he rewrote these equations, not as continuous functions, but rather as allowing radiation to be emitted only at certain discrete energy levels, they would conform to experimental evidence. Planck was further able to calculate the increment between these energy levels, a crucial measurement now known as Planck's constant. For as neatly as the mathematics was working out, however, Planck had no idea what sort of physical meaning his results could have. Indeed, the idea of energy behaving discontinuously struck him as so improbable that he had some doubts as to whether his math was right.

Already convinced by 1905 that matter is discontinuous, Einstein did not share Planck's qualms. Rather, picking up on Planck's suggestion of discrete energy levels, Einstein used these discrete levels to explain the photoelectric effect, another problem arising out of Maxwell's equations. Moving in the opposite direction as blackbody radiation—matter infused with heat energy releasing light—the photoelectric effect describes what happens when light strikes certain metals and this triggers a release of energy, in this case electrical energy taking the form of a stream of electrons; this is how photoelectric cells now operate, running everything from pocket calculators to satellites. In any case, Maxwell's equations predict that the number of electrons released should be determined by the light's intensity, or how brightly the light is shining, and thus by the sheer quantity of light waves flooding the surface of the metal. Experiments had shown, however, that if you shine a light with a low frequency—long wavelengths—on one of these metals, it will not release any electricity, at all, no matter how bright you make the light. But if you merely increase the frequency of the light—shorten its wavelength—the metal will begin emitting electrons, even as the light remains very dim. Yet, how can a dim light, containing less total energy, accomplish something that a bright light, seemingly having more energy, cannot?

Einstein's response was to suggest that light should not be considered a continuous stuff, whose total energy would therefore be fully determined by the amount of stuff present: the light's intensity. Rather, Einstein posited, light comes in discrete packets, all identical. Since every light packet is of the same size, the varying levels of energy they carry can only be determined by their frequency: the shorter a packet's wavelength, the higher its frequency, and thus the greater its energy. Drawing on Planck's notion of energy levels, moreover, Einstein posited that a metal will release electrons only when it is struck by light packets having a high-enough energy level—a high-enough frequency—to dislodge the electrons. This explains why shining a low-frequency light on a metal produces no electricity, no matter how bright the light is made. Such an attempt is like trying to topple a marble statue by shooting ping pong balls at it. Because the individual ping pong ball cannot possibly carry enough force to budge the statue, increasing the number of balls you shoot at it will not change things; they will still just bounce off. Fire just a single cannonball at the statue, however, and you can knock it down. Shining a dim light of high frequency on the metal has this same effect. Although only a small number of light packets strike the metal, each of them contains enough energy to dislodge an electron, and thus the electricity begins to flow.

Circling back to the blackbody effect, if we reverse the process just described and apply heat to the metal in the form of electromagnetic radiation, the metal will start re-gaining electrons. Each time it accepts an electron, it will shed the excess energy it receives in the form of one "photon," as Einstein's light packets came to be known. The metal, in other words, will begin to glow. Meanwhile, the leaps in the frequency of light emitted that Planck could describe mathematically, but not explain physically, now have their explanation: Because light energy only comes in discrete packets, or quanta, electrons cannot give up their energy along a continuous spectrum, but rather they will move jerkily from one energy level to the next, depending on whether a photon is being absorbed or released.

With both the photoelectric effect and blackbody radiation having therefore been explained by treating light as discrete photons, Newton's corpuscular theory of light appeared to have been vindicated, meaning the wave model of light should have collapsed. Except that it did not. Young's double-slit experiment could still be performed, after all, producing the interference patterns characteristic of waves. Maxwell's equations, moreover, still worked beautifully to describe any number of other phenomena. In fact, even within Einstein's quantized theory of light, waves still make an appearance: the energy level of an individual photon is determined by its frequency. Yet, what does it even mean for a photon to have a frequency? Does it jiggle back and forth as it travels through space, like a molecule subject to Brownian motion? How, moreover, does this square with the account of light Einstein was developing in his relativity theory, which posits that light races forward in a straight line at 300,000 kilometers per second? Einstein, himself, was not exactly sure, nor was anyone else for some twenty years after he published his seminal papers of 1905. Eventually, however, the mysteries surrounding the dual nature of light—sometimes a wave, sometimes a particle—would take scientists to the heart of quantum physics. Before we can enter this strange realm, however, we need to get caught up on some intervening developments in the atomic theory of matter. Bizarrely, it would turn out that electrons and other material particles display the same wave-particle duality as light.

Wave-Particle Weirdness

When Thomson isolated the electron in 1897, he demonstrated that electrons carry a negative electric charge. Yet, because most of the matter we encounter macroscopically is electrically neutral, Thomson theorized that atoms must be mostly composed of some positively charged form of matter, studded here and there with electrons to balance out the atom's overall electric charge. This was the so-called "plum pudding" model of the atom, with electrons being represented by the raisins that intersperse the famous English dessert. When Ernest Rutherford began shooting alpha particles at hydrogen atoms in the first decade of the twentieth century, however, he found that the particles did not bounce off the larger atoms predictably like billiard balls. Rather, most would pass right through the hydrogen atoms, although occasionally a particle would ricochet off at some odd angle. This suggested to Rutherford that atoms are composed mostly of empty space, though containing a small but very hard core at their center. In a paper of 1911, he proposed that this core, or nucleus, carries the atom's positive charge, while the negatively charged electrons occupy the atom's outer reaches, presumably orbiting the nucleus like little tiny planets traveling around a sun.

While intuitively pleasing, the problem with Rutherford's planetary model of the atom is that, according to Maxwell's equations, an orbiting electron should generate an electric current, depleting it of energy so quickly that its orbit would collapse into the nucleus in less than a second. Accordingly, in 1913, Rutherford's one-time student, Niels Bohr, proposed some changes to his professor's model of the atom. First, for whatever undetermined reason, electrons must not generate electric current as they orbit a nucleus. Second, following upon the findings of Planck and Einstein, electrons must be able to occupy only certain fixed orbital levels. This is why, when an electron drops to a lower orbital level, where it carries less energy, it must release a quantum of excess energy in the form of a photon. Conversely, when this electron gets shot by a photon, it can absorb the photon's energy and climb to the next higher orbital level.

Bohr first developed this model by studying hydrogen atoms, which contain just a single electron, but he later determined that heavier elements contain more electrons, with there being fixed numbers of electrons that can occupy any single orbital shell. As we now learn in high school chemistry class, an element's valence number—the number of electrons in its outer shell—determines how it will react with other elements, with diverse elements generally trying to reach a point where, between them, they have a complete outer shell. Thus, not only did the "Bohr atom" provide a physical basis for Einstein's accounts of blackbody radiation and the photo-electric effect. It elegantly explained why the Periodic Table that Dimitri Mendeleev had composed some half century previously is organized the way it is.

By the early 1920s, physicists had further determined that an atom's nucleus is composed of protons, which carry a positive electric charge, and neutrons, which are electri-cally neutral. The contemporary conception of the atom was thus well on its way to being developed. Nevertheless, some puzzles remained, particularly concerning the behavior of electrons. Specifically, empirical researchers had been play-ing with Young's double-slit experiment by firing electrons, instead of photons, at the two slits, and they found electrons produce an interference pattern just like light, suggesting electrons are actually waves. Or more precisely, researchers found the experiment could demonstrate that electrons are *either* particles or waves, depending on where you focused your attention. If you monitor the two slits carefully—perhaps by shooting small beams of photons at the slits and tracking their rebounds—you find that every electron passes through either Slit A or Slit B, consistent with the notion that electrons are discrete particles. But if you then look at the screen behind the slits, you see the interference pattern, indicating that waves are passing through the slits, then interfering with one another. Most bizarrely, it was found that, even if you shoot the electron beam very slowly, one electron at a time, an interference pattern will still develop. This suggests each individual electron is somehow interfering with itself in wave-like fashion—thus requiring that it pass through both slits at the same time—even as the electron could be observed passing through one slit or the other. What on earth was happening?

Struck by the similarity between electrons and photons, and specifically by their dual wave-particle character, in 1923 Louis de Broglie worked out a set of equations showing that both electrons and photons are particles that possess a harmonic resonance that gives them such wave-like properties as wavelength and frequency. This was a major advance. Nevertheless, the question remained as to what it meant for either of these particles to resonate, since it did not appear they simply vibrated back and forth in space the way entire atoms do. Werner Heisenberg began to spell out the answer to this question in 1927 with the introduction of his famous uncertainty principle—although his answer was just about as baffling as the original mystery.

Quantum Uncertainty

If you are observing a particle like an electron, Heisenberg asserted, it is impossible to determine with any precision both its velocity and its location at the same time. To get at Heisenberg's point, think about how you might take such measurements. You might, for instance, fire a photon at the electron, observing the photon's rebound to calculate exactly where the electron must have been when the two particles collided. This gives you the electron's location, but the collision will alter the electron's velocity, so you cannot use the results of the collision to determine how fast the electron was moving prior to the collision. If you then fire another photon to determine how far the electron has moved in the intervening period, this will allow you to gauge the electron's current velocity. But the second collision will also move the electron slightly, so now you have lost your fix on its location.

When Heisenberg first announced his uncertainty principle, it appeared to many physicists, including Einstein, that what Heisenberg had identified was a limit to the human ability to observe and measure very small particles. Surely an electron must *have* a determinate location and velocity at any given moment; it must just be that we cannot detect both at once due to technical limitations, such as the lack of a non-intrusive electron probe. The more researchers pushed forward on both the theoretical and empirical fronts, however, the more it became evident that the indeterminacy expressed by the Heisenberg uncertainty principle is somehow baked into nature, rather than reflecting a limit to our observational powers. It became clear, in other words, that at any given moment, an electron does *not* possess a specific location and velocity. The electron is more like a cloud, spread out over a range of possible locations and having a range of possible velocities. If you try to pin the electron down through direct observation, you can, in fact, isolate it at one location, *or* you can discern the electron to have a specific velocity. Home in on either one of these variables, however, and that just leaves the other more cloudy.

Strange as Heisenberg's notion of an uncertainty being woven right into the fabric of nature may sound, it did finally allow for a comprehensible answer to be given to the question of what it means for a particle to exhibit a wave-like behavior, assuming it is not simply vibrating back and forth in space. As it turns out, a particle's waves are probability waves. As we just saw, when an electron is not being directly observed, it will not have a single, determinate location. Rather, there is more a cloudy area across which you might find the electron if you try to pin it down through observation. This cloudy area is what has the character of a wave, with areas of higher amplitude being areas where there is a greater chance of finding the particle, and areas of lower amplitude being areas where there is less chance of finding the particle.

Admittedly, this notion of probability waves makes very little intuitive sense, which is why Einstein never lost his suspicion that some deeper, unknown principle must be at work here, lending determinacy to a situation that merely appears to be indeterminate from our vantage point. But this appears to be one thing Einstein got wrong. The mathematics of probability waves all work out, and after decades of empirical corroboration, a consensus has emerged among quantum physicists that nature really does contain an irreducible indeterminacy at the quantum level. Reality, in other words, appears to consist of statistical probabilities rather than determinate states of affairs, at least as long as we remain at a quantum scale.

The Implications of Quantum Theory

Most immediately, quantum theory revolutionized the view not just of physicists, but all of us, have of material nature. Over the millennia, the doctrine of atomism was always a minority position, overshadowed by the more widespread belief that matter is continuous, if perhaps held together in discrete bundles by certain immaterial forms. Now, however, we take it for granted that the macroscopic objects we observe are composed of physically discrete smaller parts, and that these parts are composed of parts, all the way down to microscopic atoms, themselves a product of yet smaller subatomic parts. Had these material building blocks proved to be tiny billiard balls, subject to the laws of Newtonian physics, the new atomism could have been integrated with the mechanical philosophy that began to displace Aristotelianism in the seventeenth century. As it turned out, however, the strange behavior of atoms and their constituent parts ensured the quantum revolution would complete a move away from Newtonian determinism that Boltzmann had initiated in the nineteenth century with his statistical interpretation of the second law of thermodynamics.

To be clear, Boltzmann did not predict quantum indeterminacy. When he argued that we need to use statistical methods to understand, say, the behavior of a liquid containing trillions of molecules, he doubtlessly assumed each of these molecules has a determinate location and velocity, with the need to analyze their behavior statistically stemming from the practical impossibility of tracking trillions of collisions at once. Boltzmann nevertheless demonstrated that we can use statistical analysis to identify certain objective tendencies and patterns in nature—justifiably calling them "laws of nature"—that arise out of situations that are not fully determinate in themselves, if only because they feature so many individual players interacting in so many complicated ways. Quantum theory took this indeterminacy a step farther, showing that it is not just the large number of interactions between the parts composing matter, but the fundamental nature of the parts themselves, that contains an irreducible indeterminacy.

What does the indeterminacy lying at the heart of material nature imply for the progressive worldview? At first glance, it is troubling. The progressive worldview first arose, after all, from the seventeenth-century realization that (1) nature is a rational place, governed by certain immutable, universal laws, (2) we can use our powers of reasoning to discern these laws, and (3) once we have identified these laws, we can start using them to predict how nature will behave under certain circumstances, which in turn allows us to modify these circumstances to better align the world with our human wants, needs, and aspirations. Quantum theory, however, proclaims that nature is awash in indeterminacy at its most fundamental levels, not only making it impossible to predict what its constituent parts will be doing a few moments from now but denying that these parts even exist in fully determinate fashion here and now. Yet, if nature is not the august, rational temple Newton conceived, does the progressive project fall apart?

It does not. For one thing, quantum theory makes clear that Newtonian determinism still reigns at the macroscopic level. Just as the effects of relativity are noticeable only at velocities close to the speed of light or in proximity to bodies as massive as the sun, the indeterminacy that pervades the subatomic realm dwindles as soon as we ascend even to the molecular level, all but disappearing by the time we reach the scale of everyday human life. This leaves most of the events that concern us as determinate and predictable as the scientists of the seventeenth century had envisaged. The phenomenon of radioactive decay illustrates how extreme indeterminacy on the quantum level can translate into a high degree of determinacy at the macroscopic level.

Uranium-232 has a half-life of 68.9 years. This means that if you have a single uranium-232 atom in your lab, there is a fifty-fifty chance the atom will decay into lighter elements at some point in the next 68.9 years. Over this period, there is absolutely no way of knowing whether *this particular atom* will decay. As far as scientists can determine, nature has no hidden variables that would render the decay of a single atom predictable, even in theory. The precise timing of an atom's decay rather appears to be truly random. That said, if you have a gram of uranium-232 in your lab, you can be extremely confident that, after 68.9 years, exactly half this sample will have decayed into lighter atoms, leaving half a gram of uranium. Hence, something completely random at the quantum level turns out to be fully deterministic and predictable at the macroscopic level, as soon as the probabilities associated with a huge number of quantum events have been aggregated. And since the macroscopic world is where we live, we can be confident that the objects we encounter will mostly behave as we predict—especially when we use the methods and accumulated knowledge of modern science to refine our predictions.

Why, then, even discuss the quantum revolution in connection with the progressive worldview? For one thing, on a philosophical level, the introduction, not of complete chaos, but of a certain degree of "contained" indeterminacy into our account of nature actually fits the progressive worldview better than the strict determinism of Newtonian science. Going back to the earlier chapters on the Scientific Revolution and Kant's theoretical philosophy, we saw that, even as seventeenth-century scientists began to uncover a highly determinate order of nature, they did so only by groping their way toward a scientific method that relies, not just on deduction—a highly determinate mode of judgment in which the conclusion is already determined by its premises—but also on abduction, the speculative means of generating entirely novel hypotheses. To be sure, a promising scientific hypothesis will not be completely random; it will at least be suggested by observations already made. Nevertheless, because these observations are not determinate enough to allow you, for instance, simply to read the theory of relativity off the observed motions of trains, the hypothetical stage necessarily includes a certain element of quasi-random groping in the dark—playing with ideas like chasing light beams before more rigorously deducing the consequences of these ideas and testing them out. Modern science thus owes its success to a certain degree of theoretical indeterminism, without which scientists would never be able to propose or learn anything new. Whether there is a direct link between the human mind's ability to generate novel ideas and quantum indeterminacy—with quantum fluctuations perhaps tickling a particular neuron this way or that—is not yet known. Philosophically, however, the dash of indeterminism that quantum theory adds to nature is consonant, if not with the scientific theories the seventeenth century was producing, then with the human capacity to launch such an intellectual revolution.

As scientists began to discover in the nineteenth century, moreover, abduction is not simply a mode of human reasoning. On the contrary, there are certain ways in which nature behaves abductively, and this is crucial to its progressive character. Most notably, Darwin showed that species are not fixed, but rather they gradually evolve over time as the result of a series of very small changes. And as twentieth-century advances in genetics made clear, these changes take place when parents produce an offspring with slightly different genetic material than themselves, whether due to the random shuffling of genes through sexual reproduction or the occasional genetic mutation. While a breeder may guide these changes to a certain extent, in nature, they are completely unguided or random. As a result, most genetic innovations will fail, the novel traits they produce killing their bearers before they can reproduce. Still, it is only by making large numbers of such random attempts that nature occasionally stumbles across a trait that is not only novel but useful, thereby helping its bearer live long enough to pass the new trait down to its descendants. Without this sprinkling of randomness into the reproductive process, the mechanism of natural selection could not have emerged, and life would have never evolved beyond the simplest microbes.

In fact, genetic mutation provides a realistic example of how quantum indeterminacy can cross over into the macroscopic world. As twentieth-century biologists determined, genetic information is encoded at a molecular level, within the strands of a creature's DNA. One cause of genetic mutation, moreover, is nuclear radiation. Accordingly, if a fertilized egg is exposed to a small amount of nuclear material, there may be a fifty-fifty chance whether enough material will decay to trigger a genetic mutation. This means that whether a particular species is launched on some completely novel evolutionary course may come down to quantum chance. Granted, this oversimplifies how genes operate: a species will manifest a visible change only when a large number of its genes are modified over many generations. But this just means the evolution of new traits, and new species, is the compound result of numerous random genetic events, thus ensuring that the course of evolution—while having a general logic to it—is not preordained in its details but rather has an irreducible unpredictability to it.

As twentieth-century physicists began to apply the findings of relativity theory and quantum theory to their study of the larger universe, some other instances of quantum indeterminacy crossing over into the macroscopic realm—occasionally with momentous effects—began to emerge. In fact, some astrophysicists now speculate that random quantum fluctuations are the reason we have a universe, at all. This brings us to the third major topic of this chapter, the story of an evolving, expanding universe that came together over the course of the twentieth century, a strange and exhilarating drama that likely represents the most significant contribution twentieth-century physics made to the ongoing evolution of the progressive worldview.

The Expanding Universe

In 1912, American observational astronomer Vesto Slipher made a puzzling discovery: the light coming from most of the galaxies we can observe beyond the Milky Way appears to be redshifted. Given the blackbody effect, when any element burns, it will emit electromagnetic radiation of certain distinctive wavelengths. By 1912, moreover, it was known which elements fuel various types of stars, thus making it possible to predict what mix of wavelengths should come out of large groups of stars. What Slipher found, however, is that galaxies give off radiation that is slightly redshifted, meaning its wavelengths are slightly longer—skewed more toward the red end of the spectrum—than would be expected. Typically, when an object is redshifted, this means it is moving away from the observer, for the same reason a train whistle sounds lower as the engine chugs away from you: the Doppler effect. The source emissions, that is, end up farther away from the observer by the time it has finished emitting a wave than when it first started, which essentially stretches the wave out. This makes sense in the case of trains, but in 1912, it did not make sense in the case of galaxies.

Going back to ancient times, it had always been assumed that, if anything in the universe is absolutely fixed and eternal, it is the stars above us. Of course, by the nineteenth century, the ground beneath our feet had begun to move, and just as Slipher was making his observations, Einstein was rendering space and time plastic, so perhaps the notion of galaxies moving through space should not have been entirely surprising. Nevertheless, if galaxies do move, one would expect to see some of them redshifted as they move away from Earth, but others blueshifted as they move toward Earth, and still others with little or no shift as they move transversely across our line of sight. So, unless God really did create human beings at the center of the universe—and for some reason commanded all the stars to flee from us—a uniform red shift across the sky was perplexing.

In 1927, a Belgian priest and amateur physicist, Georges Lemaître, published a paper interpreting the universal red shift in terms of Einstein's theory of general relativity. But Lemaître was not a professional astronomer, and he published in an obscure Belgian astronomical journal, so few scientists read his work. When the eminent astronomer, Edwin Hubble, then published a similar paper two years later, he did not have the same problem. Analyzing Slipher's observations, Hubble found that, not only are other galaxies retreating from us, but the farther away they are from us (as judged by such factors as the intensity of their light), the faster they recede. By this time, Einstein had gotten the world accustomed to the notion that space is pliable. Nevertheless, the theory Hubble proposed to explain the behavior of galaxies was startling: Unless the earth occupies some unique position in the center of space, it must be that galaxies are not racing *through* space, to get away from us. It must rather be that space we all occupy is expanding.

To explain Hubble's thinking, astronomy textbooks usually ask readers to envision space, not as the flat surface of a trampoline that was used to illustrate general relativity, but rather as the gently curved surface of a large balloon. To get from Point A to Point B, a rocket ship cannot travel through the center of the balloon. The rocket must rather travel across the balloon's surface, with the "straight" line forming the shortest distance between two points being a line that does not veer right or left, but which must nonetheless traverse the arc of the balloon's surface. To simulate the expansion of space and the variable redshifting it produces, let us assume I live on the surface of the balloon, in Galaxy A, but I can see two other galaxies, B and C, which are located 5 and 10 light-years from me, respectively.

Now let us suppose someone begins to inflate the balloon further. This stretches the balloon's surface, thereby increasing the total amount of space in the universe. Assuming this expansion proceeds uniformly, if the distance between Galaxies A and B increases by 1 lightyear, we would expect the distance between B and C to likewise increase by this same amount. This means, however, that the distance between my own vantage point, Galaxy A, and the more distant galaxy, Galaxy C, will increase by both lightyears put together, or 2 lightyears.

Over an equal span of time, therefore, Galaxy C will move twice as far away from me as Galaxy B. With Galaxy C receding faster, the light I receive from this more distant galaxy will have a more pronounced redshift than the light from the nearer galaxy, just as Slipher observed.

The short shrift initially paid to Lemaitre's work notwithstanding, he was the one who eventually drew the full implications of space's expansion. In 1931, Arthur Eddington went back and read Lemaitre's earlier paper, and recognizing its importance, he arranged to have it published in a more prominent journal. Enjoying some newfound recognition, Lemaitre gave a public talk at the British Association, where he suggestively noted that the current expansion of our universe could be the result of a "Cosmic Egg exploding at the moment of the creation." Lemaitre's thinking was straightforward enough. If our current universe is a large balloon that is only getting larger, presumably it was once a much smaller balloon. Or to go back still farther, all the way to the beginning, perhaps the universe started as just a single point—a Cosmic Egg—before blowing apart in a massive explosion that gave rise to the ongoing expansion of space we now observe.

Einstein is reported to have been immediately struck by Lemaitre's theory, but other contemporaries were more dubious. It is not that anyone had a more convincing account of the universe's origin. It was more that the prospect of assigning the universe any beginning, at all, was so daunting that most scientists preferred to stick with the Aristotelian notion that the universe had always been around, in essentially the same state as it always was. To account for the universe's observed expansion, a "steady state" theory was proposed suggesting that, at some point near the geographic center of the universe, both matter and space are continually created, from whence they spread outward. Fred Hoyle, one of the foremost proponents of steady state theory, was trying to be derisive when he dubbed Lemaitre's competing account the "Big Bang." Proponents of Lemaitre's theory came to embrace the name, however, and with new empirical evidence consistently coming in on the side of the Big Bang, a consensus has emerged among astrophysicists that our universe began in a cataclysmic burst some 13.8 billion years ago.

Over the second half of the twentieth century, numerous details got filled in regarding what happened between the Big Bang and the present day, with astrophysicists now being able to describe events dating as far back as 10^{-43} seconds—or $1/1\text{x}10^{43}$ of a second—after the Big Bang. Here we will merely touch on a few of the highlights of the story that emerged, a narrative that reveals our universe to have been progressively developing itself, taking on ever more sophisticated forms, for nearly 14 billion years.

It All Started with a Big Bang

In the beginning, to the best of our knowledge, was the Big Bang. It is natural to ask, "What came before the Big Bang?" or, "What caused the Big Bang?" Strictly speaking, however, these questions have no meaning. If we trace the current expansion of the universe back to the point when this expansion began, we literally do come to a point—known as a singularity—when all the current contents of the universe were packed into a geometric point having no length, breadth, or height. This point did not exist somewhere *in* space. Rather, it was the rapid expansion *of* this point, just as a balloon is blown up, that yielded the spatial universe we now know. By the same token, the initial singularity did not exist in time, such that we could ask what happened before the Big Bang. Rather, as space raced out, this took time, and thus the universe took on the temporal character familiar to us.

Obviously, this notion of space and time expanding out of nothingness cannot even be imagined without the theory of general relativity, but we can now return to one of the promised contributions quantum theory makes to the story of the expanding universe. If we cannot meaningfully discuss what happened before the universe began, or what caused the Big Bang, some physicists have nonetheless pushed up to the limits of comprehensibility by speculating that the whole universe began with a quantum fluctuation. One of the odd effects of quantum indeterminacy is that new particles will occasionally pop into existence before disappearing just as quickly, typically accompanied by an anti-particle. An electron, for instance, will normally be accompanied by an anti-electron, or a positron. This dual emergence helps keep the world's electrical charge balanced, yet the spontaneous creation of two particles out of nothing clearly violates the combined principles of conservation of matter and energy. So how can it happen?

Keeping in mind that, even under ordinary circumstances, particles do not have completely determinate locations or velocities, but rather a sort of foggy, probabilistic presence, it appears new particles are essentially able to sneak into existence, then sneak back out, before the universe has had a chance to notice their violation of the conservation laws, up to some threshold connected with the usual indeterminacy of particles. The whole of the quantum realm is so fuzzy and unpredictable, in other words, that not even nature bothers to monitor whether one more pair of particles happens to flick into and out of existence for a fraction of a nanosecond.

Normally, such random fluctuations go completely unnoticed by the larger universe. Back at the moment of the Big Bang, however, there *was* no space and no time, so a tiny phantom particle flicking into existence would have been all there was. Minuscule as this proto-particle might have been, when compressed into a geometric point devoid of extension, the pressure it generated would have been nearly infinite. Bursting outward to relieve this incredible pressure, this proto-particle would have generated a new spatiotemporal realm as it expanded, racing outward so fast that not even quantum fluctuations could keep up. Before the briefest fraction of a second had elapsed, therefore, the proto-particle would have exceeded the threshold of quantum indeterminacy. Unable to flick back out of existence, the newly created burst of matter would have been essentially stuck in reality, fully constituting a new universe as it continued to race outward in virtue of its own stupendous energy.

While the universe remains a tiny speck of energy, however, we need to mention one other conundrum that arose for astrophysicists as they attempted to fill in the details of how we got from the Big Bang to our present world. The initial singularity, again, had no extension; it was just pure energy packed into a mathematical point. Given its lack of extension, this primordial stuff was necessarily uniform and balanced: having no sides, it could not have been denser on its left side than its right. Yet, given the perfect uniformity of the universe in its initial state, once this point of energy began expanding into the space it generated, we would expect this energy to have remained perfectly uniform, just growing more diffuse as space expanded, and possibly transitioning into matter. But in this case, how did we get to our present universe, which is *not* perfectly uniform, but is rather characterized by vast stretches of empty space, punctuated here and there by galaxies and galaxy clusters? Indeed, how did the universe gain any structure, at all, if the initial state was so perfectly smooth?

This question spurred considerable debate over the second half of the twentieth century, and a final consensus was not reached until the 1990s. Cutting to the chase, it was again quantum fluctuations that saved the day. As noted above, the quantum realm is characterized by random perturbations that are usually so minuscule as to have no effect on the cosmic scale. For the first fraction of a nanosecond after the Big Bang, however, the universe was packed into a space so small that quantum perturbations *could* be felt. And this appears to be what happened: as the infant universe expanded, it somehow jiggled randomly, in the same way an ordinary particle might flutter briefly between the two slits it could pass through. This jiggling produced slight differences in the concentrations of energy that got distributed across the expanding space. While these differences were minor—maybe 1% more energy in one direction, 1% less in another—we know from relativity theory that the shape of space-time is affected by the mass it contains (with mass and energy being equivalent). As the universe continued to expand, therefore, it was now just slightly wrinkled. And just as an imperfection on the surface of a balloon may start out unnoticeable, but grow more pronounced as the balloon inflates, these wrinkles in space-time would grow in both size and consequence as the universe continued to expand, eventually seeding the universe's later large-scale structures. Before we get to this cosmic scale, however, we need to catch up on other things that were happening over the first few hectic seconds of the universe's existence.

When the universe initially popped into existence, everything was so concentrated that the four fundamental forces of gravity, electromagnetism, weak nuclear force, and strong nuclear force were likely unified as a single force. Within 10^{-36} seconds, however, the universe had grown large enough that gravity—which operates over much larger distances than the other forces—had separated out from the other three. Over this same period, the rapid expansion of space cooled the universe by diluting its energy, to the point that the first subatomic particles and anti-particles could begin coalescing out of the pure energy driving the Big Bang. When the strong nuclear force, which typically holds such particles together, then separated out from the electromagnetic and weak forces, this allowed an exponential expansion known as "cosmic inflation" to occur, swelling the universe to the size of a grapefruit within 10^{-32} seconds after the Big Bang. Over the next fractions of a second, as the expanding universe cooled still further to a mere 10 quadrillion degrees, quarks, electrons, and neutrinos began forming in large numbers, while the electromagnetic and weak nuclear forces decoupled, leaving the universe with the four fundamental forces it has today. By 10^{-6} seconds after the Big Bang, quarks began binding together to form protons and neutrons. The pace of change then finally beginning to slow, the next several seconds were dominated by particles of all sorts colliding with their anti-particles, thereby annihilating themselves and releasing photons in the process. With space expanding, temperatures continued to fall, reaching about 1 billion degrees 3 minutes after the Big Bang. This was an ideal temperature for protons and neutrons to bind together through nuclear fusion, so for the next 20 minutes, large numbers of atomic nuclei of the three lightest elements—hydrogen, helium, and lithium—came together. By the time the universe had finally cooled off enough to halt this fusion reaction, it was some half a trillion kilometers across.

Compared to the universe's initial headlong rush into existence, the next stage of its development proceeded at a glacial pace. For the next 240,000 years, electrons and atomic nuclei intermingled within a hot, opaque plasma soup. The universe's energy was concentrated in its photons at this point, but everything remained dark since these light packets could not shine through the opaque plasma. It was only at the end of this period when temperatures dropped to about 3000 degrees that energy levels were low enough for nuclei to begin capturing electrons. With the plasma now congealing into atoms of hydrogen, helium, and lithium, the photons could suddenly burst into a glow of light, the last vestiges of which are still visible to astronomers today. Nevertheless, around 300,000 years after the Big Bang, the universe grew dim again. It still contained plenty of photons, but with the space continuing to expand, the light just kept growing more diffuse, to the point that the universe slipped into a darkness that would last for the next 150 million years. It was then that the wrinkles caused by the early quantum fluctuations began to make themselves felt.

By this time, the universe contained large amounts of hydrogen, some helium, and traces of lithium. These gaseous elements are quite light, and they were growing ever more diffuse, just like the photons. Unlike photons, however, even light elements have some mass, and the principle of universal gravitation dictates that every body with any mass will mutually attract every other massive body in the universe. Due to the original wrinkles in space-time, moreover, the distribution of gases across space was not perfectly uniform. Areas of higher concentration therefore exerted a slightly stronger gravitational pull on neighboring areas than did areas of lower concentration. This drew more gases in toward the denser areas, thereby strengthening their gravitational pull even further. As the whole process snowballed, the matter within the universe began dividing itself into massive gas clouds, interspersed by much larger areas of empty space. The gravitational drive did not stop there, however. Within each gas cloud were areas of higher and lower concentration, and as gravity accentuated these differences, the superclouds broke into smaller clouds, before dividing again into yet smaller clouds. But at some point in this subdivision—starting around 300,000 million years after the Big

Bang—something different began to happen. Once gravity has compressed a gas cloud to a certain density, it will no longer subdivide, but rather all its constituent gases will be attracted to the same central point. The more the gases drift in toward this point, the stronger the central gravitation pull becomes, thereby concentrating the gases yet further. This process again snowballing, all the gases will eventually rush headlong in toward their common center until they collapse into a relatively small, central space, and a star appears.

With the birth of stars, a new dynamic—completely unprecedented in the early universe—comes into being. As gravity compresses huge amounts of matter into a very small space, internal pressures rise dramatically, pushing temperatures up to levels not seen since the early minutes of the Big Bang. At these high temperatures, individual atoms dissolve into their constituent parts, and nuclear fusion once again becomes possible. As hydrogen and helium nuclei begin fusing together to form heavier nuclei, tremendous amounts of energy are released in accord with the formula, $E=mc^2$. This released energy, in turn, blows the inward-rushing gases back out from the central core, contrary to the crush of gravity, until a point of equilibrium is reached where the outward-thrusting nuclear forces are balanced by the inward-pressing gravitational forces, and the star settles into a period of relative stability. With a sustained fusion reaction now roaring away within the star's core, most of the heavier nuclei it forges are just as quickly ripped apart by fission reactions. A few of these heavier nuclei, however, may be blown intact up to the star's surface, where temperatures are cool enough that they can recombine with electrons to form complete atoms of such heavier elements as nitrogen, carbon, oxygen, silicon, manganese, and iron.

Depending on their size, early stars lived anywhere from a few million to a few billion years. Eventually, however, a star's internal fuel supply will be so depleted that it can no longer maintain the equilibrium between fusion and gravity, and a second collapse begins. This collapse will often be followed by an explosion that temporarily creates a larger, cooler-burning star, which may, in turn, collapse into a much smaller, hotter-burning star. From here, many stars just fizzle out, going dark as they spend their remaining fuel. The very largest stars, however—typically those at least ten times the size of our own sun—will undergo one final, catastrophic collapse, exploding in a miniature version of the Big Bang: a supernova. This massive explosion strews the deceased star's contents across space, creating new clouds of gas and dust still mostly composed of hydrogen and helium, but now including small amounts of the heavier elements the star forged within it. Consequently, when a second generation of stars begins to coalesce out of the detritus of the first, again drawn together by the relentless pull of gravity, these stars will contain a wider array of elements. Some of the heavier materials, moreover, will come together in bodies not large enough to trigger fusion reactions. Depending on the size of these bodies, the elements composing them, and the orbits in which they happen to get captured by a nearby star, they may constitute space dust, comets, asteroids, meteors, or planets.

The Milky Way Galaxy is one of around 200 billion galaxies in the known universe. Located in the Laniakea supercluster, it is a nondescript spiral galaxy that contains somewhere between 100 and 400 billion stars. About 4.3 billion years ago, a second-generation yellow dwarf star formed toward the end of one of its spiral arms. Depending on how you count, this star has eight or nine planets orbiting it, the third of which contains modest amounts of water, as well as being just the right distance from its sun that this water can exist in solid, liquid, or vaporous forms. This planet further contains plentiful supplies of such heavier elements as nitrogen, silicon, sodium, potassium, and iron. It also holds carbon, a versatile atom that typically has 4 electrons filling the 8 slots in its outer electron shell, thereby leaving it eager to bond with other atoms and capable of doing so in a wide variety of ways.

If the ingredients for life were therefore in place since Earth's formation, the planet did not begin as a lush garden. On the contrary, its early atmosphere was harsh, comprising mostly carbon dioxide, mixed with methane and ammonia that spewed from the volcanoes constantly reshaping the planet's surface. Inhospitable as the early Earth therefore was, it did feature one additional prerequisite for life: copious amounts of available energy, much of it streaming down from the sun, but some of it arising from within the planet, generated by intense underground pressures and subterranean nuclear decay. Keeping in mind the thermodynamic principle that crafting order from disorder requires energy, the exact way various carbon-based compounds began organizing themselves into more complex, organic structures is still not entirely understood. The latest supposition, however, is that life began, not with lightning striking one of Darwin's tide pools, but with heat pouring from undersea vents fueling the rise of extremophiles, simple organisms that thrive under adverse conditions.

However it happened, once the first primitive organisms had established themselves and learned how to reproduce, they began improvising various means of metabolizing the energy they drew from their environment. A frequent waste product of their metabolism was oxygen, so over the next billion years, the oxygen-rich atmosphere we now breathe slowly came into existence. Single-cell organisms, meanwhile, learned how to join together to form more complex multicellular organisms. And with some of these creatures pioneering sexual reproduction—with its enhanced possibilities for genetic variation—the dynamics of natural selection we considered in Chapter 8 could come into full effect. Over the course of the next 3 billion years, ever larger, more specialized, more sophisticated plants and animals continued to evolve, ultimately producing the rich living world we inhabit today, of which human beings are only one of the latest products.

The New Foundational Narrative

Since the earliest human times, people have found themselves driven to compose creation narratives, motivated by an existential desire to grasp where their world came from, where it is headed, how it operates, and what place human beings occupy within it. The earliest of these stories were drawn from the natural world, featuring a cast that included celestial bodies, geographic features, weather events, plants and animals, even human emotions—with all these visible phenomena intermingling casually with unseen spirits and forces. As more formal religions arose and crafted their own creation narratives, these stories still tried to give people a home in a vast, often perplexing, sometimes threatening world around us. Increasingly, however, many religious narratives sought to provide this sense of belonging by describing an even better unseen, other-worldly realm to which we might one day escape.

The story that begins with the Big Bang and culminates in the evolution of human life is the creation narrative of the contemporary progressive worldview. Like the first creation myths, this story is drawn from our experience of the natural world. This time, however, it has been scripted using the abductive, evidence-based approach of modern science, whose rigorous methods give us confidence that, while the story will always be subject to further revision and refinement, it has an objective truth that transcends any particular cultures or traditions. This approach limits us to speaking about the world we can observe around us. But this has not stopped scientists from weaving a cosmic narrative more incredible than anything the most peyote-inspired shaman could have ever dreamed up, filled with bending space and time, wave-like particles that pop into and out of existence, and a universe that continually expands like a balloon.

This new foundational narrative has, moreover, turned out to be a story of progress—slow, fitful, messy progress, to be sure, but nevertheless a progress that has completely reshaped our universe, down to its most fundamental structures. This progress has included the evolution and ongoing development of a very smart primate capable of behaving in moral fashion. Indeed, having spent the last four chapters studying how various scientific advances of the nineteenth and twentieth centuries gave rise to the second iteration of the progressive worldview, we need to consider more closely how some of the social and political developments of this same period similarly transformed the progressive world-view on its moral side.

CHAPTER 11

THE ARC OF THE MORAL UNIVERSE: KING AND MORAL UNIVERSALISM

When Einstein predicted that light traveling from a distant star will bend ever so slightly as it passes by our sun, the sun's enormous mass warping the space through which the light travels, it seems unlikely he was considering the moral implications of the twentieth-century revolution in physics he was helping initiate. By the same token, when Martin Luther King proclaimed some sixty years later that "the arc of the moral universe is long but it bends toward justice," he was adapting a quote from nineteenth-century abolitionist and Unitarian minister Theodore Parker, and probably did not have Einstein's theory of general relativity in mind. Nevertheless, the resonance between these two images is striking. It reminds us that if, as the progressive worldview has emerged and evolved over the past four centuries, the single most important factor driving and shaping its ongoing development has been a series of concurrent advances in the modern sciences, reflection on the moral implications of these scientific advances has never followed far behind.

Galileo, after all, had scarcely finished articulating his law of falling bodies—a universal law of nature that treats the fall of every material body in exactly the same fashion—before Hobbes began searching for a corresponding law of human behavior. And just as Galileo's attempt to grasp some of the basic laws of motion ultimately led to Newton's depiction of the universe as an entire system of universal laws, Hobbes' search for the law of human nature inaugurated a line of moral and political inquiry that eventually led to Kant's articulation of the doctrine of moral universalism and to the founding of a new nation based on the proposition that all people are created equal—thus implying they ought to be treated in exactly the same fashion.

Taken together, the achievements just mentioned in the physical sciences and moral philosophy of the seventeenth and eighteenth centuries represent the culmination of what I am calling the first iteration of the progressive worldview. In the current chapter I will suggest that, if we view Einstein as the scientist who most decisively closed the book on the Newtonian model of the universe, thereby making him the standard bearer for the second iteration of the progressive worldview in the scientific realm, King is the twentieth-century figure most suited to playing this role in the moral sphere. Not only was King one of the most eloquent advocates for the progressive worldview of any era, but just as Einstein did not so much refute Newton's laws as show them to be special cases of a much broader and more dynamic natural system, King took the Enlightenment doctrine of moral universalism and drew out its full implications in ways its original authors would not have anticipated but that actually came closer to fulfilling their guiding intuitions than these revolutionary thinkers and statesmen themselves had managed.

Taking Our Bearings

To appreciate the precise nature of the change in progressive moral thinking King helped drive and articulate, we need to briefly review ground we have covered already—namely, the distinction between the first and second iterations of the progressive worldview, each of which has one foot in the physical sciences, the other in moral and political philosophy. As we know, the first iteration of the progressive worldview came to ground itself on Newton's portrayal of nature as a rational system governed by a relatively small set of unchanging, universal laws. These laws allow for local motion within space and time, but nature as a whole, on the Newtonian model, is augustly unchanging in its broader structures. And thus the Newtonian natural order came to serve as the stable, rational arena within which human reason could make its progress. This can include technological progress, as scientists uncover nature's universal laws and thus allow engineers to start manipulating the contents of nature to better serve our human ends. Yet, this progress can also include moral progress as we learn to treat one another in a fashion that not only better serves our collective self-interest but better aligns us with the workings of the broader universe as we begin to determine our own actions in accord with the idea of universal law.

Turning to this moral sphere, if the timeless, unchanging Newtonian physical order served as the backdrop for moral progress under the first iteration of the progressive worldview, this backdrop gave Enlightenment ethics a timeless character of its own. To be sure, moral progress is one of the types of local motion Newton's physics allows, so the moral philosophers of the seventeenth and eighteenth centuries always encouraged moral action. They fully assumed, however, that the *dictates* of morality are as timeless as the laws of physics. Hobbes and Locke, for instance, posited that the laws of human nature are invariant, which is why they not only tried to identify these unchanging laws but also sought to design systems of government that would work *with* the perennial dynamics of human nature rather than against them. Similarly, when Jefferson described certain moral truths as "self-evident," his eighteenth-century auditors would have understood him to be comparing the claim that all people are created equal or that human beings possess certain inalienable rights with another class of truths early modern philosophers regarded as self-evident: the necessary, unchanging laws of mathematics and logic. Teasing the timeless character out of Kantian ethics, meanwhile, will require a bit more work, but doing so will be particularly helpful for pinpointing the distinction with King's later approach to morality.

When Kant defines morality as acting in accord with the moral law rather than allowing our actions to be fully determined by our animal inclinations, he acknowledges the possibility that no one has yet managed to behave in fully moral fashion. Still, this does not change what it means to be moral, Kant insists, thus implying that our guiding ideal, the moral law—which is to say, the idea of universal law—stands timeless and unchanging above the flux of the everyday world. Otherwise stated, while our actions in the temporal order may either accord with the moral law or fail to, the imperatives determining what we *should* do are unaffected by the messy, ever-changing details of the precise context in which we find ourselves acting. It follows that, in any particular moral situation, I just need to perform the test of the Categorical Imperative—does the maxim of my proposed action take the form of universal law?—and, in theory, the test will return the same result every time for any given maxim, no matter under what circumstances the test is invoked.

This context-independent nature of Kantian ethics is best illustrated by a passage in which Kant explores whether it can ever be morally acceptable to lie—likely the passage for which Kant has been most roundly criticized by later critics. As a general matter, lying fails the test of the Categorical imperative, since using language to convey a falsehood contradicts the very purpose for which language was developed: sharing information with one another. Indeed, it seems that making lying universally permissible would cause the whole institution of language to fall apart. Kant raises the tricky case, however, in which I am hiding an innocent person from someone I know to have evil designs. If this aggressor knocks at my door and asks whether I am sheltering his intended victim, is it acceptable to deny that I am, thereby saving an innocent person from harm?

The answer would seem to be intuitively clear—just tell

the lie, for God's sake! Kant, however, was so convinced that a moral contradiction can never be right, any more than a logical proposition taking the form "A and not-A" can ever be true, that he concludes telling even such a well-intentioned lie cannot be morally justified, since this would require asserting something like, "I may use language, an instrument designed for conveying truth, to knowingly convey an untruth." Twentieth-century commentators have attempted to raise the stakes on this moral dilemma by proposing a context that is even more concrete and even more troubling: It is 1941 Germany, and I am hiding a Jewish person in my house when a Nazi stormtrooper knocks at the door. May I at least bend the truth in this instance? Some of Kant's defenders have attempted to show that Kant might be willing to accept a bit of creative misdirection in this extreme instance. Still, the lengths to which commentators have needed to go to "save Kant from himself" only highlight the degree to which Kant considered the imperatives of morality to be timeless and unchanging, indifferent to the precise context under which they are applied.

Setting ethics aside for a moment and moving to the second iteration of the progressive worldview, we have seen that a series of nineteenth-century scientists ranging from Lyell to Darwin to Boltzmann began calling the Newtonian model of the universe into question by demonstrating that some of the most fundamental structures of nature are capable of changing in a consequential, irreversible fashion. Then, in the early twentieth century, Einstein showed that even the rigid containers of space and time can be altered by the matter and energy passing through them, thereby driving the final nail in the coffin of the static, timeless Newtonian universe. Again, Einstein did not show Newton's laws to be false, but rather that there are special cases of a broader set of natural laws that are not only more dynamic than Newton's but more sensitive to the precise content to which they are applied, as exemplified by a massive body warping the space in which it sits. The cosmic tale of an expanding universe that arose out of Einstein's work makes clear, moreover, that nature's contents *have* been changing in dramatic ways over time, thereby altering the way the timeless laws of physics manifest themselves. Matter, for instance, behaves quite differently depending on whether it is concentrated in a superheated plasma soup, divided into individual atoms spread across a giant gas cloud, or compressed at the center of the star. Across these changing conditions—which typify different cosmic eras—the fundamental laws of physics remain constant. Nevertheless, the way in which these laws play out under such diverse circumstances is so different that we are justified in asserting, for instance, that the more specific laws of stellar dynamics simply did not exist until the first stars began to form.

In any case, this more dynamic, content-sensitive way of viewing the physical realm spurred the development, over the nineteenth and twentieth centuries, of the second iteration of the progressive worldview. According to this revised conception of progress, the universe itself and some of its most fundamental structures have been changing in dramatic ways for a very long time—since long before human beings came on the scene—with many of these changes being reasonably described as progress. And although human reason has recently come to play a prominent role in this story of progress, under the second iteration of the progressive worldview, human reason is not the sole nor even main driver of the world's progress. Human reason, rather, stands as one of the most notable products of a much larger universal progress—with human reason being so notable because, among other things, it has managed to carry the story of universal progress another step forward by pioneering the practice of thinking and acting morally.

Returning to the moral sphere, this time under the second iteration of the progressive worldview, just as Einstein showed that such basic physical structures as space and time can be affected by their material contents, King brought the doctrine of moral universalism into the twentieth century by recognizing that the struggle to realize such timeless ideals as universal equality can take place only within a particular historical context. And of logical necessity, this struggle will occur only in contexts where the proposed ideals have not yet been fully realized; otherwise, there would be no struggle. What this means is that the precise moral imperatives we find thrust upon ourselves will be shaped *partly* by the timeless ideals toward which we strive but *also* by the concrete social reality in which we find ourselves living, to include the many ways our current reality falls short of the envisioned ideals.

History has shown, moreover, that the concrete social reality we inhabit can change in profound ways over the decades, centuries, and millennia. And this means that what we are called to do in any particular instance will vary in accord with the time, place, and circumstance in which we find ourselves acting. Ignoring this context-dependent nature of morality is a luxury afforded only to those who happen to occupy the most comfortable circumstances of their place and time. This may have been true for Kant and Jefferson, but it was not true for King, who was born with dark skin into the segregated South of the late 1920s. Accordingly, while the moral vision King developed always kept itself pointed toward the timeless ideal of moral universalism, the rich detail that suffused King's understanding of what needed to be done at the precise moment in history that he was acting arose from the details of his own personal story, which were in turn strongly influenced by the larger story of the Black community into which he was born, which was itself largely determined by the role non-European people of color had long played in a global story of privilege and subjugation. To establish the context of King's moral vision, therefore, we need to touch on all three of these interwoven stories.

The Context of King's Moral Vision, Part I

Many of the defining moments in King's biography have become well-known to American schoolchildren. As a young boy, King was perplexed when a favorite playmate, who happened to be White and had begun attending an all-White school, no longer seemed interested in playing with Martin; eventually, the boy informed Martin his father had forbidden the continuation of their friendship. Nearing the end of his own career at the local Black school, King was similarly taken aback when he mentioned his plans to become a lawyer to a favorite English teacher. The teacher, aware of King's already impressive speaking abilities, gently suggested that

Martin was good with his hands, and perhaps he should consider becoming a carpenter. Ignoring this particular piece of advice, King entered Morehouse College at age 15, where he earned a degree in sociology. Ultimately deciding to follow his father into the ministry, he went on to Crozer Theological Seminary, then to Boston University's School of Theology, where he took a doctorate in systematic theology.

Although King's theological studies exposed him to the work of Kant and other classic moral philosophers, it was not abstract moral theory that filled the sermons he began preaching at Dexter Avenue Baptist Church in Montgomery, Georgia. King rather built his sermons, and later many of his political speeches, around the rich, messy stories of the Bible. King was particularly drawn to the ancient Hebrew narrative that later came to serve as the Christian Old Testament—the foundational narrative, as we know, that pioneered the linear view of time, with its cast of unique personalities who took decisive actions that could not be undone, irreversibly changing both their own lives and the world around them. Notwithstanding his own rootedness in the traditional Christianity of the American Baptist Church, the Old Testament story to which King was most drawn was not that of Adam and Eve disobeying God, committing the original sin that would get them kicked out of paradise and set humanity on a permanently downward course. Rather, the story King embraced—like many others in America's Black church before him—was that of Moses leading his people out of bondage in Egypt before guiding them on a forty-year journey through the desert until finally, on the eve of his death, he was able to climb Mount Nebo and catch a brief glimpse of Canaan, the homeland God had promised his people.

Of course, it is no mystery why, of all the stories that compose the religious narrative White American slave owners had once forced upon their Black African slaves, it was the story of the Exodus to which these slaves and their descendants gravitated. With the opening of the Atlantic slave trade in 1619, European colonists in North America inaugurated a system of race-based chattel slavery that came to serve as the basis of the colonial economy, most directly in the southern colonies, where the majority of slaves were held, but also in the north, where cotton picked by southern slaves fueled the rise of the textile industry. This slave-based economy served as a quiet backdrop to events a century and a half later when the European colonists decided they were tired of being ruled by an English king who unjustly exploited them in any number of ways while denying them any meaningful voice in their own governance. Resolving to free themselves from this oppressive rule, the colonists charged an eloquent Virginia planter with drafting a Declaration of Independence. Jefferson responded with the ringing words that have been cited here repeatedly, proclaiming that all people are created equal, endowed by their creator with certain inalienable rights.

With independence being secured on the battlefield and an initial attempt at self-governance under the Articles of Confederation starting to falter, a prominent group of former colonists called for the convening of a Constitutional Convention in 1789 to draft a stronger guiding document for the young United States. In preparation for the convention, the bookish Madison took it upon himself to design a system of government that would defy the ancient wisdom that democracies are inherently unstable while concretely realizing the universalistic ideals Jefferson had laid out in the Declaration. The convention dragged on through the heat of a Philadelphia summer, with delegates haggling over every word of every clause, but eventually, thirty-nine of them signed their names to the new Constitution of the United States, constructed largely along the lines Madison had originally proposed.

In many ways, the work of the framers was a stunning success. The stability of the democratic system they designed speaks for itself, with the United States now well into its third century. The longevity of the American experiment in democracy is due in no small part to the genius of Madison, who built on the work of Locke, Montesquieu, and others to devise a multi-part system of government that places the interests and ambitions of different individuals and groups in tension with one another, thereby balancing one another out. Not only did the Constitution establish the well-known system of checks and balances between the executive, legislative, and judicial branches of government, but it also struck similar balances between state and federal governments, big states and small states, the private sector and the public sector, and ultimately between elected leaders and the citizens who periodically vote them into or— notably— out of office. Such equilibrating mechanisms allowed the young country to establish a strong central government, capable of vigorous action, while resisting the devolution of power into small numbers of hands, itself the recipe for tyranny.

Similarly, we must acknowledge that the framers went

a considerable way toward realizing their own self-proclaimed ideal of moral universalism— or in any case, they went farther down this path than any other country had yet ventured. Otherwise stated, the United States went a fair distance toward replacing the ancient system of privilege with a modern system of rights. As prior chapters have noted, virtually every premodern society organized and governed itself in accord with some version of the system of privilege, a socio-political regime that divides society into a pyramidally shaped series of ranks, from the monarch on down, with each level of the hierarchy being accorded a distinctive mix of privileges and duties. Those near the top of the hierarchy enjoy mostly privileges, and only modest duties. Indeed, the exclusive privileges these lucky few enjoy are not only denied to those beneath them, but generally funded by the duties their subordinates perform: the king can eat his cake only because many peasants toil in his fields. Those further down the hierarchy, meanwhile, possess more duties than privileges, with the largest group at the bottom of the social hierarchy having no meaningful privileges at all, but only duties.

This system of privilege, in turn, came to be supported by an ideology of privilege, a belief system or worldview holding that the metaphysical order of the universe is similarly hierarchical in character, thus making it natural, right, and good that human beings should order themselves in similar fashion. A particular version of this ideology might hold, for instance, that an omnipotent creator stands as lord and master over his creation, and that when he fashions this world's human inhabitants, he not only grants them collective mastery over the rest of creation, but he makes some of these people noble by nature, others more servile. It follows that all is right with the world when kings and barons are ruling and peasants are serving: this is the way of the world, what God has decreed. Granted, life may be a grind for those who occupy the lowest tiers of the social hierarchy, but even they are well-advised to accept the status quo, since this is God's will, with the reward for their quiet obedience sure to come in the next life.

When certain philosophers and statesmen of the seventeenth and eighteenth centuries began arguing that the legitimacy of the sovereign derives not from divine favor but from the consent of the governed, that all people are fundamentally equal in moral worth, and that everyone possesses certain natural rights of which not even a king can dispossess them, they were proposing an alternate belief system, namely, an ideology of rights. The key difference in beliefs here is that, whereas privileges are exclusive in scope, rights are necessarily universal: if a right is limited to some particular group or individual, it is not a right, but a privilege. The Declaration of Independence offers a striking profession of the ideology of rights, proclaiming that all people naturally possess a moral dignity that was once ascribed only to the highest of social classes. The colonists then used this new dogma to justify their revolt against the English crown, and when the constitutional framers later sought to enact a system of government that would not only be stable but instantiate the ideology of rights, they enjoyed some success in this regard. This was particularly true in what we might loosely term the economic sphere, as opposed to the demographic sphere.

In the European context from which the American colonists descended, most kingdoms were relatively homogeneous in their demographics, with peasants being little different from kings in terms of their race, ethnicity, religion, language, or cultural background. Accordingly, the feudal hierarchy was defined by the different economic stations into which people were divided by the accident of birth: some people were born noble, enjoying immense power, wealth, and privilege, whereas others were born peasants, sentenced to lives of material privation and backbreaking labor. The lived experience of these two groups was therefore starkly different, but clean both groups up, and you could scarcely tell the difference between them.

When the American founders designed their new system of government, they explicitly sought to distance themselves from the system of privilege by rejecting, not just the monarchy, but the whole institution of hereditary titles. This had important economic implications, since holding a royally sanctioned title had traditionally been the only way to own land in Europe. Indeed, what it *meant* to be the Duke of Brunswick was to hold title to the lands of Brunswick. Dispensing with feudal tradition in favor of Locke's argument for the right to hold property, the framers established that, in the United States, land would be a form of private property like any other, to be bought and sold on the free market, thus making land available to anyone with the means to purchase it.

In a related break with tradition, the framers had some debate, but finally decided not to establish a property requirement for voting in federal elections. In England, voting in parliamentary elections had always been limited to property holders, on the reasoning that only the landed class possessed the wisdom, discipline, and skin in the game to vote wisely, whereas the landless masses could easily be swayed into voting for radical demagogues who would lead the country astray. Many American states still retained property requirements for voting, but delegates to the Constitutional Convention ultimately voted to make the federal franchise universal, on the argument that the right to select one's representatives was indispensable to creating a form of government that would operate in accord with the principle of government by consent.

Except, of course, that the right to vote, as originally enshrined in the Constitution, was *not* universal. On the contrary, voting was limited to white males of European descent, specifically excluding Native Americans, Black slaves, and women of any race. Nor was this exclusion from voting the worst treatment any of these demographic groups had suffered—or were continuing to suffer—at the hands of a society dominated by White European men. From the time European settlers began arriving in the New World, they had been driving Native American tribes from their homelands, decimating the indigenous population through what historian Jared Diamond has termed a deadly combination of European guns, germs, and steel. The system of chattel slavery, meanwhile, essentially took the Lockean doctrine of private property and applied it to human beings: dark-skinned people who had been kidnapped from Africa and their descendants were legally deemed to be property that their lighter-skinned owners could buy, sell, and dispose of as they saw fit. And though White women, at least, were never subject to quite the same systematic brutality as Native Americans or African

Americans, they were similarly regarded as the property of their husbands or fathers, both legally and culturally. It went without saying, therefore, that women would not be allowed to vote, despite being fully half the nation's population.

In a sense, this result is baffling. How could such intelligent men as the American founding fathers, imbued with the Enlightenment spirit of reason and inspired by a bold new ideology that celebrated government by consent, social equality, and universal rights, craft a social and political order that so obviously contradicted their own professed beliefs? The paradox is perhaps most striking in the case of Jefferson: the man who penned one of history's most remarkable manifestos of moral universalism owned slaves until the day he died, refusing even to publicly acknowledge the children he fathered by a favorite female slave. If we look back a little further, however, perhaps this result is not so surprising. Thumb through the works of Hobbes, Locke, Kant, or any of their Enlightenment colleagues, and it is not difficult to find remarks that today leap out at us as racist, xenophobic, or misogynistic. These remarks, moreover, are not presented as the well-reasoned conclusions of carefully developed arguments. They are rather just tossed off lightly, as if their authors were simply mentioning things everybody knew when they noted, for instance, the inability of women to reason about serious matters or the primitive nature of the "savages" European explorers were encountering in Africa and North America. It would seem, in other words, that these highly intelligent authors of the Enlightenment doctrine of moral universalism never even considered the possibility that the "universal" group to which they were applying their new ideology of rights might include people other than White European males like themselves.

In any case, however we choose to explain the gaping moral blind spot the framers exhibited, we can describe the socio-political results it produced in straightforward fashion. Inspired by an ideology of rights that had arisen out of the Scientific Revolution and Enlightenment, the constitutional framers sought to craft a political regime that was stable, efficient, and enduring, yet would also realize the era's new universalistic ideals. The framers, however, were all drawn from a single demographic subgroup, the group had traditionally enjoyed overwhelming dominance within European society: White males. Given the homogeneous demographic nature, therefore, not just of the Constitutional Convention, but of the young nation's entire leadership class, delegates focused their attention on dismantling the particular system of privilege that had long divided European White males into rigid, hereditary economic classes, each with its distinctive mix of privileges and duties. They replaced this particular version of the system of privilege with a surprisingly robust and enduring system of universal rights—*within the traditionally dominant subgroup of White males of European descent*. With respect to relations *between* demographic subgroups, however, the new constitutional arrangement did little to change things. Among social subgroups that were a function, not just of inherited economic station, but more fundamentally of such indelible, genetically determined traits as race, ethnicity, and gender, the system of privilege continued to prevail, with the traditionally dominant subgroup of White males of European descent continuing to assert its traditional power and privilege over everyone else.

Meanwhile, the dominant subgroup's intellectual leaders—the only subgroup with enough education to *have* an intellectual class—justified its ongoing dominance by reciting arguments drawn straight from the ideology of privilege. "Just look around you," these highly intelligent men intoned, one after another—in so many words. "Only White men attain high levels of education. Only White men serve in such esteemed professions as medicine, law, and the ministry. Only White men occupy political office. White men must therefore be the only group capable of serving as society's leaders. Indeed, many of these other groups would seem to be scarcely able to take care of themselves if not offered the paternal guidance of White men. This must therefore be the social arrangement nature intended: White men on top, with other demographic groups filling out the ranks on the social hierarchy beneath them. White men, in other words, bear the *burden* of social leadership; hence, they *deserve* whatever minor privileges this unique duty might happen to bring them."

The Context of King's Moral Vision, Part II

The schematic portrait just offered of the American socio-political system circa 1789—one demographic subgroup governing itself in accord with the new ideology of rights, even as it continued to dominate other demographic subgroups in the fashion of the old system of privilege—may be disheartening from a progressive perspective, insofar as it shows just how far short of their own universalistic goals our nation's founders fell. Nevertheless, it makes clear what shape the progressive project would take over the years and centuries that followed. And the American founders, wherever else they came up short, did create the conditions that would allow for progress to continue beyond what they had already accomplished.

For one thing, the founders did not just craft a political system that at least began to concretely instantiate the new ideology of rights, albeit within a limited subset of the population. They further managed to drive this ideology into the core of the American identity. For countless individuals over the course of more than two centuries—some of them members of the dominant demographic subgroup, others belonging to one or more marginalized subgroups, as well as many other people around the world who have looked to America aspirationally—what it has meant to *be* an American is to embrace such ideals as universal equality and individual rights. At the same time, if the founders designed what has proved to be a very stable system of government, they had the foresight to equip this system with a variety of mechanisms that allow it to change in controlled fashion over time. These mechanisms range from the regular election of lawmakers, thus giving voters ultimate control over the sorts of statutory laws that are enacted, to formal procedures for amending the Constitution, itself. And when Madison and his colleagues followed up ratification of the Constitution with a Bill of Rights that incorporated the first ten such amendments, the rights enumerated therein included many instrumental to promoting political change in democratic fashion, including the rights to assembly, free speech, and a free press.

In any case, with the American founders putting all of the concrete conditions into place—including a universalistic system of rights within a favored demographic subgroup, the continued assertion of privilege by this subgroup over others, an abiding ideology of rights, mechanisms for controlled political change—the progressive project since this time has taken the following form: slowly drawing one traditionally marginalized subgroup after another into the American mainstream, incrementally offering its members something closer to the full slate of rights, opportunities, and moral dignity promised by the Declaration of Independence, and thereby inching the country closer to its own self-proclaimed goal of crafting a socio-political system of rights that fully realizes the principles of the ideology of rights by creating a social and political community that is truly universal in scope.

Some of the individuals working to bring about such change have themselves been members of one or more particular marginalized subgroups, quite reasonably fighting for their group interests, along with any ideological motivation they might have. Others have been sympathetic members of the one or more of the relatively dominant subgroups, striving to bring American society into better alignment with its own founding ideals. Successful reform efforts have generally involved the participation of both groups, whether directly collaborating or just pulling in the same direction. This was certainly true of the country's first major social justice movement, abolitionism.

It was probably inevitable that, of all the anti-universalistic practices in which the young United States engaged, slavery would be the first to be confronted in sustained fashion. We can debate about whether the way European colonists treated North America's indigenous population or their practice of enslaving Black people from Africa was *worse*, whether qualitatively or quantitatively. By the time the United States had become an independent country, however, its Native American population had been so depleted, with most surviving members having been driven beyond the country's ever-expanding borders, that the "Indian problem" was generally a pressing matter only for frontier communities. Black slaves, conversely, were everywhere, particularly in the south but also in many northern states, and much of the nation's economy continued to depend on the institution of slavery, whether directly or indirectly. At the same time, the treatment of Black slaves by their White owners was proving to be so horrific that it became increasingly difficult to overlook the contradiction between the country's founding ideals of moral universalism and the barbaric practice of race-based slavery. Accordingly, over the first half of the nineteenth century, both Black and White abolitionists from a variety of socio-economic, intellectual, and religious backgrounds began demanding an end to slavery on moral grounds, arguing that such bondage was inimical, not just to the country's proclaimed Enlightenment ideals, but also to its Christian heritage.

Although crucial to the eventual demise of slavery in

the United States, the abolition movement was never strong enough to accomplish this result by itself. Abolitionism was always viewed as a fringe political movement, and even in the early 1860s, when the relatively liberal Abraham Lincoln won the presidency, he distanced himself from calls to immediately end slavery. Lincoln's own priority was to preserve the original union of states, some of them now proclaiming themselves free states, others still clinging to the institution of slavery. Lincoln's hand was forced only when eleven southern states moved to secede from the union to keep practicing slavery unmolested. Over the course of a devastating Civil War, Lincoln eventually concluded that "a house divided could not stand"—that a country could not endure indefinitely with two diametrically opposed policies on slavery. Ultimately coming down on the side of the nation's founding ideals, Lincoln issued the Emancipation Proclamation in 1863. It would take Union forces another two years to win the war and thus start implementing the Proclamation, with Lincoln being assassinated by a Confederate sympathizer shortly thereafter. Nevertheless, the institution of slavery did finally come to an end in the United States, and as the country began putting itself back together, three new constitutional amendments were ratified that sought to ensure that the rights and freedoms promised by the Declaration of Independence were extended to all Americans, both White and Black.

Or in any case, the Reconstruction period that followed the Civil War was characterized by an attempt to draw all American *men* into the community of those granted their full slate of promised rights. Since the country's founding, small but tenacious groups of women had been advocating for rights comparable to those of men, and particularly for the foundational right to vote. Over most of the nineteenth century, however, suffragists found little support for their position within the all-male legislatures that would need to give them this right. In fact, even the progressively leaning abolition movement split in half at one point in a dispute over whether women should be allowed to play a meaningful role in the movement, or whether they should stay home and leave the serious business of social reform to men. By the final decades of the century, however, with the all-consuming issue of slavery having finally been resolved, the suffragist movement came into its own, with protests around the country starting to grow large and colorful enough to start drawing the attention of elected leaders. In the second decade of the twentieth century, when the Progressive Party formed and gained some degree of political influence, women's suffrage was not high on its list of political priorities. As public opinion continued to shift, more and more politicians began to see the writing on the wall and—realizing that a huge new voting bloc would soon be up for grabs—began lending their support to the passage of the Twentieth Amendment, which would extend the right to vote to women. Eventually, this came to include the tepid, reluctant but politically significant support of President Woodrow Wilson, and in 1920, the Twentieth Amendment was ratified.

This brief consideration of two of the first major American social justice movements has already revealed one key characteristic most of these early movements shared: an intense focus on drawing one particular marginalized subgroup into the social mainstream, combined with a willingness to ignore or downright exclude other such groups. Indeed, one of the most graphic examples of this phenomenon took place within the suffragist movement, representing the inverse of what happened when the abolition movement was split over a disagreement on gender roles. In the decades immediately following the Civil War, freed slaves briefly enjoyed a meaningful level of political participation in the United States, even sending a handful of Black legislators to Congress. By the 1880s, however, Reconstruction had collapsed, and a series of Jim Crow laws swept across the South, including many that effectively rescinded the newly granted right of Black Americans to vote. By the early twentieth century, meanwhile, the suffragist movement was gaining enough steam that securing the franchise on behalf of women was becoming a realistic possibility. In a push to get over the finish line, some northern White suffragists actively sought the support of southern Black women, long denied the right to vote on two counts. Others in the movement, however, made the calculated decision to court southern White women by appealing to their racial fears, noting that Black men had likewise been clamoring for a meaningful right to vote, and if they were to gain this, the votes of White women would be needed to augment those of their husbands if control of southern politics was not to fall into Black hands.

Over roughly the same period we have just been discussing of the late nineteenth and early twentieth centuries, another cadre of progressives was fighting on a different front, this one defined more by economic than demographic differences, with industrial workers being the marginalized class activists were trying to draw into the American mainstream. There was good reason for this. As noted earlier in this chapter, when the American founders sought to dismantle the traditional European system of privilege, one way they did this was by replacing the institution of hereditary titles with a strong system of property rights. This provided a favorable legal environment ground for the developing market economy, which had taken on the character of full-fledged industrial capitalism by around 1870. With the United States well on its way to becoming one of the world's foremost economic powers, the resulting economic growth drove up the nation's per capita income, even as the cost of factory-produced consumer goods was coming down. Still, industrial production is not without its costs, and many of these were borne by workers in the form of grueling, dangerous work performed under unhealthy conditions, often for wages scarcely rising above the subsistence level.

Meanwhile, America's capitalist class was growing extremely wealthy, with a few "robber barons" living in absolute opulence, even as they responded to any attempts their workers made to organize for the sake of demanding higher wages or better working conditions with mass firings or even physical violence. Sometimes this intimidation was carried out by hired detective agencies such as Pinkerton, but also sometimes by National Guard troops sent in by business-friendly governors. As a result of the vast discrepancies in wealth and power arising between business owners and their workers, a new system of privilege was emerging within the United States, this time with capitalists on top, with a variety of middle managers and technicians filling out the intermediate ranks, and a vast army of semi-skilled or unskilled laborers toiling away at the bottom. Granted, the absence of hereditary titles did allow for slightly more class mobility than under feudalism, and just enough rags-to-riches stories were circulated to fuel workers' hopes of one day improving their economic station. But fortunes could be passed down to future generations just as well as titles, thus lending a hereditary aspect to this new form of privilege, and as well-monied families used their wealth to purchase political influence, this produced government policies that kept wealth concentrating into an ever-smaller number of hands. A notable feature of this particular version of the system of privilege, moreover, is that it was arising even *within* the demographic subclass that had seemingly left this system behind, at least with respect to its internal relations: White men. Indeed, by the 1890s, some White industrial workers in the North and Midwest were living and working under conditions just as bleak as those of former Black slaves now working as sharecroppers in the South.

As the American labor movement slowly galvanized over the first decades of the twentieth century, most of the heavy lifting was done by workers themselves, often at great personal cost as they mounted strikes and engaged in other forms of labor protest in the face of employer-driven violence, material deprivation, and public attitudes that were frequently unsympathetic to their cause. Gradually, however, a loose coalition of activists, intellectuals, and progressively leaning politicians came together to champion the working class as the next marginalized subgroup that needed to be accorded the same rights as those in the social mainstream, in the first case by giving workers a greater say in the terms of their employment by providing stronger protections for labor unions and requiring business owners to engage in collective bargaining. This was one of the priorities that brought the Progressive Party together, and though its time in power was short, it helped notch significant victories for the working class, to include limits on working hours, restrictions on child labor, stronger health and safety requirements for employers, and enactment of a federal income tax that would eventually allow for the creation of a social safety net.

With these progressive victories being acknowledged, it must be stressed—in keeping with the emerging theme of progressives being able to focus only on a single marginalized group at a time—that most of the gains arising from the labor struggles of the early twentieth century accrued to a single demographic group: White male workers. Granted, when the United States joined the First World War in 1917, this sent many male workers overseas, while drawing large numbers of women into American factories for the first time, thereby helping working women win some of the recognition and benefits of working men. As labor unions began to flex their newfound muscle, however, these unions were dominated by men, so they focused their efforts on issues relevant to their male members rather than the unique needs of female workers, many of whom continued to raise children and take care of their husbands in addition to working eight or more hours a day in a factory. With labor unions being concentrated in the industrial North and Midwest, moreover, the labor movement did little to touch the lives of southern Black agricultural workers. Indeed, many of the protections workers won over this period were either legally or practically denied to Black workers and other marginalized subgroups, particularly immigrants who came from parts of the world other than northern Europe.

Over the 1920s, the country enjoyed good times, with the economy booming and American social life bubbling with the excitement of the Jazz Age. But when the economic bubble burst and the Great Depression of the 1930s set in, the focus of progressively minded politicians turned back to the struggles of working Americans. In pushing through the New Deal set of reforms, Franklin Delano Roosevelt permanently altered the balance between the free market and the government within the American system, both by granting such government entities as the Federal Reserve Board a role in managing the economy and by creating a slew of redistributive programs meant to protect individuals from the worst vagaries of the market. Once again, however, most of these programs specifically targeted white Americans. The Aid to Dependent Children program, for instance—created in conjunction with the Social Security Act of 1935—provided cash benefits to families that had lost a father due to death or incapacitation. The target beneficiary was widowed middle-class White women, most of whom had never worked outside the home and were thus assumed to be incapable of supporting themselves. Black women, conversely, had long been forced to work as domestics or in other menial jobs to help support their families. Being more self-sufficient, and in any case facing lower social expectations as to the income level at which they lived, Black families were generally ineligible for Aid to Dependent Children.

A time of renewed hope for the Black community came

with World War II, when the intense need for manpower led the American military to open its doors to Black recruits. Individual units were segregated, with Black units typically having White commanders, but Black and White units fought side by side, with the heat of combat tending to melt racial distinctions away. As many Black units fought with great distinction, anticipation began to arise that, once the war was over, White America could not possibly keep denying the full measure of citizenship to a community that had just helped defend the country against fascism. This anticipation proved unfounded, however, as most American institutions remained legally segregated, while the generous programs of the GI Bill—which helped propel White workers solidly into the middle class in the 1950s by sending returning veterans to college and offering them cheap home loans—were denied to Black veterans; they were sent back to southern farms or northern ghettos with scarcely a word of thanks.

In May 1954, the Supreme Court did hand Black Americans a victory with its *Brown vs. Board of Education* decision ordering public schools to integrate, conceding its prior doctrine of "separate but equal" had been fundamentally flawed, given that—in a country that had long sanctioned race-based slavery and still featured many forms of institutionalized racism—separate Black and White institutions could never be equal. This legal decree notwithstanding, many Southern states and municipalities pointedly refused to integrate their schools or other public institutions. This included the municipal bus system in Montgomery, Georgia— which brings us, finally, the precise context under which a young Black pastor who had just taken his first preaching job in Montgomery had to pose the question, "What should I do?" when, in December 1954, a local Black woman was arrested for refusing to yield her seat at the front of the bus to a White passenger.

King's Philosophy of Nonviolence

When King began his ministerial career at Dexter Avenue Baptist Church in 1954, he had no plans to get involved in the civil rights movement that was just that beginning to coalesce at the time. It is not that he was unaware Black Americans had long been denied the universal rights promised to them by the American system of government; already as a 15-year-old student, he had won a public speaking contest with an address—his first public speech—titled, "The Negro and the Constitution." As a young pastor, however, King hoped to keep his focus more on spiritual matters, and he was looking forward to starting a family with his recent bride, Coretta. But when Rosa Parks was arrested and Black pastors in the area began meeting to discuss a response, King found himself elected President of the Montgomery Improvement Association. In this role, he led Montgomery's Black residents in a 13-month boycott of the municipal bus system, not pausing his efforts when his house was bombed or when he was convicted of violating a state injunction against the boycott. He instead appealed his case to the Supreme Court, and in *State of Alabama vs. M.L. King, Jr,* the Court deemed segregation in public transportation unconstitutional, thus bringing the boycott to a successful end.

As the events surrounding the bus boycott propelled

King into the national spotlight, he continued to develop the strategy of nonviolent protest that proved so effective in Montgomery. For King, however, nonviolence was not just a political strategy. It was a full-fledged philosophy, which he outlined in his 1958 book, *Stride Toward Freedom*. Drawing much of his inspiration from Mahatma Gandhi's non-violent struggle for independence in India, King identified six principles of non-violence. The first sets the tone for all the rest, asserting that nonviolence is *not* quiescence; it is *not* acceptance of the status quo; and its approach to changing the world is *not* for the timid. Nonviolence is rather an active, aggressive, extraordinarily demanding way of life that acknowledges two concrete facts of our world: (1) Ever since human beings began forming societies, power has been divided unequally. (2) Changing this situation will require vigorous, sustained action, since those who are in power and enjoy its privileges will not relinquish their power voluntarily. Achieving a more equitable distribution of power and other social resources will therefore require a fight. The question, however, is what sort of fight will best achieve the desired result.

King addresses this question with principles Two through Five. Nonviolence seeks to establish friendship and understanding rather than perpetuating enmity. Nonviolence opposes unjust social arrangements, not the individuals who happen to occupy the existing social structures. Nonviolence holds that suffering can be redemptive, demanding that its practitioners sometimes accept unwarranted suffering without retaliation. And nonviolence chooses love over hate, resisting violence of the spirit as much as violence of the body.

As King learned from Gandhi, these principles of nonviolence *do* have a strategic component to them. In fact, nonviolent protest is often the only strategy available to an oppressed social subgroup with a realistic chance of changing the status quo. The oppressed group will, after all, wield less power than its oppressor, so in an open fight, the oppressor is almost certain to win. The nonviolent approach therefore seeks to peel support away from the dominant group by appealing to the conscience of its individual members, typically by dramatizing the contradiction between the dominant group's own professed moral ideals and its actions on the ground, with the willingness of protestors to endure unjust public suffering without retribution only heightening the emotional impact of these appeals. The goal of this approach, accordingly, is not so much to defeat the oppressor as to build strong enough bonds of respect, trust, and even love between the two groups that the grounds for conflict begin to dissolve and the benefits of cooperation start to outweigh the benefits of domination, even for the traditionally dominant group.

The strategic value of nonviolence for waging an asymmetric battle against injustice notwithstanding, King did not view nonviolence as *merely* a strategic choice. He rather came to view adopting and living out a philosophy of non-violence as an existential imperative. To illustrate, we can ask what would happen if an oppressed group were somehow to defeat its oppressor on the battlefield. The most likely outcome would be the establishment of a tense balance of power between the two groups. This might reduce the exploitation of one group by the other, which would be a welcome result. Yet, with the violence stoking anger, fear, and hatred on both sides, the conflict would be unlikely to end. Most likely, it would rather simmer along quietly, periodically erupting back into open fighting. And as even Hobbes would recognize, such a perpetual state of war—no matter how low level—would serve nobody's interests.

Yet, the situation gets no better if the traditionally oppressed group were somehow to achieve a decisive victory and bring its former master under its heel, thereby rendering the former master a slave. Such an outcome, King insists, would defeat the whole purpose of the struggle, since the fight ought to be against *oppression*, not a specific group of oppressors. Overthrowing one's captors only to become a captor, oneself, would be tantamount to the situation Jesus warned against of gaining the world but losing your soul. In this case, however, the formerly oppressed group would *also* lose the world, or in any case, the world it had been striving to create. For the ultimate goal, as King always saw it, is to fashion a world that is not shaped by the fear, anger, and hatred that inevitably arises out of the violent exercise of power, but rather a world shaped by the love, trust, and compassion, thereby creating what King called "beloved community."

The Struggle for Basic Civil Rights in the Early 1960s and King's Dream

For all his talk of love, King was enough of a realist to understand that love, by itself, cannot bring about an end to rule by violence. The prerequisite for establishing beloved community is rather justice. Love, that is, can have a chance of prevailing over hate only if people generally treat one another as prescribed by the sort of universalistic ethic Kant articulated, as opposed to a few powerful individuals or groups systematically exploiting everyone else. And ensuring such universalistic behavior on a large scale requires that a society govern itself in accord with the egalitarian legal principles and doctrine of universal rights that Jefferson proposed in the Declaration of Independence. King and his fellow activists were well aware, meanwhile, that in a representative democracy, the most fundamental right is voting, since voting gives people the opportunity to select the leaders who will be responsible for safeguarding their other rights. And early in the 1960s, Jim Crow laws were continuing to make voting onerous, if not impossible, for Black citizens across the South, so King and the national civil rights group he organized, the Southern Christian Leadership Conference (SCLC), began to focus their political attention on passing both a Civil Rights Act and a Voting Rights Act.

The president at the time, the liberal but pragmatic John F. Kennedy, was broadly sympathetic to the goals of the SCLC, but he begged King and other civil rights leaders to slow down in the interest of national stability, assuring them equality would be achieved over time if only they would be more patient. For protestors who were getting beaten, going to jail, and running a real risk of being killed daily, however, the time for patience was past, and in 1963 the SCLC teamed up with other civil rights groups to organize a massive march on Washington to shore up support for the flagging Civil Rights Act and more generally pressure

Kennedy and other politicians to start taking concrete action on civil rights. In the opening section of King's own speech at the event—which would become the most iconic of his career—he tacitly rebuked Kennedy's hesitancy by reiterating that just because suffering may sometimes need to be borne patiently to expose injustice, this does not mean anyone should be willing to accept injustice for a moment. Protestors had therefore gathered "to remind America of the fierce urgency of now." This was no time, King proclaimed, "to engage in the luxury of cooling off or to take the tranquilizing drug of gradualism. This is rather the time to make real the promises of democracy."

Before we go on to consider the later, more famous part of King's speech in which he describes his dream for America, we should pause to note that the event at which he was speaking was officially titled the "March on Washington for Jobs and Freedom." This mention of jobs in connection with a major civil rights march struck some contemporary observers as curious. Its inclusion in the event's title, however, was largely due to King's insistence, and it fit a pattern consistent throughout his career of tying demands for racial justice to calls for economic justice. In one sense, this linking of racial and economic justice was straightforward enough. Centuries of slavery and systemic discrimination had produced huge gaps in wealth, income, and opportunity between White and Black America, so although securing such basic rights as voting was a necessary condition for bringing Black citizens into the American social mainstream, it was not sufficient. For Black Americans to enjoy the same opportunities as their

White compatriots, the unique economic barriers they faced would also need to be addressed.

That said, when King campaigned for economic justice—culminating several years later in the SCLC's launch of the Poor People's Campaign to address such issues as unemployment, housing shortages, and poverty—he made clear he was not just advocating for poor Blacks. He was rather seeking to bring about changes in economic policy that would benefit poor people of all races. In so doing, King was well aware that, while Black poverty rates were higher than White rates, the sheer size of the White population ensured that the majority of poor Americans were White, many of them living in the deep South or Appalachia. King's insistence on advocating for this particular demographic subgroup—which had traditionally been among the most hostile to Blacks—perplexed and annoyed some of his colleagues in the civil rights movement. Why risk diluting the movement's mission of securing equality for Black Americans by standing up for a community that often opposed this equality, sometimes violently?

For King, however, this advocacy aligned precisely with the ultimate goals of the movement—or what his philosophy of nonviolence said these goals should be. As with his nonviolent approach more generally, part of King's logic in linking racial justice to broader economic justice was strategic. As King frequently explained in speeches, if affluent southern Whites had used the institutions of slavery and Jim Crow to oppress Blacks to an unparalleled degree, these rich plantation owners had also badly exploited poor southern Whites. Their strategy, moreover, had always involved promoting a deep fear and hatred of Black people among "low Whites" so that the White underclass would direct its anger and frustration *down* the social ladder rather than *up*. If poor Whites could not find work at a decent wage, for instance, this must be because Blacks were stealing their jobs, not because wealthy Southern business owners were refusing to pay any of their employees a living wage. King realized that convincing poor Whites they had more in common with poor Blacks than with their fair-skinned social superiors would not be easy. But if civil rights protestors could secure some economic victories for poor people of all races, this might at least begin to diminish the rancor many poor Whites felt toward their Black neighbors, or if nothing else relieve some of the economic desperation that tended to foster such attitudes as racism.

Once again, however, seeking common ground with poor Whites was not *just* a strategic move on King's part. It rather went straight to the heart of his universalistic vision. To elucidate, we first need to recall how the progressive pursuit of social justice had typically proceeded up to this point in history. Again, virtually every premodern society had governed itself in accord with some version of the system of privilege, which concentrates power and privilege in a small number of hands atop a social hierarchy, while utilizing an ideology of privilege to metaphysically justify this social arrangement. Inspired by a novel ideology of rights coming out of the Enlightenment, the founders of the United States resolved to build a nation that would extend political power beyond a central ruling class to everyone, while trading exclusive privileges for universal rights. The founders only partially succeeded in their aims, however, by going some way toward establishing a system of rights within the traditionally dominant subgroup of White males of European descent, with this subgroup continuing to treat other demographic subgroups in accord with the system of privilege. Further progress toward realizing the ideal of moral universalism has therefore come as one traditionally marginalized subgroup after gained entrance, whether partially or fully, into the county's central in-group. This has never happened without a fight, since there have always been those within the reigning in-group more intent on defending their unique status and privilege than realizing their own putative moral ideals. In this combative atmosphere, however, neither have the marginalized groups seeking ascendency hesitated to throw elbows at one another as they compete for what must appear a limited number of open slots within the social mainstream.

To recall some of the precise examples we have witnessed of this happening, we can go all the way back to Hobbes, Locke, Kant, who began articulating the modern ideology of rights, even as they tacitly limited membership in the "universal" moral community to the traditionally dominant social subgroup, White European males, while sprinkling their writings with all manner of racist, xenophobic, and misogynistic comments. Or we can think of Jefferson so eloquently making the case that the inalienable rights of the American colonists were being trampled by their British occupiers, even as he owned a plantation full of Black slaves. Even within the abolitionist movement, moreover, there was a significant faction that refused to work with women to free slaves, just as a segment of the suffragist movement would later be willing to stoke White racism to help secure the right of women to vote. And finally, we considered a whole line of progressive politicians, running from Theodore Roosevelt to Wilson to Franklin Delano Roosevelt, who stood up for the interests of the White working class, even while paying Black Americans of any economic class scarcely a second thought.

As King saw it, this one-group-at-a-time approach to making social progress was understandable, and probably even inevitable. Unlike Kant, after all, he never viewed moral universalism as a goal that could be pursued in an abstract, context-free setting, where we simply propose a moral maxim, then use the principles of logic to determine whether it is universalizable. Fighting injustice, King always insisted, requires addressing the precise nature of the injustice that has been perpetrated. And because the concrete fact of our world is that different social subgroups have been oppressed in different ways, there is a degree to which these different cases must be handled separately: neither non-Black American women nor Native Americans were ever enslaved per se, so just as neither of these groups required an Emancipation Proclamation, neither does repealing Jim Crow laws directly address the unique ways in which they have been oppressed. That said, King's philosophy of nonviolence makes clear that the battle against injustice is not between particular social subgroups, but against unjust social structures, and ultimately against the attitudes that underlie oppressive social structures, namely, the personal greed that places Me before Us, and the tribalistic distrust and aggression that places Us before Them. And if the marginalized groups of the world cannot figure out how to transcend these combative attitudes in their dealings with one another, what hope is there that the broader society will change its thinking enough to allow any of these marginalized groups in?

Thus, if Kant's conception of moral universalism finds its most concise expression in the categorical imperative—a test for the morally acceptability of a particular, isolated action, divorced from a broader context—King's universalistic vision is better captured by two of his most famous quotes: "Unless all are free, none can be free," and "Injustice anywhere is a threat to justice everywhere." Almost like a subatomic particle with a precise state that is bound up with the states of all the other particles around it, King asserts that one individual or group can never become truly free if all others do not win a similar freedom. These two different conceptions of moral universalism do not contradict one another. In fact, King's moral vision presupposes something like the test of the categorical imperative to ensure that as one marginalized group claws its way into the social mainstream, it is lifting other groups up with it rather than raising itself up by clambering onto the shoulders of other marginalized groups and thus pushing them down. But by insisting that a light be shone on the precise and unique circumstances of oppression all these different groups have faced, King's conception of universalism guards against the moral failing that dogged Kant and virtually all his Enlightenment contemporaries: assuming the progressive project would be complete as soon as the principles of moral universalism had been extended to all the people who looked and sounded like them, those falling outside this privileged group scarcely deserving mention in a discussion on morality.

This is the spirit with which we must listen to the famous concluding section of King's "I Have a Dream Speech." By the time he built up to the climactic moment in which he describes his dream for the American future, he had already established the historical context of his remarks. He reminded his listeners that they were standing before the monument to a man who, "five score years ago," had signed the Emancipation Proclamation. With this particular choice of words, King alluded to one of Lincoln's own monumental speeches, the Gettysburg Address, which he opened by paraphrasing the words of Jefferson: "Fourscore and seven years ago our fathers brought forth, on this continent, a new nation, conceived in liberty, and dedicated to the proposition that all men are created equal."

Quickly moving to the situation one hundred years after Lincoln's address, however, King noted that Black Americans were still not free. Refusing to believe that the promises of the Declaration of Independence and the Constitution did not apply to his people, King colorfully compared these promises to a check, which had thus far been returned, marked "insufficient funds," but which he and his listeners had come to Washington to cash. He acknowledged that gains had been made in the struggle for civil rights, while also insisting on recognizing the tremendous cost at which these gains have come: "I am not unmindful that some of you have come here out of great trials and tribulations. Some of you have come from areas where your quest for freedom left you battered by the storms of persecution and staggered by the winds of police brutality." Nor would King allow that the hard work was yet done, instructing his listeners, "Go back to Mississippi, go back to Alabama, go back to Georgia, go back to South Carolina, go back to Louisiana, go back to the slums and ghettos of our northern cities, knowing that this situation can and will be changed."

The past and present having been surveyed, King went on to describe his vision for America's future, describing this vision as a dream he had for his country.

"I have a dream," King began, evoking Jefferson's words one more time, "That one day this nation will rise up and live out the true meaning of its creed: 'We hold these truths to be self-evident, that all men are created equal.'"

"I have a dream," King continued, perhaps recalling his own childhood story of being separated from a White friend, "That one day on the red hills of Georgia, the sons of former slaves and the sons of former slaveowners will be able to sit down together at the table of brotherhood."

Returning moments later to the theme of childhood, King thundered, "I have a dream that my four little children will one day live in a nation where they will not be judged by the color of their skin but by the content of their character."

What is striking about these passages is the richness of detail they quickly take on. Although King sets out from the abstract declaration that all people are created equal, he is soon offering a vivid depiction of the scenes we would need to see enacted to know this ideal had been realized in the precise context of the United States of America, with its great constitutional tradition and its long history of oppression, division, violence, and hatred along racial lines. Of necessity, the concrete specificity of King's remarks limits their scope. The images he conjures do not, that is, call to mind every social subgroup that has faced discrimination in the United States. On the contrary, the children of slaves and slaveowners who sit down with one another are unambiguously Black and White, nor is it even clear whether any of these children gathering at "the table of brotherhood" are girls. Martin Luther King, after all, was a Black man, and he found himself called to action at a time when the unavoidable social issue of the day in the United States was the ongoing exclusion of Black citizens from aspects of American life as basic as lunch counters and public drinking fountains. The specific task to which he was called was therefore that of helping to secure a place for Black Americans within the American dream. But King's dream did not exclude anyone else. On the contrary, the pictures King painted were pictures of inclusion, of exclusion being overcome. And if King's dream could come true—if White children and Black children could both be judged on equal terms in the United States of America, the country that has once designated Blacks slaves as equal to three-fifths of a White person—what was not possible for other groups that had been marginalized by the dominant group in their society?

Growing Turmoil in the Later 1960s

Some five months after the March on Washington, the nation was stunned by the assassination of President Kennedy. His successor, Lyndon B. Johnson, was another progressive at heart who nonetheless hoped to take civil rights reform at a more measured pace, in his case, so he could focus on his own broader anti-poverty agenda. Feeling the pressure of ongoing protests across the country, however, while being prodded by King and other civil rights leaders, the former Senate Majority Leader ultimately grasped the urgency of the moment and used his considerable legislative skills to help secure passage of the Civil Rights Act in 1964 and of the Voting Rights Act in 1965.

These twin legislative achievements proved to be the high-water mark of the civil rights movement. In the years that immediately followed, the Johnson Administration turned its attention to enacting a range of Great Society programs meant to prosecute the War on Poverty it had declared before the entire country became increasingly consumed by another war, that in Vietnam. As anti-war protests began to sap the civil rights movement of attention and energy, many Black leaders remained pointedly neutral on the war, not wanting to risk losing the support of White moderates by appearing to express support for the communist regime in North Vietnam. King, however, felt compelled to remain true to his universalistic vision by speaking out on behalf of all the marginalized groups he saw being harmed by the war. This included the young Black men who were being sent to fight an unnecessary war overseas and who were being drafted into the military at a much higher rate than their White counterparts. But King also lamented the deaths of hundreds of thousands of Vietnamese peasants at the hands of American troops and their South Vietnamese allies, victims of a proxy war between the United States and Soviet Union that had little to do with their simple desire for a plot of land to farm.

Deeming the propensity of the great powers to use warfare as an instrument of policy to be one more manifestation of the combative, exploitative, us-versus-them attitude that drives injustice everywhere, King lumped militarism together with racism and poverty as the "triple evils" standing in the way of America's more complete realization of its own universalistic ideals.

With nerves fraying across the country, by the second half of the 1960s many Black activists were losing patience with King's philosophy of nonviolence. From the start of the civil rights movement, there had been a debate as to whether nonviolent protest provided an adequate response to the injustices being perpetrated against the Black community, which came to include southern police cracking down on protestors in ever more violent fashion. Malcolm X emerged as the leader of a faction advocating for a more militant approach than King's. Although Malcolm's views on violence evolved over time, he always insisted that violence is justified at least in cases of self-defense, viewing King's doctrine of the redemptive power of suffering as a reversion to the slave mentality. When Malcolm was assassinated in 1965, leaders of the Black Power movement such as Stokely Carmichael stepped up their calls for Black activists to spend less time trying to make room for themselves in White society and more time building up their own power so that Blacks could start forming communities of their own, dictating the terms by which they engaged with the larger country. Then in 1966, Bobby Seale and Huey Newton formed the Black Panther Party, an Oakland-based group that advocated for an even more militant approach to fighting racial injustice, taking advantage of California's loose open carry laws to show up at demonstrations or monitor police activity fully armed.

As the civil rights movement increasingly began splitting itself among these different approaches, King made clear that he understood—and shared—the frustration that was driving some activists toward a greater tolerance for violence. He always insisted, however, that the temptation to lash out is a temptation to be resisted. In speech after speech, he implored listeners not to grow bitter, reminding them that "hatred can never drive out hatred; only love can drive out hatred." Indeed, King observed, it was during challenging times such as these that the sixth and final principle of his philosophy of nonviolence was truly needed: Nonviolence believes the universe is on the side of justice, and nonviolence believes justice will eventually win. Or as we can reformulate this principle using visual imagery we have already seen King employ: We have a moral duty to believe that while the arc of the universe is long, it bends towards justice.

King's Moral Faith

It may be surprising, as we approach the final chapters of this book, that we should zero in on a call for faith on the part of a twentieth-century Baptist minister. A key thesis of the book, after all, has been that the development of the progressive worldview has been closely tied to the emergence of the modern sciences and their crucial turn away from the blind faith in authority, religious or otherwise, and toward a rigorously empirical mode of reasoning. While this thesis still holds, I believe those who subscribe to the progressive worldview have just as much need for faith as anyone else. I believe, moreover, that King modeled a *type* of faith that progressives of any religious bent, or none at all, can embrace in good intellectual conscience. In fact, I would follow King in suggesting the type of faith he articulates is something progressives have a moral duty to embrace.

To be sure, as an American Baptist minister, King had a strong personal belief in the immortality of the soul and the ultimate coming of God's kingdom, and in his sermons at Ebenezer Baptist Church, he often preached about such specifically Christian convictions. In his addresses to broader audiences, however, although King constantly evoked the compelling stories and rich poetic language of the biblical tradition, he spent little time trying to convince his listeners of the truth of certain unknowable propositions regarding worlds beyond our own. And he most certainly did not counsel his listeners to defer their hopes for peace, justice, equality, and moral dignity to the next life. Just the opposite: King's philosophy of nonviolence demands urgent action in the here and now, and as the dream he described in Washington makes abundantly clear, when King looked forward to the time when "every valley shall be exalted, and every hill and valley shall be made low," he was not imagining some future heavenly realm. He was inviting his listeners to envision a more just, egalitarian order being established within *this* life, within *this* world. What King's sixth principle of nonviolence therefore demands is that we do not regard this vision as a mere pipe dream, nor even that we limit ourselves to fervently hoping this dream may one day come true. Instead, we must believe with all our hearts that the dream *will* come true, and moreover, *that the entire universe is straining to make this so.*

Yet how, in good intellectual conscience, can we maintain such a belief when we know, first of all, that the future is highly contingent, dependent on the actions that countless individuals will decide to take, and second, that much of the evidence available to us would appear to speak against the likelihood of King's dream being realized? Whether we look back at human history or at the world around us today, we see endless examples of oppression, intolerance, cruelty, hatred, greed, violence, and warfare. What reason, then, do we have to believe any of this will change?

To answer this question properly, we cannot just consider particular instances of historical injustice, no matter how often they may recur, nor how deeply their patterns may still be woven into our current social fabric. We must rather take a *very* long view, stepping back far enough to survey the entire arc of history so that we can discern its overall trajectory. King was a preacher, not a physicist, so when he stepped back for such a perspicacious view of things, he did not go all the way back to the Big Bang. For his starting point, he rather consulted the stories of the Bible, and particularly the story of Exodus, which establishes a paradigm for moving from bondage to freedom. Whether this particular story is rooted more in historical fact or religious myth, it illustrates that the world's most fundamental social structures are not permanently fixed, but rather they are capable of consequential, unidirectional change. And the type of change this story models—the movement from oppression to greater freedom—is something we then see repeated on numerous occasions throughout the later history about which we do have greater empirical knowledge, and particularly the history of the last few hundred years.

In fact—to view human history through the broadest possible lens—if we go back to the start of the historical era when societies first began to leave a written record of how they organized and governed themselves, virtually every one of these societies was built upon the subjugation of the weak by the strong, operating in accord with some version of the system of privilege. This top-down mode of social organization long appeared to be an immutable fact of the world, itself reflecting the hierarchical structure of the larger universe. In the seventeenth and eighteenth centuries, however, certain scientists, philosophers, and statesmen began casting off the intellectual shackles of the premodern era by abductively positing a world governed not by the power and privilege of the few, but by universal law. And when some plucky colonists in North America then resolved to smash the chains of British rule, they elected not to replace the English monarch with a king of their own but rather to establish a novel, democratic mode of governance meant to ensure that political authority would henceforth derive not from the inherited majesty of kings but in bottom-up fashion, from the consent of the governed.

As we know, the American founders did not complete the task they had set for themselves. They rather left numerous chains intact, most blatantly by continuing to sanction the race-based institution of chattel slavery. Tragic though this chapter in American history was, it set the stage for another Exodus-like journey, this one featuring escaped slaves taking the Underground Railroad north, even as abolitionists waged a moral battle for the legal end of slavery, finally culminating in Lincoln's signing of the Emancipation Proclamation. Other marginalized American subgroups then set off on similar journeys of their own, to include suffragists seeking to cast off the demographic chains imposed by their gender, while workers fought to free themselves from the economic chains of unrestrained capitalism. Meanwhile, this same story was playing out around the world, with many other countries trading monarchy for democracy in the nineteenth century, followed by scores of European colonies throwing off the chains of colonial rule over the first half of the twentieth century, whether nonviolently, as under Gandhi's leadership in India, or by more violent means. For Black Americans, however, Reconstruction had quickly descended into Jim Crow, thus requiring that another leg be added to this community's journey from bondage to freedom, this one leading right up to the legal and legislative reforms King and his fellow activists were helping push through in the 1950s and 1960s.

As we allow our gaze to run across these events, therefore, it becomes evident that the dream King articulated on the Washington Mall was not some delusional fantasy. On the contrary, if we act as scientists and diligently record all this data we have been observing, plotting it out as points on a graph, we see a curve emerging: an arc. And while the left side of this arc is characterized by oppression, violence, and greed, as we move across to the right side of the graph—plotting against time—we see the arc bend in the direction of a more just, peaceful, and universalistic social order. If we then go on to extrapolate from this data, the evidence itself suggests we should extend the curve, prompting us to offer predictions of future events that very much resemble the hopeful scenes King portrayed in his famous speech.

Yet, if the strong possibility that the future will exhibit greater justice than the past or present is firmly rooted in the empirical evidence available to us, why do we need faith? Why not just trust the evidence? The answer is that we do not always have the leisure to step back to take a perspicacious view of the world around us and its long history. As active participants in life, we are necessarily caught up in the concrete particularity of the circumstances and events in which we are enmeshed today, thereby shrinking our horizon. And at times, the evidence immediately before us is not hopeful. No matter how smooth the arc of history may appear from a great distance, in the proximity of the here and now, the data can be far messier. Sometimes, it is inconclusive, pointing in so many different directions that we cannot reasonably use it to predict where the world will go next. And sometimes, as we look at the evidence around us, intellectual honesty demands that we acknowledge the world does not appear to be moving in the direction we might hope. The world of our immediate, concrete experience may well appear to be standing stubbornly still, if not moving backward. The evidence before us, in other words, may appear to council despair—that we give up our dreams of realizing a more just social order and instead reconcile ourselves to the colder, bleaker, more violent reality in which we live.

In fact, if we are being completely honest with ourselves, we must concede that, even when we get the opportunity to step back and run our gaze over the grand sweep of history, we could choose different data points to highlight, and we could tie them together using a different narrative than King's favorite story of the journey from bondage to freedom. Taking a different chapter of the Old Testament as our starting point, for instance, we could posit that the story of Adam's sin and punishment was the episode that established the pattern for the universal drama that has since followed. If we then scan the events of the distant and recent past with this meta-narrative in mind, we will doubtless be able to find ample evidence to bolster our conviction that the world around us is sliding ever deeper into sin, depravity, and dissolution. And when this is precisely what the events of the present moment would appear to suggest, we may well conclude—not entirely without empirical justification—that we are wise to give up any hopes we have of fundamentally changing the present order for the better, reserving whatever hope we do have left for some future life, set in some future world.

The problem with taking such a despairing view of the world around us is that it can be a self-fulfilling prophecy. The future, after all, is not determined entirely by what precedes it. Though strongly influenced by past events and the present configuration of circumstances, the future is ultimately determined by the actions we decide to take today. And these actions are strongly informed by our beliefs about the world. If we are convinced tomorrow cannot possibly be better than today, we may collapse into quietism, abandoning any dreams we may have once had of changing the world for the better, instead resigning ourselves to living with whatever injustices persist. Alternatively, despair can lead us to militancy, where we conclude the social order will always be defined by unbalanced power relations—particularly of the sort that arise between social subgroups defined along demographic or economic lines—and thus we resolve to make sure our group will come out on top, indulging whatever anger, hatred, or violence this struggle may occasion. In either case, however, our despair is leading us to stop straining to bend the arc of the moral universe in the direction of justice. Yet, because the arc *has been bending* in this direction only because countless individuals have been straining with all their might for generations, if enough people stop straining today, the arc will spring back, and history will settle back into its old pattern of oppression and violence without apparent end.

That being said, if despair can be a self-fulfilling prophecy, so too can faith. And that is why, if we subscribe to the progressive worldview, we have a moral duty not just to predict with scientific detachment that tomorrow will be better than today, nor even just to *hope* for a future that more fully realizes our moral ideals than the present moment. We have a moral duty to embrace this hope so tightly it becomes a sincere conviction that the future *will* be better—that our world *will* grow more just over time. And this faith, in turn, can give us the confidence, courage, energy, and inspiration we need to get to work and start doing our part to ensure that the world *does* become more just. Especially when times are dark—when the evidence immediately before us suggests the world is standing still or moving backward—our faith in a brighter future can act as a bridge that carries us across the chasm of despair. One leg of this bridge is anchored in the perspicuous view we take of the past, providing us with solid empirical evidence of a historical trend away from relations of bondage and in the direction of freedom and universal equality. The other leg of the bridge rests on our dream of a future in which human freedom is fully realized, not just for a privileged few, but for everyone. It is faith, however, that spans the distance between these two visions, stretching over the choppy waters of the present and thereby allowing us to keep moving forward even when the waves rising around us might incline us to turn back.

Yet, if our faith in a more just future can give us the resolve we need to help make this future a reality, why ought we believe, as King suggests, that the entire universe is already striving in this direction? And is such a belief even helpful to the cause of justice? Some of King's critics have argued it is not, suggesting his expansive notion of a faith in the entire universe lets us off the hook too easily: If the arc of the moral universe is going to bend toward justice, anyway, why should we go to any trouble to help bend it? Clearly, however, this is not the message King intended to convey. His philosophy of nonviolence expressly rejects quiescence, demanding that we take vigorous action with the fierce urgency of now. A more charitable interpretation of King's call for faith in the broader universe is therefore something like the following.

As we consider our current situation, reflecting on all the barriers that still stand in the way of our realizing a more just social order, another temptation to despair can arise from the fact that each one of us is so small, whereas the world's injustices are so large. What can we possibly do, as individuals who have just a few score years to act, to dismantle a tradition of domination, exploitation, and violence that defined human society for almost all recorded history, the better part of ten thousand years? An answer to this question begins to come into view when we combine the faith King prescribes in the arc of the moral universe bending toward justice with the insight that this universal straining toward justice comprises the personal strivings of innumerable individuals, all straining in the same direction over many generations. What this insight tells us is that we do not have to do everything ourselves; none of us is called to save the world on our own. All we are called to do is to look around ourselves, determine what point we occupy on history's moral arc, ask what changes we could help bring about to bend this arc one fraction of a degree further in the direction of justice, then do whatever is in our power to effect these changes.

The results of our personal efforts will, of course, be infinitesimal. Yet, as is true in Newton's differential calculus, when you take a vast number of infinitesimal line segments and add them up, you get a finite curve: an arc. And when we place our faith, not just in the broad arc of history, but in the individuals who fashion this arc, this assures us we are not alone. It tells us we do not have to carry the universe on our back for mile after mile. We just need to build on the tremendous amount of work our predecessors have already done and help the universe take its next step or two on its journey. Nor must we bear even this temporary burden alone. Even when things seem lonely, our faith in the broader universe assures us many others are walking alongside us. This means that, if any one of us should stumble, this will not trigger a worldwide slide into desolation; rather, others will be there to pick up the load until we can regain our footing. And when, finally, any of us approaches the end of the finite span we are given to act, we need not despair that all the gains we have made will be lost upon our demise. We can instead rest secure in the faith that our companions and successors will take up the journey where we have left off, building on our own work and thereby giving our actions in this lifetime a sort of immortality.

This, in any case, was the faith King had. On April 4, 1968, he was in Memphis to support a strike by city sanitation workers when he was felled by an assassin's bullet. The evening before, he had given what turned out to be his final speech. King had no foreknowledge of the events coming the next day, but he had been facing death threats for so long that he well understood he might not live long enough to see every aspect of his dream fulfilled. Perhaps this made him wistful, for near the end of his speech, he returned to his favorite biblical story of Moses and the Israelites, specifically invoking the occasion near the end of Moses's life when he climbed Mount Nebo and finally, after forty years of leading his people through the desert, he was able to look over and see the homeland God had promised his people. Given his advanced age and frail condition, Moses knew he would not be able to make the final journey into the promised land. But he did not need to. The goal for which he had been laboring for so long on behalf of his people was in sight. Moses had answered his unique call, and with the arc of history being long, he knew there were others who could pick up his staff and lead the Israelites the final steps of the way—at which point they would need to start a new chapter in their story, learning to live under conditions of freedom.

Reflecting on this story, King acknowledged the threats to his own life that hung in the air, but he went on to muse, "It really doesn't matter to me now, because I've been to the mountaintop. And I don't mind. Like anybody, I would like to live a long life—longevity has its place. But I'm not concerned about that now. I just want to do God's will. And he's allowed me to go up on the mountain. And I've looked over, and I've seen the Promised Land."

Going on to offer a final profession of his faith in the direction that the moral universe bends, King noted to his listeners, "I may not get there with you. But I want you to know tonight, that we, as a people, will get to the Promised Land. And so I'm happy tonight; I'm not worried about anything; I'm not fearing any man. Mine eyes have seen the glory of the coming of the Lord."

CHAPTER 12

A NEW FOUNDATIONAL NARRATIVE: THE SECOND ITERATION OF THE PROGRESSIVE WORLDVIEW

———

As the end of the twentieth century approached, it is safe to say that few people in the United States or elsewhere were feeling the unbridled sense of optimism that had been so pervasive at the beginning of the century. The intervening hundred years had just been too brutal, in too many ways, for anyone to believe the world was on an inexorable path to peace, prosperity, and enlightenment. Nevertheless, by the final decade of the century, things were starting to look up, at least from the perspective of many Americans who leaned Left in their political and moral sensibilities. Accordingly, we might best describe the mood that prevailed among American progressives as the twentieth century drew to a close as one of "wary optimism."

The decades following King's assassination had been a mixed bag for progressives. In the wake of the cultural turbulence of the 1960s and a series of economic crises in the 1970s, the entire country lurched to the political right, culminating in the election of President Ronald Reagan in 1980. The staunchly conservative Reagan oversaw cuts to many of the surviving programs of the New Deal and Great Society, while rejecting their underlying rationale—namely, that vigorous government intervention in the market is a legitimate tool for fighting poverty and otherwise ensuring social welfare. Instead championing a supply-side economic theory that promised strong economic growth would cause wealth to trickle down from a successful producer class to the rest of society, Reagan—together with his Vice President and successor, George H.W. Bush—presided over twelve years of tax cuts, deregulation, and reduced social spending. These *laissez-faire* policies spurred some economic growth, but the rising tide did not, as advertised, raise all boats, or in any case, it did not raise them all equally. On the contrary, following a fifty-year period when American wealth and income gaps had been steadily shrinking, the 1980s saw measures of inequality start to rise again, as those near the top of the American economic ladder did extraordinarily well—and kept doing better year after year—even as real wages for working Americans entered a decades-long period of stagnation.

With respect to the sorts of inequality that rest more on demographic identity, most of the legislative and legal victories civil rights activists had won in the 1950s and 1960s endured throughout the remainder of the century, and they proved to be life-changing for Black Americans, with the most overt forms of institutionalized discrimination having been outlawed. Nevertheless, more subtle forms of racial discrimination continued to pervade American life, even as the civil rights movement proper wound down in the early 1970s. The Fair Housing Act of 1968, for instance, had forbidden such practices as writing clauses into home deeds that prohibited resale to racial or ethnic minorities. Still, unequal mortgage lending practices, appraisals reflecting the race of the applicant, and other unspoken forms of redlining continued to keep many of the country's neighborhoods and schools highly segregated. And there were some real setbacks for America's Black community over the post–civil rights period. Most notably, when President Richard Nixon first declared a War on Drugs in 1971, he was channeling conservative exhaustion with the psychedelic hippie culture of the 1960s, largely a White phenomenon. But when President Reagan— supported by many other politicians, including some liberal Democrats—cited rising inner-city crime as a justification for ramping up the War on Drugs in the 1980s, the law enforcement effort targeted young Black men, sentencing Black offenders more frequently and to much longer prison terms than their White co-offenders, thus inaugurating an era of mass incarceration that depleted many Black communities of their sons and fathers.

While the civil rights movement had focused on securing the constitutional rights of Black Americans, one of its most profound legacies for American society ended up being the degree to which it inspired other traditionally marginalized groups to launch similar rights movements of their own. Even before the 1960s had ended, the contemporary women's movement had launched, aiming to harness the voting power earlier generations of suffragists had secured to establish true equality for women in the workplace, the legal sphere, and even the family. In 1973, the Supreme Court decision on *Roe vs. Wade* established a federal right to abortion, thereby giving women greater control over their bodies and freeing them from total dependence on men for making such major life decisions as when to marry or have children. The movement did suffer a notable setback in the 1970s when the Equal Rights Amendment narrowly failed to gain the support of enough states for ratification. Nevertheless, many of the specific protections the amendment sought to ensure came to be enacted in more piecemeal fashion over subsequent decades, particularly as a growing number of women began to win political office.

With issues of sex and gender on the table, the Stonewall Riots in Greenwich Village sparked the modern gay rights movement in 1969. Gay men and lesbians had long faced some of the most repressive discrimination of any demographic subgroup in America, with both private and government employers routinely firing employees suspected of homosexual tendencies, landlords evicting gay tenants, and anti-sodomy laws in many states rendering homosexual conduct illegal, even when occurring between consenting adults behind closed doors. For decades, small groups of activists had campaigned against the most restrictive of these laws, generally making a point of both dressing and acting quite conservatively to convince their straight neighbors that homosexuals were no different from everyone else. By the late 1960s, however, a younger generation of activists—inspired by the Black Panthers and their militant version of Black Pride—began to embrace a more brash, in-your-face exultation of the gay identity, as celebrated exuberantly at colorful Pride Parades that began to spring up around the country. The entire gay rights movement was brought to a wrenching standstill in the 1980s by the outbreak of the AIDS epidemic, which particularly devastated the community of gay men. But as treatments began to emerge in the early 1990s that increasingly allowed AIDS victims to live with, if not cure, their disease, activists began to turn their desperate calls for increased medical research back to broader demands for equal rights for gays and lesbians.

In other corners of American life, Cesar Chavez led the struggle for the rights of American farm workers over the late 1960s and 1970s. These migratory laborers, occupying one of the lowest rungs on the American economic ladder, had long been invisible to the rest of the country, so Chavez and his fellow activists spent much of their time educating the broader public about the inhumane conditions under which their food was harvested. And because many of these work-ers had long been immigrants from Mexico or other Latin American countries, over the final decades of the twentieth century, the farm workers' movement gradually evolved into a broader immigrants' rights movement. Over this same period, advocacy by the country's disabled community led to the passage of the Americans with Disabilities Act in 1990, which mandated significant changes to building codes to make public spaces more accessible to all Americans. Meanwhile, America's environmental movement came into its own in the 1970s, with many activists citing a concern for the right of future generations to enjoy a clean, healthy planet as one of the key motivators of their environmental-ism. Indeed, even non-human species found their advocates over the final decades of the twentieth century, with animal rights activists winning significant changes to the laws that regulate how both farm and laboratory animals are treated.

These gains on the part of various traditionally marginalized communities notwithstanding, perhaps the development of the late twentieth century that paid greatest tribute to King's legacy was the fact that many of the country's different marginalized communities finally began to recognize that they had common cause with one another, not only making them natural political allies but also providing their various members with a new sense of spiritual solidarity. Given the long history these diverse subgroups had of ignoring one another's struggles, when not actively throwing other marginalized groups under the bus, this new progressive ecumenicalism did not come easy. For an example of the rocky path that had to be traversed toward a better realization of King's mantra that "unless all are free, none can be free," we can consider what happened in and around the gay rights movement over the final decades of the twentieth century.

As noted earlier, the gay rights movement—which had always been overwhelmingly White—underwent a split in the late 1960s between its conservative old guard, who had spent decades trying to carve out a space for homosexuals within the *Ozzie and Harriet* picture of America, and younger radicals, who explicitly modeled themselves after such militant civil rights groups as the Black Panthers. This homage to Black activism notwithstanding, many veterans of the civil rights movement—who often, like King, had strong roots in the Black church—resented what they viewed as an attempt to co-opt their legitimate struggle on the part of sexual deviants. Many lesbians, meanwhile, had long resented the male dominance of the gay rights movement, noting—in the rising spirit of feminism—that gay men were just as prone to being male chauvinists as their straight counterparts. Still, this did not win lesbians quick acceptance within feminist circles. National Organization for Women founder Barbara Frieden, in particular, was terrified the women's movement would be crippled if it came to be associated with lesbians sporting butch haircuts, so lesbians were not welcomed into the group for many years.

It may have been the AIDS tragedy that first prompted an informal truce among all these warring progressive factions. The disease targeted gay men, but its human toll was so overwhelming as to spur a flow of compassion across demographic lines. And thus, by the time in the early 1990s when most major cities were hosting AIDS Walks to fight stigmatization and raise money for AIDS research, these walks had become a melting pot for progressives of all stripes, with straight White grandmothers marching alongside gay Black teenagers and bisexual Latinas. Indeed, this was the decade when the term "LGBT community" came into use, thus signaling that gay men, lesbians, bisexuals, and trans individuals had begun—really for the first time—to view themselves as a *community*, bound by their common experiences, political interests, and guiding ideals. And as ever more non-heterosexuals of color began to join their White counterparts in coming out of the closet, this not only made the LGBT community more diverse but also began to win the entire community a measure of acceptance within various other traditionally marginalized groups.

Thus, for all the ups and downs of the twentieth century, by the 1990s many progressively leaning Americans were seeing more reasons for hope than despair. This was the decade, in fact, when some of these people began to explicitly adopt the label of "progressive," seeking to distance themselves from the outworn "liberal." In part, this rebranding effort testified to the success of a campaign on the part of Reagan-era conservatives to tar "liberal" as a dirty word, while establishing that those on the right could be "proud to be a conservative." Many on the left began to feel that they, too, needed an identifier in which they could take pride. "Progressive" worked well for this purpose, partly because it set aside some of the historical messiness that had always been associated with "liberal"—contemporary conservatism of the sort Reagan espoused was actually an outgrowth of the "classical liberalism" associated with such *laissez-faire* economic thinkers as Smith. More significant, however, was the fact that "progressive" draws such a sharp contrast with "conservative." Do you really want to remain stuck in the status quo, this new label seemed to ask, with all the problems and injustices it has inherited from the past, or do you want to make progress toward realizing a better, more just future?

Ironically, the growing sense of progressive identity got another key boost from conservatives during the 1992 presidential campaign, which not only ended with Bill Clinton—a charismatic Democrat from Hope, Arkansas—defeating the incumbent President Bush, thereby bringing the Reagan-

Bush years to an official end. It also saw social conservatives declare war on the progressive worldview.

The Culture Wars

In 1991, James Davison Hunter published *Culture Wars: The Struggle to Define America*, in which he considered the different moral understandings that cultural traditionalists and progressives bring to such hot-button social issues as abortion, gay rights, and school prayer. The following year, Pat Buchanan gave a fiery speech at the Republican National Convention—a parting shot in his unsuccessful bid to wrest the party's nomination from the incumbent President Bush—flatly asserting that the United States was locked in a culture war. On one side of this war were social conservatives, with their moorings in the traditional Christian worldview. On the other side were not just individual liberal politicians and activists but the broader, more secular, worldview they embraced, which Buchanan portrayed as a post-1960s, relativistic, anything-goes sort of moral nihilism that rejects, not just traditional Christianity and its socially conservative moral values, but any enduring moral values, at all.

To make a case for a return to "family values," Buchanan and his fellow culture warriors frequently invoked the foundational narrative upon which their own worldview rested, the story of God creating Adam and Eve into the Garden of Eden, the first couple falling into sin, and their descendants then following inexorably behind, leaving those of us today with little hope for the future other than to be among the elect who are taken up by Jesus at the end of days and transported to heaven. While this traditional story does not directly address such contemporary issues as abortion or school prayer, once its basic metaphysics of sin and guilt is stipulated, it does not take much of a leap to determine, for instance, that because God creates each of us innocent—even if we are inevitably bound to fall into sin of our own accord—abortion amounts to the murder of innocent children not even given a chance to stand or fall on their own. And because the Old Testament does, in fact, condemn homosexual behavior in a handful of verses—which is hardly surprising, given that the Israelites at the time were struggling to multiply their population so as to avoid being overrun by their larger neighbors—it does not take any leap, at all, to conclude that an inerrant, timeless God is not going to change his mind on such a fundamental moral issue.

While progressives had long understood that religious fundamentalists viewed the world differently than they did, this declaration of war against the progressive worldview came as somewhat of a surprise to many on the American left, in no small part because few on the left had ever given much thought to *having* a worldview of their own. That is not to say progressives of the late twentieth century lacked a guiding political philosophy. Most could trace their political convictions back to such Enlightenment figures as Locke, Montesquieu, or Jefferson, or to more recent progressives such as Gandhi, King, or Malcolm X. The term "worldview," however—a translation of the German *Weltanschauung*—had gotten a bad name earlier in the twentieth century through its association with totalitarian visions such as Hitler's and Stalin's. Like many older religious worldviews, these more recent secular attempts to capture how the entire world works in a single narrative tended to leave little room for those who did not hew the party line. Accordingly, as twentieth-century progressives of a more intellectual bent increasingly came under the influence of French postmodernism, many resolved to demonstrate their respect for cultural pluralism by refusing to make any all-encompassing proclamations about how the world is put together, knowing that any such account would contradict—and thus devalue—the foundational narratives of many other traditions, most of which had long been marginalized by the dominant Western culture.

Among American progressives of the later twentieth century, King probably went the farthest toward articulating a sweeping worldview, although to do this he needed to draw heavily on traditional Christian imagery—something more secular progressives likely accepted only because it came out of King's experience in the Black church, itself a marginalized institution. But when an explicit challenge to progressivism was launched by a group that had long been socially dominant—White American Christians, under a leadership that was overwhelmingly male—progressives were increasingly anxious to push back. And what many began to realize is that, their generally unfavorable view of worldviews notwithstanding, they *did* have a worldview of their own. This was a worldview, moreover, from which they did not have to shy away on grounds of non-inclusivity, given that some of its most recent and essential chapters had been devoted precisely to expanding their society's circle of inclusion.

A worldview, again, is a sweeping characterization of

the entire metaphysical order of things, typically grounding itself on a foundational narrative that details where the world came from, where it is headed, how it operates, and what role human beings occupy within it. This was something the progressives of the Enlightenment era certainly had. By the early eighteenth century, most intellectually-inclined Europeans had accepted that Newtonian physics provides a correct account of how the physical order operates, while such moral philosophers as Hobbes, Locke, and Kant had begun to identify the proper role for human beings within this rational order—namely, to be the primary agents of progress within an otherwise-unchanging world, whether this progress occurred in the scientific, technological, political, economic, or moral spheres. At the same time, nobody had yet come up with a better explanation of where the world comes from than the Genesis creation story, so even most scientists of the seventeenth and eighteenth centuries continued to believe that the world was created several thousand years ago by an omnipotent, omniscient God—albeit a non-interventionist watchmaker God who set the world in motion, and has since allowed it to operate in accord with its own timeless laws.

By the nineteenth century, however, even this stripped-down version of the foundational Christian narrative had begun to falter as ongoing scientific progress was making clear not only that our world is both far older than the biblical narrative would suggest and in constant flux, down to its most fundamental structures, but also that nature is far more complex and messy than previously imagined, thereby resisting any easy encapsulation by a single narrative, whether mythical, scientific, or otherwise. Accordingly, most progressives who gave the matter any thought moved away from the whole notion of articulating a grand worldview, suspecting that any effort to wrap such an incredibly complex subject as our world into a neat, tidy package would smack more of religion or totalitarian propaganda than science. Nevertheless, over the course of the nineteenth and twentieth centuries, scientists from across a variety of disciplines—together with an array of progressively minded politicians, social theorists, and activists—were quietly piecing together a comprehensive story of our world that meets all the criteria of a foundational narrative. And when the worldview this narrative suggests was explicitly attacked in the 1990s, the foundational narrative, itself, began coming into clearer focus.

This narrative was not a supernatural tale cobbled together by ancient prophets, themselves struggling to get a handle on the vast, perplexing, often-terrifying world in which they lived. Nor was it the propaganda of a modern dictator trying to convince the people he oppressed that it was right and good for him to possess so much power. This was, rather, a story rising out of the combined efforts of the modern physical and human sciences, and particularly those sciences of the nineteenth and twentieth centuries that had been casting light on the evolving nature of our universe. It was a story that begins with a cataclysmic fireball, continues through the formation of stars and planets, gains momentum with the evolution of life on earth, then traces the evolution of ever more sophisticated species of living creatures, finally to include a highly intelligent bipedal primate that has undergone its own series of intellectual, social, political, economic, and moral developments—all leading up to the current effort to realize a more just and universalistic social order.

To be sure, there are numerous reasons why a grand narrative coming out of the modern sciences does not readily lend itself to grounding a comprehensive worldview. For one thing, the story modern science has to tell about our world is long—extremely long. Granted, the Bible is also a long book. Nevertheless, the traditional Christian narrative of creation, fall, sin, and redemption can easily be compressed into a twenty-minute sermon, and while such a synopsis may not capture all the nuance of the Christian story, it is sufficient to reveal this narrative's overriding trajectory. By way of contrast, the current volume has attempted to offer only the briefest summary of the modern scientific story of our world—told alongside the story, inseparable from it, of how this particular narrative came to be scripted—and it runs well over 400 pages, having left out, not just numerous key details, but entire chapters that could have rightfully been included.

The modern scientific story, moreover, is far more intellectually challenging than most traditional foundational narratives. Setting aside the difficulty of imagining space bending or photons simultaneously being waves and particles, most contemporary science is conducted in a language of higher mathematics that few laypeople can speak, leaving the details of the modern narrative accessible only to an elite priesthood of scientists. Even among scientists, moreover, research has grown so specialized that few contemporary researchers have any detailed knowledge of what is happening in the next sub-field over, much less in completely different disciplines. Thus, if a worldview generally rests on a foundational narrative that provides its listeners with a compelling, intuitively graspable account of where the world came from, where it is headed, how it operates, and what role human beings occupy within it, whatever the modern scientific narrative has delivered in the way of "compelling," it lacks in "intuitively graspable."

This all being said, it is also true that no single one of us needs to know every detail of the story by which our world reached its current state to discern this story's plotline. There are plenty of Americans today, moreover, who may have forgotten whatever calculus they have once learned, if any, and who never studied any science beyond the high school or undergraduate levels, but who grew up paging through *National Geographic* and *Discover* magazines, watched *Cosmos* and *Nova* as teenagers, then graduated to reading such works of popular science as Stephen Hawking's *A Brief History of Time* or any of Richard Dawkins's numerous books on evolution. Piecing together such snippets of modern science, even those of us who are laypeople can begin to wrap our heads around a story that is still incomplete and still subject to revision as scientists continue to make observations and refine their theories accordingly, but that nonetheless has a discernible trajectory to it.

This story contains numerous cyclical elements, from the orbit of planets around their suns to the metabolic cycles of living organisms to the rise and fall of empires. In its broadest outlines, however, the scientific story of our world is decidedly linear in character, beginning at a particular point in time—or rather, with time itself coming into being at a particular point—and the story then unfolding over the next 14 billion years through a series of one-time, irreversible events. This linear story does not, however, have the declinist sense of the Christian narrative, with the universe having been created in a state of perfection, then going downhill ever since. Precisely the opposite: this new foundational narrative starts with an infernal fireball, then moves through a series of developments in which the inhabitants of nature grow ever more sophisticated—from quarks to atoms and molecules, to stars and planets, to single-cell organisms, to multicell organisms, finally to include one highly intelligent primate that progressively organizes itself into tribes, villages, city-states, nation-states, empires, and finally rights-based democracies—all giving this narrative an unmistakable trajectory of progress.

Yet, what exactly is progress? What does it mean to say the world has gradually been getting *better* over time, or moving forward and upward? These are questions worthy of further philosophical discussion, and future volumes of this three-volume exploration of the progressive worldview will address them in depth. As the twentieth century drew to a close, however, certain general lessons about the nature of progress were starting to come into view for those inclined to reflect on such matters, thereby rounding out what we have labeled the second iteration of the progressive worldview. These lessons include the following:

1. Progress is real, and it has been

occurring for a very long time.

Although we always have some choice as to what interpretation to give the historical information available to us—Have things been getting better over time? Worse? Stayed the same? Are they going round and round?—the evidence before us strongly suggests a trajectory of progress. This is true even if we limit our gaze to the history of the United States through the end of the twentieth century. Without diminishing the injustices that still permeated American society as the twentieth century ended, the United States was indisputably farther along in 2000—as measured against the yardstick of moral universalism—than it was in 1950 when Black Americans frequently could not attend White schools, buy property in White neighborhoods, or use White drinking fountains. And the country was farther along in 1950 than it was in 1890 when women could not vote, Jim Crow laws dominated the South, worker protection laws did not exist, and a few fabulously wealthy families ran a significant portion of the nation's economy. But conditions in 1890 nonetheless represented a significant advance over 1820 when slavery was legal and widespread, federal troops were frequently employed to drive Native Americans off their lands, and women had virtually no legal status of their own. And if we step back even farther to contrast the American democratic order that was crafted, however imperfectly, in 1789 with the feudal order or other versions of the system of privilege that had ruled the world for some ten thousand years prior, the progress is almost immeasurable. Yet, life under even the most brutal of these inegalitarian regimes was probably more secure in many ways than under the pre-civic condition that preceded the Agricultural Revolution, when migratory tribes of hunter-gatherers were entirely dependent on the beneficence of nature for their survival, while not infrequently clashing with one another.

Nor, as the sciences of the nineteenth and twentieth centuries have revealed, has progress merely been a human affair. Pushing back even earlier in the story of universal progress, *homo sapiens* and their relatives in the family of great apes are among the most sophisticated descendants of the warm-blooded, furry mammals that gained a foothold in the biosphere several hundred million years ago, likely helped along by a meteor strike that cleared the landscape of dinosaurs. Yet, even the dinosaurs embodied a few billion years' worth of evolutionary progress, tracing their lineage back from their own genus of lizards through amphibians, fish, and various more primitive types of multicell organisms, all the way back to the first single-cell creatures that somehow managed to assemble themselves out of randomly drifting amino acids and other organic compounds. The very earth, moreover—which provided both the stage upon which life could emerge and its constitutive elements—first came together in a dynamic process of planetary formation some 4 billion years ago. And while the Earth took shape in the neighborhood of a later-generation star we call the sun, the heavier elements giving the planet its solidity had been forged within the cauldrons of even earlier generation stars. These stars were, in turn, produced by massive gas clouds collapsing, themselves having come together when the universe first cooled enough for lighter atoms such as hydrogen and helium to form out of the subatomic particles that had themselves condensed out of the fiery aftermath of the Big Bang.

Even this very brief recounting of the story of universal progress—here told in reverse—points to a second lesson that has emerged over the past two hundred years with respect to the nature of progress.

2. The various instances of progress we have considered here have all been of a piece with one another, sharing a similar dynamic. Specifically, they have all involved a movement from smaller and simpler to larger and more complex.

To run through the story of our universe's progress once more, now traveling forward in time, when the raw energy of the Big Bang had cooled enough to condense into matter, it first formed tiny sub-subatomic particles, whether quarks or something even smaller, such as superstrings—physicists are still not entirely sure. Whatever their precise composition, these tiny bits of matter came together to generate somewhat larger subatomic particles, to include electrons, protons, and neutrons. Many of these subatomic particles, in turn, bonded to form such light atoms as hydrogen and helium. A huge number of these hydrogen and helium atoms, drawn together by the pull of gravity, then began to coalesce into massive gas clouds. Some of these gas clouds grew large and dense enough that they collapsed under their own weight to form the first generation of stars: discrete, self-sustaining objects that are not only massive in size, but which maintain themselves over time through a complex dynamic that balances the inward-pulling force of gravity with the outward-thrusting force of a sustained nuclear explosion. Likewise drawn to one another by gravity, huge numbers of stars assembled themselves into galaxies, which in turn formed galaxy clusters and superclusters. Thus was established the large-scale architecture of our universe—a massive, complex whole containing an incalculable number of parts, within parts, within parts.

But the universe was not yet finished moving from smaller and simpler toward larger and more complex. As stars began to burn, this "burning" was actually an ongoing nuclear fusion reaction, which fused many smaller, lighter hydrogen and helium atoms into larger, heavier, more complex atoms such as oxygen, silicon, carbon, and iron. Eventually, these first-generation stars burned themselves out and exploded, thus spewing their constituent atoms across space. Accordingly, when gravity then drew the next generation of gas clouds together, these clouds were seeded with traces of many heavier elements. And when these "dirty" gas clouds ultimately collapsed into stars, some of their heavier elements clumped together to form discrete celestial bodies that fell into orbit around a neighboring star, thereby generating whole stellar systems populated by comets, asteroids, and planets. Then, on at least one of these planets, the familiar movement from smaller and simpler toward larger and more complex began once again.

In its very earliest days, the planet Earth did not host anything resembling life. The thin band immediately above and below the planet's surface merely contained a few molecules that happened to be a bit larger and more complex than usual, many of them built around carbon atoms, particularly flexible in their bonding capabilities. Over time, some of these carbon-based molecules stumbled together to form chains of molecules that were even longer and more complex. Drawing on some source of energy—whether the sun, geothermal heat vents, or radioactive minerals deep within the earth—groups of these more intricate molecules began organizing themselves into amino acids and proteins. Eventually, through a process scientists are still unraveling, some of these organic compounds began joining together to form single-celled organisms capable of reproducing themselves. Then, after another very long stretch of time, a few of these single-cell organisms figured out how to merge into multi-cell organisms, which themselves gradually evolved into ever larger and more sophisticated varieties of plant and animal. Some animal species, meanwhile, did not just evolve novel physical attributes. They also evolved social behaviors that allowed their individual members to live together coopera-tively in larger, more complex groups, whether hives, packs, herds, or flocks. Among these social animals was a bipedal primate with an unusually large brain.

In the present volume, we have filled the gap between the first appearance of human beings and the rise of some of the world's earliest civilizations—as marked by such events as the scripting of the world's great religious narratives and the handing down of the first law codes—with the conjectural story the contract theorists offered of how the inhabitants of the state of nature came together to sign a social contract. Even this hypothetical story follows the familiar pattern of moving from smaller and simpler to larger and more complex, as the solitary residents of the state of nature used their collective powers of reasoning to found larger states governed by the rule of law. The same is true of the slightly different hypothetical tale Smith proposed when he analyzed the transition from individuals behaving as solitary jacks-of-all-trades to entering into informal exchange relations with one another, then later coming together to form complex markets featuring multiple buyers and sellers.

As it turns out, advances in twentieth-century sciences such as paleontology, anthropology, and archeology have shown that these Enlightenment-era stories were empirically inaccurate in any number of ways. What the later research has confirmed, however, is the general movement among early humans from smaller and simpler to larger and more complex. As we can now be empirically confident, our earliest ancestors huddled together in small family troops for millions of years. Somewhat later, they came to form larger tribes of migratory foragers composed of multiple unrelated families. Finally, around ten thousand years ago, people who had learned to domesticate various species of plants and animals began establishing permanent agricultural villages, which themselves ultimately grew into ever larger and more complex towns, city-states, kingdoms, nation-states, and empires.

All the instances just cited of movement from smaller and simpler to larger and more complex have played themselves out in the concrete world of nature, yet we can observe a similar dynamic if we consider some of the key conceptual structures people have used over the millennia to make better sense of the world around them. Skipping past the mythical age, the first concerted effort in the Western tradition to develop a rational account of the world came with the birth of Greek philosophy in the sixth century BCE. The earliest of these accounts were the simplest, with various presocratic philosophers attempting to reduce the complexity of the observed world to the simplicity of a single element, whether water, fire, seeds, or the interplay between love and hate. A later Greek metaphysical account proposed by Aristotle proved to be particularly consequential for European society when later revived by the scholastic scholars of the late medieval period. Organized around the concept of substance—the discrete, self-contained thing defined by its properties—Aristotelian physics and metaphysics suggest the study of nature should consist of observing individual objects in isolation from one another, cataloging their distinct properties. It was therefore a major revolution in thought when seventeenth-century investigators like Galileo began turning their attention from discrete objects to the relations between these objects, seeking to uncover the universal laws governing these relations. Newton then took this approach to its logical conclusion by portraying nature as a vast, interconnected system of universal laws, a whole comprising not only a huge number of parts but also the rules determining their complex interactions down to the last detail.

Not long after Galileo and his colleagues initiated this conceptual shift in the study of physical nature, the modern human sciences were born when philosophers such as Hobbes, Locke, and Smith developed their various accounts of how isolated individuals in a state of nature—subject to the universal law of human behavior, self-interest—might come together to form larger, more complex social units governed by novel laws of their own. Although later shown to be inaccurate descriptions of past events, the stories these philosophers told drove very real future developments by providing the conceptual underpinnings for an emerging set of modern political and economic institutions, with the conceptual shift in question again running in the direction from smaller and simpler toward larger and more complex.

As noted numerous times already, prior to the eighteenth century, virtually every major society had organized itself around some version of the system of privilege. This socio-political system, in turn, rested on an ideology of privilege, a belief system holding that every individual is born with their own, hereditarily determined nature. The individual, in other words, is an Aristotelian substance endowed with certain inherited properties, with these properties determining the precise mix of privileges and duties the individual should rightfully enjoy. On this account, the sovereign's legitimacy lies within the person of the monarch, himself, in the form of a regal nature ultimately inherited from Adam. Hobbes, following Galileo's lead, broke with this Aristotelian conception of human social relations in two crucial ways.

First, he argued that "human nature" is to be found, not in the individual natures people carry around within them but in the universal law of nature that governs the behavior of every living being, which he identified as the law of self-interest. Second, Hobbes proposed that the sovereign does not derive its legitimacy from the monarch's individual nature but from the actions and interactions of the many individuals over whom the sovereign rules, and specifically from their collective act of submitting to the rule of law, as administered by the sovereign. In this case, the social unit—the state, or civic society—is a complex whole that is prior to its parts, not in the sense that the state exists before the individual human beings that comprise it, but in the sense that they attain their full character *as citizens* only by entering into a larger political order that recognizes them as possessing certain inalienable, universal rights. Locke then expanded on Hobbes's account by increasing the number of these rights, while sketching out a political system in which power would not end up devolving back to a single individual but rather be spread across multiple individuals and institutions in self-balancing, self-sustaining fashion.

When the young United States made the world's first enduring attempt to instantiate the new ideology of rights within a democratic political order, this was an extraordinary achievement in itself, insofar as it placed humanity on a different path than it had been traveling for the previous ten thousand years. To be sure, the American founders did not make it all the way down this path: they failed to fully realize their own universalistic ideals by systematically excluding whole groups of people from full participation in the larger society. Nevertheless, they did set the stage for one more progression from smaller and simpler to larger and more complex, which we traced out in the last chapter. In this case, the nation's dominant ingroup—those individuals granted their full slate of rights and otherwise accorded full participation in the nation's democratic political order—comprised a relatively small, homogeneous demographic subgroup: basically the straight, white, able-bodied, Christian males of some means who had long dominated European society under the system of privilege. That said, over the years, more and more traditionally marginalized groups have been drawn within the American social and political mainstream, which has correspondingly grown both larger and more diverse than it once was. The ideal that continues to guide this movement, as so eloquently portrayed by King, is the vision of a society in which there are no longer any "outsiders," but rather the group of social insiders is fully universal in scope, thereby incorporating all the rich diversity of humanity within it.

Admittedly, this ideal has still not been reached, even after generations of striving in this direction. Indeed, this points us to a third lesson that has emerged regarding the nature of progress.

3. Progress is hard.
It has always been hard.

If we have learned anything about progress over the course of this book, it is that progress does not simply churn itself out, like cars rolling off an assembly line. Progress is hard. It has *always* been hard. Progress has always been slow, exhausting, wasteful, and often tragic. At the most fundamental levels of physics, the second law of thermodynamics tells us why this is so.

If progress, in its most general sense, involves a movement from smaller and simpler to larger and more complex, this further implies a movement from lesser toward greater order. The second law of thermodynamics, however, stipulates that nature's overriding tendency is to move in precisely the opposite direction, from more order to less. This explains why a steam engine can never be fully efficient. The engine performs work, which somehow imposes greater order on the world around it, perhaps by running a loom and organizing many scattered threads into a coherent piece of cloth. This increased order must be paid for through an even greater increase in disorder somewhere else, in this case taking the form of unusable heat energy the engine must dissipate to keep running. This wastefulness may well distress the industrialist who must pay for the coal being shoveled into the engine's firebox. But in our universe, both the energy expended and the resulting waste are simply the cost of doing work, including the sort of work we are calling "progress," moving from smaller and simpler to larger and more complex.

In the story of universal progress presented here, one of the most graphic examples we have witnessed of the extravagant wastefulness of nature involves the mechanism of natural selection. When the random workings of genetic mutation or sexual reproduction invest an individual with some novel trait, this new trait *could* give the individual an advantage over its neighbors, thereby increasing the odds the individual will survive and pass the new trait down to its offspring. And if the new trait is advantageous enough, it may come to be adopted by the entire species, thereby giving the species a new competitive advantage in its own struggle for survival within the broader ecosystem. For every new trait that proves to be advantageous in this way, however, hundreds will fail to pan out, literally killing their bearers. This waste is unavoidable, in the sense that if no waste was permitted—if no failed attempts at adaptation were allowed—no successful adaptations could ever be struck upon, and evolution would grind to a halt. Once again, therefore, waste is simply one of the costs of making progress in our universe. It just happens that, in the case of natural selection, the waste factor is particularly large, while the particular form of waste that results has a real element of tragedy to it. This final observation, however, bears elucidation.

The tragedy of natural selection is not merely that the appearance of some new trait is often a matter of life and death for the individuals who happen to be born with it. The tragedy is that those individuals who are cursed with an unsuitable adaptation will perish without ever benefiting from the progress to which their own failure has contributed, even if indirectly. This same tragic element can be found in other chapters of our story of universal progress, including those that involve human progress.

For the southern Black slave born in 1750, there was simply nothing redeeming about the fact that a group of her White contemporaries would gather to sign a document declaring that all people are created equal, possessed of certain inalienable rights. The Declaration of Independence, after all, would soon be followed by a Constitution that legally granted people like its signatories the privilege of owning and disposing of people like the slave. To be sure, if the American founders had never made this first highly imperfect attempt to institute a democratic regime based on the concepts of equality and universal rights, there is little chance life would have been much better for the slave's great-great-grandchildren than it had been for her. So, from the perspective of the grand sweep of history, the signing of both the Declaration of Independence and the Constitution were tremendously important steps toward progress. This was progress, moreover, to which the slave born in 1750 contributed, not just by helping build the economy of the young United States but by suffering a treatment that would eventually come to be regarded as antithetical to the country's founding ideals, thereby finally spurring some meaningful changes in the way people of all races are treated in the United States. Still, for this slave born in 1750, she would never taste the fruits of this later progress for which she had helped pay. From her individual perspective, she was born a slave, had no realistic hope of escaping slavery, and ultimately died a slave, with this being the end of her personal story.

To be emphatically clear, there is nothing fair about this arrangement. That some people should bear a very high cost for progress, and others very little…

That some people should benefit immediately from progress, whereas others should have to wait a long time to earn any reward for their efforts, and still others may never taste any of the fruits of the progress to which they have contributed…

That the man who wrote, "All men are created equal" should have had a monument built to him, whereas the slaves who tidied his writing desk at night should be forgotten…

This, however, is the way progress is. It is just a fact of our universe that, in addition to progress being slow and exhausting, it is almost always wasteful, and very often tragic—and thus grossly unfair. Indeed, the concept of fairness is a distinctly human concept, found almost nowhere else in nature, with only a handful of the most sophisticated primates displaying anything remotely close to a sense of fairness. Even among humans, moreover, the concerted effort to make life more fair—treating everyone more or less equally, irrespective of demographic identity or economic station—is a recent development, part and parcel of the push toward universalism that forms the latest chapter in the story of human progress. And this chapter has still not been fully written, with there still being much about how we organize and govern ourselves that is grossly unfair. Nevertheless, the very fact that large segments of the human population are now at least *trying* to make life more fair represents one of the highest forms of progress our universe has yet seen. That said, we must always keep in mind just how hard-fought the gains to date have been, if for no other reason than not to be surprised or disheartened when future progress proves to be just as slow, hard, exhausting, messy, wasteful, tragic, and unfair as that already achieved.

The general messiness of progress, including that which has extended into our own day, tends to obscure another key lesson that has emerged regarding progress. This lesson comes into view only when we step back far enough to view the very big picture.

4. The pace of progress has actually been accelerating over time.

As progressives, we tend to grow impatient at how agonizingly slow progress often seems to be. And it is certainly true, as we gaze back over the story of a developing universe that scientists have pieced together over the past two hundred years, that the first few chapters of this story cover very long stretches of time. Consider, however, what happens with the general timeframe of each chapter as we work our way forward through this story.

Setting aside the flurry of activity that took place in the first few milliseconds after the Big Bang, some ten billion years then elapsed before the rocky planet we now inhabit first formed. It took another 4 billion years for life on Earth to emerge and evolve to a high enough level of sophistication that our earliest ancestors could break off from the larger line of primates. Over the next 6 million years, anatomically modern humans took shape, spending most of this period wandering the savannahs of Africa as migratory hunter-gatherers. Only about ten thousand years ago did our more recent ancestors begin settling down into towns and cities, thereby giving rise to civic society as we know it. These early civilizations all governed themselves in accord with some version of the system of privilege, a system that was codified when early lawgivers began handing down the first written law codes somewhere around three thousand years ago.

With the timescales continuing to shrink, it was only about four hundred years ago that an alternate governing ideology, one based on the twin concepts of universal rights and equality, was first theoretically conceived. And less than two and a half centuries have passed since the first, imperfect attempts were made to instantiate this new ideology of rights within a democratic system of government. Since that time, the progressive project of giving the ideal of moral universalism greater concrete reality by drawing ever more individuals and groups within the sphere of those granted their full slate of rights, opportunities, and moral dignity has been slow and arduous, not to mention incomplete. Nevertheless, the pace even of this progress has been accelerating. To cite just one example, from the time when the first slave ships landed in colonial America, it took some three hundred fifty years before Congress passed the Civil Rights Act of 1964, thereby giving Black Americans a real measure of legal equality for the first time. In contrast, following the Stonewall Riots of 1969, which launched the contemporary gay rights movement, scarcely thirty years had passed before the first states began to recognize civil unions between same-sex couples in the late 1990s, with a constitutional right to marry not being too many years in the offing.

To be sure, the fact that meaningful social change can now take place in a matter of decades—whereas getting us to this point took our universe nearly 14 billion years—still does not make it *feel* like the social progress for which we yearn is coming at anything other than a glacial pace, especially to those most affected by the injustices that still persist. Such impatience is understandable, and indeed inevitable for human beings like ourselves: no matter how rapidly, in cosmic terms, our world may have transformed itself over the past few thousand or few hundred years, we are mortal creatures who rarely live over a century, so we cannot help but measure progress by the yardstick of a human lifetime. And even for the longest-lived of us, the forty-six years that passed between the Stonewall Riots and the *Obergefall vs. Hodges* decision legalizing same-sex marriage was half a lifetime.

Before we despair about how slowly progress seems to be going these days, however, we need to remind ourselves that for most of human history, life changed at such an imperceptible pace that people had no expectation that the world would transform itself in any significant way over the course of their lifetimes beyond the cyclical turning of the days and seasons. Most people throughout history, in other words, *had* no conception of progress. Now, conversely, our world changes so rapidly that we not only expect but demand change: even people born before the introduction of personal computers get antsy waiting for the next iPhone to come out. By the same token, the frustration we now feel at how slowly our political and cultural institutions seem to be embracing the sorts of progressive changes we would like to see—while real and justified—itself serves as evidence of the degree to which moral progress has accelerated, to the point that we now expect and demand significant gains, not just from decade to decade, but from year to year, if not more rapidly.

The particularly rapid pace at which universal progress has been accelerating since human beings first took the global stage itself holds one final lesson that we can draw about the nature of progress.

5. In the most recent chapters of the story of universal progress, human reason has played a leading role.

This book has stressed that the key point differentiating the first and second iterations of the progressive worldview is that, whereas progressively minded thinkers of the seventeenth and eighteenth centuries tended to view human reason as the primary driver of progress within an otherwise static world, the scientists of the nineteenth and twentieth centuries came to see the entire universe as highly dynamic in character, with some of the most consequential changes it has undergone including the evolution of life on earth, and ultimately human life. As this revised conception of progress suggests, the unique human ability to engage in higher forms of reasoning is more the outcome of a very long story of universal progress than the original author of this story. But this does not diminish the role human reason eventually comes to play in the story of progress once human beings finally take the global stage. Indeed, if anything, the second iteration of the progressive worldview binds us even more tightly to the larger universe than the first: because human reason manifests itself as an ability to understand and act upon the world in ways that are increasingly complex and sophisticated, not only we are *products* of a universal movement from smaller and simpler to larger and more complex that has already been going on for billions of years, but we *carry this movement forward* when we utilize and continue to develop our powers of reasoning.

As we reflect on the place human reason occupies in a progressively developing universe, we need to keep in mind something that was emphasized in the chapter on Kant's theoretical philosophy: the human mind is not a mere calculating machine, capable of nothing more than accepting input, manipulating the received data in accord with certain established rules, then spitting out a predetermined output. To be sure, our brains *have* developed this sort of calculating ability, and it is indispensable to many forms of thinking. But this essentially deductive mode of judgment does not exhaust our reasoning capacity, nor is it the primary means by which human reason drives progress forward. By the same token, while our complementary inductive mode of judgment is indispensable for daily life, allowing us to make generalizations based on past experiences and thereby predict the future with passable success, this backward-looking orientation prevents induction from being reason's primary engine of progress. What really allows the human mind to drive progress forward is rather its ability to scan the present situation, then creatively, abductively propose some new means of organizing what lies before it, whether conceptually, by suggesting some new concept or rule that better ties the observed data together, or physically, by manipulating and reshaping the objects it encounters to endow them with some novel form.

Of course, this abductive, trial and error mode of judgment is guaranteed to go awry with some frequency, yielding incorrect hypotheses about the world or recommending actions that do not pan out as predicted. And these failures can be wasteful, painful, or even tragic. In this way, the human power of abductive reasoning exhibits a dynamic quite similar to that of natural selection—which is hardly surprising, given that human reason is itself a product of natural selection. But while this possibility for error likely accounts for much of the pain and tragedy in human life, it also makes human progress possible, since if we were not allowed to make guesses that turned out to be wrong, we could never make guesses that turned out to be right. As in the case of natural selection, therefore, progress driven by human reason does not so much depend on an ability to avoid every mistake as the ability to distinguish bad guesses from the good guesses, committing both to our individual or collective memories so that we need not commit the same mistakes again, but rather we can build on our accumulated knowledge to make still more abductive leaps forward, this time of an even more sophisticated and productive variety.

In the present volume, again, we skipped over the story that paleontologists, archaeologists, and evolutionary anthropologists have recently been unearthing as to how prehistoric human beings evolved and progressively developed their cognitive powers. Nevertheless, the broad outlines of this story will be familiar to many readers, so we can here touch on just a few highlights to emphasize the role human reason has played in reshaping the world around us since our ancestors first broke off from the larger line of great apes some 6 million years ago. When hominins—as anthropologists now refer to these first proto-humans—began leaving Africa's dense forests for the open savannah, they possessed a handful of physiological traits that gave them some degree of competitive advantage over other species in their new environment. Most notably, whereas their closest genetic cousins continued to be knuckle-walkers, in the fashion of contemporary chimpanzees, hominins adopted a bipedal, upright stance that allowed them to scan the distant horizon for both predators and prey. Meanwhile, the opposable thumbs hominins inherited from their tree-dwelling ancestors allowed them to carry various objects around with them as they walked, including the tools they would eventually invent. This mention of tools, however, points to the most potent physiological advantage hominins enjoyed over their potential competitors: large, well-developed brains, which only tripled in size over the subsequent course of human evolution.

One way hominins put their large brains to work was by observing how the larger world functions, then using this knowledge to develop novel technologies that, in turn, allowed them to better meet their natural wants and needs—a very early version of what would later happen at a much faster pace over the periods of the Scientific and Industrial Revolutions. Some 3.3 million years ago, for instance, hominins learned how to chip rocks to make sharp blades, thus helping compensate for their lack of sharp teeth or claws. Around 1 million years ago, our more recent ancestors figured out how to tame the power of fire, thereby unlocking many previously unavailable calories in the food they ate—calories our ancestors desperately needed to fuel their growing, energy-guzzling brains. And at an unknown later date, probably within the past few hundred thousand years, *Homo sapiens* developed the first oral languages, thereby making it easier—among many other things—to transmit new technologies from one tribemate to another or down through the generations.

As this final observation suggests, if the invention of various physical technologies was crucial to our ancestors' evolutionary success, just as significant was their ability to master the social technology of living together in ever larger groups, thereby providing the group with a stronger common defense, while allowing its members to reap the benefits of doing many things cooperatively that one or two individuals could never accomplish on their own. For the first hominins, this probably meant organizing themselves into troops composed mostly of extended family, much as we see among contemporary chimpanzees. And at some later date—again unknown with any precision, but at least several hundred thousand years ago—our more recent ancestors began to form migratory, foraging tribes that numbered somewhere between one and two hundred members, with many of these members sharing no direct ties of blood. To appreciate both the advantages and challenges associated with this communal, cooperative form of living, we can consider the development of one relatively late technology: the group hunting of such very large game as wooly mammoth.

A single mammoth could feed an entire tribe for weeks, so hunting this type of large game was a far more efficient means of obtaining calories than sending everyone out to hunt small game on their own. But luring such a large, dangerous beast toward a cliff before driving it over the edge requires a great deal of planning and well-coordinated execution on the part of the entire hunting party. And more challenging is reaching a point where the hunter charged with luring the mammoth to the side of the ravine is willing to entrust his life to his tribemates, placing himself before the charging beast in the faith that they will jump out of the bushes to divert it. Establishing this level of trust requires many generations' worth of establishing social norms and expectations, aided by the development of such social technologies as harsh sanctions for tribal members who placed their natural concern for personal safety above the interests of the larger group.

The human ability to simultaneously develop new material and social technologies was again on display over the period of the Agricultural Revolution when some clever hunter-gatherers figured out how to domesticate various species of wild plants and animals, thereby allowing them to give up their ceaseless wandering in search of food and establish permanent agricultural settlements. As these settlements grew in size, different groups experimented with various means of organizing and governing themselves, some of these more egalitarian and bottom-up in character, not unlike the migratory tribes from which they sprang, others more hierarchical in structure, featuring the top-down rule of a powerful chieftain. Over the course of several thousand years, the hierarchical model emerged the winner, such that, by the time we here picked up the story of recorded human history with the appearance of the major world religions and the handing down of law codes by the world's first lawgivers, virtually every major society featured a steep socio-political hierarchy. The resulting inequalities of wealth and power set the stage for the mode of governance here termed the system of privilege, according to which individuals on different levels of the hierarchy were accorded different mixes of privileges and duties. As a rule, those near the top of the hierarchy used the power they wielded to assign themselves mostly privileges, while charging those near the bottom of the hierarchy almost entirely with duties—most of them geared toward underwriting the privileges of those on top.

Admittedly, the extent to which the innovation of top-down rule made life "better" for the vast majority of individuals stuck at the bottom of the social pyramid is debatable. Granted, even these people were probably less likely to fall into deadly quarrels with one another now that the sovereign's sword was hanging over their heads. Meanwhile, the shift to domestic agriculture provided a better return on caloric investment than hunting and gathering, so there was at least the potential for greater material security. Those near the top of the hierarchy, however, generally confiscated all but the barest subsistence living from those on the bottom, so for millennia, most of the tangible progress arising from the domestication of agriculture and the establishment of what the contract theorists would call civic society accrued to a very small segment of the population. That said, the innovation of top-down governance did, at least, allow the size of the standard social unit to multiply many times over: village, town, city-state, kingdom, nation-state, empire. Improving agricultural efficiency, meanwhile, freed some of the social unit's members from the need to devote all their time to food acquisition, thus allowing them to pursue such more cerebral professions as scribe, accountant, astronomer, priest, poet, and philosopher. Taken together, these developments promoted the acquisition of yet more learning, while assisting in its transmission from one part of the world to another, and from one generation to the next.

To be sure, much of the learning that took place over the period dominated by the system of privilege could probably be better characterized as rationalization than as a proud display of human reason. The explanation for this was simple. Priests, scholars, and other members of the intellectual classes were almost all dependent on the king for their sustenance, their physical safety, and their esteemed social status. It follows that when one of these learned people preached a sermon or wrote a scholarly tract, he was most likely to be rewarded—or in any case, to avoid being burned at the stake—not for revealing the objective truth of things, but for giving a convincing account as to why the prevailing socio-political arrangements were right and good, with the king and his nobles being on top and everyone else obediently serving them. That said, even under such relatively sterile intellectual conditions as those found within the scholastic university, enough genuine learning took place eventually to inspire certain visionaries to imagine a different approach to the study of nature that would more accurately discern the objective workings of nature. Thus was sparked the Scientific Revolution, which prompted all the developments in the intellectual, technological, social, political, economic, and moral realms that we have considered throughout this book.

Notably, this more recent burst of reason-driven progress included replacing the ancient ideology of privilege with a modern ideology of rights while attempting to lend this novel ideology concrete reality by experimenting with a new bottom-up, democratic mode of social organization and governance. As we know, the American pioneers of this new political system, though obviously highly intelligent, did not make the best show of reason when they failed, for instance, to grasp the incongruity of promoting a doctrine of universal rights while personally owning slaves. Nevertheless, one of the crucial functions of human reason is what Kant labeled critique: the ability to come back and assess whether your abductive stabs in the dark are panning out. This can involve gathering additional empirical data to determine whether a proposed scientific theory is being borne out. Yet, it can also mean reassessing your actions—whether personally or at the level of the larger society—to determine whether these actions are truly aligning with the moral principles to which you have committed.

In the social, political, and moral realms, the process of critique and correction is generally much slower, messier, and more painful than in the scientific or engineering laboratory. But progress of this sort is not only possible, it is real; it has been happening for a very long time; and it continues to occur at an ever quickening pace. And as our world continues its progress toward better realizing the ideal of moral universalism, it is generally our faculty of reason—aided by healthy doses of courage, determination, inspiration, and faith—that drives this progress forward, even as this progress then renders our reason more acute by shining a light on past errors and suggesting ways we can do better in the future.

This, in any case, was the view of the world—where it

comes from, where it is headed, and how it operates—that was coming together and gaining some public recognition by the end of the twentieth century. And progressives' growing awareness of their own worldview, in turn, allowed them to begin reflecting more consciously on the place they occupy within this world, whether in a very general sense, as human beings, or more specifically as progressively inclined individuals called to the global stage around the turn of the twenty-first century.

CHAPTER 13

OUR PLACE IN THE WORLD: THE PROGRESSIVE CALLING

If it is true that by the close of the twentieth century, progressively leaning Americans were becoming increasingly aware, first, that they have a comprehensive worldview; second, that this worldview rests on a foundational narrative that is compelling in plot, epic in scope, and strongly backed by empirical evidence; and third, that this narrative exudes the hopeful message that our entire universe is moving forward and upward, displaying a bias in favor of progress, what good has this done? How has it helped the progressive cause? Has our new foundational narrative, for instance, given us a powerful new weapon to wield in the culture war social conservatives declared against us?

Perhaps. It is possible that the captivating, still evolving, empirically based story of a universe that has been already making progress for billions of years has drawn some American voters in the direction of a progressive outlook more generally, thus leading them to lend their political support to more specific progressive causes. If this is true, such a draw has probably been felt most strongly among voters with higher levels of education, who are most likely to have been exposed to various chapters in the universal story of progress, whether in school or leisure time. And in fact, voters with college degrees have been moving steadily leftward over the past decades, doubtless for a whole variety of reasons, but perhaps this is one of them. Over this same period, however, rural and working-class voters—who tend to have lower levels of education—have drifted politically rightward. Many of these voters, meanwhile, have attributed their change of political orientation to a resentment they feel that liberal elites—to include the sorts of intellectual elites who dominate American higher education and the sciences—have been trying to shove a nontraditional, politically correct, secular worldview down their throats. For these voters, the fact that progressives have begun trumpeting a long, complicated, technically challenging foundational narrative has probably just added to the sense that scientific gobbledygook is one more tool the liberal establishment is using to extend its control over ordinary folks.

All told, therefore, it is probably an open question whether growing public awareness of the progressive foundational narrative has produced a net gain or loss of support for progressive politics. That said, as I have spent the past twenty years sorting through my own thoughts on the progressive worldview, it has become increasingly clear to me that any political benefits we may derive from holding a well-articulated worldview are of secondary importance, at best, whether for progressives or anyone else. When our tribal ancestors first began telling stories about their world, after all—perhaps sitting around the communal fire at night, finally getting a chance to step outside the stimulus-and-response mode in which they necessarily spent most of their lives, possibly looking up at the stars and wondering at their majesty—they did not have a particular political agenda in mind. They were just trying to make sense of their experience. They were trying to get a handle on the vast, confusing, often terrifying world into which they had been thrown. Faced with this bewildering reality, they began asking such questions as: Where does the world come from? Where is it headed? How does it operate? And what role do human beings play within it? And in a groping, grasping attempt to answer these questions, our ancestors began telling stories about their world.

As they told these stories, our tribal ancestors wove unseen forces and actors seamlessly together with the objects and events they could observe around them. Why should they not? The distinction between visible and invisible probably did not strike them as relevant, nor could they ever begin to make sense of the world around them merely on the basis of the available data. So, they told stories about earth spirits and river spirits, sun gods and moon goddesses, abductively throwing out the best explanations they could conjure as to why, for instance, the hunt succeeded one day but failed the next. Perhaps when the antelope offered himself up to the tribe's hunters, his spirit was pleased with the tribe, whereas on days the antelope stayed away, his spirit was angry. Such explanations may not have eased the hunger pangs our ancestors felt on nights when the hunt had failed, but they did make some sense of this suffering; they gave it some meaning.

Such stories, moreover, gave our tribal ancestors a degree of agency within a world that was otherwise largely beyond their control. These stories, that is, suggested certain "technologies," with a technology being nothing but an insight into how the larger world operates that gives its bearer some control over the world. Understanding, for instance, that the antelope has a fickle spirit, an ancient hunter might have painted a picture of the antelope on a cave wall, or his entire tribe might have performed a ritual dance the night before a hunt. Nor did it discredit such technologies when the hunt still sometimes failed. Who was to say the tribe had not failed to perform the dance with sufficient vigor?

In any case, such stories and their accompanying rituals informed our ancestors as to what they should be doing in particular instances. And this likely helped them achieve certain tangible ends: early hunting parties probably *did* enjoy greater success when they danced the night before a hunt, whether because of the increased confidence this gave them or because such communal rites strengthened the bonds of tribal solidarity, thereby promoting cooperation among the hunters. Perhaps even more significantly, however, by telling our ancestors what they should be doing—what the natural order demanded of them—these stories gave our tribal forebears a place in the world. They assigned both individuals and tribes a role to play in the global drama. And hence these stories answered to the deepest longing our ancestors felt as they sat around the fire at night, looking up at the stars: the existential desire to be part of something larger than themselves.

It was a similar urge to make sense of the world—and particularly to make sense of the suffering that pervades the world—that led later Vedic mystics to compose a grand cyclical drama featuring fantastic characters that were part human, part animal, and part god. With the ever-recurring cycles of the sun, moon, and stars teaching that nothing ever really changes in the visible order, the Vedics concluded that the only way to escape the mundane cycle of joy and suffering is through the otherworldly release of *nirvana*, thus transporting us back to our true home in *brahman*, the ground of all things. Somewhat later, as small Semitic tribes wandered the Middle Eastern desert, facing the hostility of both nature and their larger, more powerful neighbors, their prophets crafted a linear, unidirectional narrative in which Yahweh ultimately leads his people to a promised land, thereby lending cosmic significance to their mundane quest for a home in the world. Finally, it was a similar longing for a secure, respected, and even exalted place in the world that drove the rise of a small movement centered around the charismatic Jewish prophet, Jesus. Persecuted by their Roman occupiers and the entrenched Hebrew religious establishment, the first Christians viewed Jesus as the messiah who would provide them with the safe, esteemed, metaphysically significant place in the world for which they yearned—even if constructing this new home might require destroying the current order and building a New Jerusalem.

It is certainly true that, once this last foundational story had been appropriated by the Roman political authorities, it began to be reshaped in subtle ways to serve an overt political purpose—namely, keeping the ruling classes in power, while convincing everyone else to accept their place at the bottom of the social hierarchy. Particularly once the Augustinian doctrine of original sin had been enshrined as orthodoxy, this story's declinist trajectory counseled those who were oppressed to relinquish any hope of changing the present order for the better, and to instead place their hopes in a future world that might be reached through patient obedience in this life. Even under these circumstances, however, the Christian foundational narrative was not merely, or even primarily, serving a political purpose. The Christian story was also doing what foundational narratives had always done: providing its hearers with a meaningful place in an otherwise hostile world. Indeed, had the Christian narrative not given medieval peasants a sense of metaphysical comfort, reassuring them that they had a place in God's plan, the story could not have fulfilled its political purpose of promoting quiet obedience, since no one would have cared much about what it said.

For those of us who find ourselves living in the vicinity of the turn of the twenty-first century, there is no reason we should not feel the same existential longing to have a place in the world—to be an integral part of something much larger than ourselves—that people have always felt. Little about the human condition has changed, after all, since our tribal ancestors first sat around the fire at night, looking up at the stars. We still find ourselves existing within a much larger world that we did not create, nor can we even remember when we first came into this world. Unlike other animals, moreover, we are painfully aware that our time on earth is limited, running no more than a few score years, at most. Indeed, with several thousand years of collective philosophical reflection under our belts, we are even better equipped than our tribal ancestors were to step outside the stimulus-and-response mode of daily life and shift into the more abstract mode of thinking required for existential reflection. Yet, this just heightens the potential we have to be stopped dead in our tracks, staggered by the wonder of the world around us. The night sky may not shine as brightly as it did for our ancestors, given modern light pollution, and some of us may go for weeks on end without even glancing up at the stars. But this does not render the sight of the glistening heavens any less extraordinary when we do occasionally stop to gaze skyward. Nor is there any reason why our longing to have a place in this immense whole should be any less urgent than it was for our ancestors.

As we reflect on the vast, confusing, occasionally terrifying world that surrounds us, we continue to respond to our longing for a place in this world in the same way our tribal ancestors did: we tell stories. In fact, a large portion of the world's population still gravitates toward the traditional religious stories that have served generations of our predecessors perfectly well for thousands of years. For many of us who identify as progressives, however, we find these older stories simply do not work anymore, at least not as literal accounts of how our world is put together. We may appreciate that, at the time they were scripted, these traditional stories were authentic responses to our ancestors' existential longing for a place in the larger universe. Accordingly, we may find these stories still brimming with nuggets of truth or inspiration. Some of us, moreover, may find that participating in traditional religious rituals still helps us step outside of daily life and enter the more reflective space of existential contemplation. Yet, given our conviction that the evidence-based mode of reasoning that arose along with the modern sciences is the most reliable path humankind has yet found to Truth, many of us find we simply cannot, in good intellectual conscience, take the traditional religious narratives at face value, or as literal accounts of where our world comes from, where it is headed, and how it operates.

For centuries, defenders of these religious narratives have been charging that the modern, scientific way of viewing the world cannot but lead to a complete loss of meaning in human life. This charge of nihilism assumes, however, that in setting aside some particular religious story, we are leaving ourselves with no stories to tell about our world, or at least none with any spiritual import. From the progressive perspective, however, precisely the opposite has happened. The same empirical approach to the study of nature that has caused traditional religious stories to fall flat for us has not only increased our collective understanding of our world hundreds of times over—leading to all manner of tangible, material benefits—but modern science has given us a new mode of storytelling that is every bit as compelling as the earlier mythic and religious modes. Indeed, many of us would argue this new mode of storytelling is even more compelling. This is partly because, with the line between the visible and invisible having now been drawn more carefully, scientific stories are made to rest on demonstrable, empirical facts. But it is also because many of the empirical facts modern science has uncovered have turned out to be more breathtakingly remarkable than even the most inspired mystical visions on the part of ancient prophets.

This last point bears emphasizing, for it helps us respond to another charge frequently lodged against modern science, not just by proponents of traditional religion, but by romantics of all stripes. This is the charge that modern science has demystified nature, purging it of all the spirits, vitality, passion, and mystery that once permeated everything, thereby reducing our world to the sort of lifeless, empty shell suggested by a cursory glance at the graphs and equations of Newton's *Principia*. This charge actually has something to it, and many scientists have done their best to lend it credence. In fact, we would probably need to concede the charge that science had rendered nature lifeless if the modern scientific project had played out the way Descartes originally conceived it.

Descartes, again, pioneered the reductionist approach to science by arguing that the best way to learn about complex objects is by breaking them into simpler parts, then doing so again until finally we arrive at parts so simple we can grasp them clearly and distinctly, leaving no room for ambiguity, error, or mystery. More specifically in the realm of physics, Descartes believed we could reduce every material object to its geometric shape, thus transforming the study of nature into an exercise in analytic geometry and allowing researchers to learn everything there is to know about the world by sitting in their armchairs and working through geometric demonstrations like those of Euclid. The modern scientific project, on this conception, was so straightforward that Descartes believed the work of science might be completed in a few decades, quite possibly within his own lifetime.

This is not, once again, how things turned out. It is true that most scientists spend most of their time moving in a reductionist direction, taking some complex phenomenon and analyzing it into simpler parts, typically making heavy use of mathematics. Throughout this book, however, we have seen that the routine work of science is periodically interrupted by some mind-blowing discovery that completely changes the prevailing way of viewing things, often yielding a picture of the world far richer than anything previously imagined. Take, for example, what happened when Galileo first trained his telescope on Jupiter. Most likely, Galileo was just planning to use his new optical device to render our knowledge of a particular dot in the sky more clear and distinct. What he discovered, however, is that Jupiter is not a lone body orbiting the sun, but rather it is circled by multiple moons of its own, almost like a tiny solar system, thus opening a whole new astronomical frontier for further exploration. Leeuwenhoek had a similar experience a few decades later when he first peered into his microscope. To his surprise, Leeuwenhoek discovered that nature is not empty, at all, but rather the tiniest drop of water is teeming with life—and not just unseen, animistic spirits, but actual living creatures on a diminutive scale.

Thus it has been throughout the history of modern science: the more deeply scientists have probed nature, trying to reduce its workings to simpler, more graspable terms, the more they have stumbled into new realms never before dreamed of, each of them more mysterious and fascinating than the last. Just think here of the quantum and relativistic revolutions of the early twentieth century, or of the deep-space images the Hubble Telescope began transmitting back to earth late in that same century. And thus, far from telling a story that renders our world a lifeless, empty shell, modern science has spun a tale that only grows richer with each generation, continually opening new doors that earlier storytellers did not even know were there. If anything, therefore, the old religious narratives are prone to growing stale and lifeless, having been separated from the ancient experiences of awe and wonder that originally inspired them by centuries of verbatim repetition. In the modern sciences, conversely, the foundational story is forever being revised and augmented, with the discoveries of one generation providing not only the concrete knowledge upon which the next generation can build, but also the fresh experiences of awe and wonder that can inspire scientists and non-scientists alike to continue probing the world around them ever more deeply.

Nor, to address one final charge the proponents of traditional religion have been lodging against the modern sciences for centuries, has the scientific account of nature left human beings without a meaningful place in the world. To be sure, developments in the sciences have repeatedly dislodged humankind from the central, starring role it once played in older foundational narratives, to include that of traditional Christianity. This displacement began with Copernicus's suggestion that the earth orbits the sun, rather than vice versa, thereby shoving humankind from the center of the cosmos to its periphery. The displacement then continued when Darwin showed *homo sapiens* to be not a unique, exalted species given mastery over all others but just one more strain of primate that evolved through the blind workings of natural selection. And finally, when twentieth-century cosmologists populated the universe with billions of galaxies, each of them containing billions of stars, this only confirmed how tiny and insignificant humankind is on the cosmic scale.

Each of these displacements was existentially wrenching, forcing those who accept the science to rethink what sort of meaningful role human beings might play within such a large, impersonal universe. But as the story of a progressively developing universe came together over the nineteenth and twentieth centuries—driven largely by the work of natural scientists, but also by the thoughts, words, and deeds of philosophers, politicians, social activists, and ordinary citizens—this story has come to show that human beings still occupy a place in the world that is entirely unique, and even exalted. We have simply needed to carve this place out for ourselves, rather than having it handed to us by an even more exalted being.

Our Place in the World

As we begin to consider the place human beings might occupy within the world portrayed by modern science, the first point to note is that the modern scientific narrative treats humankind as being tied far more closely to the rest of nature than was true under such earlier foundational narratives as that of traditional Christianity. In Genesis, God gives Adam dominion over all the earth, including over every living creature. But this just set Adam apart from the rest of creation, rendering him a lonely outsider. And when Adam then falls, prompting his expulsion from paradise, this underscores the message that the rest of us are living in a world for which we were never truly intended, our real home being the paradise to which we hope one day to return.

According to the modern scientific story, conversely, human beings are fully products of the world around us, composed of the exact same stuff as stars, planets, rocks, trees, bacteria, fish, and chimpanzees, our constituent parts merely being arranged in somewhat different fashion. Indeed, while Darwin had already proposed that all living creatures share a common ancestor, genetic sequencing techniques developed over the final decades of the twentieth century have made clear just how much DNA we share, not merely with one another, but with every other species of animal, and even plants. The spectrographic analysis of ancient supernovae, moreover, has confirmed that the heavier elements out of which both the earth and its living inhabitants are composed were once forged within distant stars. Proponents of traditional religion may complain this drags humankind down into the mud, much as Darwin's critics once charged that he was reducing human beings to apes. But from the progressive perspective, the continuity modern science has established between people and the rest of nature only serves to draw us that much more intimately into a grand narrative as old and large as the universe, itself—thus beginning to answer to our deepest existential longing to be part of something much larger than ourselves.

Yet, if modern science therefore places human beings on

a continuum with the rest of nature, it *also* remains true, on the modern scientific account, that we are an entirely unique variety of existent. Indeed, the modern scientific story gives us meaningful grounds for asserting that human beings are not just *different* from the other inhabitants of nature, but that we have *transcended* the rest of nature. That being said, *even this act of transcendence serves to bind us all the more tightly to the larger universe.* This claim sounds paradoxical until we recall that the history of our universe is nothing but the story of one such transcendence after the next, with these acts of transcendence typically taking the form of many smaller, simpler parts coming together to form larger, more complex wholes, thereby transforming both their constituent parts and the world around them.

This was already happening, for instance, when huge numbers of hydrogen and helium atoms began falling together under the force of gravity. The stars that resulted continued to be card-carrying members of the natural order from which they sprang, obeying the same laws of physics that had always been in effect. At the same time, however, these stars developed an inner dynamic more complex than anything the universe had yet seen, balancing the inward-pressing force of gravity against an outward-rushing blast of nuclear energy in a fashion stable enough to allow many stars to burn for billions of years. These new massive, complex, enduring objects then went on to dramatically alter the cosmic landscape around them, providing the universe with its large-scale architecture of galaxies and galaxy clusters, while forging the heavier elements out of which solid celestial bodies could one day form—themselves providing the platforms upon which even more complex entities, some of them living, could eventually evolve.

This same movement in the direction of greater complexity was still taking place some 6 million years ago when a small population of bipedal primates began walking the African savannah. With nearly fourteen billion years' worth of compounding complexity going into their production, hominins were already exceedingly complex when they first took the global stage. Granted, beyond their upright stance and opposable thumbs, our first ancestors may not have been physiologically remarkable, at least as compared to many other species of their day. Neurologically, however, hominins were already on nature's cutting edge, and as their descendants then tripled their brain size over the next 6 million years—the neural networks these brains could support growing more complex and sophisticated all the while—the mental acuity this produced allowed later humans not only to think and act at uniquely high levels of complexity and sophistication but to continue generating yet more complexity, whether within their own thoughts, in the material order around them, or in their relations with one another. And this power to innovate has allowed human beings to repeatedly transcend, not just the other inhabitants of nature but themselves—or their predecessors—thereby launching humanity on a course of continuous progress that is *both* unprecedented in the larger universe *and* faithful to the basic script that has given the universal drama of progress its upward trajectory from the beginning.

To illustrate this point, we can touch on just a few of the many realms of experience in which human beings may have started out standing on a common spectrum with other living creatures but through repeated acts of self-transcendence, established ourselves as a fully unique species. Beginning in the intellectual realm, cognition is something we presumably share with every other type of animal. Like most things in nature, however, cognition would appear to come in degrees, and human cognition is simply off the charts in terms of the analytic power it confers on its bearers. Perhaps most significantly, human thinkers have developed what would appear to be a unique variety of self-consciousness. Like other sentient beings, we devote the bulk of our attention to the objects immediately before us, yet we are also capable of turning our attention back upon ourselves, recognizing ourselves to be the perceivers who are cognizing these objects. This self-awareness opens a separation between knower and known that allows us to step back from the things or events before us and consider the abstract properties or behaviors that might bind many of them together as instances of common phenomena.

By struggling to make sense of their world in this fashion, our predecessors worked their way through a series of increasingly complex and sophisticated explanations for such natural phenomena as why a rock will roll downhill, first invoking the mood of some unseen spirit, then citing the inner nature of individual rocks and their tendency to strive earthward, and finally subjecting rocks and everything else in nature to the universal laws of physics. This same power of abstract reasoning is also what allowed our tribal ancestors occasionally to step outside the stimulus-and-response mode of daily life and reflect on the abstract, all-encompassing concept of "world" or "All," thereby generating the world's first worldviews—a completely unprecedented instance, we could say, of our universe becoming conscious of itself.

Turning to the technological realm, we are far from being the only species that has learned how to manipulate the material order to better serve our own ends. Spiders spin webs to catch their prey, while beavers dam streams to create the still ponds in which to build their lodges. Presumably, these behaviors are completely instinctive, learned over many generations by means of natural selection, but individual chimpanzees have been observed using their more human-like powers of abductive reasoning to figure out that dipping a stick into a termite mound allows the dipper to extract its tasty inhabitants. Still, even at this upper end of the animal cognitive spectrum, most non-human species tend to stumble their way into a few technologies that work well for them, then cling to these same innovations indefinitely. Human beings, in contrast, have made a practice of continually innovating and re-innovating, often using the results of one technology as the platform upon which to build the next.

Thus our earliest ancestor surpassed their primate cousins by learning how to chip rocks to create sharp blades. They did not stop here, but rather went on to develop such increasingly complex and sophisticated technologies as controlled fire and oral language; then ploughs, written language, aqueducts, and sailing ships; and still later power looms, airplanes, digital computers, and cell phones. The invention of language, both oral and written, proved particularly significant in the development and diffusion of other technologies, since it gives both individuals and communities a means of sharing their innovations with other groups, while passing the associated knowledge down through the generations. By the same token, the more recent invention of transistors and microchips has spurred another wave of innovation, partly through the computing power these devices confer, but also through the ease and rapidity with which they allow information and ideas to be shared around the world.

As noted in prior chapters, of all the technologies human beings have developed, likely the most consequential have been the series of social technologies—customs, rules, political and legal institutions, shared understandings, and values—that have allowed people to live and work together in ever larger social units. Here again, we are not the only species to have discovered the benefits of cooperation. Social insects such as ants and bees form communities so tightly interwoven as to function almost as single organisms. Many birds and mammals, meanwhile, come together to form flocks, herds, packs, or troops, each of these groups featuring increasingly complex social dynamics. Hominins, in fact, probably started out living in small family troops comparable to what we observe among contemporary chimpanzees. But whereas other species have generally settled into an optimal group size and remained there, human beings have distinguished themselves by continually expanding the social units to which they belong.

As we have touched on here—and will consider in much greater detail in the next volume—if hominins began living in small family troops, multiple families eventually came together to form somewhat larger migratory tribes. With the invention of domestic agriculture, some of these tribes then settled down to form permanent agricultural villages, which themselves grew into towns, city-states, nation-states, and empires. And while empires have recently fallen out of fashion, leaving the nation-state as the current standard unit of human social organization, dramatic advances in transportation and communications technologies have combined with robust international trade and the establishment of various supernational institutions to create an increasingly interconnected global order. It is not yet clear whether this global order will ever achieve the unity and coherence required to qualify as a social unit in its own right, but should this happen, it would represent the logical culmination of movement from smaller and simpler to larger and more complex in the socio-political realm that has been playing out for the past 6 million years.

Turning, on this note, to the closely related moral realm, recent research has shown that, even here, human beings fall on a continuum with other members of the animal kingdom—and that all of us, human and non-human animals alike, have a psychology far more complex than Hobbes envisioned when he reduced all possible motivations to personal self-interest. Many birds and mammals, for instance, make great sacrifices to nurture and defend their offspring, displaying an altruism seemingly at odds with their personal survival instinct. Some mammals, moreover, behave in ways that strongly suggest they feel compassion for those around them, including sometimes for non-family members, and occasionally even for members of other species. And a handful of primates appear to possess an innate sense of fairness comparable to what developmental psychologists have found in very young human children. Chimpanzees, for example, have been observed rejecting highly valued food treats when they see researchers offering fellow test subjects less desirable snacks for no apparent reason.

With all these examples of proto-moral behavior in the animal kingdom being acknowledged, morality would *also* appear to be one of the realms in which human beings at least have the potential to completely transcend even our closest genetic cousins, behaving in a fashion that does not just represent a difference in degree from other animals, but a difference in kind. Specifically, observation would suggest that other animals run almost completely on instinct, including when they make their seemingly "moral" decisions. The altruism a mother bird displays, for instance, would appear to be an evolved behavior driven by the release of certain biochemicals in her brain, with the mother throwing herself before the fox that threatens her hatchlings because this just feels right, not because she has made any conscious decision to behave morally. As human beings, we doubtless operate in this same instinctive fashion much of the time, including when we engage in many behaviors we typically regard as moral, such as sacrificing for our children, compassionately reaching out to others who are suffering, or bristling at the sight of some unfair situation. Nevertheless, our ability to engage in self-conscious, abstract reasoning gives us what would appear to be a unique ability to step back from the particular circumstances in which we find ourselves enmeshed—where we are constantly asking ourselves what we should be doing to achieve some particular end, generally as suggested to us by some instinct or inclination—and instead pose the question of what we *ought* to be doing, in a moral sense.

This, in any case, is what Kant argued. As we saw back in Chapter 6, Kant freely allowed that we are constantly bombarded with bodily inclinations, most of which are nakedly self-interested. He insisted, however, that whereas other animals are fully determined by their inclinations, human beings have the capacity, if not to turn off our inclinations, then to override them, at least on occasion. And this gives us the potential to freely chart our own course, as opposed to having all our actions determined by whatever appetites, urges, or passions happen to strike us, as if from beyond. To achieve this autonomy from our own bodily condition in a manner that does not just come down to acting randomly—an empty freedom, as Kant saw it—we must use our powers of reasoning to pose a question taking the form of "What is the *right* thing to do?" or equivalently, "What is my duty?" As Kant again acknowledged, nothing compels us even to raise such moral questions, much less to act on the answers reason suggests to them. We can always revert to our default mode of doing whatever our inclinations tell us to do, thus behaving as the animals we are. But if we can resist the pull of the inclinations and determine our actions in accord with the moral law—which is to say, in accord with the idea of universal law—we transcend our animal nature and thereby invest ourselves with moral dignity found nowhere else in nature.

As we saw in Chapter 6, this account of *how* we go about acting morally also ended up serving as Kant's ultimate answer to the metaethical question of *why* we ought to be moral, specifically in the sense of determining our actions in accord with the universal moral law. As that earlier chapter noted, this was not an easy question for Kant to answer, given his particular approach to ethics. He had rejected the British approach initiated by Hobbes, which rests on the premise that all voluntary action is determined by the law of self-interest, such that promoting moral action requires finding ways to channel self-interest into socially beneficial behaviors. Having dispensed with the need for the Hobbesian premise in his theoretical philosophy, Kant went on, in his moral writings, to insist that if our actions are to be moral in character, they *cannot* be guided by self-interest, at least not exclusively, no matter how pro-social they might be in effect. What, after all, would distinguish certain pro-social actions as right or good if we took them merely because we calculated they would make us feel good inside, or they would maximize the long-term benefit we ultimately receive back from others, just as we might reason when making any of our other self-interested decisions? To be moral, therefore, our actions must rather accord with the moral law, which is to say the maxims guiding them must take the form of universality. Crucially, moreover, we must perform these actions *for the sake of* following the moral law, whether or not they also happen to serve our material interests.

But this is what made it challenging for Kant to answer to the question of, "Why be moral?" By the terms of his own argument, he could not respond, "Because, as a general rule, behaving morally is in our long-term best interest." Certainly, it *may* be in our enlightened self-interest to live in accord with the moral law, since doing so will generally help us win friends, avoid fights, and escape social sanction, not to mention promoting a more peaceful, cooperative social order. Still, these beneficial outcomes cannot be the *motive* of our moral actions, or at least not our sole motive, or this would rob our actions of their morality. So why, then, be moral, particularly in the sense prescribed by Kant's doctrine of moral universalism?

As we saw, Kant did make one direct attempt to answer this question. He noted that even if moral actions cannot—by definition—be motivated by self-interest, observing the moral law responds to a certain "interest of reason" we innately possess. As rational beings, that is, we constantly strive to make sense of the world around us. We perpetually attempt to unify the manifold with which we are confronted by drawing as many diverse phenomena as possible under the unity of particular concepts or principles, whether by bundling multiple sensations together under the concept of "my desk," subsuming numerous instances of heavy objects falling under the law of falling bodies, or—at a very high level—viewing the entire world through the lens of a particular worldview. Our bodily inclinations, however, are not only numerous, disjointed, and disorganized, but they can contradict one another, with one inclination pulling us one way, even as another pushes in the opposite direction. It follows that when we allow ourselves to be governed by our inclinations, our thoughts and actions can have little coherence to them, such that we end up living contrary to our essential vocation of unifying the manifold. When, conversely, we determine our actions in accord with the idea of universal law, we give our many diverse actions the unity of a common principle, thus answering to our deepest calling as rational, unifying beings.

Now, perhaps this suggestion that we ought to be moral because this will help us keep our lives in a neat, tidy order will be inspiring to a born rationalist like Kant—whose neighbors, again, could set their watches by the time he walked to the university each morning. But after scientists have spent the past two hundred years showing us how gloriously complex, dynamic, and messy nature is—to include, as we are now learning, our own psychology—the notion that we could tidy up any of this does not seem particularly relevant anymore, much less morally compelling. In fact, given the relatively small amount of space Kant devotes to the interest of reason, it does not appear even he found this to be one of his stronger arguments. For Kant's ultimate answer to the question of why we should be moral, therefore, he appears to have fallen back on the more existential argument referenced above, which we could paraphrase more completely as follows:

We find ourselves existing, and more specifically—to borrow Aristotle's formulation—we find ourselves existing as rational animals. Given this dual nature, we are subject to a wide range of passions or inclinations we share with other animals. Arising from our bodily form, these inclinations are presumably determined by the laws of nature, so we cannot avoid feeling their strong pull. What distinguishes us from other animals, however, is that we need not let these inclinations fully determine our actions. In virtue of our rational capacity, we can also determine our actions in accord with a law we discover through rational reflection: the moral law.

Because the moral law—which is to say, the idea of universal law—is a law of our own giving, when we observe it, we cease to be controlled by the inclinations with which we are constantly pelted, as if from beyond, and instead take ownership of our actions. Thus we achieve a moral autonomy—and along with it a moral dignity—completely unknown to the rest of nature. As we step outside the stimulus-and-response mode of daily life and engage in moral reflection, therefore, the existential question we find ourselves facing is: Given that we are here for a finite span of time, do we really want to live like beasts, at the mercy of our disjointed, chaotic inclinations? Or would we prefer to attain the dignity of rational, autonomous moral agents, to be achieved by submitting our actions to the test of universalizability—which, in turn, demands that we recognize and respect the moral dignity of every other rational, autonomous, moral agent?

This is not, by any means, a bad answer to the question, "Why be moral?" And at the end of the day, it may be enough to convince us to behave in moral fashion, specifically in the sense of observing a doctrine of moral universalism. Still, this argument for behaving morally that Kant advanced as he was helping round out the first iteration of the progressive worldview is not fully satisfying, particularly given the perspective we now enjoy in virtue of having access to the foundational narrative associated with the second iteration of the progressive worldview. The problem, specifically, is that Kant's argument for morality rests all its weight on the notion that acting in universalizable fashion is how we differentiate ourselves from other animals. This argument is still persuasive under the second iteration of the progressive worldview—which, as I have been arguing throughout this chapter, continues to provide human beings with a unique, transcendent, and even exalted place in the world. Yet, the second iteration of the progressive worldview *also* celebrates the fact of how closely we are bound up with the larger world we occupy. This suggests we have an existential incentive, not just to distinguish ourselves from the rest of nature, but also to tie ourselves back to the larger world at some higher level. Does behaving morally, specifically in the sense of embracing the progressive project of moral universalism as it has taken shape over the past two centuries, allow us to do this?

I believe it does. Indeed, if the current chapter began by asking what good has come from the fact that, by the close of the twentieth century, progressives were achieving a greater self-awareness of their own worldview—the fully matured second iteration of the progressive worldview—I believe one of the most compelling answers we can give to this question is that the second iteration's story of a progressively developing universe can help us formulate a more compelling answer than Kant ever managed to the metaethical question of "Why be moral?" It does so, not by rejecting Kant's answer, but by complementing it with a second argument for behaving morally. I will use the remainder of this chapter to sketch out this argument, although by this point, its basic thrust should be clear. If pursuing the progressive moral project allows us to transcend our own animal nature, thereby setting us apart from the rest of nature, this same act of transcendence ties us back to the larger world in an even more profound fashion by weaving the story of human moral progress into a much larger story of universal progress—itself a story of one transcendence after the next.

Why Be Progressive?

The plotline of the universal story of progress is by now familiar to us. Since our universe began nearly 14 billion years ago, it has been on a path of progress, with the most general form this progress has taken being the movement from smaller and simpler to larger and more complex. A glance back at human history, meanwhile, makes clear that humankind has made considerable progress of its own, including in the moral realm. Torture, for instance, was once routinely used as an instrument of state power. Now, the practice is both legally banned and publicly reviled, at least in most democratic countries, which feels like progress. Still, the way moral progress fits with the general pattern of progress is not quite as obvious as in some other realms of experience. The historical movement from smaller and simpler to larger and more complex in the moral realm, moreover, includes one massive jog that disrupted this pattern for a significant period. Accordingly, as we begin to think through the relationship between moral progress and our world's progress more generally, it will be worth briefly re-traversing the path our collective moral progress has taken to date.

If one way of entering the moral realm is by asking the question, "What is my duty?" then one way we can track the progress humankind has made in this realm is by considering the answer most people would give to the closely related question of, "*To whom* do I owe certain duties?" The standard answer to this question has evolved over the ages, roughly in keeping with the size of the standard social unit of the day, or with the answer that would be expected to a third question, "Who are my people?"—or as social scientists might now phrase it, "Who is my social ingroup?" These latter questions are particularly useful for discerning what people would have understood by the concept of duty at any given point in history, for they contain a built-in presumption: fellow ingroup members are to be treated with compassion, trust, loyalty, fairness, and respect, whereas outsiders are to be regarded with suspicion and aggression, if not downright hatred. Fellow ingroup members, that is, are owed a variety of more specific duties, whereas outsiders are owed nothing. Given our evolutionary heritage—most primates live in some sort of family troop—this presumption was probably baked into the human psyche from the time our earliest ancestors first arrived on the scene, with family members comprising the initial ingroup that was to be loved, nurtured, treated fairly, and defended. As multiple family troops then began joining together to form larger migratory tribes, and as people later settled into even larger villages, towns, city-states, nation-states, and empires, the circle to whom a person owed certain moral duties likewise grew larger, even as the interconnected web of mutual duties grew more complex— though also as those falling outside the growing ingroup continued to merit nothing but suspicion and aggression.

If the size of one's social ingroup, or of the group to whom one owes certain moral duties, has therefore generally grown in keeping with the standard social unit of the day, the major jog that occurred in this progression was crucial to shaping human society from the time of the Agricultural Revolution through roughly the end of the eighteenth century—which is to say, for most of recorded human history. Specifically, when migratory tribes began settling down to form permanent agricultural villages, which then began to grow, these expanding communities maintained social order by dividing themselves into multiple social subgroups, with the more powerful subgroups forcibly imposing an order on everyone else, generally one favorable to their own interests. Thus was born the mode of social organization we have here termed the system of privilege, whereby those in power grant themselves any number of exclusive privileges, made possible by the corresponding array of duties they impose on their subordinates; the king's privilege of receiving feudal dues, for instance, is made possible by the duty his subjects have to pay such taxes. Given these asymmetric relations, we could say the society's relatively small ruling class formed its one true social ingroup, or the one group to whom anyone owed a variety of specific duties. And because the members of this ruling ingroup tended to view their subordinates with suspicion or even animosity, these social insiders effectively relegated everyone else to the status of outsiders—even if they were "internal outsiders," still members of the society for certain purposes, such as fighting wars with foreign enemies, but excluded from the subset of the population recognized to possess any claim to moral treatment.

This jog in the path of moral progress lasted a good ten thousand years, with the effective social ingroup failing to grow as rapidly as the social unit as a whole. Then, however, the size of the community viewed as possessing certain inalienable rights—thus implying a duty on the part of others to respect these rights—took a sudden, dramatic leap forward. This happened when such Enlightenment figures as Locke, Kant, and Jefferson took the progression in the moral realm from smaller and simpler to larger and more complex all the way to its logical conclusion, at least in theory, by proposing that the community to whom we owe certain duties is universal: our social ingroup is everyone. As we know, this abstract articulation of the ideal of universalism did not instantly change the way particular societies treated the various subgroups composing them. It did, however, set in motion another movement from smaller and simpler to larger and more complex, this time within particular societies, and this time involving concrete changes to the size and composition of their recognized social ingroups.

In the case of the United States, for instance, when the constitutional framers crafted a system of democratic governance meant to instantiate the proposition that all people are created equal, they took important steps toward achieving this goal, such as eliminating the system of hereditary titles that had long divided European society into permanent, hierarchically ordered economic classes. This expansion of the recognized social ingroup was limited, however, to the traditionally dominant demographic subgroup of White males, which continued to treat other subgroups as "internal outsiders" to be controlled and exploited for its own benefit. Still, if the forces in favor of maintaining some version of this modified system of privilege have always been strong, the contradiction between the country's founding ideals and its concrete social reality eventually proved too egregious for many to overlook. And thus, over many generations of hard, bitter struggle, one traditionally marginalized subgroup after another has won entry into the country's recognized social ingroup. Though slow, exhausting, messy, painful, and sometimes tragic, the progress in this direction has been real, it has been significant, and it has been accelerating, thereby not only swelling the ranks of the community of recognized moral equals but also rendering this community more economically and demographically diverse, and hence more complex—in keeping with the general pattern of universal progress.

Certainly, this concrete moral progress still has a long way to go before reaching its own logical endpoint of a social reality in which the recognized social ingroup is as large, diverse, and inclusive as its guiding ideal—which is to say, universal. But our country and others around the world have made enough progress in this direction for us to realistically envision the possibility of the progressive moral ideal one day being realized, thereby giving us the hope, inspiration, and faith to keep pressing forward. The distance still left to travel down this path, meanwhile, indicates the role we have been assigned to play in the universal drama of progress. As we find ourselves taking the global stage around the turn of the twenty-first century, the thinkers and statesmen of the Enlightenment have already articulated the abstract ideal of moral universalism, while a long line of social activists has already been working tirelessly, in some cases giving their lives, to lend this ideal a measure of concrete reality. The task to which we have been called, therefore, is to do everything in our power to take this progressive moral project closer to completion by continuing to expand the circle of those to whom our society grants their full slate of rights, opportunities, and moral dignity, with the ultimate goal of rendering this circle fully universal.

To be sure, we do not have to accept this assigned task. Nothing compels us to make the project of continuously expanding the circle of inclusion our own. We can always devote ourselves to preserving whatever power, wealth, or privilege we might already possess, or we can strive to acquire more of these goods, whether for ourselves or for one of the social subgroups to which we belong. Why, then, dedicate ourselves to the progressive moral project when the work promises to be difficult, exhausting, messy, painful, and even tragic, while for some of us, success in this project might actually run contrary to our immediate interests? Why be moral, in the sense of being moral universalists? Why be progressive?

One answer to this question, already suggested by Kant, is that when we rise above our instincts and inclinations and instead use our reason to determine our actions in accord with the idea of universal law, we distinguish ourselves from other living creatures and the entire natural order in the most profound, transcendent, noble fashion anyone has yet proposed. The second, complementary answer we can now give to this question is that, when we commit ourselves to the project of moral universalism—and more specifically, when we work to expand the community of recognized moral equals, ultimately to include everyone, while excluding no one—we are participating in a universal movement from smaller and simpler to larger and more complex that stretches back to the Big Bang and will presumably continue long after our deaths.

And thus, by embracing the unique role into which we have been cast in the universal drama of progress, we are responding to our existential urge to be part of something larger than ourselves.

By making the human social order more inclusive, we are not just finding a place for ourselves in the world. We are *making* a place for ourselves by reshaping our world in a fashion that is both fully unprecedented and fully in keeping with the world's long history of progress.

By helping our universe take its next step or two forward in its long journey of progress, we are investing our lives with a meaning that transcends the limits of our own finite, transitory existence—which is to say, we are investing our lives with a bit of eternity.

CHAPTER 14

INTO A NEW CENTURY:
THE HEADWINDS REAPPEAR

As the twenty-first century dawned, it quickly became clear that the wary optimism American progressives had felt toward the close of the last century was well justified—both the optimism and the wariness. The new century had scarcely begun when, on September 11, 2001, Islamist terrorists crashed three passenger jets into the World Trade Center and the Pentagon, with brave passengers bringing down a fourth plane likely headed for the U.S. Capitol. As the nation came together in grief and shock, many progressives supported President George W. Bush's decision to invade Afghanistan for the purpose of shutting down the terrorist safe havens from which the 9/11 attacks had originated. But when this defensive action morphed into a preemptive invasion of Iraq on the grounds—which turned out to be false—that Saddam Hussein was hiding weapons of mass destruction, progressives were outraged, and partisan rancor shot back to pre-9/11 levels.

But then, in 2008, the United States did something that

would have scarcely been conceivable even a decade or two prior: it elected a Black man to the presidency. Barack Obama was elected president, moreover, by inspiring huge, diverse crowds with rousing speeches that touted a progressive mantra of Hope and Change, even as the country was heading into its worst economic crisis since the Great Depression. Obama's victory so inspired progressives around the world that the Nobel Committee awarded Obama its Peace Prize in 2009—well before the new president had been on the job long enough to accomplish much of anything, as even the slightly embarrassed Obama noted. In 2010, he did log the signature achievement of his presidency by signing the Affordable Care Act (ACA), referred to as "Obamacare" by supporters and detractors alike. The ACA did not create the system of universal health care for which many progressives had long advocated, but it did take a step in that direction by offering government-supported health insurance to millions of Americans who had never had it. In another progressive victory that year, Obama signed a law repealing the military's "Don't Ask, Don't Tell" policy, which had prohibited gays and lesbians from openly serving their country. Two years later, he went a step further on LGBTQ rights by announcing his support for same-sex marriage. This caused a brief flare-up of the culture war, but Obama and his policies proved popular enough that he cruised to reelection in 2012, and in the middle of his second term, the Supreme Court handed down its *Obergefell vs. Hodges* decision extending to same-sex couples the right to marry.

Flush with these successes, few progressives grasped just how much of a backlash the Obama presidency was generating. Granted, Republicans had been unanimous in opposing the Affordable Care Act, and the formation of the informal Tea Party in the wake of the Great Recession gave Republicans enough momentum to claim a substantial House majority in the midterm elections of 2010. Still, midterms often go against the sitting president, and the populist Tea Party—still seething that the government had bailed out big banks and insurance companies in 2008 and 2009, while letting working people bear the brunt of the financial collapse—spent just as much time attacking the Republican establishment as it did Democrats. Indeed, as more than one pundit noted, the Tea Party's right-wing, anti-establishment, anti-elitist rhetoric was not always discernible from that being offered by such left-wing populist movements as Occupy Wall Street.

That something deeper than economic resentment was simmering across the American landscape did not become clear until the 2016 presidential campaign, when the candidacy of real estate magnate and reality television star Donald Trump unexpectedly took off. Trump had been a fixture in American business and popular culture since the 1980s, and he first teased a possible presidential run in 2011, when he also began promoting the Obama "birther" conspiracy. As the sitting president freely shared, he had been born in Hawaii, the product of a brief marriage between a Black man from Kenya and a White woman from Kansas. Trump began suggesting, however—without evidence—that perhaps Obama had really been born in Africa, while hinting that the president's middle name of "Hussein" indicated he might be a Muslim. When Trump dogged Obama with demands that he prove his American citizenship by producing the long-form version of his birth certificate, the president took the unusual step of releasing this private document, although even this did not stop Trump and his growing legion of admirers from musing that perhaps the document had been faked. The whole affair proved to be an indication of things to come.

In 2015, Trump did mount a run for the presidency, launching his candidacy in decidedly un-populist fashion by riding down a gold escalator at the opulent Trump Tower. Soon after, he made the case for stricter enforcement of the nation's southern border by declaring that most of the Mexican immigrants trying to enter the country illegally were probably rapists. The sentiment struck a chord, and at the raucous campaign rallies Trump began to hold, one of his biggest applause lines came to be the promise to build a wall between the United States and Mexico. Similarly channeling residual anti-Muslim anger from 9/11, Trump pledged to impose a complete travel ban on Muslims seeking to enter the country. The intentionally inflammatory rhetoric continuing, Trump openly mocked a disabled reporter who had been critical of him, performing a junior high-level impression of the reporter's muscular disorder. And when Black Lives Matter protestors began decrying the disproportionate use of lethal force by police against unarmed suspects of color, Trump unambiguously sided with police, echoing an appeal Richard Nixon had once issued to southern segregationists by promising to be the country's "law and order candidate."

Securing his party's nomination and moving on to the general election, Trump faced off against Democrat Hillary Clinton in her bid to become the country's first female president. At campaign rallies, Trump repeatedly called for Clinton to be prosecuted on grounds she had used a private email server to conduct official business while serving as secretary of state, generally smirking as this launched frothing supporters into chants of "Lock her up!" And then, just as the MeToo movement was starting to call out powerful men for using their positions of authority to make unwanted sexual advances against women, video footage surfaced showing a slightly younger Trump boasting about how his celebrity status gave him the ability to sexually assault women with impunity.

With each of these incidents, progressives were both outraged and relieved. They were outraged that such divisive, fear-mongering, exclusionary rhetoric was even part of an American presidential campaign in 2015. They were relieved, however, because *this time* Trump had finally gone too far. Now he could not possibly win the general election; his words and actions were simply disqualificatory for any American political leader in the twenty-first century.

Except that, after every such statement, Trump either did not dip in the polls or he quickly bounced back. And then, in November of 2016—to the disbelief of Democrats, pundits, pollsters, and even the candidate himself—he won.

Back Into the Desert

The Trump presidency proved to be everything progressives had feared, and worse. A Muslim travel ban did go into effect, only slightly less sweeping than what candidate Trump had promised. As president, Trump never won the congressional support he needed to build significant stretches of a new wall with Mexico, but a few miles of existing border fence were upgraded to impressive concrete walls. And more contentiously, the Trump administration implemented a policy aimed at deterring migrant families from crossing the border by separating apprehended children from their parents, holding these children in overcrowded detention facilities under conditions that grew increasingly squalid as apprehensions increased. Then, in 2017, when White supremacists held a rally in Charlottesville, North Carolina that turned deadly as a rally participant deliberately drove his car into a crowd of counter-demonstrators, killing one woman and injuring 35 other people, Trump remarked, "I think there's blame on both sides, and I have no doubt about it... you also had people that were very fine people on both sides." This suggestion of a moral equivalence between protestors advocating for and against White supremacism confirmed for many progressives that, whether or not Trump was deeply racist in his own ideology—and many observers have suggested his presidency was guided by no other belief system than the promotion of his own interests and ego—Trump was perfectly willing to stoke the racist, nationalist, nativist passions of his supporters to win their votes and adulation.

If Trump's obsession with building a wall to keep out "the other" provided the most graphic contrast between his moral views—such as they were—and the progressive vision of welcoming ever more traditionally marginalized groups into the social mainstream, a second, even more insidious rejection of progressive values began to manifest itself over the course of the Trump presidency, accelerating and exploding toward its end. This was his administration's complete disregard for any notion of a common, objective truth upon which observers of good faith could agree. Trump's personal disdain for the truth was already clear when he fanned the birther conspiracy, but an indication that his entire administration would similarly hold objective, empirical facts in low regard came just a few days into his presidency.

Following Trump's inauguration ceremony, both the president and his press secretary, Sean Spicer, falsely claimed Trump's inaugural crowd had been larger than either of Obama's, with Spicer refusing to back down even when reporters produced aerial photography clearly showing the opposite. When Trump advisor Kellyanne Conway was then pressed as to why Spicer would cling to a claim so clearly refuted by the facts, Conway memorably noted that the press secretary had been citing "alternative facts." Incredulous at this rejection of a common standard of truth, mainstream media outlets gradually began calling the administration out for its more egregious falsehoods. But as conservative outlets like Fox News uncritically repeated whatever unfounded assertions Trump made, there was a real sense in which the Administration's alternative facts were taking on an objective character. Trump's supporters, in any case, believed these falsehoods to be true, and this was starting to have objective, measurable effects on the world.

At first, Trump's embrace of alternative facts mostly served as fodder for late-night comedians. In 2020, however, it took on a deadly seriousness when the COVID-19 pandemic hit. Worried that the mounting public health crisis would interfere with his reelection campaign, Trump consistently downplayed the seriousness of the disease, suggesting it could be treated with a variety of existing medicines or home remedies, while being openly dismissive of the notion that wearing a mask might be an effective means of protecting oneself and others against what was proving to be a highly transmissible respiratory disease. As the pandemic wore on, Trump pressured state governors to ease up on lockdowns meant to curb the spread of the disease. And as emboldened pandemic doubters and deniers began to openly question whether the disease was even real, or if the vaccines that ultimately became available might not be a government plot to implant unsuspecting citizens with tracking devices, the president did little to tamp down these conspiracy theories. With over 1 million Americans ultimately dying from COVID, there is no way of knowing how many of these deaths could have been prevented through stronger presidential leadership and a greater public willingness to follow basic public health measures, but estimates range in the hundreds of thousands.

The sheer magnitude of the COVID death toll notwithstanding, likely an even graver threat to the United States arose at the end of 2020, when Democrat Joe Biden decisively beat Trump in his bid for reelection. Refusing to concede defeat, Trump and his more vociferous supporters claimed the election had been rigged, putting forward numerous theories to support this claim. None of these theories proved strong enough to stand up in court, with over fifty lawsuits filed by Trump allies being thrown out. Trump, however, was undeterred, and he began pressing his vice president, Mike Pence, to refuse to certify the electoral votes from six states Trump had lost when these votes were presented at a ceremonial joint session of Congress to be held at the Capitol on

January 6, 2021. As Congress then prepared to meet on the morning of January 6, Trump gave a fiery speech at a rally near the White House, encouraging his supporters to march down to the Capitol and "keep fighting." Many of them did, violently storming the Capitol, disrupting the vote certification process, assaulting hundreds of police officers, and erecting a scaffold on the Capitol steps, purportedly to hang the disobedient Pence. As the riot raged on and lawmakers were chased into hiding, Trump refused to call his supporters off for several hours, later lauding these would-be insurrectionists as patriots, while continuing to deny the election results even long after Biden was eventually sworn in.

As I write in 2023, no credible evidence of substantial fraud in the 2020 presidential election has ever been produced. Nevertheless, a majority of Republican voters have come to embrace some form of election denialism, not only refusing to accept the legitimacy of the Biden presidency, but in some cases preemptively doubting the results of future elections.

The Progressive Crisis

Over the course of the Trump years—which feel like they have dragged on, even after their namesake reluctantly left the Oval Office—not even the wary optimism that had characterized the progressive mood of just a few years ago has been anywhere to be found. On the contrary, since the 2016 presidential election, the prevailing sense among progressives has been one of crisis, even existential crisis. It is not that we think the world around us is literally coming to an end. Rather, we fear the demise of the vision we have for our world and its future: we fear for our worldview.

This language of existential crisis may sound overblown, but to put the threat the progressive worldview faces in context, recall that this worldview first arose four hundred years ago when certain brave scholars began setting aside their blind faith in authority and applying their own eyes, ears, and reasoning abilities to the study of nature. Prior to this time, Truth had always been, essentially, whatever the authorities said it was. There were religious authorities, intellectual authorities, cultural authorities, and bureaucratic authorities, but since every lower authority ultimately reported to the king, the Truths these authorities promulgated all generally ended up favoring the interests of the king—whose own interest lay in maintaining or augmenting the power he already possessed.

It was therefore revolutionary, not just epistemologically, but politically, when scientists like Galileo foreswore their reliance on authority and instead launched an empirically based search for Truth. Indeed, even before such political thinkers as Hobbes and Locke had begun to apply the methods and concepts of modern science to the specific topic of human beings and the societies they form, this new insistence that truth-claims be grounded in empirical evidence was *democratizing*, for it implied that anyone who turned their careful attention to a particular subject matter would arrive at exactly the same facts, no matter whether this observer was a king, priest, scholar, or peasant. This new approach to learning thus deprived the king and his mouthpieces of their long-held monopoly on Truth, which in turn dramatically reduced the opportunities these authorities had to slant the Truth in favor of safeguarding their own power and status.

As we know, once the philosophers and statesmen of the seventeenth and eighteenth centuries did begin to apply the approach of the modern physical sciences to political science and moral philosophy, they took this democratizing trend even farther. The contract theorists established that the only legitimate form of sovereignty is rule by the consent of the governed, with every individual possessing certain natural rights of which they cannot reasonably be deprived. Kant argued that behaving morally requires that we determine our actions in accord with the idea of universal law—which itself requires that we treat every other human being as our moral equal. And the American founders at least attempted to give these universalistic ideals concrete reality by designing a system of government that would recognize the inherent equality of all people and secure their inalienable, universal rights. Granted, the American founders came up short in this regard, offering full equality only to the traditionally dominant subgroup of White males. Nevertheless, they established a stable governing system with enough flexibility to allow for future change, and over the subsequent centuries, the United States has slowly—if reluctantly and imperfectly—drawn one marginalized group after another into the social mainstream, thereby rendering the community of social equals progressively larger and more diverse.

But then, just as those of us who cheer this movement in the direction of greater inclusivity thought we had caught a glimpse of the promised land, our country lurched back in precisely the opposite direction. Nor is what concerns us merely that many of our contemporaries appear to have rejected the progressive vision of a continually expanding circle of social insiders, instead latching onto the contrary image of a wall meant to keep strangers out. At an even deeper level, many of our fellow citizens would seem to be walking away from the conviction that launched the progressive worldview in the first place: the belief that there exists a set of objective, empirical facts that are accessible to us all, and upon which we should all be able to agree provided we apply our powers of reasoning to them. In recent years, many of our fellow citizens have increasingly come to insist on their right to arrive at their own determination of the facts, perhaps after "doing their own research"—even if such research amounts to watching a favorite cable news show or consulting the social media posts of like-minded partisans. To be sure, this increasingly casual attitude toward Truth is not limited to the political right. Nevertheless, the embrace of alternative facts has become particularly prominent on the right, especially since it took its populist turn with the rise of the Tea Party and Donald Trump. I would argue, moreover, that there is a direct connection between the Right's abandonment of traditional standards of objective Truth and its rejection of the progressive moral vision of continually expanding the circle of social insiders.

Let us go back for a moment to the 1950s. The United States had emerged from World War II as the world's leading manufacturer, so the economy was booming and blue-collar jobs were plentiful and well-paying. This meant that, for the first time in American history, having a high school diploma and a willingness to work hard were enough to guarantee a comfortable, respected, middle-class living—for White men, that is. Indeed, because White men still enjoyed an unquestioned social dominance, even White factory workers found themselves fairly high up the American social ladder. Over the 1960s and 1970s, however, things began to change. Most significantly, the American economy underwent a series of structural adjustments, including an increase in automation and outsourcing. This led to sharp declines in manufacturing jobs, thus making it harder for blue-collar workers to earn the secure, middle-class living to which they had grown accustomed. At the same time, the civil rights movement of the 1960s, followed by the other rights movements it helped inspire, allowed a variety of traditionally marginalized groups to begin making significant economic and social gains, often by moving into traditionally White communities and filling some of the lower-end jobs White men had traditionally held.

Against this backdrop of economic anxiety and rapid demographic change, many rural and working-class White men found themselves increasingly receptive to a narrative—a Truth—that first began to be heard on conservative talk radio in the late 1980s, gained a wider audience on Fox News over the 1990s and 2000s, then exploded onto right-wing social media in the 2010s. According to this narrative, the 1950s had been a sort of Golden Age: a time when America was great, hard work and a high school education were all you needed to join the middle class, and no one questioned the dominant status of White men. But then the country began to change, and working-class White men started to see both their economic security and social status threatened.

This could only mean, the narrative ran, that someone was taking what rightfully belonged to them. And this "someone" was generally understood to be people who looked, sounded, or behaved differently than they did.

This soil having been tilled, when a brash anti-politician came on the scene who promised to make America great again, he was warmly embraced by any number of demographic groups, but most prominently by working-class White men. And as attendees at Trump's campaign rallies consistently told reporters, what drew them to Trump was his refreshing willingness to "tell it like it is." This did not, of course, mean that the candidate limited himself to citing carefully researched, objectively verifiable facts. Rather, "telling it like it is" meant coming out and *saying* what his listeners had long been *feeling*, which is that other people had been making off with the economic opportunity, political power, and social prestige that rightfully belonged to them.

Clearly, Trump was not himself "one of them." He did not pretend to come from the working class. Trump was rather a natural-born authority figure: charismatic, unimaginably rich, and extremely powerful, particularly once he had won the presidency. This could have been a turn-off for working-class voters, many of whom instinctively resist any form of authority, as evidenced by the "Don't Tread on Me" flags they like to fly in the backs of their pickup trucks. Yet, because Trump was a powerful figure willing to proclaim a Truth that justified and celebrated their own vision of reestablishing the economic stability, political power, and dominant social status they had once enjoyed in virtue of their race and gender, they willingly submitted to his authority. This, in turn, primed them to accept as fact any of the more specific truth claims he put forward, whether or not they had any basis in empirical reality. This proved to be convenient, for when Trump later found his own power threatened by the fact that he had lost a democratic election, his supporters were quick to embrace a set of alternative facts he put forward to try to remain in power—that the 2020 election had been fraudulent, that American democracy was now rigged against real Americans, that true patriots had a moral duty to keep him in office by any means necessary, up to and including physical violence.

As those of us in the progressive camp have watched this series of events unfold—marked not just by the actions of one particular man, but by the willingness of so many Americans to vote for him, then to continue supporting him even after Charlottesville, the COVID-19 pandemic, and January 6—we have been forced to confront some very uncomfortable questions. First among these: Was the progressive project upon which we have been collectively embarked for the past four hundred years ever truly sustainable? Or has this whole effort been a flash in the pan, a brilliant yet brief experiment in organizing and governing ourselves universalistically that was always destined to burn itself out and collapse back into some version—no matter how high tech—of the premodern system of privilege? Or to frame these questions slightly differently: Given that the progressive worldview has always taken human reason to be the primary driver of progress, at least in the human realm, was our faculty of reasoning ever really up to this task? Or have we always been just another species of self-interested animal, incapable of steering ourselves other than by our most primordial instincts and inclinations, many of which would appear to be quite suspicious, angry, and violent in character?

Of course, as progressives, we would like to believe that if the progressive project is, in fact, falling apart, the failure lies with our political opponents, and specifically with their inability to reason more clearly. If only these dupes would stop listening to Trump's lies and start applying their own powers of reasoning to the evidence before them, we would like to say, our country could get back on its path toward better realizing the progressive ideal of moral universalism. And yet, as we have seen over the past several chapters, even progressives—and even the most intelligent and committed progressives of their day—have always had massive moral blind spots, leading them to slip into such blatant contradictions as proclaiming that all people are created equal, even while personally owning slaves, or advocating for the rights of one particular marginalized group, even while support- ing the larger society's continued oppression of other groups.

Even today, as we congratulate ourselves on finally having grasped King's message that unless all are free, none can be free—many of us proudly displaying yard signs that proclaim our support for all the various demo- graphic subgroups our country has traditionally marginal- ized—contemporary psychological research shows that we continue to carry plenty of prejudices around with us, most of them directed against people who do not look, sound, or behave like us. This includes, not incidentally, biases we harbor against our political opponents—or against anyone who happens to look, sound, or behave like the stereotypical picture we have formed of these opponents. And with many Trump voters attributing their support for him to the scorn and condescension they have long felt coming from the entire liberal establishment, whether in Washington or the Ivory Tower or Hollywood, this gives rise to the uncomfortable question of whether progressives, through our own prejudiced behavior, have helped fuel the rise, if not of Donald Trump, then of the phenomenon of Trumpism.

Faced with these developments, it is impossible for those of us who are progressives not to be tempted to despair. Such despair may take the form of quietism, where we lose any hope of the world ever fundamentally changing for the better, and thus we stop struggling to make this change happen. Or our despair could take the form of militancy, where we grow tired of always taking the high road and instead allow ourselves to indulge all the anger, aggression, and even hatred our opponents have been stirring up in us—even if this means that, by submitting to the urge to divide into groups and use whatever power we have to crush our opponents, we are actually handing our opponents a victory by allowing their violent, exclusionary worldview to triumph over our vision of peaceful inclusion.

What Do We Do Now?

So, what do we do now, faced with this temptation to despair? I believe the study we have made of the history of progress over the course of this volume holds two key lessons for us here.

The first is that it is precisely in times like these, when

things appear their darkest—when all the evidence before us appears to be pointing in the direction, not of progress, but of reversion and decline—that we must follow King's admonition to maintain our faith.

Our faith in the power of nonviolence.

Our faith that while the arc of the universe is long, it bends toward justice.

Our faith in progress.

Of course, maintaining this faith does not require that we check our powers of reasoning at the door, latching onto some unrealizable pipe dream rather than facing up to reality. Nor does it require that we look beyond the present order to pin our hopes on some future life, set in some future world. Rather, maintaining our faith in progress requires that we step back from the present moment, with its overwhelming rush of events and circumstances, and allow our gaze to return to the very big picture: the story of universal progress as it stretches back, not just to the beginning of the progressive worldview some four hundred years ago, but to the birth of our universe some 14 billion years ago. When we then allow our gaze to wander back forward over the events of this story, it becomes obvious that our faith in progress is not a blind faith, at all. On the contrary, it rests on a tremendous amount of evidence derived from many distinct fields of empirical study, covering many different chapters in the story of progress. And all this evidence tells us progress is real, it has been going on for a very long time, and its pace has been accelerating.

To be sure, our look back at the history of progress does not provide us with any guarantees of how future events will pan out. If anything, the story of universal progress teaches us progress is hard. Progress has always been hard. It has always been messy, exhausting, wasteful, painful, and often tragic. And if we are being completely honest with ourselves, this means our current efforts at progress in the social, political, and moral realms could fail, just as countless other attempts at progress over the ages have failed. But this just underscores why we need to maintain our faith: if we stop believing progress is possible, and thus we stop striving to make this progress a reality, progress *will* stop, since like it or not, we are the authors of the current chapter in the story of universal progress. Still, the hope we can derive from earlier chapters in this story is that the challenges we currently face are nothing new; they are nothing progress has not seen many times before, and overcome. So, while the struggles ahead promise to be difficult, and probably none of us alive today will ever reach the promised land, we as a people—as a universal people—have already climbed high enough that we can look over and see the possibility of our moral vision being realized.

The second lesson we can draw from the story of universal progress lies more specifically in the way this foundational narrative has developed over the past four hundred years. As I have stressed throughout this book, as the progressive worldview has emerged and evolved since the early seventeenth century, the single most significant factor driving its ongoing development has been a series of concomitant advances taking place in the modern sciences. What this suggests is that, if the version of the progressive worldview that had come together and achieved some degree of public visibility by the close of the twentieth century—what we are here calling the second iteration of the progressive worldview—is leaving us at a loss, unable to make complete sense of our world and unsure of how to respond to the events pummeling us, one place we can turn is back to the sciences.

This could mean revisiting the scientific developments of the past four centuries with fresh eyes, perhaps focusing on certain areas of research we had previously overlooked. If history is any guide, however, we are more likely to find the insights we will need to make sense of our contemporary world by looking to the cutting-edge sciences of our own day. And the hopeful news on this front is that the past few decades have witnessed the emergence of not just one, but two, young sciences that promise to lend us both the empirical facts and conceptual structures needed to draw the progressive worldview into the twenty-first century, quite possibly marking the start of a third iteration of this worldview.

The first of these young sciences goes by the title of "moral psychology." A subdiscipline of cognitive psychology, moral psychology uses laboratory equipment and research techniques that have only become available over the past few decades to do something such early philosophers of human psychology as Hobbes, Hume, and Kant never could: make an empirical study of how people go about making those decisions we commonly label "moral," to include those decisions that affect how we view and treat other people. The results coming back are forcing progressives to ask whether the tremendous faith our worldview has always placed in the power of human reason to master the passions has been justified, and indeed, whether it ever made sense to separate reason and the passions so cleanly. These are the questions that will guide Volume II of *The Progressive Worldview*.

The second of these young sciences is the science of complex adaptive systems, more commonly known as the science of complexity. Highly interdisciplinary in its approach, the science of complexity makes a rigorous study of a phenomenon we have observed in numerous contexts throughout this volume, to the point that it has come to provide us with a sort of working definition of progress: the movement whereby many smaller, simpler parts come together to form some larger, more complex whole that is somehow more than just the sum of its parts. The scientific, metaphysical, and moral implications of this new line of research will form the subject matter of *Volume III of The Progressive Worldview*.

*　　*　　*　　*　　*

Did you find this book compelling? If so, please join me at theprogressiveworldview.com. There you can email me with your feedback on the book or your own thoughts on what it means to be a progressive. You can also sign up to be notified when *Volumes II and III* of *The Progressive Worldview* are released, as well as keeping up with *The Progressive World-view Blog*, where I'll be periodically sharing my thoughts on progressivism in a more informal setting, whether as spurred by my work on the final two volumes, the events of the day, or the comments you share.

ACKNOWLEDGMENTS

I have many people to thank for their assistance in making this book a reality. Cynthia Gwynne Yaudes provided me with invaluable editorial guidance. Jozsef Balazs-Hegedus composed all the technical drawings. Mirko Pohle designed the cover and produced the interior layout. And Shawn Dressler shepherded the book through the entire publication process.

I also need to thank my parents, Chuck and Nancy Carlson, for first setting me on the twin paths of intellectual inquiry and moral concern; I miss them both deeply. And finally, I must thank my wife, Amy, for her years of support and encouragement as I slowly—from her perspective no doubt *really* slowly—turned some ideas that had been bouncing around in my head for decades into the book you now have before you.

www.ingramcontent.com/pod-product-compliance
Lightning Source LLC
Chambersburg PA
CBHW060103170726
48004CB00013B/2